✳ *Highlights* ✳
of this
Study Guide

✳ Each Chapter of this **Study Guide** includes—

✳ Chapter **Introduction**

✳ Easy to Read & Understand, Comprehensive **Outline**

✳ **True-False** Questions

✳ **Fill-In** Questions

✳ **Multiple-Choice** Questions

✳ **Short Essay** Questions

✳ **Issue Spotters**—hypothetical fact problems & black letter law questions on key issues

✳ Each Unit of this **Study Guide** ends with a **Cumulative Hypothetical** and corresponding **Multiple-Choice** Questions

✳ This **Study Guide** also contains an **Answer Appendix** with answers to all of the Questions & explanations of the Answers

Study Guide

to Accompany

Fundamentals of Business Law
Sixth Edition

ROGER LeROY MILLER
Institute for University Studies
Arlington, Texas

GAYLORD A. JENTZ
Herbert D. Kelleher
Emeritus Professor in Business Law
University of Texas at Austin

Prepared by

William Eric Hollowell
Member of
   U.S. Supreme Court Bar
   Minnesota State Bar
   Florida State Bar

Roger LeRoy Miller
Institute for University Studies
Arlington, Texas

THOMSON
SOUTH-WESTERN
WEST

Australia · Canada · Mexico · Singapore · Spain · United Kingdom · United States

THOMSON

SOUTH-WESTERN

WEST

Study Guide to Accompany *Fundamentals of Business Law*, Sixth Edition
by Roger LeRoy Miller and Gaylord A. Jentz,

Vice President/Editorial Director:
Jack W. Calhoun

Vice President/Editor-in-Chief:
George Werthman

Publisher for Business Law & Accounting:
Rob Dewey

Senior Developmental Editor:
Jan Lamar

Marketing Manager:
Steven Silverstein

Production Editors:
Bill Stryker and Anne Sheroff

Manufacturing Coordinator:
Rhonda Utley

Printer:
Globus Printing Company

ISBN: 0-324-27095-x

Table of Contents

Preface vii

UNIT ONE: The Legal Environment of Business

1   Sources of Business Law and the Global Legal Environment 1
2   Traditional and Online Dispute Resolution.. 8
3   Ethics and Social Responsibility 16

UNIT TWO: Torts and Crimes

4   Torts and Cyber Torts.. 23
5   Intellectual Property and Internet Law 31
6   Criminal Law and Cyber Crimes... 38

UNIT THREE: Contracts

7   Nature and Classification... 48
8   Agreement and Consideration... 54
9   Capacity and Legality 62
10   Defenses against Contract Enforceability 68
11   Third Party Rights and Discharge... 74
12   Breach and Remedies... 81
13   E-Contracts 87

UNIT FOUR: Sales and Lease Contracts

14   The Formation of Sales and Lease Contracts.. 94
15   Title and Risk of Loss 103
16   Performance and Breach of Sales and Lease Contracts..................................110
17   Warranties and Product Liability..118

UNIT FIVE: Negotiable Instruments

18   Negotiability, Transferability, and Liability 127
19   Checks, the Banking System, and E-Money 135

UNIT SIX: Debtor-Creditor Relationships

20   Secured Transactions...145
21   Creditors' Rights and Bankruptcy..153

UNIT SEVEN: Employment Relations

22   Agency Relationships 164
23   Employment Law 171

UNIT EIGHT: Business Organizations

24   Sole Proprietorships, Partnerships, and Limited Liability Companies 181
25   Corporate Formation, Financing and Termination...190
26   Corporate Directors, Officers, and Shareholders..199
27   Investor Protection and Online Securities Offerings 206

UNIT NINE: Property and Its Protection

28   Personal Property and Bailments...215
29   Real Property 222
30   Insurance, Wills, and Trusts...229

UNIT TEN: Special Topics

31   Professional Liability 237

Appendix A: Answers A-1

Preface

To the Student

This *Study Guide* is designed to help you read and understand *Fundamentals of Business Law,* **Sixth Edition**.

How this Study Guide Can Help You

This study guide can help you maximize your learning, subject to the constraints and the amount of time you can allot to this course. There are at least six specific ways in which you can benefit from using this guide.

1. This study guide can help you concentrate on the *crucial topics* in each chapter.

2. If you are forced to miss a class, you can use this study guide to help you learn the material discussed in your absence.

3. There is a possibility that the questions that you are required to answer in this study guide are representative of the types of questions that you will be asked during examinations.

4. You can use this study guide to help you review for examinations.

5. This study guide can help you decide whether you really understand the material. Don't wait until examination time to find out!

6. Finally, the questions in this study guide will help you develop critical thinking skills that you can use in other classes and throughout your career.

The Contents of this *Study Guide*

Business law sometimes is considered a difficult subject because it uses a specialized vocabulary and also takes most people much time and effort to learn. Those who work with and teach business law believe that the subject matter is exciting and definitely worthy of your efforts. Your text, *Fundamentals of Business Law,* **Sixth Edition**, and this student learning guide have been written for the precise purpose of helping you learn the most important aspects of business law. We always try to keep you, the student, in mind.

Every chapter includes the following sections:

1. What This Chapter Is About: You are introduced to the main subject matter of each chapter in this section.

2.   Chapter Outline: Using an outline format, the salient points in each chapter are presented.

3.   True-False Questions: Ten true-false questions are included for each chapter. Generally, these questions test knowledge of terminology and principles. The answers are given at the back of the book. Whenever an answer is false, the reasons why it is false are presented at the back of the book also.

4.   Fill-in Questions: Here you are asked to choose between two alternatives for each space that needs to be filled in. Answers are included at the back of the book.

5.   Multiple-Choice Questions: Ten multiple-choice questions are given for each chapter. The answers, along with an explanation, are included at the back of this book.

6.   Short Essay Questions: Two essay questions are presented for each chapter.

7.   Issue Spotters: These questions alert you to certain principles within the chapter. Brief answers to these questions are included at the end of this text.

How to Use This Study Guide

What follows is a recommended strategy for improving your grade in your business law class. It may seem like a lot of work, but the payoffs will be high. Try the entire program for the first three or four chapters. If you then feel you can skip some steps safely, try doing so and see what happens.

For each chapter we recommend you follow the sequence of steps below:

1.   Read the What This Chapter Is About and Chapter Outline.

2.   Read about half the textbook chapter (unless it is very long), being sure to underline only the most important topics (which you should be able to recognize after having read no more than two chapter outlines in this study guide). Put a check mark by the material that you do not understand.

3.   If you find the textbook's chapter easy to understand, you might want to finish reading it. Otherwise, rest for a sufficient period before you read the second half of the chapter. Again, be sure to underline only the most important points and to put a check mark by the material you find difficult to understand.

4.   After you have completed the entire textbook chapter, take a break. Then read only what you have underlined throughout the entire chapter.

5.   Now concentrate on the difficult material, for which you have left check marks. Reread this material and *think about it*; you will find that it is very exciting to figure out difficult material on your own.

6. Now reread the Issue Spotters. Answer them in the book and compare your answers with those at the back of this book. Next, do the True-False Questions, Fill-In Questions, and Multiple-Choice Questions. Compare your answers with those at the back of this book. Make a note of the questions you have missed and find the pages in your textbook upon which these questions are based. If you still don't understand, ask your instructor.

7. If you still have time, do one or both of the essay questions.

9. Before your examination, study your class notes. Then review the chapter outline in the text. Reread the Chapter Outline in this *Study Guide*, then redo all of the questions within each chapter. Compare your answers with the answers at the back of this *Study Guide*. Identify your problem areas and reread the relevant pages in **Fundamentals of Business Law, Sixth Edition**. Think through the answers on your own.

If you have followed the strategy outlined above, you should feel sufficiently confident and be relaxed enough to do well on your exam.

Study Skills for *Fundamentals of Business Law,* Sixth Edition

Every student has a different way to study. We give several study hints below that we think will help any student to better master the textbook **Fundamentals of Business Law, Sixth Edition**. These skills involve outlining, marking, taking notes, and summarizing. You may not need to use all these skills. Nonetheless, if you do improve your ability to use them, you will be able to understand more easily the information in **Fundamentals of Business Law, Sixth Edition**.

MAKING AN OUTLINE

An outline is simply a method for organizing information. The reason an outline can be helpful is that it shows how concepts relate to each other. Outlining can be done as part of your reading or at the end of your reading, or as a rereading of each section within a chapter before you go on to the next section. Even if you do not believe that you need to outline, our experience has been that the act of *physically* writing an outline for a chapter helps most students to improve greatly their ability to retain the material in **Fundamentals of Business Law, Sixth Edition,** and master it, thereby obtaining a higher grade in the class, with less effort.

To make an effective outline you have to be selective. Outlines that contain all the information in the text are not very useful. Your objective in outlining is to identify main concepts and to subordinate details to those main concepts. Therefore, your first goal is to *identify the main concepts in each section*. Often the large first-level headings within your textbook are sufficient as identifiers of the major concepts within each section. You may decide, however, that you want to phrase an identifier in a way that is more meaningful to you. In any event, your outline should consist of several levels written in a standard outline format. The most important concepts are assigned a roman numeral; the second most important a capital letter; the third most important, numbers; and the fourth most important, lower-case letters. Even if you make an outline that is no more than the headings in the text, you will be studying more efficiently than you would be otherwise. As we stated above, the process of physically writing the words will help you master the material.

MARKING A TEXT

From kindergarten through high school you typically did not own your own textbooks. They were made available by the school system. You were told not to mark in them. Now that you own your own text for a course, your learning can be greatly improved by marking your text. There is a trade-off here. The more you mark up your textbook, the less you will receive from your bookstore when you sell it back at the end of the semester. The benefit is a better understanding of the subject matter, and the cost is the reduction in the price you receive for the resale of the text. Additionally, if you want a text that you can mark with your own notations, you necessarily have to buy a new one or a used one that has no markings. Both carry a higher price tag than a used textbook with markings. Again there is a trade-off.

Different Ways of Marking   The most commonly used form of marking is to underline important points. The second most commonly used method is to use a felt-tipped highlighter, or marker, in yellow or some other transparent color. Marking also includes circling, numbering, using arrows, brief notes, or any other method that allows you to remember things when you go back to skim the pages in your textbook prior to an exam.

Why Marking is Important   Marking is important for the same reason that outlining is—it helps you to organize better the information in the text. It allows you to become an *active* participant in the mastery of the material. Researchers have shown that the physical act of marking, just like the physical act of outlining, helps you better retain the material. The better the material is organized in your mind, the more you will remember. There are two types of readers—passive and active. The active reader outlines and/or marks. Active readers typically do better on exams. Perhaps one of the reasons that active readers retain more is because the physical act of outlining and/or marking requires greater concentration. It is through greater concentration that more is remembered.

Points to Remember When Marking

1. Read one section at a time before you do any extensive marking. You can't mark a section until you know what is important and you can't know what is important until you read the whole section.

2. Don't over mark. Just as an outline cannot contain everything that is in a text (or in a lecture), marking can't be of the whole book. Don't fool yourself into thinking you've done a good job just because each page is filled up with arrows, asterisks, circles, and underlines. When you go back to review the material you won't remember what was important. The key is *selective* activity. Mark each page in a way that allows you to see the most important points at a glance. You can follow up your marking by writing out more in your subject outline.

SUMMARIZING THE MATERIAL

Even if each chapter has a chapter summary, it is still worthwhile for you to make your own summary points. The reason is that the more active you are as a reader, the better you will understand the material.

Summarization helps you in your reading comprehension. It is the final step in reviewing the book. There is probably nothing else you can do that works as well to help you remember what your textbook has to say.

The importance of summarization is that the notes you make are in your own words, not in the words of the author. Writing down a summary in your own words is the most effective use of your time. This allows you to process the information into your own memory by being required to think about it. You also have to make it part of your vocabulary. Whenever you cannot state important legal concepts in your own words, you probably haven't understood the concepts necessary to master the material. Indeed, summary notes are a good way to determine whether you have actually understood something. Don't simply make a mechanical listing of quotes taken right out of the textbook. Rather, you should make summary notes using complete sentences with correct grammar. This forces you to develop your ideas logically and clearly. Also, summary notes written in this matter can be more easily remembered.

Be Brief. Your notes should condense the information in the text into statements that summarize the concepts. It is when you force yourself to make the statements brief that you best learn the material. By making only brief summary notes, you have to think about the essence of each concept and present it in a form that is compact enough to remember. You should typically have no more than a one-paragraph summary for each important topic in the chapter.

What Format to Use? The authors find that using 5" x 8" cards is the best way to take summary notes. Don't fill up each note card. You need to leave room to make additional notes later on when you are reviewing for the final exam. That is to say, leave margins for further notes and study markings. Additionally, if you leave enough room, you can integrate the notes that you take during lectures on to these summary note cards.

Another reason to place your summary notes on 5" x 8" cards is because in so doing you have a set of flash cards that you can use in studying for a final exam.

HOW TO STUDY AND TAKE EXAMS

There is basically one reason why you have purchased this *Study Guide*—to improve your exam grade. By using this study guide assiduously, you will have the confidence to take your mid-terms and final examinations and to do well. The study guide, however, should not just be used a day before each exam. Rather, the guide is most helpful if you use it at the time that you read the chapter. That is to say, after you read a chapter in *Fundamentals of Business Law,* **Sixth Edition,** you should directly go to the appropriate chapter in the study guide. This systematic review technique is the most effective study technique you can use.

Besides learning the concepts in each chapter as well as possible, there are additional strategies for taking exams. You need to know in advance what type of exam you are going to take—essay or objective or both. You need to know which reading materials and lectures will be covered. For both objective and essay exams (but more importantly for the former) you need to know if there is a penalty for guessing incorrectly. If there is, your strategy will be different: you will usually only mark what you are certain of. Finally, you need to know how much time will be allowed for the exam.

FOLLOWING DIRECTIONS

Students are often in a hurry to start an exam so they take little time to read the instructions. The instructions can be critical, however. In a multiple-choice exam, for example, if there is no indication that there is a penalty for guessing, then you should never leave a question unanswered. Even if there only remains a few minutes at the end of the exam, you should guess for those questions about which you are uncertain.

Additionally, you need to know the weight given to each section of an exam. In a typical multiple-choice exam, all questions have equal weight. In some exams, particularly those involving essay questions, different parts of the exam carry different weights. You should use these weights to apportion your time accordingly. If an essay part of an exam accounts for only 20 percent of the total points on the exam, you should not spend 60 percent of your time on the essay.

You need to make sure you are answering the question correctly. Some exams require a No. 2 lead pencil to fill in the dots on a machine-graded answer sheet. Other exams require underlining or circling. In short, you have to look at the instructions carefully.

Lastly, check to make sure that you have all the pages of the examination. If you are uncertain, ask the instructor or the exam proctor. It is hard to justify not having done your exam correctly because you failed to answer all the questions. Simply stating that you did not have them will pose a problem for both you and your instructor. Don't take a chance. Double check to make sure.

TAKING OBJECTIVE EXAMINATIONS

The most important point to discover initially with any objective test is if there is a penalty for guessing. If there is none, you have nothing to lose by guessing. In contrast, if a half-point is subtracted for each incorrect answer, then you probably should not answer any question for which you are purely guessing.

Students usually commit one of two errors when they read objective-exam questions: (1) they read into the questions things that don't exist, or (2) they skip over words or phrases.

Most test questions include key words such as:

- all
- always

- never
- only

If you miss these key words you will be missing the "trick" part of the question. Also, you must look for questions that are only *partly* correct, particularly if you are answering true/false questions.

Never answer a question without reading all of the alternatives. More than one of them may be correct. If more than one of them seems correct, make sure you select the answer that seems the most correct.

Whenever the answer to an objective question is not obvious, start with the process of elimination. Throw out the answers that are clearly incorrect. Even with objective exams in which there is a penalty for guessing, if you can throw out several obviously incorrect answers, then you may wish to guess among the remaining ones because your probability of choosing the correct answer is high.

Typically, the easiest way to eliminate incorrect answers is to look for those that are meaningless, illogical, or inconsistent. Often test authors put in choices that make perfect sense and are indeed true, but they are not the answer to the question under study.

WRITING ESSAY EXAMS

To write an essay exam, you should be prepared. One way of being prepared is to practice writing timed essays. In other words, find out in advance how much time you will have for each essay question, say 15 minutes, and then practice writing an answer to a sample essay question during a 15-minute time period. This is the only way you will develop the skills needed to pace yourself for an essay exam. Do your timed essay practice without using the book, since most essay exams are closed book.

Usually you can anticipate certain essay exam questions. You do this by going over the major concept headings, either in your lecture notes or in your text; search for the themes that tie the materials together and then think about questions that your instructor might ask you. You might even list possible essay questions as a review device; then write a short outline for each of those most likely questions.

As with objective exams, you need to read the directions to the essay questions carefully. It's best to write out a brief outline *before* you start writing. The outline should present your conclusion in one or two sentences, then your supporting argument. It is important to stay on the subject. We can tell you from first hand experience that no instructor likes to read answers to unasked questions.

Finally, make a strong attempt to write legibly. Again speaking from experience, we can tell you that it's easier to be favorably inclined to a student's essay if we don't have to reread it five times to decipher the handwriting.

Acknowledgments

We wish to thank Suzanne Jasin of K & M Consulting for her expert design and composition of this guide.

We welcome comments and criticisms to help us make this guide even more useful. All errors are our sole responsibility.

W. E. H.
R. L. M.

Chapter 1:
Sources of Business Law and the Global Legal Environment

WHAT THIS CHAPTER IS ABOUT

The first chapters in Unit 1 provide the background for the entire course. Chapter 1 sets the stage. From this chapter, you must understand that (1) the law is a set of general rules, (2) in applying these general rules, a judge cannot fit a case to suit a rule, but must fit (or find) a rule to suit the case, and (3) in fitting (or finding) a rule, a judge must also supply reasons for the decision. The chapter also covers constitutional law.

CHAPTER OUTLINE

I. THE NATURE OF LAW
Law consists of enforceable rules governing relationships among individuals and between individuals and their society.

II. THE COMMON LAW TRADITION

A. COMMON LAW
The American legal system, based on the decisions judges make in cases, is a **common law** system, which involves the application of principles applied in earlier cases with similar facts.

B. *STARE DECISIS*
The use of precedent in a common law system is known as the doctrine of *stare decisis*. *Stare decisis* makes the legal system more efficient, just, uniform, stable, and predictable. When there is no precedent, a court may look at other legal principles and policies, social values, or scientific data.

C. EQUITABLE REMEDIES
As a rule, courts grant an equitable remedy only when the remedy at law is inadequate.

1. Remedies at Law
Remedies at law include awards of land, money, and items of value. A jury trial is available only in an action at law.

2. Remedies in Equity
Remedies in equity include decrees of specific performance, injunctions, and rescission. Decisions to award equitable remedies are guided by equitable maxims.

III. SOURCES OF AMERICAN LAW

A. CONSTITUTIONAL LAW
The U.S. Constitution distributes power among the branches of government. It is the supreme law of the land. Any law that conflicts with it is invalid. The states also have constitutions, but the federal constitution prevails if their provisions conflict.

1

B. STATUTORY LAW

Statutes and ordinances are enacted by Congress and by state and local legislative bodies. Uniform laws and model codes are created by panels of experts and scholars and adopted at the option of each state's legislature.

C. ADMINISTRATIVE LAW

Administrative law consists of the rules, orders, and decisions of administrative agencies. Congress creates a federal agency through enabling legislation, which specifies the powers of the agency. These powers may include rulemaking, investigation and enforcement, and adjudication.

D. CASE LAW

Case law includes courts' interpretations of constitutional provisions, statutes, and administrative rules. Because statutes often codify common law rules, courts often rely on the common law as a guide to the intent and purpose of a statute. Case law governs all areas not covered by statutes.

IV. CLASSIFICATIONS OF LAW

A. SUBSTANTIVE AND PROCEDURAL LAW

Substantive law includes laws that define, describe, regulate, and create rights and duties. *Procedural law* includes rules for enforcing those rights.

B. CRIMINAL AND CIVIL LAW

Criminal law regulates relationships between individuals and society. *Civil law* regulates relationships between individuals.

C. NATIONAL AND INTERNATIONAL LAW

1. National Law

National law is the law of a particular nation. Laws vary from country to country, but generally each nation has either a common law or civil law system. A common law system, like ours, is based on case law. A civil law system is based on codified law (statutes).

2. International Law

International law consists of written and unwritten laws observed by independent nations and governing the acts of individuals and governments. Sources include treaties and international organizations.

a. Treaties

Agreements or contracts between two or more nations that must be authorized and ratified by the supreme power of each. A bilateral agreement occurs when only two nations form an agreement; multilateral agreements are those formed by several nations.

b. International Organizations

Composed mainly of nations; usually established by treaty; such entities adopt resolutions that require particular behavior.

3. Contracts in an International Setting

Special provisions avoid problems in international contracts.

a. Choice-of-Language Clause

Designates the official language by which a contract will be interpreted in the event of disagreement. Clauses may also provide for translations and arbitration in certain languages.

b. Choice-of-Forum Clause

Designates the jurisdiction, including the specific court, in which a dispute will be litigated. The forum may be anywhere—it does not have to be in the nations of the parties to the contract.

    c. **Choice-of -Law Clause**
Designates what law to apply in a dispute. There is no limit on the parties' choice. If no law is specified, the governing law is that of the seller's place of business.

V.   THE CONSTITUTION AS IT AFFECTS BUSINESS

A.   THE COMMERCE CLAUSE
The Constitution (Article I, Section 8) gives Congress the power to regulate commerce among the states.

1.   The Commerce Power Today
The national government can regulate every commercial enterprise in the United States. The United States Supreme Court has held, however, that this does not justify regulation of areas that have "nothing to do with commerce."

2.   The Regulatory Powers of the States
States possess police powers (the right to regulate private activities to protect or promote the public order, health, safety, morals, and general welfare). Statutes covering almost every aspect of life have been enacted under the police powers.

3.   The "Dormant" Commerce Clause
When state laws impinge on interstate commerce, courts balance the state's interest in regulating a certain matter against the burden on interstate commerce. State laws that *substantially* interfere with interstate commerce violate the commerce clause.

B.   BUSINESS AND THE BILL OF RIGHTS
The first ten amendments to the Constitution protect individuals and businesses against some interference by the federal government. Under the due process clause of the Fourteenth Amendment, many rights also apply to the states.

C.   FREEDOM OF SPEECH
The First Amendment guaranty of freedom of speech applies to the federal and state governments.

1.   Freedom of Speech
The First Amendment guaranty of freedom of speech applies to the federal and state governments.

a.   Speech with Limited Protection

1)   Political Speech
States can prohibit corporations from using corporate funds for independent expressions of opinion about political candidates.

2)   Commercial Speech
A state restriction on commercial speech (advertising) is valid if it (1) seeks to implement a substantial government interest, (2) directly advances that interest, and (3) goes no further than necessary to accomplish its objective.

b.   Speech That the Constitution Does Not Protect

1)   Defamatory Speech
Speech that harms another's good reputation can take the form of libel (if it is in writing) or slander (if it is oral).

2)   Lewd and Obscene Speech
States can ban child pornography. One court has banned lewd speech and pornographic pinups in the workplace.

3)   "Fighting Words"
Words that are likely to incite others to violence.

4)   **Online Obscenity**
Attempts to regulate obscene materials on the Internet have been challenged, and some have been struck, as unconstitutional.

2.   **Freedom of Religion**
Under the First Amendment, the government may not establish a religion (the establishment clause) nor prohibit the exercise of religion (the free exercise clause). Restrictions on commerce on Sunday have been upheld on the ground it is a legitimate government function to provide a day of rest.

3.   **Due Process**
Both the Fifth and Fourteenth Amendments provide no person shall be deprived "of life, liberty, or property, without due process of law."

a.   **Procedural Due Process**
Procedural due process requires that any government decision to take away the life, liberty, or property of an individual be accompanied by procedural safeguards to ensure fairness.

b.   **Substantive Due Process**
Substantive due process focuses on the content (substance) of legislation.

1)   **Compelling Interest Test**
A statute can restrict an individual's fundamental right (such as all First Amendment rights) only if the statute promotes a compelling or overriding governmental interest.

2)   **Rational Basis Test**
Restrictions on business activities must relate rationally to a legitimate government purpose. Most regulations qualify.

VI.   FINDING AND ANALYZING THE LAW

A.   FINDING STATUTORY AND ADMINISTRATIVE LAW

1.   **Publication of Statutes**
Federal statutes are arranged by date of enactment in *United States Statutes at Large*. State statutes are collected in similar state publications. Statutes are also published in codified form (the form in which they appear in the federal and state codes) in other publications.

2.   **Finding a Statute in a Publication**
Statutes are usually referred to in their codified form. In the codes, laws are compiled by subject. For example, the *United States Code* (U.S.C.) arranges by subject most federal laws. Each subject is assigned a title number and each statute a section number within a title.

3.   **Publication of Administrative Rules**
Rules and regulations adopted by federal administrative agencies are published initially in the *Federal Register*. They are also compiled by subject in the *Code of Federal Regulations* (C.F.R.).

4.   **Finding an Administrative Rule in a Publication**
In the C.F.R., administrative rules are arranged by subject. Each subject is assigned a title number and each rule a section number within a title.

B.   FINDING CASE LAW

1.   **Publication of Court Opinions**
State appellate court opinions are often published by the state in consecutively numbered volumes. They may also be published in units of the *National Reporter System*, by West Publishing Company. Federal court opinions appear in other West publications.

2. **Finding a Court Opinion in a Publication**
   After a decision is published, it can be referred to by the name of the case and the volume, name, and page number of one or more reporters. This information is called the **citation**.

C. **READING AND UNDERSTANDING CASE LAW**

1. **Plaintiffs and Defendants**
   In the title of a case (*Adams v. Jones*), the *v.* means **versus** (against). Adams is the **plaintiff** (the person who filed the suit) and Jones the **defendant** (the person against whom the suit was brought). An appellate court may place the name of the appellant first (*Jones v. Adams*.).

2. **Appellants and Appellees**
   An **appellant** (or **petitioner**) is the party who appeals a case to another court or jurisdiction from the one in which the case was brought. An **appellee** (or **respondent**) is the party against whom an appeal is taken.

3. **Judges and Justices**
   These terms are designations given to judges in different courts.

4. **Decisions and Opinions**
   An opinion contains a court's reasons for its decision, the rules of law that apply, and the judgment.

TRUE-FALSE QUESTIONS

(Answers at the Back of the Book)

____ 1. Law is a body of enforceable rules governing relationships among individuals and between individuals and their society.

____ 2. The doctrine of *stare decisis* obligates judges to follow precedents established within their jurisdictions.

____ 3. Common law develops from rules of law announced in court decisions.

____ 4. Statutory law is legislation.

____ 5. Congress enacted the Uniform Commercial Code for adoption by the states.

____ 6. Criminal law covers disputes between persons, and between persons and their governments.

____ 7. In most states, the same courts can grant legal or equitable remedies.

____ 8. Congress can regulate any activity that substantially affects commerce.

____ 9. A state law that substantially impinges on interstate commerce is unconstitutional.

____ 10. Any restriction on commercial speech is unconstitutional.

FILL-IN QUESTIONS

(Answers at the Back of the Book)

The common law system, on which the American legal system is based, involves the application of principles applied in earlier cases _____(with similar facts/whether or not the facts are similar). This use of previous case law, or _____ (precedent/preeminent), is known as the doctrine of *stare decisis*, and _____ _____ (emphasizes a flexible/permits a predictable) resolution of cases.

MULTIPLE-CHOICE QUESTIONS

(Answers at the Back of the Book)

____ **1.** According to the doctrine of *stare decisis,* a court must follow rules of law established by

a. all courts.
b. courts of higher rank only.
c. courts of lower rank only.
d. none of the above.

____ **2.** Applying the doctrine of *stare decisis* requires a court to find cases that, compared to a case before it, has

a. entirely different facts.
b. identical facts.
c. similar facts.
d. none of the above.

____ **3.** Rescission is

a. an action to cancel a contract and return the parties to the positions they held before the contract's formation.
b. an award of damages.
c. an order to do or refrain from doing a particular act.
d. an order to perform what was promised.

____ **4.** In a given case, most courts may grant

a. equitable remedies only.
b. legal remedies only.
c. equitable or legal remedies, but not both.
d. equitable remedies, legal remedies, or both.

____ **5.** The U.S. Constitution takes precedence over

a. a provision in a state constitution or statute only.
b. a state supreme court decision only.
c. a state constitution, statute, and court decision.
d. none of the above.

____ **6.** Case law includes interpretations of federal and state

a. administrative rules and statutes only.
b. constitutions only.
c. administrative rules, statutes, and constitutions.
d. none of the above.

____ **7.** Civil law concerns

a. disputes between persons, and between persons and their governments.
b. only laws that define, describe, regulate, and create rights and duties.
c. only laws that establish methods for enforcing rights.
d. wrongs committed against society for which society demands redress.

____ **8.** The sources of international law include

    a. customs that have evolved among nations in their relations only.
    b. international organizations and treaties only.
    c. laws of individual nations only.
    d. international customs, organizations, and treaties, and national law.

____ **9.** A state statute that bans certain advertising practices to prevent consumers from being misled is likely unconstitutional under

    a. the commerce clause.
    b. the First Amendment.
    c. the Uniform Commercial Code.
    d. none of the above.

____ **10.** Under the First Amendment, protected speech includes

    a. dissemination of obscene materials.
    b. "fighting words."
    c. speech that harms the good reputation of another.
    d. none of the above.

SHORT ESSAY QUESTIONS

1. What is the primary function of law?

2. What is the significance of the commerce clause?

ISSUE SPOTTERS

(Answers at the Back of the Book)

1. Under what circumstance might a judge rely on case law to determine the intent and purpose of a statute?

2. Apples & Oranges Corporation learns that a federal administrative agency is considering a rule that will have a negative impact on the firm's ability to do business. Does the firm have any opportunity to express its opinion about the pending rule?

3. Would a state law imposing a fifteen-year term of imprisonment without allowing a trial on all businesspersons who appear in their own television commercials be a violation of substantive due process? Would it violate procedural due process?

Chapter 2:
Traditional and Online Dispute Resolution

WHAT THIS CHAPTER IS ABOUT

This chapter explains which courts have power to hear what disputes and when and outlines what happens before, during, and after a civil trial. The chapter also covers alternative dispute resolution and online dispute resolution.

CHAPTER OUTLINE

I. THE JUDICIARY'S ROLE IN AMERICAN GOVERNMENT

The power of **judicial review**: the courts can decide whether the laws or actions of the executive branch and the legislative branch are constitutional.

II. BASIC JUDICIAL REQUIREMENTS

A. JURISDICTION

To hear a case, a court must have jurisdiction over (1) the defendant or the property involved and (2) the subject matter.

1. Jurisdiction over Persons or Property

A court has *in personam* (personal) jurisdiction over state residents. Long arm statutes permit courts to exercise jurisdiction over nonresidents who have *minimum contacts* with the state (e.g., do business there). A court has *in rem* jurisdiction over property within its borders.

2. Jurisdiction over Subject Matter

A court of **general jurisdiction** can decide virtually any type of case. A court's jurisdiction may be **limited** by the subject of a suit, the amount of money in controversy, or whether a proceeding is a trial or appeal.

3. Jurisdiction of the Federal Courts

a. Federal Questions

Any suit based on the Constitution, a treaty, or a federal law can originate in a federal court.

b. Diversity of Citizenship

Federal jurisdiction covers cases involving (1) citizens of different states, (2) a foreign government and citizens of a state or of different states, or (3) citizens of a state and citizens or subjects of a foreign government. The amount in controversy must be more than $75,000.

4. Exclusive v. Concurrent Jurisdiction

Exclusive: when cases can be tried only in federal courts or only in state courts. Concurrent: When both federal and state courts can hear a case.

B. JURISDICTION IN CYBERSPACE

Whether a court can compel the appearance of a party *outside* the physical limits of the court's jurisdiction depends on the amount of business the party transacts over the Internet with parties *within* the court's jurisdiction.

C. VENUE
Venue is concerned with the most appropriate location for a trial.

D. STANDING TO SUE
Standing is the interest (injury or threat) that a plaintiff has in a case. A plaintiff must have standing to bring a suit, and the controversy must be justiciable (real, as opposed to hypothetical or purely academic).

III.   THE STATE AND FEDERAL COURT SYSTEMS

A. STATE COURT SYSTEMS

1. Trial Courts
Trial courts are courts in which trials are held and testimony is taken.

2. Courts of Appeals
Courts that hear appeals from trial courts look at *questions of law* (what law governs a dispute) but not *questions of fact* (what occurred in the dispute), unless a trial court's finding of fact is clearly contrary to the evidence. Decision of a state's highest court on state law is final.

B. THE FEDERAL COURT SYSTEM

1. U.S. District Courts
The federal equivalent of a state trial court of general jurisdiction. There is at least one federal district court in every state. Other federal trial courts include the U.S. Tax Court and the U.S. Bankruptcy Court.

2. U.S. Courts of Appeals
The U.S. (circuit) courts of appeals for twelve of the circuits hear appeals from the federal district courts located within their respective circuits. The court of appeals for the thirteenth circuit (the federal circuit) has national jurisdiction over certain cases.

3. The United States Supreme Court
The Supreme Court, the highest level of the federal court system, can review any case decided by any of the federal courts of appeals, and it has authority over some cases decided in state courts. To appeal a case to the Supreme Court, a party asks for a writ of *certiorari*. Whether the Court issues the writ is within its discretion.

IV.   FOLLOWING A STATE COURT CASE

A. THE PLEADINGS

1. The Plaintiff's Complaint
Filed by the plaintiff with the clerk of the trial court. Contains (1) a statement alleging the facts for the court to take jurisdiction, (2) a short statement of the facts necessary to show that the plaintiff is entitled to a remedy, and (3) a statement of the remedy the plaintiff is seeking.

2. The Summons
Served on the defendant, with the complaint. Notifies the defendant to answer the complaint (usually within twenty to thirty days).

3. The Defendant's Response
No response results in a default judgment for the plaintiff.

a. Answer
Admits the allegations in the complaint or denies them and sets out any defenses. May include a counterclaim against the plaintiff.

b. Motion to Dismiss
The defendant may file a motion to dismiss. If the court denies the motion, the defendant must file an answer. If the court grants the motion, the plaintiff must file an amended complaint.

B. PRETRIAL MOTIONS

1. Motion to Dismiss
(See above.) Either party may file a motion to dismiss if they have agreed to settle the case. A court may file such a motion on its own.

2. Motion for Judgment on the Pleadings
Any party can file this motion (after the pleadings have been filed), when no facts are disputed and only questions of law are at issue. A court may consider only those facts stated in the pleadings.

3. Motion for Summary Judgment
Any party can file this motion, if there is no disagreement about the facts and the only question is which laws apply. A court can consider evidence outside the pleadings.

C. DISCOVERY
The process of obtaining information from the opposing party or from witnesses. May include depositions; interrogatories; requests for admissions, documents, objects, entry on land, and physical or mental examinations.

D. PRETRIAL CONFERENCE
This is an informal discussion between the judge and the attorneys, after discovery, to identify the issues, consider a settlement, and plan the trial.

E. JURY SELECTION
The process by which a jury is chosen is *voir dire*—the jurors are questioned, and a party may ask that some not be sworn.

F. AT THE TRIAL
First, each side presents opening statements. Second, the plaintiff presents his or her case, offering evidence, including the testimony of witnesses. The defendant can challenge the evidence and cross-examine the witnesses.

1. Motion for a Directed Verdict
After the plaintiff's case, the defendant can ask the judge to direct a verdict on the ground the plaintiff presented no evidence to justify relief. If the motion is not granted, the defendant presents his or her case, after which this motion can be filed again.

2. Jury Verdict
In a jury trial, the jury decides the facts and the amount of the award, if any, to be paid by the losing party. This is the verdict.

G. POSTTRIAL MOTIONS

1. Motion for Judgment *N.O.V.*
The defendant can file this motion, if he or she previously moved for a directed verdict. The standards for granting this motion are the same as those for granting a motion to dismiss or for a directed verdict.

2. Motion for a New Trial
This motion is granted if the judge believes that the jury erred but that it is not appropriate to grant a judgment for the other side.

H. THE APPEAL

1. **Filing the Appeal**
Appellant files a notice of appeal with the clerk of the trial court, and the record on appeal, an abstract, and a brief with the reviewing court. Appellee files an answering brief. The parties can give oral arguments.

2. **Appellate Review**
Appellate courts do not usually reverse findings of fact unless they are contradicted by the evidence presented at the trial in the lower court.

a. **Options of an Appellate Court**
(1) Affirm: enforce the lower court's order; (2) reverse (if an error was committed during the trial); or (3) remand: send back to the court that originally heard the case for a new trial.

b. **Appeal to a Higher Appellate Court**
If the reviewing court is an intermediate appellate court, the case may be appealed to the state's highest court. If a federal question is involved, the case may go to the United States Supreme Court.

I. **ENFORCING THE JUDGMENT**
A judgment may not be enforceable, particularly if a losing party does not have sufficient assets or insurance to cover it.

V. THE COURTS ADAPT TO THE ONLINE WORLD

A. **Electronic Filing**
To save time, storage space, etc., courts are switching from paper to electronic document filing, using the Internet, e-mail, and CD-ROMs.

B. **Courts Online**
Most courts have Web sites. What is available on the sites varies.

C. **Cyber Courts and Proceedings**
The future may see the use of virtual courtrooms, in which proceedings take place only on the Internet.

VI. ALTERNATIVE DISPUTE RESOLUTION (ADR)

A. **NEGOTIATION**
Parties come together informally, with or without attorneys, to try to settle or resolve their differences without involving independent third parties.

B. **MEDIATION**
Parties come together informally with a mediator, who may propose solutions for the parties. A mediator is often an expert in a particular field.

C. **ARBITRATION**
An arbitrator—the third party hearing the dispute—decides the dispute. The decision may be legally binding.

1. **Arbitration Clauses**
Disputes are often arbitrated because of an arbitration clause in a contract entered into before the dispute. Courts generally enforce such clauses.

2. **Arbitration Statutes**
Most states have statutes under which arbitration clauses are enforced. The Federal Arbitration Act (FAA) enforces arbitration clauses in contracts involving interstate commerce.

3. **The Arbitration Process**
At an arbitration hearing, the parties make their arguments, present evidence, and call and examine witnesses, and the arbitrator makes a decision. The decision is called an award, even if no money is involved.

D. **OTHER TYPES OF ADR**

1. **Early Neutral Case Evaluation**
Parties select a neutral third party (generally an expert) to evaluate their positions, with no hearing and no discovery. The evaluation is a basis for negotiating a settlement.

2. **Mini-trial**
A private proceeding in which attorneys briefly argue each party's case. A third party indicates how a court would likely decide the issue.

3. **Summary Jury Trial**
Like a mini-trial, but a jury renders a nonbinding verdict. Negotiations follow. If no settlement is reached, either side can seek a full trial.

VII.   ONLINE DISPUTE RESOLUTION
Many Web sites offer online dispute resolution (ODR) services to help resolve small- to medium-sized business liability claims.

A. **WHAT LAW APPLIES IN AN ODR PROCEEDING?**
Most ODR services do not apply the law of a specific jurisdiction. Results are based on general, common legal principles.

B. **NEGOTIATION AND MEDIATION SERVICES**

1. **Online Negotiation**
A settlement may be negotiated through blind bidding: one party submits an offer to be shown to the other party if it falls within a previously agreed range. There is a limited time to respond.

2. **Mediation Providers—SquareTrade**
SquareTrade resolves, as part of a free pilot program, disputes involving $100 or more between eBay customers. SquareTrade also resolves other disputes related to online transactions, using software to walk participants through a step-by-step resolution process.

C. **ARBITRATION PROGRAMS**

1. **Internet Corporation for Assigned Names and Numbers (ICANN)**
The federal government set up ICANN as a nonprofit corporation to oversee the distribution of domain names. ICANN has issued rules and authorized organizations to resolve related disputes.

2. **Resolution Forum, Inc. (RFI)**
RFI, a nonprofit entity associated with the Center for Legal Responsibility at South Texas College of Law, offers arbitration in an online conference room via a standard browser, using a password.

3. **Virtual Magistrate Project (VMAG)**
VMAG resolves disputes involving users of online systems; victims of wrongful messages, postings and files; and system operators subject to complaints or similar demands. Online-related contract, intellectual property, property, and tort disputes. The goal is resolution within seventy-two hours. Appeal of a result may be made to a court.

TRUE-FALSE QUESTIONS

(Answers at the Back of the Book)

____ 1. Under a long arm statute, a state court can compel someone outside the state to appear in the court.

____ 2. Doing substantial business in a jurisdiction over the Internet can be enough to support a court's jurisdiction over a nonresident defendant.

____ 3. The United States Supreme Court is the final authority for any case decided by a state court.

____ 4. Suits involving federal questions originate in federal district courts.

____ 5. An answer may admit or deny the statements or allegations in a complaint.

____ 6. Before a trial, if there are no issues of fact, and only questions of law, a court may grant a summary judgment.

____ 7. Only a losing party may appeal to a higher court.

____ 8. Most lawsuits go to trial.

____ 9. In mediation, a mediator makes a decision on the matter in dispute.

____ 10. A party to an arbitration agreement may never be compelled to arbitrate a dispute.

FILL-IN QUESTIONS

(Answers at the Back of the Book)

A motion _____ (to dismiss/for summary judgment) alleges that even if the facts in a complaint are true, their legal consequences are such that there is no reason to go on with the suit and no need for the defendant to file an answer. A motion _____ (to dismiss/for judgment on the pleadings) is filed after the complaint, answer, and any counterclaim and reply have been filed, when no facts are disputed and only questions of law are at issue. A motion for _____ (summary judgment/a new trial) is proper if there is no disagreement on the facts and the only question is which laws apply to the facts.

MULTIPLE-CHOICE QUESTIONS

(Answers at the Back of the Book)

____ 1. Bob, who lives in Texas, advertises his business on the Web. Bob's page receives hundreds of "hits" by residents of Ohio. If a resident of Ohio files a suit against Bob in an Ohio state court, the court can compel Bob to appear, under the "sliding scale" test, if

a. Bob conducted substantial business with Ohio residents at his Web site.
b. there was any interactivity with any Ohio resident at Bob's Web site.
c. Bob's Web site was only a passive ad.
d. any of the above.

____ 2. In Alpha Company's suit against Beta Corporation, before the trial Alpha can obtain from Beta access to

a. all related documents in Beta's files.
b. everything in Beta's files.
c. nothing in Beta's files.
d. only material in Beta's files that Beta is willing to make available.

____ 3. General Business, Inc. (GBI), has its offices in Virginia, but owns property in Maryland, where Ann files a suit against GBI concerning that property. In this suit, Maryland has

a. diversity jurisdiction.
b. *in personam* jurisdiction.
c. *in rem* jurisdiction.
d. no jurisdiction.

____ 4. National Service Corporation was incorporated in Delaware, has its main office in California, and does business in New York. National is subject to the jurisdiction of

a. Delaware, California, or New York.
b. Delaware or California, but not New York.
c. Delaware or New York, but not California.
d. California or New York, but not Delaware.

____ 5. Ace Manufacturing, Inc., loses its suit against Best Products, Inc., and files an appeal. The appellate court is most likely to review the trial court's

a. application of the law.
b. consideration of the credibility of the evidence.
c. findings of fact.
d. interpretation of the conduct of the witnesses.

____ 6. The United States Supreme Court is required to hear John's suit against Kay if

a. it comes from a federal court.
b. it is an appeal.
c. John lost in a lower court.
d. none of the above.

____ 7. Grant serves a complaint on Lee, who files a motion to dismiss. Lee will also need to file an answer to the complaint if

a. the motion to dismiss is granted.
b. the motion to dismiss is denied.
c. Grant files a motion for judgment on the pleadings.
d. none of the above.

____ 8. In Carol's suit against Don, before going to trial, the parties meet, with their attorneys, to try to resolve the dispute without a third party. This is

a. arbitration.
b. litigation.
c. mediation.
d. negotiation.

____ 9. In Sara's suit against Tim, their attorneys present the case to a judge and jury. The jury renders an advisory verdict. The judge then meets with the parties to encourage a settlement. This is

a. a mini-trial.
b. a summary jury trial.
c. early neutral case evaluation.
d. mediation.

___ **10.** Small Business Company submits a claim against Medium Market Supplier, Inc., to an online dispute resolution forum. An appeal of this dispute may be made to a court by

a. Small only.
b. Medium only.
c. Small or Medium.
d. none of the above.

SHORT ESSAY QUESTIONS

1. What is jurisdiction? How does jurisdiction over a person or property differ from subject matter jurisdiction? What does a long arm statute do?

2. What are the advantages and disadvantages of alternative dispute resolution?

ISSUE SPOTTERS

(Answers at the Back of the Book)

Jan contracted with Dean to deliver a quantity of computers to Jan's Computer Store. They disagree over the amount, the delivery date, the price, and the quality.

1. Their state requires that their dispute be submitted to mediation or nonbinding arbitration. If the dispute is not resolved, or if either party disagrees with the decision of the mediator or arbitrator, will a court hear the case?

2. At the trial, after Jan calls her witnesses, offers her evidence, and otherwise presents her side of the case, Dean has at least two choices between courses of actions. Dean can call his first witness. What else might Dean do?

3. After the trial, the judge issues a judgment that includes a grant of relief for Jan, but the relief is not as much as Jan wanted. Neither Jan nor Dean are satisfied with this result. Can either party—or both—appeal to a higher court?

Chapter 3
Ethics and Social Responsibility

WHAT THIS CHAPTER IS ABOUT

The concepts set out in this chapter include the nature of business ethics and the relationship between ethics and business. Ultimately, the goal of this chapter is to provide you with basic tools for analyzing ethical issues in a business context.

CHAPTER OUTLINE

I. BUSINESS ETHICS
Ethics is the study of what constitutes right and wrong behavior. Ethics focuses on morality and the application of moral principles in everyday life.

A. WHAT IS BUSINESS ETHICS?
Business ethics focuses on what constitutes ethical behavior in the world of business. Business ethics is *not* a separate kind of ethics.

B. WHY IS BUSINESS ETHICS IMPORTANT?
An understanding of business ethics is important to the long-run viability of a business, the well being of its officers and directors, and the welfare of its employees.

II. SETTING THE RIGHT ETHICAL TONE
Some unethical conduct is founded on the lack of sanctions.

A. THE IMPORTANCE OF ETHICAL LEADERSHIP
Management must set and apply ethical standards to which they are committed. Employees will likely follow their example. Ethical conduct can be furthered by not tolerating unethical behavior, setting realistic employee goals, and periodic employee review.

B. CREATING ETHICAL CODES OF CONDUCT
Most large corporations have codes of conduct that indicate the firm's commitment to legal compliance and to the welfare of those who are affected by corporate decisions and practices. Large firms may also emphasize ethics in other ways (for example, with training programs).

C. CORPORATE COMPLIANCE PROGRAMS
Components of a comprehensive corporate ethical-compliance program include an ethical code of conduct, an ethics committee, training programs, and internal audits to monitor compliance. These components should be integrated. The Sarbanes-Oxley Act of 2002 requires firms to set up confidential systems for employees to report suspected illegal or unethical financial practices.

D. CONFLICTS AND TRADE-OFFS
A firm's duty to its shareholders should be weighed against duties to others who may have a greater stake in a particular decision. For example, an employer should consider whether it has an ethical duty to loyal, long-term employees not to replace them with workers who will accept lower pay and whether this duty prevails over a duty to improve profitability by restructuring.

III. DEFYING THE RULES: THE ENRON CASE
Unethical conduct resulted in the single largest bankruptcy of a U.S. business firm.

A. THE UNETHICAL CONDUCT
Managers took advantage of accounting standards to overestimate future earnings, which resulted in inflated reports of current earnings. To maintain these exaggerations, the company created subsidiaries to which it could shift unreported losses and assets with inflated values. Many of these shifts occurred outside the U.S. to avoid federal income taxes. When questioned, management refused to investigate and reveal financial improprieties.

B. WHO WAS AFFECTED
This misconduct affected the firm's managers, employees, suppliers, and shareholders, and the community and society in general.

IV. BUSINESS ETHICS AND THE LAW
The minimal acceptable standard for ethical business behavior is compliance with the law. Ethical standards, such as those in a company's policies or codes of ethics, must also guide decisions.

A. LAWS REGULATING BUSINESS
Because there are many laws regulating business, it is possible to violate one without realizing it. Ignorance of the law is no excuse.

B. "GRAY AREAS"
There are many "gray areas" in which it is difficult to predict how a court will rule. For example, if a consumer's misuse of a product harms the consumer, should the manufacturer bear the responsibility? The best course is to act responsibly and in good faith.

C. TECHNOLOGICAL DEVELOPMENTS AND LEGAL UNCERTAINTIES
How laws apply in the context of cyberspace is not certain.

V. APPROACHES TO ETHICAL REASONING
Ethical reasoning is the process by which an individual examines a situation according to his or her moral convictions or ethical standards. Fundamental ethical reasoning approaches include the following.

A. DUTY-BASED ETHICS

1. Religious Ethical Standards
Religious standards provide that when an act is prohibited by religious teachings, it is unethical and should not be undertaken, regardless of the consequences. Religious standards also involve compassion.

2. Kantian Ethics
Immanual Kant believed that people should be respected because they are qualitatively different from other physical objects. Kant's *categorical imperative* is that individuals should evaluate their actions in light of what would happen if everyone acted the same way.

3. Principle of Rights
According to the principle that persons have rights (to life and liberty, for example), a key factor in determining whether a business decision is ethical is how that decision affects the rights of others, including employees, customers and society.

B. OUTCOME-BASED ETHICS
Utilitarianism is a belief that an action is ethical if it produces the greatest good for the greatest number. This approach is often criticized, because it tends to reduce the welfare of people to plus and minus signs on a cost-benefit worksheet.

VI.   CORPORATE SOCIAL RESPONSIBILITY

A. VIEWS ON CORPORATE SOCIAL RESPONSIBILITY

1. Profit Maximization
Corporate directors and officers must act in the shareholders' interest, which is to maximize profits. Some reason that this is also in society's interest, and thus that generating income is acting ethically.

2. The Stakeholder Approach
Under this approach, a firm's duty to its shareholders should be weighed against duties to others (employees, etc.) who may have a greater stake in a particular decision.

3. Corporate Citizenship
This theory argues that business firms should pursue goals that society deems important, because firms have so much wealth and power.

B. MAXIMUM VERSUS OPTIMUM PROFITS
Behaving ethically can protect a firm's reputation and profits. Many firms thus attempt to strike a balance between ethics and profits, and aim for optimum, rather than maximum, profits.

C. THE ROLE OF PUBLIC OPINION
Being ethical can protect a firm's reputation and profits, in light of public opinion.

VII.   BUSINESS ETHICS ON A GLOBAL LEVEL

A. MONITORING THE EMPLOYMENT PRACTICES OF FOREIGN SUPPLIERS
Concerns include the treatment of foreign workers who make goods imported and sold in the United States by U.S. firms. Should a U.S firm refuse to deal with certain suppliers or monitor their workplaces to make sure that the workers are not being mistreated?

B. THE FOREIGN CORRUPT PRACTICES ACT
The Foreign Corrupt Practices Act (FCPA) of 1977 applies to—

1. U.S. Companies
Including their directors, officers, shareholders, employees, and agents.

    a. What Is Prohibited
The FCPA prohibits the bribery of most foreign government officials to get an official to act in an official capacity to provide business opportunities.

    b. What Is Permitted
The FCPA permits payments to (1) minor officials whose duties are ministerial, (2) foreign officials if the payments are lawful in the foreign country, or (3) private foreign companies or other third parties unless the U.S. firm knows payments will be made to a foreign government.

2. Accountants

    a. What Is Required
All companies must (1) keep detailed records that "accurately and fairly" reflect the company's financial activities and (2) have an accounting system that provides "reasonable assurance" that all transactions are accounted for and legal.

    b. What Is Prohibited
The FCPA prohibits false statements to accountants and false entries in accounts.

3. Penalties
Firms: fines up to $2 million. Officers or directors: fines up to $100,000 (cannot be paid by the company); imprisonment up to five years.

C. OTHER NATIONS

A treaty signed by members of the Organization for Economic Cooperation and Development makes the bribery of foreign officials a crime.

TRUE-FALSE QUESTIONS

(Answers at the Back of the Book)

____ 1. Ethics is the study of what constitutes right and wrong behavior.

____ 2. A background in business ethics is as important as knowledge of specific laws.

____ 3. The *minimal* acceptable standard for ethical behavior is compliance with the law.

____ 4. According to utilitarianism, it does not matter how many people benefit from an act.

____ 5. The best course towards accomplishing legal and ethical behavior is to act responsibly and in good faith.

____ 6. The ethics of a particular act is always clear.

____ 7. Optimum profits are the maximum profits that a firm can earn while staying within legal *and* ethical limits.

____ 8. If an act is legal, it is ethical.

____ 9. If a corporation fails to act ethically, its profits may suffer.

____ 10. Bribery of public officials is only an ethical issue.

FILL-IN QUESTIONS

(Answers at the Back of the Book)

_____ (Religious standards/ Kantian ethics/ The principle of rights) provide that when an act is prohibited by religious teachings, it is unethical and should not be undertaken, regardless of the consequences. According to _____ (religious standards/ Kantian ethics/ the principle of rights), individuals should evaluate their actions in light of what would happen if everyone acted the same way. According to _____ (religious standards/ Kantian ethics/ the principle of rights), a key factor in determining whether a business decision is ethical is how that decision affects the rights of others.

MULTIPLE-CHOICE QUESTIONS

(Answers at the Back of the Book)

____ 1. Beth is a marketing executive for Consumer Goods Company. Compared to Beth's personal actions, her business actions require the application of ethical standards that are

a. more complex.
b. simpler.
c. the same.
d. none of the above.

____   2. Pat, an employee of Quality Products, Inc., takes a duty-based approach to ethics. Pat believes that regardless of the consequences, he must

  a. avoid unethical behavior.
  b. conform to society's standards.
  c. place his employer's interest first.
  d. produce the greatest good for the most people.

____   3. Joy adopts religious ethical standards. These involve an element of

  a. compassion.
  b. cost-benefit analysis.
  c. discretion.
  d. utilitarianism.

____   4. Eve, an employee of Fine Sales Company, takes an outcome-based approach to ethics. Eve believes that she must

  a. avoid unethical behavior.
  b. conform to society's standards.
  c. place her employer's interest first.
  d. produce the greatest good for the most people.

____   5. In a debate, Ed's best criticism of utilitarianism is that it

  a. encourages unethical behavior.
  b. fosters conformance with society's standards.
  c. mandates acting in an employer's best interest.
  d. results in human costs many persons find unacceptable.

____   6. In resolving an ethical problem, in most cases a decision by a business firm will have a negative effect on

  a. one group as opposed to another.
  b. the firm's competitors.
  c. the government.
  d. none of the above.

____   7. Ethical standards would most likely be considered to have been violated if Acme Services, Inc., represents to Best Production Company that certain services will be performed for a stated fee, but it is apparent at the time of the representation that

  a. Acme cannot perform the services alone.
  b. the actual charge will be substantially higher.
  c. the actual charge will be substantially lower.
  d. the fee is a competitive bid.

____   8. Tina, the president of United Sales, Inc., tries to ensure that United's actions are legal and ethical. To ensure this result, the best course of Tina and United is to act in

  a. good faith.
  b. ignorance of the law.
  c. regard for the firm's shareholders only.
  d. their own self interest.

____ 9. Alan, an executive with Beta Corporation, follows the "principle of rights" theory, under which an action may be ethical depending on how it affects

a. the right determination under a cost-benefit analysis.
b. the right of Alan to maintain his dignity.
c. the right of Beta to make a profit.
d. the rights of others.

____ 10. Gamma, Inc., a U.S. corporation, makes a side payment to the minister of commerce of another country for a favorable business contract. In the United States, this payment would be considered

a. illegal only.
b. unethical only.
c. illegal and unethical.
d. none of the above.

SHORT ESSAY QUESTIONS

What is the difference between legal and ethical standards? How are legal standards affected by ethical standards?

ISSUE SPOTTERS

(Answers at the Back of the Book)

1. If, like Robin Hood, a person robs the rich to pay the poor, does his or her benevolent intent make his or her actions ethical?

2. Delta Tools, Inc., markets a product that under some circumstances is capable of seriously injuring consumers. Does Delta owe an ethical duty to remove this product from the market, even if the injuries result only from misuse?

3. Acme Corporation decides to respond to what it sees as a moral obligation to correct for past discrimination by adjusting pay differences among its employees. Does this raise an ethical conflict between Acme's employees? Between Acme and its employees? Between Acme and its shareholders?

CUMULATIVE HYPOTHETICAL PROBLEM FOR UNIT ONE—INCLUDING CHAPTERS 1–3

(Answers at the Back of the Book)

Computer Data, Inc. (CDI), incorporated and based in California, signs a contract with Digital Products Corporation (DPC), incorporated and based in Arizona, to make and sell customized software for DPC to, in turn, sell to its clients. CDI ships defective software to DPC, which sells it to Eagle Distribution Corporation. The defective software causes losses to Eagle estimated at $100,000.

____ 1. Federal authorities file charges against CDI, alleging that the shipment of defective software violated a federal statute. CDI asks the court to exercise its power of judicial review. This means that the court can review

a. the actions of the federal authorities and declare them excessive.
b. the charges against CDI and declare them unfounded.
c. the statute and declare it unconstitutional.
d. the totality of the situation and declare it unethical.

____ **2.** Eagle and DPC enter into mediation. In mediation, the parties

a. may come to an agreement by mutual consent.
b. must accept a winner-take-all result.
c. settle their dispute without the assistance of a third party.
d. submit their dispute to a mediator for a legally binding decision.

____ **3.** Eagle is located in Tennessee. Eagle could file a suit against DPC in

a. Arizona only.
b. Tennessee only.
c. a federal court only.
d. Arizona, Tennessee, or a federal court.

____ **4.** Eagle files a suit against DPC, seeking the amount of its losses as damages. Damages is a remedy

a. at law.
b. in equity.
c. at law or in equity, depending on how the plaintiff phrases its complaint.
d. at law or in equity, depending on whether there was any actual "damage."

____ **5.** CDI's managers evaluate the shipment of defective software in terms of CDI's ethical obligations, if any. In other words, CDI's managers are considering the firm's

a. legal liability.
b. maximum profitability.
c. optimum profitability.
d. right or wrong behavior.

QUESTIONS ON THE FOCUS ON LEGAL REASONING FOR UNIT ONE— *KASKY V. NIKE, INC.*

(Answers at the Back of the Book)

____ **1.** In *Kasky v. Nike, Inc.*, in the majority's opinion, commercial speech is distinguished from other speech in part by

a. its capacity to inform the public.
b. its contribution to the marketplace of ideas.
c. its inherent worth.
d. the identity of the speaker.

____ **2.** In the dissent's opinion, commercial speech should be distinguished from other speech by

a. its capacity to inform the public.
b. its content.
c. its inherent worth in the marketplace of ideas.
d. the identity of the speaker.

____ **3.** According to the majority, its holding regarding the defendant would have a chilling effect on

a. commercial speech only.
b. public debate only.
c. commercial speech and public debate.
d. none of the above.

Chapter 4:
Torts and Cyber Torts

WHAT THIS CHAPTER IS ABOUT

Torts consist of wrongful conduct by one person that causes injury to another. *Tort* is French for "wrong." For acts that cause physical injury or that interfere with physical security and freedom of movement, tort law provides remedies, typically damages.

This chapter outlines intentional torts, negligence, and strict liability. These categories include torts that are specifically related to business and cyber torts.

CHAPTER OUTLINE

I. THE BASIS OF TORT LAW
Two notions serve as the basis of all torts: wrongs and compensation. Tort law recognizes that some acts are wrong because they cause injuries to others. Most crimes involve torts, but not all torts are crimes. A tort action is a *civil* action in which one person brings a personal suit against another, usually for damages.

II. INTENTIONAL TORTS AGAINST PERSONS
Intentional torts involve acts that were intended or could be expected to bring about consequences that are the basis of the tort. A **tortfeasor** (one committing a tort) must intend to commit an act, the consequences of which interfere with the personal or business interests of another in a way not permitted by law.

A. ASSAULT AND BATTERY

1. **Assault**
An intentional act that creates in another person a reasonable apprehension or fear of immediate harmful or offensive contact.

2. **Battery**
An intentional and harmful or offensive physical contact. Physical injury need not occur. Whether the contact is offensive is determined by the reasonable person standard.

3. **Compensation**
A plaintiff may be compensated for emotional harm or loss of reputation resulting from a battery, as well as for physical harm.

4. **Defenses to Assault and Battery**

   a. **Consent**
   When a person consents to an act that damages him or her, there is generally no liability for the damage.

   b. **Self-Defense**
   An individual who is defending his or her life or physical well-being can claim self-defense.

   c. **Defense of Others**
   An individual can act in a reasonable manner to protect others who are in real or apparent danger.

    d. Defense of Property
    Reasonable force may be used in attempting to remove intruders from one's home, although force that is likely to cause death or great bodily injury can never be used just to protect property.

B. FALSE IMPRISONMENT

1. What False Imprisonment Is
The intentional confinement or restraint of another person without justification. The confinement can be accomplished through the use of physical barriers, physical restraint, or threats of physical force.

2. The Defense of Probable Cause
In some states, a merchant is justified in delaying a suspected shoplifter if the merchant has probable cause. The detention must be conducted in a reasonable manner and for only a reasonable length of time.

C. INFLICTION OF EMOTIONAL DISTRESS
Infliction of emotional distress is an intentional act that amounts to extreme and outrageous conduct resulting in severe emotional distress to another (a few states require physical symptoms). Stalking is one way to commit it. Repeated annoyance, with threats, is another.

D. DEFAMATION
Defamation is wrongfully hurting another's good reputation through false statements. Doing it orally is **slander**; doing it in writing is **libel**.

1. Types of False Utterances That Are Torts *Per Se*
Proof of injury is not required when one falsely states that another has a loathsome communicable disease, has committed improprieties while engaging in a profession or trade, or has committed or been imprisoned for a serious crime, or that a woman is unchaste.

2. The Publication Requirement
The statement must be published (communicated to a third party). Anyone who republishes or repeats a defamatory statement is liable.

3. Defenses against Defamation

    a. Truth
    The statement is true. It must be true in whole, not in part.

    b. Privilege
    The statement is privileged: absolute (made in a judicial or legislative proceeding) or qualified (for example, made by one corporate director to another and was about corporate business).

    c. Public Figure
    The statement is about a public figure, made in a public medium, and related to a matter of general public interest. To recover damages, a public figure must prove a statement was made with **actual malice** (knowledge of its falsity or reckless disregard for the truth).

E. INVASION OF PRIVACY
Four acts qualify as invasions of privacy:

1. The use of a person's name, picture, or other likeness for commercial purposes without permission. (This is **appropriation**—see below.)

2. Intrusion on an individual's affairs or seclusion.

3. Publication of information that places a person in a false light.

4. Public disclosure of private facts about an individual that an ordinary person would find objectionable.

F. APPROPRIATION

The use of one person's name or likeness by another, without permission and for the benefit of the user. An individual's right to privacy includes the right to the exclusive use of his or her identity.

G. MISREPRESENTATION (FRAUD)

Fraud is the use of misrepresentation and deceit for personal gain. Puffery (seller's talk) is not fraud. The elements of fraudulent misrepresentation—

1. **Misrepresentation** of material facts or conditions with knowledge that they are false or with reckless disregard for the truth.

2. **Intent** to induce another to rely on the misrepresentation.

3. **Justifiable reliance** by the deceived party.

4. **Damages** suffered as a result of reliance.

5. **Causal connection** between the misrepresentation and the injury.

H. WRONGFUL INTERFERENCE

1. **Wrongful Interference with a Contractual Relationship**
   Occurs when there is a contract between two parties and a third party who knows of the contract intentionally causes either of the two parties to break it.

2. **Wrongful Interference with a Business Relationship**
   If there are two yogurt stores in a mall, placing an employee of Store A in front of Store B to divert customers to Store A constitutes the tort of wrongful interference with a business relationship.

3. **Defenses to Wrongful Interference**
   A person is not liable if the interference is justified or permissible (such as bona fide competitive behavior).

III. INTENTIONAL TORTS AGAINST PROPERTY

A. TRESPASS TO LAND

Trespass to land occurs if a person, without permission, enters onto, above, or below the surface of land owned by another; causes anything to enter onto the land; or remains on the land or permits anything to remain on it.

1. **Trespass Criteria, Rights, and Duties**
   Posted signs *expressly* establish trespass. Entering onto property to commit an illegal act *impliedly* does so. Trespassers are liable for any property damage. Owners may have a duty to post notice of any danger.

2. **Defenses against Trespass to Land**
   Defenses against trespass include that the trespass was warranted or that the purported owner had no right to possess the land in question.

B. TRESPASS TO PERSONAL PROPERTY

Occurs when an individual unlawfully harms the personal property of another or interferes with an owner's right to exclusive possession and enjoyment. Defenses include that the interference was warranted.

C. CONVERSION

1. **What Conversion Is**

An act depriving an owner of personal property without the owner's permission and without just cause. Conversion is the civil side of crimes related to theft. Buying stolen goods is conversion.

2. **Defenses**

Defenses to conversion include that the purported owner does not own the property or does not have a right to possess it that is superior to the right of the holder. Necessity is also a defense.

D. DISPARAGEMENT OF PROPERTY

Occurs when economically injurious falsehoods are made about another's product or ownership of property. Torts can be specifically referred to as **slander of quality** (product) or **slander of title** (ownership of property).

IV.   UNINTENTIONAL TORTS (NEGLIGENCE)

A. THE ELEMENTS OF NEGLIGENCE

1. **What Negligence Is**

Someone's failure to live up to a required duty of care, causing another to suffer injury. The breach of the duty must create a risk of certain harmful consequences, whether or not that was the intent.

2. **The Elements of Negligence**

(1) A duty of care, (2) breach of the duty of care, (3) damage or injury as a result of the breach, and (4) the breach causes the damage or injury.

B. THE DUTY OF CARE AND ITS BREACH

1. **The Reasonable Person Standard**

The duty of care is measured by the **reasonable person standard** (how a reasonable person would have acted in the same circumstances).

2. **Duty of Landowners**

Owners are expected to use reasonable care (guard against some risks and warn of others) to protect persons coming onto their property.

3. **Duty of Professionals**

A professional's duty is consistent with his or her knowledge, skill, and intelligence, including what is reasonable for that professional.

4. **Factors for Determining a Breach of the Duty of Care**

The nature of the act (whether it is outrageous or commonplace), the manner in which the act is performed (cautiously versus heedlessly), and the nature of the injury (whether it is serious or slight). Note: Failing to rescue a stranger in peril is not a breach of a duty of care.

C. THE INJURY REQUIREMENT AND DAMAGES

To recover damages (receive compensation), the plaintiff must have suffered some loss, harm, wrong, or invasion of a protected interest. Punitive damages (to punish the wrongdoer and deter others) may also be awarded.

D. CAUSATION

1. **Causation in Fact**

The breach of the duty of care must cause the injury—that is, "but for" the wrongful act, the injury would not have occurred.

2. **Proximate Cause**
   There must be a connection between the act and the injury strong enough to justify imposing liability. Generally, the harm or the victim of the harm must have been foreseeable in light of all of the circumstances.

3. **Superseding Cause**
   An unforeseeable intervening force breaks the connection between the breach of the duty of care and the injury or damage. Taking a defensive action (such as swerving to avoid an oncoming car) does not break the connection. Nor does someone else's attempt to rescue the injured party.

E. **DEFENSES TO NEGLIGENCE**

1. **Assumption of Risk**
   One who voluntarily enters a risky situation, knowing the risk, cannot recover. This does not include a risk different from or greater than the risk normally involved in the situation.

2. **Contributory Negligence**
   In some states, a plaintiff cannot recover for an injury if he or she was negligent. The last-clear-chance rule allows a negligent plaintiff to recover if the defendant had the last chance to avoid the damage.

3. **Comparative Negligence**
   In most states, the plaintiff's and the defendant's negligence is compared and liability prorated. Some states allow a plaintiff to recover even if his or her fault is greater than the defendant's. In many states, the plaintiff gets nothing if he or she is more than 50 percent at fault.

F. **SPECIAL NEGLIGENCE DOCTRINES AND STATUTES**

1. *Res Ipsa Loquitur*
   If negligence is very difficult to prove, a court may infer it, and the defendant must prove he or she was *not* negligent. This is only if the event causing the harm is one that normally does not occur in the absence of negligence and is caused by something within the defendant's control.

2. **Negligence *Per Se***
   A person who violates a statute providing for a criminal penalty is liable when the violation causes another to be injured, if (1) the statute sets out a standard of conduct, and when, where, and of whom it is expected; (2) the injured person is in the class protected by the statute; and (3) the statute was designed to prevent the type of injury suffered.

3. **Special Negligence Statutes**
   Good Samaritan statutes protect those who aid others from being sued for negligence. Dram shop acts impose liability on bar owners for injuries caused by intoxicated persons who are served by those owners. A statute may impose liability on social hosts for acts of their guests.

V. **STRICT LIABILITY**
   Under this doctrine, liability for injury is imposed for reasons other than fault.

A. **ABNORMALLY DANGEROUS OR EXCEPTIONAL ACTIVITIES**
   The basis for imposing strict liability on an abnormally dangerous activity is that the activity creates an extreme risk. Balancing the risk against the potential for harm, it is fair to ask the person engaged in the activity to pay for injury caused by that activity.

B. **DANGEROUS ANIMALS**
   A person who keeps a dangerous animal is strictly liable for any harm inflicted by the animal.

C. PRODUCT LIABILITY

A significant application of strict liability is in the area of product liability—liability of manufacturers, sellers, and others for harmful or defective products. Product liability is outlined in Chapter 18.

VI. CYBER TORTS

A. DEFAMATION ONLINE

Under the Communications Decency Act of 1996, Internet service providers (ISPs) are not liable for the defamatory remarks of those who use their services.

B. SPAM

Spam is junk e-mail. Some states ban or regulate its use, which may constitute trespass to personal property. The First Amendment may also limit what the government can do to restrict it.

TRUE-FALSE QUESTIONS

(Answers at the Back of the Book)

____ 1. To commit an intentional tort, a person must intend the consequences of his or her act or know with substantial certainty that certain consequences will result.

____ 2. A reasonable apprehension or fear of harmful or offensive contact at some time in the future is an assault.

____ 3. A defamatory statement must be communicated to a third party to be actionable.

____ 4. Puffery is fraud.

____ 5. Depriving an owner of personal property without permission and without just cause, to place it in another's service, is conversion.

____ 6. To determine whether a duty of care has been breached, a judge asks how he or she would have acted in the same circumstances.

____ 7. Strict liability is liability imposed for reasons other than fault.

____ 8. Bona fide competitive behavior can constitute wrongful interference with a contractual relationship.

____ 9. Internet service providers are not normally liable for the defamatory remarks of those who use their services.

____ 10. The government cannot regulate spam.

FILL-IN QUESTIONS

(Answers at the Back of the Book)

1. Basic defenses to _____ (negligence/intentional torts) include comparative negligence, contributory negligence, and assumption of risk.

2. One who voluntarily and knowingly enters into a risky situation normally cannot recover damages. This is the _____ (defense of contributory negligence/defense of assumption of risk).

3.   When both parties' failure to use reasonable care combines to cause injury, in some states the injured party's recovery is precluded by his or her own negligence. This is the _____ (comparative/ contributory) negligence doctrine.

4.   When both parties' failure to use reasonable care combines to cause injury, in most states damages are reduced by a percentage that represents the degree of the plaintiff's negligence. This is the _____ _____ (comparative/contributory) negligence doctrine.

MULTIPLE-CHOICE QUESTIONS

(Answers at the Back of the Book)

_____   1.   Joe shoves Kay, who falls and suffers a concussion. This is an intentional tort

a.   if Joe had a bad motive for shoving Kay.
b.   if Joe intended to shove Kay.
c.   if Kay was afraid of Joe.
d.   only if Joe intended that Kay suffer a concussion.

_____   2.   Alan, the owner of Beta Computer Store, detains Cathy, a customer, whom Alan suspects of shoplifting. This is false imprisonment if

a.   Alan detains Cathy for an unreasonably long time.
b.   Cathy did not shoplift.
c.   Cathy has probable cause to suspect Alan of deceit.
d.   Cathy protests her innocence.

_____   3.   Fred drives across Gail's land. This is a trespass to land only if

a.   Fred damages the land.
b.   Fred does not have Gail's permission to drive on her land.
c.   Fred makes disparaging remarks about Gail's land.
d.   Gail is aware of Fred's driving on her land.

_____   4.   Gil sends a letter to Holly in which he falsely accuses her of embezzling. This is defamation only if the letter is read by

a.   a public figure.
b.   any third person.
c.   Holly.
d.   Holly's employer.

_____   5.   To protect its customers and other business invitees, Grocers Market must warn them of

a.   hidden dangers.
b.   obvious dangers.
c.   hidden and obvious dangers.
d.   none of the above.

_____   6.   Lee, a salesperson for Midsize Corporation, causes a car accident while on business. Lee and Midsize are liable to all persons

a.   who are injured.
b.   who do not have insurance to pay for their injuries.
c.   whose injuries could have been reasonably foreseen.
d.   with whom Lee was doing business.

____   **7.** Apex Mining Company engages in blasting as part of its operations. This is subject to strict liability because

a. Apex is a mining company.
b. blasting is a dangerous activity.
c. blasting is a negligent activity.
d. mining can be done without blasting.

____   **8.** Best Box Company advertises so effectively that National Products, Inc., stops doing business with Good Cartons Corporation. Best is liable for

a. appropriation.
b. wrongful interference with a business relationship.
c. wrongful interference with a contractual relationship.
d. none of the above.

____   **9.** Internet Services, Inc. (ISI), is an Internet service provider. ISI does not create, but disseminates, a defamatory statement by Jill, its customer, about Ron. Liability for the remark may be imposed on

a. ISI and Jill.
b. ISI or Jill, but not both.
c. ISI only.
d. Jill only.

____   **10.** Online Services Company (OSC) is an Internet service provider. Ads Unlimited, Inc., sends spam to OSC's customers, some of whom then cancel OSC's services. Ads Unlimited is liable for

a. battery.
b. conversion.
c. infliction of emotional distress.
d. trespass to personal property.

SHORT ESSAY QUESTIONS

1. What is a *tort*?

2. Identify and describe the elements of a cause of action based on negligence.

ISSUE SPOTTERS

(Answers at the Back of the Book)

1. Adam kisses the sleeve of Eve's blouse, to which she did not consent and which she finds offensive. Is Adam guilty of a tort?

2. If a student takes another student's business law textbook as a practical joke and hides it for several days before the final examination, has a tort been committed?

3. After less than a year in business, Superior Club surpasses Ordinary Club in number of members. Superior's marketing strategies attract many Ordinary members, who then change clubs. Does Ordinary have any recourse against Superior?

Chapter 5
Intellectual Property and Internet Law

WHAT THIS CHAPTER IS ABOUT

Intellectual property consists of the products of intellectual, creative processes. Many of these products (such as inventions, books, software, movies, and songs) are protected by the law of trademarks, patents, copyrights, and related concepts. This chapter outlines the laws that protect these products, including their use in cyberspace.

CHAPTER OUTLINE

I. **TRADEMARKS AND RELATED PROPERTY**

A. **TRADEMARKS**
The Lanham Act protects trademarks at the federal level. Many states also have statutes that protect trademarks.

1. **What a Trademark Is**
A distinctive mark, motto, device, or emblem that a manufacturer stamps, prints, or otherwise affixes to the goods it produces to distinguish them from the goods of other manufacturers.

2. **The Federal Trademark Dilution Act of 1995**
Prohibits dilution (unauthorized use of marks on goods or services, even if they do not compete directly with products whose marks are copied).

3. **Trademark Registration**
A trademark may be registered with a state or the federal government. Trademarks do not need to be registered to be protected.

a. **Requirements for Federal Registration**
A trademark may be filed with the U.S. Patent and Trademark Office on the basis of (1) use or (2) the intent to use the mark within six months (which may be extended to thirty months).

b. **Renewal of Federal Registration**
Between the fifth and sixth years and then every ten years (twenty years for marks registered before 1990).

4. **Requirements for Trademark Protection**
The extent to which the law protects a trademark is normally determined by how distinctive the mark is.

a. **Strong Marks**
Fanciful, arbitrary, or suggestive marks are considered most distinctive.

b. **Descriptive Terms, Geographic Terms, and Personal Names**
Descriptive terms, geographic terms, and personal names are not inherently distinctive and are not protected until they acquire a secondary meaning (which means that customers associate the mark with the source of a product)

  c. Generic Terms
  Terms such as *bicycle* or *computer* receive no protection, even if they acquire secondary meaning.

 5. Trademark Infringement
 When a trademark is copied to a substantial degree or used in its entirety by another, the trademark is infringed.

B. SERVICE, CERTIFICATION, AND COLLECTIVE MARKS
Laws that apply to trademarks normally also apply to—

 1. Service Marks
 Used to distinguish the services of one person or company from those of another. Registered in the same manner as trademarks.

 2. Certification Marks
 Used by one or more persons, other than the owner, to certify the region, materials, mode of manufacture, quality, or accuracy of the owner's goods or services.

 3. Collective Marks
 Certification marks used by members of a cooperative, association, or other organization.

C. TRADE NAMES
Used to indicate part or all of a business's name. Trade names cannot be registered with the federal government but may be protected under the common law if they are used as trademarks or service marks.

D. TRADE DRESS
Trade dress is the image and appearance of a product, and is subject to the same protection as trademarks.

II. CYBER MARKS

A. ANTICYBERSQUATTING LEGISLATION
The Anticybersquatting Consumer Reform Act (ACRA) of 1999 amended the Lanham Act to make cybersquatting clearly illegal. Bad faith intent is an element (the ACRA lists "bad faith" factors). Damages may be awarded.

B. META TAGS
Words in a Web site's key-word field that determine the site's appearance in search engine results. Using others' marks as tags without permission constitutes trademark infringement.

C. DILUTION IN THE ONLINE WORLD
Using a mark, without permission, in a way that diminishes its distinctive quality. Tech-related cases have concerned the use of marks as domain names and spamming under another's logo.

III. PATENTS

A. WHAT A PATENT IS
A grant from the federal government that conveys and secures to an inventor the exclusive right to make, use, and sell an invention for a period of twenty years (fourteen years for a design).

B. REQUIREMENTS FOR A PATENT
An invention, discovery, or design must be genuine, novel, useful, and not obvious in light of the technology of the time. A patent is given to the first person to invent a product, not to the first person to file for a patent.

C. PATENTS FOR SOFTWARE
The basis for software is often a mathematical equation or formula, which is not patentable, but a patent can be obtained for a process that incorporates a computer program.

D. PATENT INFRINGEMENT
Making, using, or selling another's patented design, product, or process without the patent owner's permission. The owner may obtain an injunction, damages, destruction of all infringing copies, attorneys' fees, and court costs.

E. BUSINESS PROCESS PATENTS
Business processes are patentable (laws of nature, natural phenomena, and abstract ideas are not patentable).

IV. COPYRIGHTS

A. WHAT A COPYRIGHT IS
An intangible right granted by statute to the author or originator of certain literary or artistic productions. Protection is automatic; registration is not required.

B. COPYRIGHT PROTECTION
Automatic for the life of the author plus fifty years. Copyrights owned by publishing houses expire seventy-five years from the date of publication or a hundred years from the date of creation, whichever is first. For works by more than one author, copyright expires fifty years after the death of the last surviving author.

C. WHAT IS PROTECTED EXPRESSION?
To be protected, a work must meet these requirements—

1. **Fit a Certain Category**
   It must be a (1) literary work; (2) musical work; (3) dramatic work; (4) pantomime or choreographic work; (5) pictorial, graphic, or sculptural work; (6) film or other audiovisual work; or (7) a sound recording. The Copyright Act also protects computer software and architectural plans.

2. **Be Fixed in a Durable Medium**
   From which it can be perceived, reproduced, or communicated.

3. **Be Original**
   A compilation of facts (formed by the collection and assembling of preexisting materials of data) is copyrightable if it is original.

D. WHAT IS NOT PROTECTED
Ideas, facts, and related concepts. If an idea and an expression cannot be separated, the expression cannot be copyrighted.

E. COPYRIGHT INFRINGEMENT
A copyright is infringed if a work is copied without the copyright holder's permission. A copy does not have to be exactly the same as the original—copying a substantial part of the original is enough.

1. **Penalties**
   Actual damages (based on the harm to the copyright holder); damages under the Copyright Act, not to exceed $150,000; and criminal proceedings (which may result in fines or imprisonment).

2. **Exception—Fair Use Doctrine**
   The Copyright Act permits the fair use of a work for purposes such as criticism, comment, news reporting, teaching (including multiple copies for classroom use), scholarship, or research.

F. COPYRIGHT PROTECTION FOR SOFTWARE
The Computer Software Copyright Act of 1980 provides protection.

1. **What Is Protected**
   The binary object code (the part of a software program readable only by computer); the source code (the part of a program readable by people); and the program structure, sequence, and organization.

2. What May or May Not Be Protected

The "look and feel"—the general appearance, command structure, video images, menus, windows, and other displays—of a program.

G. COPYRIGHTS IN DIGITAL INFORMATION

Copyright law is important in cyberspace in part because the nature of the Internet means that data is "copied" before being transferred online.

1. The Copyright Act of 1976

Copyright law requires the copyright holder's permission to sell a "copy" of a work. For these purposes, loading a file or program into a computer's random access memory (RAM) is the making of a "copy."

2. Further Developments in Copyright Law

a. No Electronic Theft Act of 1997

Extends criminal liability to the exchange of pirated, copyrighted materials, even if no profit is realized from the exchange, and to the unauthorized copying of works for personal use.

b. Digital Millennium Copyright Act of 1998

Imposes penalties on anyone who circumvents encryption software or other technological anti-piracy protection. Also prohibits the manufacture, import, sale, or distribution of devices or services for circumvention. ISP s are not liable for their customers' violations.

c. MP3 and File-Sharing Technology

MP3 file compression and music file sharing occur over the Internet through peer-to-peer (P2P) networking. Doing this without the permission of the owner of the music's copyright is infringement.

V. TRADE SECRETS

A. WHAT A TRADE SECRET IS

Customer lists, formulas, plans, research and development, pricing information, marketing techniques, production techniques, and generally anything that provides an opportunity to obtain an advantage over competitors who do not know or use it.

B. TRADE SECRET PROTECTION

Protection of trade secrets extends both to ideas and their expression. Liability extends to those who misappropriate trade secrets by any means. Trade secret theft is also a federal crime.

C. TRADE SECRETS IN CYBERSPACE

The nature of technology (especially e-mail) undercuts a firm's ability to protect its confidential information, including trade secrets.

VI. LICENSING

Permitting the use of a mark, copyright, patent, or trade secret for certain purposes, often for a payment of royalties. Use for other purposes is a breach of the license agreement.

VII. INTERNATIONAL PROTECTION

A. THE BERNE CONVENTION

The Berne Convention is an international copyright treaty.

1. For Citizens of Countries That Have Signed the Berne Convention

If, for example, an American writes a book, the copyright in the book is recognized by every country that has signed the convention.

2. **For Citizens of Other Countries**

   If a citizen of a country that has not signed the convention publishes a book first in a country that has signed, all other countries that have signed the convention recognize that author's copyright.

B. **THE TRIPS AGREEMENT**

Trade-Related Aspects of Intellectual Property Rights (TRIPS) Agreement is part of the agreement creating the World Trade Organization (WTO). Each member nation must not discriminate (in administration, regulation, or adjudication of intellectual property rights) against owners of such rights.

TRUE-FALSE QUESTIONS

(Answers at the Back of the Book)

____ 1. To receive a patent, an applicant must show that an invention is genuine, novel, useful, and not obvious in light of current technology.

____ 2. To obtain a copyright, an author must show that a work is genuine, novel, useful, and not a copy of a current copyrighted work.

____ 3. In determining whether the use of a copyrighted work is infringement under the fair use doctrine, one factor is the effect of that use on the market for the copyrighted work.

____ 4. A personal name is protected under trademark law if it acquires a secondary meaning.

____ 5. A formula for a chemical compound is not a trade secret.

____ 6. A trade name, like a trademark, can be registered with the federal government.

____ 7. A copy must be exactly the same as an original work to infringe on its copyright.

____ 8. Only the *intentional* use of another's trademark is trademark infringement.

____ 9. Using another's trademark in a domain name without permission violates federal law.

____ 10. Trademark dilution requires proof that consumers are likely to be confused by the unauthorized use of the mark.

FILL-IN QUESTIONS

(Answers at the Back of the Book)

Copyright protection is automatic for the life of the author of a work plus _____ (70/95/120) years. Copyrights owned by publishing houses expire _____ (70/95/120) years from the date of the publication of a work or _____ (70/95/120) years from the date of its creation, whichever is first. For works by more than one author, a copyright expires _____ (70/95/120) years after the death of the last surviving author.

MULTIPLE-CHOICE QUESTIONS

(Answers at the Back of the Book)

____ 1. Alpha, Inc., makes computer chips identical to Beta Corporation's patented chip, except for slight differences in the "look," without Beta's permission. This is

a. copyright infringement.
b. patent infringement.
c. trademark infringement.
d. none of the above.

____   **2.** Omega, Inc., uses a trademark on its products that no one, including Omega, has registered with the government. Under federal trademark law, Omega

a. can register the mark for protection.
b. cannot register a mark that has been used in commerce.
c. is guilty of trademark infringement.
d. must postpone registration until the mark has been out of use for three years.

____   **3.** Ken invents a light bulb that lasts longer than ordinary bulbs and applies for a patent. If the patent is granted, the invention will be protected

a. for ten years.
b. for twenty years.
c. for Ken's life plus seventy years.
d. forever.

____   **4.** The graphics used in "Grave Raiders," a computer game, are protected by

a. copyright law.
b. patent law.
c. trademark law.
d. trade secrets law.

____   **5.** Production techniques used to make "Grave Raiders," a computer game, are protected by

a. copyright law.
b. patent law.
c. trademark law.
d. trade secrets law.

____   **6.** National Products Company uses USA Goods, Inc.'s trademark in National's advertising without USA's permission. This is

a. copyright infringement.
b. patent infringement.
c. trademark infringement.
d. none of the above.

____   **7.** Clothes made by workers who are members of the Clothes Makers Union are sold with tags that identify this fact. This is a

a. certification mark.
b. collective mark.
c. service mark.
d. trade name.

____   **8.** Tony owns Antonio's, a pub in a small town in Iowa. Universal Dining, Inc., opens a chain of pizza places in California called "Antonio's" and, without Tony's consent, uses "antoniosincalifornia" as part of the URL for the chain's Web site. This is

a. copyright infringement.
b. cybersquatting.
c. trademark dilution.
d. none of the above.

___ **9.** Data Corporation created and sells "Economix," financial computer software. Data's copyright in Economix is best protected under

    a. the Berne Convention.
    b. the Paris Convention.
    c. the TRIPS Agreement.
    d. none of the above.

___ **10.** International Media, Inc. (IMI), publishes *Opinion* magazine, which contains an article by Carl. Without Carl's permission, IMI puts the article into an online database. This is

    a. copyright infringement.
    b. patent infringement.
    c. trademark infringement.
    d. none of the above.

SHORT ESSAY QUESTIONS

1. What does a copyright protect?

2. What is a trade secret and how is it protected?

ISSUE SPOTTERS

(Answers at the Back of the Book)

1. Delta Company discovers that it can extract data from the computer of Gamma, Inc., its major competitor, by making a series of phone calls over a high-speed modem. When Delta uses its discovery to extract Gamma's customer list, without permission, what recourse does Gamma have?

2. Global Products develops, patents, and markets software. World Copies, Inc., sells Global's software without the maker's permission. Is this patent infringement? If so, how might Global save the cost of suing World for infringement and at the same time profit from World's sales?

3. Eagle Corporation began marketing software in 1990 under the mark "Eagle." In 2002, Eagle.com, Inc., a different company selling different products, begins to use "eagle" as part of its URL and registers it as a domain name. Can Eagle Corporation stop this use of "eagle"? If so, what must the company show?

Chapter 6:
Criminal Law and Cyber Crimes

WHAT THIS CHAPTER IS ABOUT

This chapter defines what makes an act a crime, describes crimes that affect business (including cyber crimes), lists defenses to crimes, and outlines criminal procedure. Sanctions for crimes are different from those for torts or breaches of contract. Another difference between civil and criminal law is that an individual can bring a civil suit, but only the government can prosecute a criminal.

CHAPTER OUTLINE

I. CIVIL LAW AND CRIMINAL LAW

    A. CIVIL LAW
    Civil law consists of the duties that exist between persons or between citizens and their governments, excluding the duty not to commit crimes.

    B. CRIMINAL LAW
    A **crime** is a wrong against society proclaimed in a statute and, if committed, punishable by society through fines, imprisonment, or death. Crimes are offenses against society as a whole and are prosecuted by public officials, not victims.

II. CLASSIFICATION OF CRIMES

    Felonies are serious crimes punishable by death or by imprisonment in a federal or state penitentiary for more than a year. A crime that is not a felony is a **misdemeanor**—punishable by a fine or by confinement (in a local jail) for up to a year. Petty offenses are minor misdemeanors.

III. CRIMINAL LIABILITY

    Two elements must exist for a person to be convicted of a crime—

    A. CRIMINAL ACT
    A criminal statute prohibits certain behavior—an act of commission (doing something) or an act of omission (not doing something that is a legal duty).

    B. INTENT TO COMMIT A CRIME
    The wrongful mental state required to establish guilt depends on the crime.

IV. CORPORATE CRIMINAL LIABILITY

    Corporations are liable for crimes committed by their agents and employees within the course and scope of employment. Directors and officers are personally liable for crimes they commit and may be liable for the actions of employees under their supervision.

V. TYPES OF CRIMES

A. **VIOLENT CRIME**

These include murder, rape, assault and battery (see Chapter 4), and *robbery* (forcefully and unlawfully taking personal property from another). Classified by degree, depending on intent, weapon, and victim's suffering.

B. **PROPERTY CRIME**

Robbery could also be in this category.

1. **Burglary**

Unlawful entry into a building with the intent to commit a felony.

2. **Larceny**

Wrongfully taking and carrying away another's personal property with the intent of depriving the owner permanently of the property (without force or intimidation, which are elements of robbery).

   a. **Property**

   Property includes computer programs, computer time, trade secrets, cellular phone numbers, long-distance phone time, and natural gas.

   b. **Grand Larceny and Petit Larceny**

   In some states, grand larceny is a felony and petit larceny a misdemeanor. The difference depends on the value of the property taken.

3. **Receiving Stolen Goods**

The recipient need not know the identity of the true owner of the goods.

4. **Arson**

The willful and malicious burning, by fire or explosion, of a building (and in some states, personal property) owned by another. Every state has a statute that covers burning a building to collect insurance.

5. **Forgery**

Fraudulently making or altering any writing in a way that changes the legal rights and liabilities of another.

C. **PUBLIC ORDER CRIME**

Examples: public drunkenness, prostitution, gambling, and illegal drug use.

D. **WHITE-COLLAR CRIME**

1. **Embezzlement**

Fraudulently appropriating another's property or money by one who has been entrusted with it (without force or intimidation).

2. **Mail and Wire Fraud**

   a. **The Crime**

   It is a federal crime to (1) mail or cause someone else to mail something written, printed, or photocopied for the purpose of executing (2) a scheme to defraud (even if no one is defrauded). Also a crime to use wire, radio, or television transmissions to defraud.

   b. **The Punishment**

   Fine of up to $1,000, imprisonment for up to five years, or both. If the violation affects a financial institution, the fine may be up to $1 million, the imprisonment up to thirty years, or both.

3. **Bribery**

a. **Bribery of Public Officials**
Attempting to influence a public official to act in a way that serves a private interest by offering the official a bribe. Committed when the bribe (anything the recipient considers valuable) is offered.

b. **Commercial Bribery**
Attempting, by a bribe, to obtain proprietary information, cover up an inferior product, or secure new business.

c. **Bribery of Foreign Officials**
Attempting, by bribing foreign officials, to obtain business contracts. Banned by Foreign Corrupt Practices Act of 1977 (see Chapter 7).

4. **Bankruptcy Fraud**
Filing a false claim against a debtor; fraudulently transferring assets to favored parties; or fraudulently concealing property before or after a petition for bankruptcy is filed.

5. **Theft of Trade Secrets**
Under the Economic Espionage Act of 1996, it is a federal crime to steal trade secrets, or to knowingly buy or possess another's stolen secrets. Penalties include up to ten years' imprisonment, fines up to $500,000 (individual) or $5 million (corporation), and forfeiture of property.

6. **Insider Trading**
Using inside information (information not available to the general public) about a publicly traded corporation to profit from the purchase or sale of the corporation's securities (see Chapter 29).

E. **ORGANIZED CRIME**

1. **Money Laundering**
Transferring the proceeds of crime through legitimate businesses. Financial institutions must report transactions of more than $10,000.

2. **RICO**
Two offenses under the Racketeer Influenced and Corrupt Organizations Act (RICO) of 1970 constitute "racketeering activity."

a. **Activities Prohibited by RICO**
(1) Use income from racketeering to buy an interest in an enterprise, (2) acquire or maintain such an interest through racketeering activity' (3) conduct or participate in an enterprise through racketeering activity, or 4) conspire to do any of the above.

b. **Civil Liability**
Civil penalties include divestiture of a defendant's interest in a business or dissolution of the business. Private individuals can recover treble damages, plus attorneys' fees, for business injuries.

c. **Criminal Liability**
RICO can be used to attack white-collar crime. Penalties include fines of up to $25,000 per violation, imprisonment for up to 20 years, or both.

VI. DEFENSES TO CRIMES

A. **INFANCY**
Cases involving persons who have not reached the age of majority are handled in juvenile courts. In some states, a child over a certain age (usually fourteen) and charged with a felony may be tried in an adult court.

B. **INTOXICATION**

Involuntary intoxication is a defense to a crime if it makes a person incapable of understanding that the act committed was wrong or incapable of obeying the law. *Voluntary* intoxication may be a defense if the person was so intoxicated as to lack the required state of mind.

C. **INSANITY**

1. **The Model Penal Code Test**

Most federal courts and some states use this test: a person is not responsible for criminal conduct if at the time, as a result of mental disease or defect, the person lacks substantial capacity either to appreciate the wrongfulness of the conduct or to conform his or her conduct to the law.

2. **The *M'Naghten* Test**

Some states use this test: a person is not responsible if at the time of the offense, he or she did not know the nature and quality of the act or did not know that the act was wrong.

3. **The Irresistible Impulse Test**

Some states use this test: a person operating under an irresistible impulse may know an act is wrong but cannot refrain from doing it.

D. **MISTAKE**

1. **Mistake of Fact**

Defense if it negates the mental state necessary to commit a crime.

2. **Mistake of Law**

A person not knowing a law was broken may have a defense if (1) the law was not published or reasonably made known to the public or (2) the person relied on an official statement of the law that was wrong.

E. **CONSENT**

Defense if it cancels the harm that the law is designed to prevent, unless the law forbids an act without regard to the victim's consent.

F. **DURESS**

1. **What Duress Is**

When a person's threat induces another person to perform an act that he or she would not otherwise perform.

2. **When Duress Is a Defense**

(1) The threat is one of serious bodily harm, (2) the threat is immediate and inescapable, (3) the threatened harm is greater than the harm caused by the crime, (4) the defendant is involved through no fault of his or her own, and (5) the crime is not murder.

G. **JUSTIFIABLE USE OF FORCE**

1. **Nondeadly Force**

People can use as much nondeadly force as seems necessary to protect themselves, their dwellings, or other property or to prevent a crime.

2. **Deadly Force**

Can be used in self-defense if there is a reasonable belief that imminent death or serious bodily harm will otherwise result, if the attacker is using unlawful force, and if the defender did not provoke the attack.

H. **ENTRAPMENT**

When a law enforcement agent suggests that a crime be committed, pressures or induces an individual to commit it, and arrests the individual for it.

I.   STATUTE OF LIMITATIONS
Provides that the state has only a certain amount of time to prosecute a crime. Most statutes of limitations do not apply to murder.

J.   IMMUNITY
A state can grant immunity from prosecution or agree to prosecute for a less serious offense in exchange for information. This is often part of a plea bargain between the defendant and the prosecutor.

VII. CONSTITUTIONAL SAFEGUARDS
Most of these safeguards apply not only in federal but also in state courts by virtue of the due process clause of the Fourteenth Amendment.

A.   FOURTH AMENDMENT
Protection from unreasonable searches and seizures. No warrants for a search or an arrest can be issued without probable cause.

B.   FIFTH AMENDMENT
No one can be deprived of "life, liberty, or property without due process of law." No one can be tried twice (double jeopardy) for the same offense. No one can be required to incriminate himself or herself.

C.   SIXTH AMENDMENT
Guarantees a speedy trial, trial by jury, a public trial, the right to confront witnesses, and the right to a lawyer in some proceedings.

D.   EIGHTH AMENDMENT
Prohibits excessive bail and fines, and cruel and unusual punishment.

E.   EXCLUSIONARY RULE
Evidence obtained in violation of the Fourth, Fifth, and Sixth Amendments, as well as all "fruit of the poisonous tree" (evidence derived from illegally obtained evidence), must be excluded.

F.   *MIRANDA* RULE
A person in custody who is to be interrogated must be informed that he or she has the right to remain silent; anything said can and will be used against him or her in court; he or she has the right to consult with an attorney; and if he or she is indigent, a lawyer will be appointed.

VIII. CRIMINAL PROCESS

A.   ARREST
Requires a warrant based on probable cause (a substantial likelihood that the person has committed or is about to commit a crime). To make an arrest without a warrant, an officer must also have probable cause.

B.   INDICTMENT OR INFORMATION
A formal charge is called an **indictment** if issued by a grand jury and an **information** if issued by a public prosecutor.

C.   TRIAL
Criminal trial procedures are similar to those of a civil trial, but the standard of proof is higher: the prosecutor must establish guilt beyond a reasonable doubt.

D.   SENTENCING GUIDELINES

1.   Federal Sentencing Guidelines
Possible penalties for federal crimes. Sentence is based on a defendant's criminal record, seriousness of the offense, and other factors.

2. **"Three Strikes" Laws**
    Federal law and many states' laws provide that a criminal with two violent felony convictions goes to jail (in some states, for life and without parole) if convicted of a third similar felony.

IX. CYBER CRIME

A. CYBER THEFT
Computers make it possible for employees, and others, to commit crimes (such as fraud) involving serious financial losses. The Internet has made identity theft and crimes committed with stolen identities easier.

B. CYBER STALKING
Harassing a person in cyberspace (such as via e-mail). Prohibited by federal law and most states. Some states require a "credible threat" that puts the person in reasonable fear for his or her safety or the safety of the person's family.

C. HACKING
Using one computer to break into another. Often part of cyber theft.

D. CYBER TERRORISM
Exploiting computers for such serious impacts as the exploding of a "bomb" to shut down a central computer.

E. PROSECUTING CYBER CRIMES
Jurisdictional issues and the anonymous nature of technology can hinder the investigation and prosecution of crimes committed in cyberspace.

1. **The Computer Fraud and Abuse Act**
    The Computer Access Device and Computer Fraud and Abuse Act of 1984 provides for criminal prosecution of a person who accesses a computer online, without authority, to obtain classified, restricted, or protected data (restricted government info, financial records, etc.), or attempts to do. Penalties include fines and up to five years' imprisonment.

2. **Other Federal Statutes**
    Electronic Fund Transfer Act of 1978, Anticounterfeiting Consumer Protection Act of 1996, National Stolen Property Act of 1988, and more.

TRUE-FALSE QUESTIONS

(Answers at the Back of the Book)

_____ 1. Only the government prosecutes criminal defendants.

_____ 2. A crime punishable by imprisonment is a felony.

_____ 3. Burglary involves taking another's personal property from his or her person or immediate presence.

_____ 4. Embezzlement requires physically taking property for another's possession.

_____ 5. Stealing a computer program is larceny.

_____ 6. Offering a bribe is only one element of the crime of bribery.

_____ 7. Receiving stolen goods is a crime only if the recipient knows the true owner.

_____ 8. Generally, a person is not responsible for a criminal act if, as a result of a mental defect, he or she lacked substantial capacity to appreciate the wrongfulness of the act or to conform the conduct to the law.

____   9.   A person who accesses a computer online, without authorization, to obtain protected data commits a federal crime.

____   10.   RICO is often used to prosecute acts classified as white-collar crimes.

FILL-IN QUESTIONS

(Answers at the Back of the Book)

Specific constitutional safeguards for those accused of crimes apply in all federal courts, and most of them also apply in state courts under the due process clause of the Fourteenth Amendment. The safeguards include (1) the Fourth Amendment protection from _____ (unexpected/unreasonable) searches and seizures, (2) the Fourth Amendment requirement that no warrants for a search or an arrest can be issued without _____ (probable/possible) cause, (3) the Fifth Amendment requirement that no one can be deprived of "life, liberty, or property without _____ (consent/due process of law)," (4) the Fifth Amendment prohibition against double _____ (immunity/jeopardy), (5) the Sixth Amendment guaranties of a speedy _____ (appeal/trial), _____ _____ (appeal to/trial by) a jury, a public trial, the right to confront _____ (counsel/witnesses), and the right to legal counsel, and (6) the Eighth Amendment prohibitions against excessive _____(bail/bail and fines) and cruel and unusual punishment.

MULTIPLE-CHOICE QUESTIONS

(Answers at the Back of the Book)

____   1.   Carl wrongfully takes a box from a Delta, Inc., shipping container, puts it in his truck, and drives away. This is

a.   burglary.
b.   embezzlement.
c.   forgery.
d.   larceny.

____   2.   Nora is charged with the commission of a crime. For a conviction, most crimes require

a.   only a specified state of mind or intent on the part of the actor.
b.   only the performance of a prohibited act.
c.   a specified state of mind and performance of a prohibited act.
d.   none of the above.

____   3.   Adam signs Beth's name, without her consent, to the back of a check payable to Beth. This is

a.   burglary.
b.   embezzlement.
c.   forgery.
d.   larceny.

____   4.   Owen, a bank teller, deposits into his account checks that bank customers give to him to deposit into their accounts. This is

a.   burglary.
b.   embezzlement.
c.   forgery.
d.   larceny.

____ 5. Jay is charged with the commission of a crime. For a conviction, Jay must be found guilty beyond

    a. a clear and convincing doubt.
    b. all doubt.
    c. a preponderance of doubt.
    d. a reasonable doubt.

____ 6. Nick is charged with the crime of mail fraud. For a conviction, Nick must be found to have

    a. had a scheme to defraud.
    b. used the mails.
    c. had a scheme to defraud and used the mails.
    d. none of the above.

____ 7. Sue, a government agent, arrests Tim for the commission of a crime. Tim claims that Sue entrapped him. This is a valid defense if Sue

    a. did not tell Tim that she was a government agent.
    b. pressured Tim into committing the crime.
    c. set a trap for Tim, who was looking to commit the crime.
    d. was predisposed to commit the crime.

____ 8. John is arrested on suspicion of the commission of a crime. Individuals who are arrested must be told of their right to

    a. confront witnesses.
    b. protection against unreasonable searches.
    c. remain silent.
    d. trial by jury.

____ 9. While away from her business, Kate is arrested on the suspicion of the commission of a crime. At Kate's trial, under the exclusionary rule

    a. biased individuals must be excluded from the jury.
    b. business records must be excluded from admission as evidence.
    c. illegally obtained evidence must be excluded from admission as evidence.
    d. the arresting officer must be excluded from testifying.

____ 10. Eve is arrested on suspicion of the commission of a crime. A grand jury issues a formal charge against Eve. This is

    a. an arraignment.
    b. an indictment.
    c. an information.
    d. an inquisition.

SHORT ESSAY QUESTIONS

1. What are some of the significant differences between criminal law and civil law?

2. What constitutes civil liability under the Racketeer Influenced and Corrupt Organizations Act (RICO) of 1968 and what are the penalties?

ISSUE SPOTTERS

(Answers at the Back of the Book)

1.   Bob drives off in Fred's car mistakenly believing that it is his. Is this theft?

2.   Ellen takes her roommate's credit card, intending to charge expenses that she incurs on a vacation. Her first stop is a gas station, where she uses the card to pay for gas. With respect to the gas station, has she committed a crime? If so, what is it?

3.   Ben downloads consumer credit files from a computer of Consumer Credit Agency, without permission, over the Internet. Ben sells the data to Donna. Has Ben committed a crime? If so, what is it?

CUMULATIVE HYPOTHETICAL PROBLEM FOR UNIT TWO—INCLUDING CHAPTERS 4–6

(Answers at the Back of the Book)

Computer Data, Inc. (CDI), incorporated and based in California, signs a contract with Digital Products Corporation (DPC), incorporated and based in Arizona, to make and sell customized software for DPC to, in turn, sell to its clients.

_____   **1.**   To protect the rights that CDI has in the software it produces, CDI's best protection is offered by

a. criminal law.
b. intellectual property law.
c. tort law.
d. none of the above.

_____   **2.**   CDI ships defective software to DPC, which sells it to a customer, Eagle Distribution Corporation. The defective software causes losses that Eagle estimates at $100,000. With respect to Eagle, CDI has likely violated

a. criminal law.
b. intellectual property law.
c. tort law.
d. none of the above.

_____   **3.**   DPC's officers order some employees to access CDI's computers online to obtain its data without CDI's permission. This is

a. cyber fraud.
b. cyber theft.
c. cyber trespass.
d. none of the above.

_____   **4.**   During an investigation into DPC's activities, some of its officers are suspected of having committed crimes. As a corporation, DPC can

a. be fined or denied certain privileges if it is held criminally liable.
b. be imprisoned if it is held criminally liable.
c. be fined, denied privileges, or imprisoned if it is held criminally liable.
d. not be found to be criminally liable.

____ 5. DPC's officers who are suspected of having committed crimes can

a. be fined or denied certain privileges if they are held criminally liable.
b. be imprisoned if they are held criminally liable.
c. be fined, denied privileges, or imprisoned if they are held criminally liable.
d. not be held criminally liable.

QUESTIONS ON THE FOCUS ON LEGAL REASONING FOR UNIT TWO—*PINSONNEAULT V. MERCHANTS & FARMERS BANK & TRUST CO.*

(Answers at the Back of the Book)

____ 1. In *Pinsonneault v. Merchants & Farmers Bank & Trust Co.*, in the majority's opinion, a business must take security precautions if harm is foreseeable to

a. its employees.
b. its patrons.
c. members of the community.
d. passersby.

____ 2. In the majority's opinion, under a negligence theory, the business in this case had

a. a duty and breached it.
b. a duty and satisfied it.
c. a duty but did not breach it or satisfy it.
d. no duty.

____ 3. In the dissent's opinion, under a negligence theory, the business in this case had

a. a duty and breached it.
b. a duty and satisfied it.
c. a duty but did not breach it or satisfy it.
d. no duty.

Chapter 7:
Nature and Classification

WHAT THIS CHAPTER IS ABOUT

Contract law concerns the formation and keeping of promises, the excuses our society accepts for breaking such promises, and what promises are considered contrary to public policy and therefore legally void. This chapter introduces the basic terms and concepts of contract law, including the rules for interpreting contract language.

CHAPTER OUTLINE

I. THE FUNCTION OF CONTRACTS

A. ENFORCE PROMISES
Contract law assures the parties to private agreements that the promises they make will be enforceable.

B. AVOID PROBLEMS
The law of contracts is followed in business agreements to avoid problems.

C. SUPPORT THE EXISTENCE OF A MARKET ECONOMY
Businesspersons can usually rely on the good faith of others to keep their promises, but when price changes or adverse economic factors make it costly to comply with a promise, good faith may not be enough.

II. DEFINITION OF A CONTRACT

A. WHAT A CONTRACT IS
A **contract** is an agreement that can be enforced in court. It is formed by two or more parties who promise to perform or refrain from performing some act now or in the future.

B. THE OBJECTIVE THEORY OF CONTRACTS
Intention to enter into a contract is judged by objective (outward) facts as interpreted by a reasonable person, rather than by a party's subjective intention. Objective facts include (1) what the party said when entering into the contract, (2) how the party acted or appeared, and (3) the circumstances surrounding the transaction.

III. REQUIREMENTS OF A CONTRACT

A. THE ELEMENTS OF A CONTRACT

1. **Agreement**
   Includes an offer and an acceptance. One party must offer to enter into a legal agreement, and another party must accept the offer.

2. **Consideration**
   Promises must be supported by legally sufficient and bargained-for consideration.

3. **Contractual Capacity**
   Characteristics that qualify the parties to a contract as competent.

4. **Legality**
A contract's purpose must be to accomplish a goal that is not against public policy.

B. DEFENSES TO THE ENFORCEMENT OF A CONTRACT

1. **Genuineness of Assent**
The apparent consent of both parties must be genuine.

2. **Form**
A contract must be in whatever form the law requires (some contracts must be in writing).

IV. FREEDOM OF CONTRACT AND FREEDOM FROM CONTRACT

A. FREEDOM OF CONTRACT

Generally, everyone may enter freely into contracts. This freedom is a strongly held public policy, and courts rarely interfere with contracts that have been voluntarily made.

B. FREEDOM FROM CONTRACT

Illegal bargains, agreements unreasonably in restraint of trade, and unfair contracts between one party with a great amount of bargaining power and another with little power are generally not enforced. Contracts are not enforceable if they are contrary to public policy, fairness, and justice.

V. TYPES OF CONTRACTS

A. BILATERAL VERSUS UNILATERAL CONTRACTS

1. **Bilateral Contract**
A promise for a promise—to accept the offer, the offeree need only promise to perform.

2. **Unilateral Contract**
A promise for an act—the offeree can accept only by completing the contract performance. A problem arises when the promisor attempts to revoke the offer after the promisee has begun performance but before the act has been completed.

   a. **Revocation—Traditional View**
   The promisee can accept the offer only by performing fully. Offers are revocable until accepted.

   b. **Revocation—Modern-Day View**
   The offer becomes irrevocable once performance begins. Thus, even though it has not yet been accepted, the offeror cannot revoke it.

B. EXPRESS VERSUS IMPLIED CONTRACTS

1. **Express Contract**
The terms of the agreement are fully and explicitly stated in words (oral or written).

2. **Implied-in-Fact Contract**
Implied from the conduct of the parties.

C. QUASI CONTRACTS—CONTRACTS IMPLIED IN LAW

In the absence of an actual contract, a quasi contract is imposed by a court to avoid the unjust enrichment of one party at the expense of another. Cannot be invoked if there is an actual contract that covers the area in controversy.

D. FORMAL VERSUS INFORMAL CONTRACTS

1. **Formal Contract**
Requires a special form or method of creation to be enforceable (such as a contract under seal, a formal writing with a special seal attached).

2. **Informal Contract**

All contracts that are not formal. Except for certain contracts that must be in writing, no special form is required.

E. **EXECUTED VERSUS EXECUTORY CONTRACTS**

1. **Executed Contract**

A contract that has been fully performed on both sides.

2. **Executory Contract**

A contract that has not been fully performed by one or more parties.

F. **VALID, VOID, VOIDABLE, AND UNENFORCEABLE CONTRACTS**

1. **Valid Contract**

Has all the elements necessary for contract formation.

2. **Void Contract**

Has no legal force or binding effect (for example, a contract is void if its purpose was illegal).

3. **Voidable Contract**

Valid contract that can be avoided by one or more parties (for example, contracts by minors are voidable at the minor's option).

4. **Unenforceable Contract**

Contract that cannot be enforced because of certain legal defenses (for example, if a contract that must be in writing is not in writing).

VI. INTERPRETATION OF CONTRACTS

Rules of contract interpretation provide guidelines for determining the meaning of contracts. The primary purpose of these rules is to determine the parties' intent from the language of their agreement and to give effect to that intent.

A. **THE PLAIN MEANING RULE**

When the writing is clear and unequivocal, it will be enforced according to its plain terms. The meaning of the terms is determined from the written document alone.

B. **OTHER RULES OF INTERPRETATION**

When the writing contains unclear terms, courts use the following rules—

1. A reasonable, lawful, and effective meaning is given to all terms.

2. A contract is interpreted as a whole; individual, specific clauses are considered subordinate to the contract's general intent. All writings that are part of the same transaction are interpreted together.

3. Terms that were negotiated separately are given greater consideration than standard terms and terms that were not negotiated separately.

4. A word is given its ordinary, common meaning, and a technical word its technical meaning, unless the parties clearly intended otherwise.

5. Specific, exact wording is given greater weight than general language.

6. Written or typewritten terms prevail over preprinted ones.

7. When the language has more than one meaning, it is interpreted against the party who drafted the contract.

8. Evidence of trade usage, prior dealing, and course of performance may be admitted to clarify meaning.

TRUE-FALSE QUESTIONS

(Answers at the Back of the Book)

____ 1. All promises are legal contracts.

____ 2. An agreement includes an offer and an acceptance.

____ 3. A promisor is a person who makes a promise.

____ 4. A unilateral contract is accepted by a promise to perform.

____ 5. An oral contract is an implied contract.

____ 6. An unenforceable contract is a valid contract that can be avoided by at least one of the parties to it.

____ 7. Under the plain meaning rule, a court will enforce a contract in which the writing is clear and unequivocal.

____ 8. When the language in a contract has more than one meaning, it will be interpreted against the party who drafted the contract.

____ 9. An executory contract is one that has not been fully performed.

____ 10. A quasi contract arises from a mutual agreement between two parties.

FILL-IN QUESTIONS

(Answers at the Back of the Book)

Whether or not a party intended to enter into a contract is determined by the _____ (objective/subjective) theory of contracts. The theory is that a party's intention to enter into a contract is judged by _____ (objective/subjective) facts as they would be interpreted by a reasonable person. Relevant facts include: (1) what the party said; (2) what the party _____ _____ (did/secretly believed); and (3) the _____ _____ (circumstances surrounding/party's personal thoughts concerning) the transaction.

MULTIPLE-CHOICE QUESTIONS

(Answers at the Back of the Book)

____ 1. Bob files a suit against Carol, claiming that she freely entered into a contract with him. Freedom of contract is

a. a concept no longer followed by the courts.
b. a foundation for an ethical business practice.
c. a fundamental public policy in the United States.
d. a principle that describes contracting parties' intent.

____ 2. National Supplies, Inc., agrees to deliver a truckload of paper to Office Products Company on Office's promise to pay for the paper. National delivers the paper. This contract is

   a. executory on National's part.
   b. executory on Office's part.
   c. fully executed.
   d. fully non-executed.

____ 3. Mary files a suit against Nick, alleging an implied-in-fact contract. The court will examine their conduct only to determine

   a. the terms of the contract.
   b. whether they intended to form a contract.
   c. the terms of the contract and whether they intended to form a contract.
   d. none of the above.

____ 4. Dan, a doctor, renders aid to Eve, who is injured. Dan can recover the cost of from Eve

   a. even if Eve was not aware of Dan's help.
   b. only if Eve was aware of Dan's help.
   c. only if Eve was not aware of Dan's help.
   d. none of the above.

____ 5. Ann claims that she and Brian entered into a contract. The intent to enter into a contract is determined with reference to

   a. the apparent theory of contracts.
   b. the objective theory of contracts.
   c. the personal theory of contracts.
   d. the subjective theory of contracts.

____ 6. Rita calls Sam on the phone and agrees to buy his laptop computer for $500. This is

   a. an express contract.
   b. an implied-in-fact contract.
   c. an implied-in-law contract.
   d. a quasi contract.

____ 7. Owen files a suit against Pam, disputing the meaning of their contract. If the terms are unclear, under the common law rules of contract interpretation, the court will give effect to

   a. the parties' intent as expressed in their contract.
   b. what Owen claims was the parties' intent.
   c. what Pam claims was the parties' intent.
   d. what the parties commonly claim they intended.

____ 8. Lora files a suit against Mike, disputing the meaning of their contract. If the terms are unclear, the contract's express terms take priority over

   a. course of performance and course of dealing only.
   b. custom and usage of trade only.
   c. course of performance, course of dealing, and custom and usage of trade.
   d. none of the above.

____   **9.** Adam's contract with Ben is voidable. This means that if the contract is avoided, with respect to the contract's obligations

    a. both parties must perform.
    b. neither party must perform.
    c. only Adam must perform.
    d. only Ben must perform.

____   **10.** Matt makes a promise to Nora. A promise is a declaration

    a. only that something will happen in the future.
    b. only that something will not happen in the future.
    c. that something will or will not happen in the future.
    d. none of the above.

SHORT ESSAY QUESTIONS

1. What are the basic elements of a contract?

2. What is the function of contract law?

ISSUE SPOTTERS

(Answers at the Back of the Book)

1. Jill signs and returns a letter from Kyle, referring to a book and its price. When Kyle delivers the book, Jill sends it back, claiming that they have no contract. Kyle claims they do. What standard determines whether these parties have a contract?

2. Ira receives from the local tax collector a notice of property taxes due. The notice is for tax on Jan's property, but Ira believes that the tax is his and pays it. Can Ira recover from Jan the amount paid?

3. Dora tells Ed that she will pay Ed $1,000 to set fire to Dora's store, so that she can collect money under a fire insurance policy. Ed sets fire to the store, but Dora refuses to pay. Can Ed recover?

Chapter 8:
Agreement and Consideration

WHAT THIS CHAPTER IS ABOUT

An agreement is the essence of every contract. The parties to a contract are the **offeror** (who makes an offer) and the **offeree** (to whom the offer is made). If, through the process of offer and acceptance, an agreement is reached, and the other elements are present (consideration, capacity, legality), a valid contract is formed.

Good reasons for enforcing promises include a benefit that the promisor received and a detriment that the promisee incurred. These are referred to as *consideration*. No contract is enforceable without it. This chapter outlines the concepts and principles of agreement and consideration.

CHAPTER OUTLINE

I. AGREEMENT
The elements of an agreement are an offer and an acceptance—one party offers a bargain to another, who accepts.

A. REQUIREMENTS OF THE OFFER
An **offer** is a promise or commitment to do or refrain from doing some specified thing in the future. An offer has three elements—

1. Intention
The offeror must intend to be bound by the offer.

a. How to Determine the Offeror's Intent
The offeror's intent is what a reasonable person in the offeree's position would conclude the offeror's words and actions meant. Offers in obvious anger, jest, or undue excitement do not qualify.

b. What Does Not Constitute an Offer?
Nonoffers include: (1) expressions of opinion, (2) statements of intention, (3) preliminary negotiations, and (4) advertisements, catalogues, price lists, and circulars. Auctions are a special situation—the bidder is the offeror; the seller is the offeree.

c. Agreements to Agree
Agreements to agree to a material term of a contract at some future date may be enforced if the parties clearly intended to be bound.

2. Definiteness
All of the major terms must be stated with reasonable definiteness in the offer (or, if the offeror directs, in the offeree's acceptance).

3. Communication
The offeree must know of the offer.

B. TERMINATION OF THE OFFER

1. Termination by Action of the Parties

a. Revocation of the Offer

The offeror usually can revoke the offer (even if he or she has promised to keep it open), by express repudiation or by acts that are inconsistent with the offer and that are made known to the offeree.

1) Communicated to the Offeree

A revocation becomes effective when the offeree or offeree's agent receives it.

2) Offers to the General Public

An offer made to the general public can be revoked in the same manner the offer was originally communicated.

b. Irrevocable Offers

1) When an Offeree Changes Position in Justifiable Reliance

The offer may not be revoked, under the doctrine of promissory estoppel (see below).

2) A Merchant's Firm Offer

The offer may be irrevocable (see Chapter 14).

3) Option Contract

An option contract is a promise to hold an offer open for a period of time. If no time is specified, a reasonable time is implied.

c. Rejection of the Offer by the Offeree

The offeree may reject an offer by words or conduct evidencing intent not to accept. A rejection is effective on receipt. Asking about an offer is not a rejection.

d. Counteroffer by the Offeree

The offeree's attempt to include different terms is a rejection of the original offer and a simultaneous making of a new offer. The **mirror image rule** requires the acceptance to match the offer exactly.

2. Termination by Operation of Law

a. Lapse of Time

An offer terminates automatically when the period of time specified in the offer has passed.

1) When the Time Begins to Run

Time begins to run when the offeree receives the offer. If there is delay and the offeree knows or should know of it, it does not affect when the offer lapses. If the offeree does not know, the moment of the lapse may be different, but the length of the time is the same.

2) If No Time Is Specified

If no time is specified, a reasonable time is implied.

b. Destruction of the Subject Matter

An offer is automatically terminated.

c. Death or Incompetence of the Offeror or Offeree

An offeree's power of acceptance is terminated. Exceptions include irrevocable offers (see above).

d. Supervening Illegality of the Proposed Contract

When a statute or court decision makes an offer illegal, the offer is automatically terminated.

C. ACCEPTANCE

1. Who Can Accept?

Usually, only the offeree (or the offeree's agent) can accept.

2. **Unequivocal Acceptance**
   The offeree must accept the offer unequivocally. This is the mirror image rule (see above).

3. **Silence as Acceptance**
   Ordinarily, silence cannot operate as an acceptance. Silence or inaction can constitute acceptance in the following circumstances—

   a. **Receipt of Offered Services**
      If an offeree receives the benefit of offered services even though he or she had an opportunity to reject them and knew that they were offered with the expectation of compensation.

   b. **Prior Dealings**
      The offeree had prior dealings with the offeror that lead the offeror to understand silence will constitute acceptance.

4. **Communication of Acceptance**

   a. **Bilateral Contract**
      A bilateral contract is formed when acceptance is communicated. The offeree must use reasonable efforts to communicate acceptance.

   b. **Unilateral Contract**
      Communication is normally unnecessary, unless the offeror requests it or has no way of knowing the act has been performed.

5. **Mode and Timeliness of Acceptance (in Bilateral Contracts)**
   Acceptance is timely if it is made before the offer is terminated.

   a. **Authorized Means of Communication**
      If an offeree uses a mode of communication expressly or impliedly authorized by the offeror, acceptance is effective on dispatch. This is the **mailbox rule** (deposited acceptance rule).

      1) **Express**
         When an offeror specifies how acceptance should be made and the offeree uses that mode, the acceptance is effective even if the offeror never receives it.

      2) **Implied**
         When an offeror does not specify how acceptance should be made, the offeree may use the same means the offeror used to make the offer or a faster means.

      3) **Exceptions**

         a) If an acceptance is not properly dispatched, in most states it will not be effective until it is received.

         b) If an offeror conditions an offer on receipt of acceptance by a certain time, acceptance is effective only on timely receipt.

         c) If both a rejection and an acceptance are sent, whichever is received first is effective.

   b. **Unauthorized Means of Communication**
      If an offeree uses a mode of communication that was not authorized by the offeror, acceptance is effective when received.

II. CONSIDERATION AND ITS REQUIREMENTS
Consideration is the value given in return for a promise.

A. ELEMENTS OF CONSIDERATION
There are two elements to consideration: something of legal value and a bargained-for exchange.

1. **Something of Legal Value**
   Something of legal value must be given in exchange for a promise. It may be (1) a promise to do something that one had no legal duty to do, (2) performing an act that one had no legal duty to perform, or (3) refraining from doing something that one could otherwise do.

2. **Bargained-for Exchange**
   The consideration given by the promisor must induce the promisee to incur legal detriment, and the detriment incurred must induce the promisor to make the promise. A gift does not have this element.

B. ADEQUACY OF CONSIDERATION

Adequacy of consideration refers to the fairness of a bargain. Normally, a court will not question the adequacy of consideration.

1. **Extreme Cases**
   Extremely inadequate consideration may indicate fraud, duress, incapacity, undue influence, or a lack of bargained-for exchange.

2. **Unconscionability**
   A contract may be unconscionable (and unenforceable) if consideration is so one-sided under the circumstances as to be unfair. (See Chapter 9.)

C. CONTRACTS THAT LACK CONSIDERATION

1. **Preexisting Duty**
   A promise to do what one already has a legal duty to do does not constitute consideration (no legal detriment is incurred). Exceptions include—

   a. **Unforeseen Difficulties**
      If a party runs into extraordinary difficulties that were unforeseen when a contract was formed, some courts will enforce an agreement to pay more. Ordinary business risks are not included.

   b. **Rescission and New Contract**
      The parties can rescind a contract to the extent that it is executory.

2. **Past Consideration**
   An act already done cannot be consideration for a later promise.

3. **Illusory Promises**
   If a contract expresses such uncertainty of performance that the promisor has not definitely promised anything, it is unenforceable.

D. SETTLEMENT OF CLAIMS

1. **Accord and Satisfaction**
   Concerns a debtor's offer of payment and a creditor's acceptance of a lesser amount than the creditor originally purported to be owed.

   a. **Accord**
      The agreement under which one of the parties undertakes to give or perform, and the other to accept, in satisfaction of a claim, something other than that which was originally agreed on.

   b. **Satisfaction**
      Takes place when the accord is executed.

   c. **The Amount of the Debt Must Be Unliquidated (in Dispute)**

1) **Unliquidated Debt—Consideration**

When the amount of a debt is in dispute, acceptance of a lesser sum discharges the debt. Consideration is given by the parties' giving up a legal right to contest the amount of debt.

2) **Liquidated Debt—No Consideration**

Acceptance of less than the entire amount of a liquidated debt is not satisfaction, and the balance of the debt is still owed. No consideration is given by the debtor, because he or she has a preexisting obligation to pay the entire debt.

2. **Release**

A **release** (a promise to refrain from pursuing a valid claim) bars any further recovery beyond the terms stated in the release. Releases are generally binding if they are (1) given in good faith, (2) stated in a signed writing, and (3) accompanied by consideration.

3. **Covenant Not to Sue**

The parties substitute a contractual obligation for some other type of legal action based on a valid claim. If the obligation is not met, an action can be brought for breach of contract.

E. **PROMISES ENFORCEABLE WITHOUT CONSIDERATION**

Under the doctrine of **promissory estoppel** (detrimental reliance), a person who relies on the promise of another may be able to recover if—

1. The promise was clear and definite.
2. The reliance is justifiable.
3. The reliance is of a substantial and definite character.
4. Justice will be better served by enforcement of the promise.

TRUE-FALSE QUESTIONS

(Answers at the Back of the Book)

_____ 1. An agreement is normally evidenced by an offer and an acceptance.

_____ 2. A contract does not need to contain reasonably definite terms to be enforced.

_____ 3. Rejection of an offer by the offeree will terminate it.

_____ 4. There are no irrevocable offers.

_____ 5. Under the mirror image rule, an offeree's acceptance does not need to adhere exactly to the terms of the offeror's offer to create a contract.

_____ 6. It is not possible for an offeree to accept an offer in silence.

_____ 7. Ordinarily, a court will evaluate the adequacy of consideration even if the consideration is legally sufficient.

_____ 8. Usually, a later promise to do what one already has a legal duty to do is not legally sufficient consideration.

_____ 9. Past consideration is consideration.

_____ 10. Unlike a release, a covenant not to sue does not always bar further recovery.

FILL-IN QUESTIONS

(Answers at the Back of the Book)

The elements necessary for an effective offer are (1) a _____ (serious/subjective) intent by the _____ (offeror/offeree) to be bound by the offer; (2) _____ (detailed/reasonably definite) contractual terms; and (3) communication of the offer to the _____ (offeror/offeree).

MULTIPLE-CHOICE QUESTIONS

(Answers at the Back of the Book)

____ **1.** Jay offers to buy from Kate a used computer, with a monitor and printer, for $400. Kate says, "Yes, but $200 more for the monitor and printer." Kate has

    a. accepted the offer.
    b. rejected the offer only.
    c. made a counteroffer only.
    d. rejected the offer and made a counteroffer.

____ **2.** Lee offers to sell his car to Mary, stating that the offer will stay open for thirty days. Lee may revoke the offer

    a. before Mary accepts the offer.
    b. only after Mary accepts the offer.
    c. only after thirty days.
    d. within thirty days, whether or not Mary has accepted the offer.

____ **3.** Jill offers to sell Ken a laptop computer. Ken's acceptance is sent via the mail. This acceptance is effective when

    a. it is halfway between Jill and Ken.
    b. Jill receives it.
    c. Ken sends it.
    d. none of the above.

____ **4.** Gail promises to pay Harry $400 to repair the roof on Gail's office building. Harry fixes the roof. The act of fixing the roof is

    a. consideration that creates Gail's obligation to pay Harry.
    b. not consideration because Gail had a legal duty to pay Harry.
    c. not consideration because it is not goods or money.
    d. not consideration unless Gail is entirely satisfied with the job.

____ **5.** Max agrees to supervise a construction project for Nora for a certain fee. In mid-project, Max asks for more money, claiming an increase in the ordinary business expenses to complete the project. Nora agrees. This agreement is

    a. enforceable as an accord and satisfaction.
    b. enforceable because of unforeseen difficulties.
    c. unenforceable under the preexisting duty rule.
    d. unenforceable as an illusory promise.

____ 6. Sue contracts with Todd to build two warehouses on two lots. After constructing the first warehouse, they decide to build a store on the second lot. Sue and Todd

   a. may rescind the original contract and make a new contract to build a store.
   b. may rescind the original contract but cannot make a new one to build a store.
   c. must perform the executory part of the original contract.
   d. must perform the original contract completely.

____ 7. Pat causes an accident in which Ruth is injured. Ruth accepts Pat's offer of $5,000 to release Pat from further liability. Later, Ruth learns that her injuries are more serious than she realized. Ruth's release of Pat will

   a. not bar a suit against Pat to recover for the injuries.
   b. not bar a suit against Pat to recover for the injuries if Pat is insured.
   c. not bar a suit against Pat to recover for the injuries if Ruth is insured.
   d. prevent Ruth from suing Pat.

____ 8. Jim promises to pay Kay to work for Jim. Kay agrees and quits her job. Jim does not hire Kay. Jim is liable to Kay based on

   a. the concept of accord and satisfaction.
   b. the concepts of rescission and new contract.
   c. the doctrine of promissory estoppel.
   d. Jim's illusory promise.

____ 9. Eve questions whether there is consideration for her contract with Frank. Consideration has two elements—there must be a bargained-for exchange and the value of whatever is exchanged must be

   a. adequately sufficient.
   b. economically sufficient.
   c. legally sufficient.
   d. significantly sufficient.

____ 10. Don has a cause to sue Edna in a tort action, but agrees not to sue her if she will pay for the damage. If she fails to pay, Ed can bring an action against her for breach of contract. This is

   a. a covenant not to sue.
   b. an accord and satisfaction.
   c. a release.
   d. an unenforceable contract.

SHORT ESSAY QUESTIONS

1. What is an "offer" and what are the elements necessary for an effective offer?

2. What is "consideration," what are its elements, and what, in this context, is "legal sufficiency"?

ISSUE SPOTTERS

(Answers at the Back of the Book)

1. One morning, when Ben's new car—with an $18,000 market value—doesn't start, he yells in anger, "I'd sell this car to anyone for $500." Carl drops $500 in Ben's lap. Is the car Ben's?

2.   Alpha Corporation offers to hire Beth to replace Curt, who has given Alpha a month's notice. Alpha gives Beth a week to decide whether to accept. Two days later, Curt signs an employment contract with Alpha for another year. The next day, Curt tells Beth of the new contract. Beth immediately sends a letter of acceptance to Alpha. Do Alpha and Beth have a contract?

3.   Before Paula starts her first year of college, Ross promises to pay her $5,000 if she graduates. She goes to college, borrowing and spending more than $5,000. At the start of he last semester, she reminds Ross of the promise. Ross sends her a note that says, "I revoke the promise." Is Ross's promise binding?

Chapter 9:
Capacity and Legality

WHAT THIS CHAPTER IS ABOUT

If a party to a contract lacks capacity, an essential element for a valid contract is missing, and the contract is void. Some persons have capacity to enter into a contract, but if they wish, they can avoid liability under the contract. Also, to be enforceable, a contract must not violate any statutes or public policy.

CHAPTER OUTLINE

I. CONTRACTUAL CAPACITY

A. MINORS
A minor can enter into any contract that an adult can enter into, as long as it is not prohibited by law (for example, the sale of alcoholic beverages).

1. Disaffirmance
A minor can disaffirm a contract by manifesting an intent not to be bound. A contract can ordinarily be disaffirmed at any time during minority or for a reasonable time after a minor comes of age.

2. Obligations on Disaffirmance
A minor cannot disaffirm a fully executed contract without returning whatever goods have been received or paying their reasonable value.

a. What the Adult Recovers

1) **In Most States**
   If the goods (or other consideration) are in the minor's control, the minor must return them (without added compensation).

2) **In a Growing Number of States**
   If the goods have been used, damaged, or ruined, the adult must be restored to the position he or she held before the contract.

b. What the Minor Recovers
All property that a minor has transferred to an adult as consideration, even if it is in the hands of a third party. If the property cannot be returned, the adult must pay the minor its value.

3. Disaffirmance and Misrepresentation of Age

a. In Most States
A minor who misrepresents his or her age can still disaffirm a contract. In some states, he or she is not liable for fraud, because indirectly that might force the minor to perform the contract.

b. In Some States
Some states prohibit disaffirmance; some courts refuse to allow minors to disaffirm executed contracts unless they can return the consideration; some courts allow a minor to disaffirm but hold the minor liable for damages for fraud.

   4. **Liability for Necessaries**
   Necessaries are food, clothing, shelter, medicine, and hospital care—whatever a court believes is necessary to maintain a person's status. A minor may disaffirm a contract for necessaries but will be liable for the reasonable value.

   5. **Ratification**
   Ratification is the act of accepting and thereby giving legal force to an obligation that was previously unenforceable.

      a. **Express Ratification**
      When a minor states orally or in writing that he or she intends to be bound by a contract.

      b. **Implied Ratification**
      When a minor performs acts inconsistent with disaffirmance or fails to disaffirm an executed contract within a reasonable time after reaching the age of majority.

   6. **Parents' Liability**
   Generally, parents are not liable for contracts made by their minor children acting on their own.

   7. **Emancipation**
   Minors, over whom parents have relinquished control, have full contractual capacity and do not have the right to disaffirm.

B. **INTOXICATED PERSONS**

   1. **If a Person Is Sufficiently Intoxicated to Lack Mental Capacity**
   Any contract he or she enters into is voidable at the option of the intoxicated person, even if the intoxication was voluntary.

   2. **If a Person Understands the Legal Consequences of a Contract**
   Despite intoxication, the contract is usually enforceable.

C. **MENTALLY INCOMPETENT PERSONS**

   1. **Persons Adjudged Mentally Incompetent by a Court**
   If a person has been adjudged mentally incompetent by a court of law and a guardian has been appointed, a contract by the person is void.

   2. **Incompetent Persons Not So Adjudged by a Court**

      a. **Those Who Do Not Understand Their Contracts**
      A contract is voidable (at the option of the person) if a person does not know he or she is entering into the contract or lacks the capacity to comprehend its nature, purpose, and consequences.

      b. **Those Who Understand Their Contracts**
      If a mentally incompetent person understands the nature and effect of entering into a certain contract, the contract will be valid.

II. LEGALITY

A. **CONTRACTS CONTRARY TO STATUTE**

   1. **Usury**
   All states limit the rate of interest that may be charged for a loan.

   2. **Gambling**
   All states regulate gambling.

   3. **Sabbath (Sunday) Laws**

a. Prohibited Contracts
In some states, all contracts entered into on a Sunday are illegal. Other states prohibit only the sale of certain merchandise (such as alcoholic beverages) on a Sunday.

b. Exceptions
Contracts for necessities and works of charity; executed contracts.

4. Licensing Statutes
In some states, the lack of a required business license bars the enforcement of work-related contracts.

a. Illegal Contracts
If the statute's purpose is to protect the public from unauthorized practitioners, a contract with an unlicensed individual is illegal.

b. Enforceable Contracts
If the purpose of the statute is to raise revenue, a contract entered into with an unlicensed practitioner is enforceable.

B. CONTRACTS CONTRARY TO PUBLIC POLICY

1. Contracts in Restraint of Trade
Competition in the economy is favored so contracts that restrain trade or violate an antitrust statute are prohibited.

a. Covenant Not to Compete
Enforceable if it is reasonable, determined by the length of time and the size of the area in which the party agrees not to compete.

b. Reformation of an Illegal Covenant Not to Compete
A court may reform an unreasonable covenant not to compete by changing it to reflect the true intentions of the parties.

2. Unconscionable Contracts or Clauses
A bargain that is unfairly one-sided is **unconscionable**.

a. Procedural Unconscionability
Relates to a party's lack of knowledge or understanding of contract terms because of small print, "legalese," etc. An **adhesion contract** (drafted by one party for his benefit) may be held unconscionable.

b. Substantive Unconscionability
Relates to the parts of a contract that are so unfairly one-sided they "shock the conscience" of the court.

3. Exculpatory Clauses
Contract clauses attempting to release parties of negligence or other wrongs. Usually held to be contrary to public policy.

C. THE EFFECT OF ILLEGALITY
Generally, an illegal contract is void. No party can sue to enforce it and no party can recover for its breach. Exceptions include—

1. Justifiable Ignorance of the Facts
A party who is innocent may recover benefits conferred in a partially executed contract or enforce a fully performed contract.

2. Members of Protected Classes
When a statute is designed to protect a certain class of people, a member of that class can enforce a contract in violation of the statute (the other party to the contract cannot enforce it).

3. **Withdrawal from an Illegal Agreement**
   If the illegal part of an agreement has not been performed, the party rendering performance can withdraw and recover the performance or its value.

4. **Fraud, Duress, or Undue Influence**
   A party induced to enter into an illegal bargain by fraud, duress, or undue influence can enforce the contract or recover for its value.

TRUE-FALSE QUESTIONS

(Answers at the Back of the Book)

____ 1. An adult may not generally disaffirm a contract entered into with a minor.

____ 2. In some states, a minor who disaffirms a contract must restore the adult party to the position he or she held before the contract was made.

____ 3. An intoxicated person who enters into a contract can void it.

____ 4. A minor can disaffirm his or her liability for tortious conduct.

____ 5. A person who has been adjudged mentally incompetent by a court cannot enter into legally binding contracts on his or her own.

____ 6. A contract clause that exculpates one party for negligence or other wrongdoing will usually be considered unconscionable.

____ 7. An adhesion contract is a contract in which the dominant party dictates the terms.

____ 8. If an illegal contract is executory, it may be enforced.

____ 9. If the purpose of a licensing statute is to protect the public from unlicensed practitioners, a contract entered into with an unlicensed practitioner is enforceable.

____ 10. Covenants not to compete are never enforceable because they are unreasonable restraints of trade.

FILL-IN QUESTIONS

(Answers at the Back of the Book)

The act of accepting and giving legal force to an obligation that previously was not enforceable is _____ (disaffirmance/ratification). In relation to contracts entered into by minors or persons who are intoxicated or mentally incompetent, this is an act or an expression in words by which the person, on or after reaching majority or regaining sobriety or mental competence, indicates intent to be bound by a contract.

Disaffirmance or ratification may be express or implied. For example, a person's continued use and payments on something bought when he or she was incompetent is inconsistent with a desire to _____ (disaffirm/ratify) and _____ (indicates/does not indicate) an intent to be bound by the contract. In general, any act or conduct showing an intent to affirm the contract will be deemed _____ (disaffirmance/ratification).

MULTIPLE-CHOICE QUESTIONS

(Answers at the Back of the Book)

____ 1. While a minor, Kay buys a car. After reaching the age of majority, Kay still maintains and operates the car. With regard to Kay's contract to buy the car, a court would likely hold that Kay

a. disaffirmed it.
b. ratified it.
c. rescinded it.
d. none of the above.

____ 2. While intoxicated, Don agrees to sell his warehouse for half its assessed value. The contract is

a. enforceable even if Don did not understand its legal consequences.
b. enforceable only if Don understood its legal consequences.
c. unenforceable because it obviously favors the buyer.
d. unenforceable under any circumstances.

____ 3. Ed is adjudged mentally incompetent. Fran is appointed to act as Ed's guardian. Ed signs a contract to sell his house. The contract is enforceable

a. only if Ed knew he was entering into a contract.
b. only if Ed had the mental capacity to comprehend the consequences.
c. if Ed knew he was entering into a contract or had the mental capacity to comprehend the consequences.
d. none of the above.

____ 4. Eve, a sixteen-year-old minor, buys a car from Fine Autos and wrecks it. To disaffirm the contract and satisfy a duty of restitution, Eve must

a. only return the car.
b. only pay for the damage.
c. return the car and pay for the damage.
d. none of the above.

____ 5. Bob bets Carl on the outcome of the SuperBowl. Gambling on sports events is illegal in their state. Before the game is over, Bob's attempt to withdraw from the bet is

a. invalid if it comes in the second half.
b. invalid without Carl's consent.
c. invalid unless Bob's team was ahead at the time of the withdrawal.
d. valid.

____ 6. Jill sells her business to Kyle and, as part of the agreement, promises not to engage in a business of the same kind within thirty miles for three years. This promise is

a. an unreasonable restraint of trade.
b. unreasonable in terms of geographic area and time.
c. unreasonable in terms of Kyle's "goodwill" and "reputation."
d. valid and enforceable.

____ 7. Luke is an unlicensed contractor in a state that requires a license to protect the public from unauthorized contractors. Mary hires Luke to build an office building. This contract is

a. enforceable only after Mary learns of Luke's status.
b. enforceable only before Mary learns of Luke's status.
c. enforceable only if no problems arise.
d. unenforceable.

____ 8. Fred signs a covenant not to compete with his employer, General Sales Corporation. This covenant is enforceable if it

a. is not ancillary to the sale of a business.
b. is reasonable in terms of geographic area and time.
c. is supported by consideration.
d. requires both parties to obtain business licenses.

____ 9. Sam leases real property from Tina under an agreement that includes an exculpatory clause. This clause is likely unenforceable

a. as a matter of public policy.
b. if either party is in a business important to the public interest.
c. if the lease involves commercial property.
d. none of the above.

____ 10. Ann contracts with Bob, a financial planner who is required by the state to have a license. Bob does not have a license. Their contract is enforceable if

a. Ann does not know that Bob is required to have a license.
b. Bob does not know that he is required to have a license.
c. the purpose of the statute is to protect the public from unlicensed practitioners.
d. the purpose of the statute is to raise government revenue.

SHORT ESSAY QUESTIONS

1. Who has protection under the law relating to contractual capacity and what protection do they have?

2. What makes an agreement illegal? What is the effect of an illegal agreement?

ISSUE SPOTTERS

(Answers at the Back of the Book)

1. Tom, a minor, enters into a contract with Diane. How might Tom effectively ratify this contract?

2. Joan runs a business through which she sells stolen goods. Joan pays Kim, a police officer, not to shut down her operation. When the crimes are discovered, Joan and Kim are jailed. Joan sues Kim to recover her payments to him. How much can she recover?

3. International Airlines, Inc., prints on its tickets that it is not liable for any injury to a passenger caused by the airline's negligence. If the cause of an accident is found to be the airline's negligence, can it use the clause as a defense to liability?

Chapter 10:
Defenses against Contract Enforceability

WHAT THIS CHAPTER IS ABOUT

A contract may be unenforceable if the parties have not genuinely assented to its terms. Under the Statute of Frauds, certain types of contracts must be in writing to be enforceable. This chapter covers both of those topics and the parol evidence rule.

CHAPTER OUTLINE

I. GENUINENESS OF ASSENT

In most cases in which assent is not genuine, the innocent party can choose to rescind the contract, or enforce it and seek damages.

A. MISTAKES

1. Unilateral Mistakes

When one contracting party makes a mistake as to some material fact, he or she is not entitled to relief from the contract. Exceptions are—

a. Other Party's Knowledge

A contract may not be enforceable if the other party to the contract knows or should have known that a mistake was made.

b. Mathematical Mistakes

A contract may not be enforceable if a substantial mistake in addition, subtraction, division, or multiplication was inadvertent.

2. Bilateral Mistakes

When both parties make a mistake as to some material fact, either party can rescind the contract. (If the mistake concerns the later value or quality of the object of the contract, however, either party can enforce the contract.)

B. FRAUDULENT MISREPRESENTATION

1. The Elements of Fraud

(1) Misrepresentation of a material fact, (2) an intent to deceive, and (3) an innocent party's justifiable reliance on the misrepresentation.

2. Misrepresentation Must Occur

a. Statements of Opinion

Statements of opinion are generally not subject to claims of fraud. But when a naïve purchaser relies on an expert's opinion, the innocent party may be entitled to rescission or reformation.

b. Misrepresentation by Conduct

Misrepresentation can occur by, for example, concealment, which prevents the other party from learning of a material fact.

c. Misrepresentation of Law

Misrepresentation of law does not entitle a party to relief, unless the misrepresenting party is in a profession that is known to require greater knowledge of the law than the average person has.

   d. **Misrepresentation by Silence**
       No party to a contract has a duty to disclose facts, unless a serious defect known to one could not reasonably be suspected by the other.

3. **Intent to Deceive (*Scienter*)**
    The misrepresenting party must know that facts have been falsely represented. This occurs when a party (1) knows a fact is not as stated; (2) makes a statement that he or she believes not to be true or makes it recklessly, without regard to the truth; or (3) says or implies that a statement is made on a basis such as personal knowledge when it is not.

4. **Reliance on the Misrepresentation**
    The misrepresentation must be an important factor in inducing the party to contract. Reliance is not justified if the party knows the true facts or relies on obviously extravagant statements, or the defect is obvious.

5. **Injury to the Innocent Party**
    To rescind a contract, most courts do not require proof of injury. To recover damages, proof of injury is required.

C. UNDUE INFLUENCE

If a contract enriches a party at the expense of another who is dominated by the enriched party, the contract is voidable. The essential feature is that the party taken advantage of does not exercise free will.

D. DURESS

Duress involves coercive conduct—forcing a party to enter into a contract by threatening the party with a wrongful act. Economic need is not enough.

II. THE STATUTE OF FRAUDS—REQUIREMENT OF A WRITING

The Statute of Frauds stipulates what types of contracts must be in writing to be enforceable. If one of these contracts is not in writing, it is not void but the Statute of Frauds is a defense to its enforcement.

A. CONTRACTS INVOLVING INTERESTS IN LAND

Land includes all objects permanently attached, such as trees. Contracts for transfer of interests in land, such as leases, must be in writing.

B. THE ONE-YEAR RULE

1. **When a Contract Must Be in Writing to Be Enforceable**
    A contract must be in writing if performance is objectively impossible within a year of the date of the contract's formation.

2. **When a Contract Need Not Be in Writing to Be Enforceable**
    A contract need not be in writing if performance within one year is possible—even if it is improbable, unlikely, or takes longer.

C. COLLATERAL PROMISES

1. **What Collateral Promises Must Be in Writing to Be Enforceable**
    A promise ancillary to a principal transaction and made by a third party to assume the debts or obligations of the primary party (only if the primary party does not perform).

2. **Exception—"Main Purpose" Rule**
    An oral promise to answer for the debt of another is enforceable if the guarantor's main purpose is to secure a personal benefit.

D. PROMISES MADE IN CONSIDERATION OF MARRIAGE

Prenuptial agreements must be in writing to be enforceable.

E. **CONTRACTS FOR SALES OF GOODS**
The Uniform Commercial Code (UCC) requires a writing for a sale of goods priced at $500 or more [UCC 2–201].

F. **EXCEPTIONS TO THE STATUTE OF FRAUDS**

1. **Partial Performance**

   a. **Contracts for the Transfer of Interests in Land**
   If a buyer pays part of the price, takes possession, and makes permanent improvements and the parties cannot be returned to their pre-contract status quo, a court may grant specific performance.

   b. **Contracts Covered by the UCC**
   Under the UCC, an oral contract is enforceable to the extent that a seller accepts payment or a buyer accepts delivery of the goods.

2. **Admissions**
   In some states, if a party admits in pleadings, testimony, or in court that a contract was made, the contract will be enforceable.

3. **Promissory Estoppel**
   An oral contract may be enforced if (1) a promisor makes a promise on which the promisee justifiably relies to his or her detriment, (2) the reliance was foreseeable to the promisor, and (3) injustice can be avoided only by enforcing the promise.

4. **Special Exceptions under the UCC**
   Oral contracts that may be enforceable under the UCC include those for customized goods and those between merchants that have been confirmed in writing (see Chapter 14).

III. THE STATUTE OF FRAUDS—SUFFICIENCY OF A WRITING
There must be at least a memo, confirmation, invoice, sales slip, check, fax, or several documents stapled together or in the same envelope that include—

A. **THE SIGNATURE OF THE PARTY TO BE CHARGED**
The writing must be signed (initialed) by the party who refuses to perform. The signature can be anywhere in the writing.

B. **ESSENTIAL TERMS**

1. **Contracts Covered by the UCC**
   The writing must include a quantity term. Other terms need not be stated exactly, if they adequately reflect the parties' intentions.

2. **Other Contracts**
   The writing must name the parties, subject matter, consideration, and quantity. In some states, a sale of land must include the price and a description of the property.

IV. THE PAROL EVIDENCE RULE

A. **THE RULE**
If the parties' written contract is integrated (the final expression of their agreement), evidence of their prior negotiations, prior agreements, or contemporaneous oral agreements that contradicts or varies the terms of the contract is not admissible at trial.

B. **EXCEPTIONS**
Parol evidence is admissible to show—

1. **Subsequent Modification of a Contract**
   Evidence of subsequent modification (oral or written) of a written contract is admissible (but oral modifications may not be enforceable if they bring the contract under the Statute of Frauds).

2. **A Contract Is Voidable or Void**

3. **Meaning of Ambiguous Terms**

4. **Essential Term Lacking in an Incomplete Contract**

5. **Prior Dealing, Course of Performance, or Usage of Trade**
   Under the UCC, evidence can be introduced to explain or supplement a contract by showing a prior dealing, course of performance, or usage of trade (see Chapter 15).

6. **Orally Agreed-on Condition**
   Proof of such a condition is admissible if it does not modify the written terms but involves the enforceability of the written contract.

7. **An Obvious or Gross Clerical Error**

TRUE-FALSE QUESTIONS

(Answers at the Back of the Book)

____ 1. A unilateral mistake does not generally afford the mistaken party a right to relief from the contract.

____ 2. When both parties are mistaken as to the same material fact, the contract cannot be rescinded by either party.

____ 3. To constitute fraud, misleading statements must be consciously false and have been made with the intent to mislead another.

____ 4. To rescind a contract for fraud, a plaintiff must prove that he or she suffered an injury.

____ 5. A contract entered into under undue influence is voidable.

____ 6. A contract involving an interest in land need not be in writing to be enforceable under the Statute of Frauds.

____ 7. To be enforceable, a contract for a sale of goods priced at $300 or more must be in writing.

____ 8. An act of concealment, without an affirmative misrepresentation, does not give rise to an action for fraud.

____ 9. A contract that cannot, by its own terms, possibly be performed within a year must be in writing to be enforceable.

____ 10. The parol evidence rule permits the introduction at trial of evidence of the parties' negotiations or agreements that contradicts or varies their contract.

FILL-IN QUESTIONS

(Answers at the Back of the Book)

A collateral promise is a promise that is _____ (superior/ancillary) to a _____ (primary/secondary) contractual relationship.

A promise by one person to pay the debts or discharge the duties of another person if the other fails to perform _____ (must/need not) be in writing to be enforceable under the Statute of Frauds. If the main purpose of a promise to pay another's debts or perform another's duties is to benefit the promisor, however, the agreement _____ (must/need not) be in writing to be enforceable.

MULTIPLE-CHOICE QUESTIONS

(Answers at the Back of the Book)

_____   1.   EZ Construction Company understates its bid on a project for Fine Properties, Inc., due to an addition error that Fine does not notice. EZ can most likely

a.   recover damages from Fine for not noticing the error.
b.   require Fine to pay the difference between the bid and the actual cost.
c.   rescind the contract.
d.   none of the above.

_____   2.   Adam persuades Beth to contract for his company's services by telling her that his employees are the "best and the brightest." Adam's statement is

a.   duress.
b.   fraud.
c.   puffery.
d.   undue influence.

_____   3.   Carol sells to Dan ten shares of Eagle Corporation stock. Dan believes that it will increase in value, but it later drops in price. From Carol, Dan can most likely recover

a.   the difference between the stock's purchase price and its later value.
b.   the stock's later value only.
c.   the stock's purchase price only.
d.   none of the above.

_____   4.   In offering to sell amplifiers to Eve for her theater, Fred intentionally misstates their capacity. In reliance, Eve buys the amplifiers. Frank's statement is

a.   duress.
b.   fraud.
c.   puffery.
d.   undue influence.

_____   5.   Ken sells Larry a parcel of land, claiming that it is "perfect" for commercial development. Larry later learns that it is not zoned for commercial uses. Larry may rescind the contract only if

a.   Ken knew about the zoning law.
b.   Larry did not know about the zoning law.
c.   the zoning law was not common knowledge.
d.   none of the above.

_____   6.   Standard Business Company agrees to hire Tim as a sales representative for six months. Their contract is oral. This contract is enforceable by

a.   Standard only.
b.   Tim only.
c.   Standard or Tim.
d.   none of the above.

_____ 7. Alpha Properties and Beta Corporation enter into an oral contract for the sale of a warehouse. Before Beta takes possession, this contract is enforceable by

   a. Alpha only.
   b. Beta only.
   c. Alpha or Beta.
   d. none of the above.

_____ 8. Ed borrows $1,000 from First State Bank. Fran orally promises the bank that she will repay the debt if Ed does not. This promise is enforceable by

   a. Ed only.
   b. First State Bank only.
   c. Ed or First State Bank.
   d. none of the above.

_____ 9. Greg agrees to make bookshelves for Holly, who tells Ira that she will guarantee payment for whatever supplies Greg orders from Ira for the shelves. Holly's promise is enforceable

   a. only if it is in writing.
   b. only if it is oral.
   c. whether it is oral or in writing.
   d. none of the above.

_____ 10. Jay and Kim enter into a contract for Jay's sale to Kim of ten computers for $500 each. After Kim takes possession, but before she makes payment, this contract is enforceable

   a. only if it is in writing.
   b. only if it is oral.
   c. whether it is oral or in writing.
   d. none of the above.

SHORT ESSAY QUESTIONS

1. What are the elements of fraudulent misrepresentation?

2. What is required to satisfy the writing requirement of the Statute of Frauds?

ISSUE SPOTTERS

(Answers at the Back of the Book)

1. In selling a house, Matt tells Nora that the wiring is of a certain quality. Matt knows nothing about the quality, until he later learns that it is not as he represented. He says nothing to Nora, who buys the house. When she discovers the truth, can she rescind the deal?

2. Curt, an accountant, files Donna's tax returns. When the Internal Revenue Service (IRS) assesses a large tax against Donna, she retains Curt to resist the assessment. The day before the deadline for replying to the IRS, Curt tells Donna that unless she pays a higher fee, he will withdraw. If she agrees to pay, is the contract enforceable?

3. Paula orally agrees with Quality Corporation to work in New York for two years. She moves her family to New York and begins work. Three months later, she is fired for no stated cause. Could she successfully sue for reinstatement or pay?

Chapter 11:
Third Party Rights and Discharge

WHAT THIS CHAPTER IS ABOUT

A party to a contract can assign the rights arising from it to another party or delegate the duties of the contract by having another person perform them. A third party also acquires rights to enforce a contract when the contracting parties intend that the contract benefit the third party (who is known as an *intended* beneficiary). This chapter also discusses performance and discharge of contracts.

CHAPTER OUTLINE

I. ASSIGNMENTS AND DELEGATIONS
Assignment and delegation occur after the original contract is made, when one of the parties transfers to another party an interest or duty in the contract.

A. ASSIGNMENTS

1. What an Assignment Is
Parties to a contract have rights and duties. One party has a *right* to require the other to perform, and the other has a *duty* to perform. The transfer of the *right* to a third person is an assignment.

2. Rights That Cannot Be Assigned

a. Statute Prohibits Assignment
(Such as assignment of future workers' compensation benefits.)

b. Contract Is Personal
The rights under the contract cannot be assigned unless all that remains is a money payment.

c. Assignment Materially Increases or Alters Risk or Duties of Obligor

d. Contract Stipulates That It Cannot Be Assigned
Exceptions: a contract cannot prevent an assignment of (1) a right to receive money, (2) rights in real property (known as restraints against alienation), (3) rights in negotiable instruments (see Chapter 18), or (4) a right to receive damages for breach of a sales contract or for payment of an amount owed under the contract.

3. Notice of Assignment
An assignment is effective immediately, with or without notice.

a. Same Right Assigned to More Than One Party
If the assignor assigns the same right to different persons, in most states, the first assignment in time is the first in right. In some states, priority is given to the first assignee who gives notice.

b. Discharge before Notice
Until an obligor has notice, his or her obligation can be discharged by performance to the assignor. Once the obligor has notice, only performance to the assignee can act as a discharge.

B. **DELEGATIONS**

Duties are delegated. The party making the delegation is the delegator; the party to whom the duty is delegated is the delegatee.

1. **Duties That Cannot Be Delegated**

Any duty can be delegated, unless (1) performance depends on the personal skill or talents of the obligor, (2) special trust has been placed in the obligor, (3) performance by a third party will vary materially from that expected by the obligee (the one to whom performance is owed) under the contract, or (4) the contract expressly prohibits it.

2. **Effect of a Delegation**

The obligee (the one to whom performance is owed) must accept performance from the delegatee, unless the duty is one that cannot be delegated. If the delegatee fails to perform, the delegator is still liable.

3. **Liability of the Delegatee**

If the delegatee makes a promise of performance that will directly benefit the obligee, there is an "assumption of duty." Breach of this duty makes the delegatee liable to the obligee, and the obligee can sue both the delegatee and the delegator.

C. **ASSIGNMENT OF ALL RIGHTS**

A contract that provides in general words for an assignment of all rights (for example, "I assign the contract" or "I assign all my rights under the contract") is both an assignment of rights and a delegation of duties.

II. THIRD PARTY BENEFICIARIES

Only intended beneficiaries acquire legal rights in a contract.

A. **INTENDED BENEFICIARIES**

An intended beneficiary is one for whose benefit a contract is made. If the contract is breached, he or she can sue the promisor.

1. **Types of Intended Beneficiaries**

a. **Creditor Beneficiaries**

A creditor beneficiary benefits from a contract in which a promisor promises to pay a debt that the promisee owes to him or her.

b. **Donee Beneficiaries**

A donee beneficiary benefits from a contract made for the express purpose of giving a gift to him or her.

2. **When the Rights of an Intended Beneficiary Vest**

To enforce a contract against the original parties, the rights of the third party must first vest (take effect). The rights vest when (1) the third party manifests assent to the contract or (2) the third party materially alters his or her position in detrimental reliance

3. **Modification or Rescission of the Contract**

Until the third party's rights vest, the others can modify or rescind the contract without the third party's consent. If the contract reserves the power to rescind or modify, vesting does not terminate the power.

B. **INCIDENTAL BENEFICIARIES**

The benefit that an incidental beneficiary receives from a contract between other parties is unintentional. An incidental beneficiary cannot enforce a contract to which he or she is not a party.

C. **INTENDED OR INCIDENTAL BENEFICIARY?**

1. **Reasonable Person Test**
   A beneficiary is intended if a reasonable person in his or her position would believe that the promisee intended to confer on the beneficiary the right to sue to enforce the contract.

2. **Other Factors Indicating an Intended Beneficiary**
   (1) Performance is rendered directly to the third party, (2) the third party has the right to control the performance, or (3) the third party is expressly designated as beneficiary in the contract.

III. CONTRACT DISCHARGE

A. CONDITIONS OF PERFORMANCE
If performance is contingent on a condition and it is not satisfied, a party does not have to perform.

1. **Condition Precedent**
   A condition that must be fulfilled before a party's performance can be required. Such conditions are common.

2. **Condition Subsequent**
   A condition that operates to terminate an obligation to perform. The condition follows a duty to perform. Such conditions are rare.

3. **Concurrent Condition**
   When each party's duty to perform is conditioned on the other party's duty to perform. Occurs only when the parties are to perform their duties simultaneously (for example, paying for goods on delivery). No party can recover for breach unless he or she first tenders performance.

B. DISCHARGE BY PERFORMANCE
Most contracts are discharged by the parties' doing what they promised to do. Discharge can be accomplished by tender. If performance has been tendered and the other party refuses to perform, the party making the tender can sue for breach.

1. **Complete versus Substantial Performance**

   a. **Complete Performance**
      Express conditions fully occur in all aspects. Any deviation is a breach of contract and discharges the other party.

   b. **Substantial Performance**
      Performance that does not vary greatly from the performance promised in the contract. If one party fulfills the terms of the contract with substantial performance, the other party is obligated to perform (but may obtain damages for the minor deviations).

2. **Performance to the Satisfaction of Another**

   a. **Personal Satisfaction of One of the Parties**
      When the subject matter of the contract is personal, performance must actually satisfy the party (a condition precedent).

   b. **Satisfaction of a Reasonable Person**
      Contracts involving mechanical fitness, utility, or marketability need only be performed to the satisfaction of a reasonable person.

   c. **Satisfaction of a Third Party**
      When the satisfaction of a third party is required, most courts require the work to be satisfactory to a reasonable person.

3. **Material Breach of Contract**
   A **breach of contract** is the nonperformance of a contractual duty. A breach is material when performance is not at least substantial. The nonbreaching party is excused from performing.

4. **Anticipatory Repudiation**
   Occurs when, before either party has a duty to perform, one party refuses to perform. This can discharge the nonbreaching party, who can sue to recover damages and can also seek a similar contract elsewhere.

C. **DISCHARGE BY AGREEMENT**
   Any contract can be discharged by an agreement of the parties.

   1. **Discharge by Rescission**
      Rescission is the process by which a contract is canceled and the parties are returned to the positions they occupied prior to forming it.

      a. **Executory Contracts**
         Can be rescinded. The parties must make another agreement, which must satisfy the legal requirements for a contract. Their promises not to perform are consideration for the second contract.

      b. **Enforceable Even if Made Orally**
         Unless the new agreement falls within the Statute of Frauds, or the original contract was subject to the UCC and required a writing.

      c. **Executed Contracts**
         Can be rescinded only if the party who has performed receives consideration to call off the deal.

   2. **Discharge by Novation**
      Occurs when the parties to a contract and a new party get together and agree to substitute the new party for one of the original parties. Requirements are (1) a previous valid obligation, (2) an agreement of all the parties to a new contract, (3) the extinguishment of the old obligation (discharge of the prior party), and (4) a new, valid contract .

   3. **Discharge by Accord and Satisfaction**
      The parties agree to accept performance that is different from the performance originally promised.

      a. **Accord**
         An executory contract to perform an act that will satisfy an existing duty. An accord suspends, but does not discharge, the duty.

      b. **Satisfaction**
         The performance of the accord discharges the original contract.

      c. **If the Obligor Refuses to Perform**
         The obligee can sue on the original obligation or seek a decree for specific performance on the accord.

D. **DISCHARGE BY OPERATION OF LAW**

   1. **Contract Alteration**
      An innocent party can treat a contract as discharged if the other party materially alters a term (such as quantity or price) without consent.

   2. **Statutes of Limitations**
      Statutes of limitations limit the period during which a party can sue based on a breach of contract.

3. **Bankruptcy**
   A discharge in bankruptcy (see Chapter 21) will ordinarily bar enforcement of most of a debtor's contracts.

4. **When Performance Is Impossible**

   a. **Objective Impossibility**
      Performance is objectively impossible in the event of (1) a party's death or incapacity, (2) destruction of the specific subject matter of a contract, or (3) change in law that makes performance illegal.

   b. **Commercial Impracticability**
      Performance may be excused if it becomes much more difficult or expensive than contemplated when the contract was formed.

   c. **Temporary Impossibility**
      An event that makes it temporarily impossible to perform will suspend performance until the impossibility ceases.

TRUE-FALSE QUESTIONS

(Answers at the Back of the Book)

_____ 1. Third parties have no rights under contracts to which they are not parties.

_____ 2. The party who makes an assignment is the assignee.

_____ 3. Rights under a personal service contract normally can be assigned.

_____ 4. An assignee can compel an obligor with notice of the assignment to perform.

_____ 5. A delegation does not relieve the delegator of the obligation to perform if the delegatee fails to perform.

_____ 6. A promise to perform subject to obtaining financing is a condition precedent.

_____ 7. Complete performance occurs when a contract's conditions fully occur.

_____ 8. A material breach of contract does not excuse the nonbreaching party from further performance.

_____ 9. An executory contract cannot be rescinded.

_____ 10. Objective impossibility discharges a contract.

FILL-IN QUESTIONS

(Answers at the Back of the Book)

The transfer of rights to a third person is _____(an assignment/a delegation) and the transfer of duties to a third person is _____ (an assignment/a delegation). Probably the most common contractual right that is _____ (assigned/delegated) is the right to the payment of money. For instance, Alpha Corporation sells its products on credit. Alpha has the right to installment payments from its customers. To obtain funds to buy more inventory, Alpha can _____ (assign/delegate) the right to the payments to a financing agency, which will pay Alpha for the right.

MULTIPLE-CHOICE QUESTIONS

(Answers at the Back of the Book)

____ 1. Greg enters into a contract with Holly that indirectly benefits Ira, although neither Greg nor Holly intended that result. Ira is

a. a delegatee.
b. an assignee.
c. an incidental beneficiary.
d. an intended beneficiary.

____ 2. Jim and Kay enter into a contract that intentionally benefits Lora. Lora's rights under this contract will vest

a. only if she manifests assent to it.
b. only if she materially alters her position in detrimental reliance on it.
c. if she manifest assent to it or if she materially alters her position in detrimental reliance on it.
d. none of the above.

____ 3. Dan and Eve sign a contract under which Dan agrees to repair Eve's computer for $150. Later, they agree that Eve will pay the $150 directly to Dan's creditor, First State Bank. The bank is

a. a delegatee.
b. an assignee.
c. an incidental beneficiary.
d. an intended beneficiary.

____ 4. Jill insures her warehouse under a policy with Kappa Insurance Company. Jill assigns the policy to Lyle, who also owns a warehouse. Kappa's best argument against the assignment of the policy is that

a. it did not consent to the assignment.
b. it was not paid for the assignment.
c. the assignment will materially alter its risk.
d. this is a personal service contract.

____ 5. Nora signs a contract to provide lawn mowing services to Owen. Nora delegates her duty under the contract to Pat. Owen can compel performance from

a. Nora only.
b. Pat only.
c. Pat or, if Pat does not perform, Nora.
d. none of the above.

____ 6. Ann enters a contract with Bill. Before either party performs, rescission of their contract requires

a. additional consideration.
b. a mutual agreement to rescind.
c. performance by both parties.
d. restitution.

____ 7. Sam and Tony want to discharge their obligations under a prior contract by executing and performing a new agreement. They must execute and perform

a. an accord and satisfaction.
b. an assignment.
c. a novation.
d. a nullification.

____   8. Lee and Mary want Nick to replace Lee as a party to their contract. They can best accomplish this by agreeing to

  a. an accord and satisfaction.
  b. an assignment.
  c. a novation.
  d. a nullification.

____   9. Adam contracts with Beth to deliver Beth's goods to her customers. This contract will, like most contracts, be discharged by

  a. accord and satisfaction.
  b. agreement.
  c. operation of law.
  d. performance.

____   10. Carl contracts with Diane to build a store on her property. If, before construction begins, the county enacts a law that prohibits building a store on that property, then

  a. Carl is in breach of contract.
  b. Diane is in breach of contract.
  c. the contract is suspended until the parties choose a new location.
  d. the contract is discharged.

SHORT ESSAY QUESTIONS

1.   Who are the parties in an assignment? What are their rights and duties?

2.   What effect does a material breach have on the nonbreaching party? What is the effect of a nonmaterial breach?

ISSUE SPOTTERS

(Answers at the Back of the Book)

1.   Ron owes Sally $100. Tim tells Ron to give him the money and he'll pay Sally. Ron gives Tim the money. Tim never pays Sally. Can she successfully sue Tim for the money?

2.   Vicky owes Warren $100. Vicky assigns her right to the money to Maria. Can Maria successfully sue Warren for the money?

3.   Eagle Construction contracts with Fred to build a store. The work is to begin on May 1 and be done by November 1, so that Fred can open for the holiday buying season. Eagle does not finish until November 15. Fred opens but, due to the delay, loses some sales. Is Fred's duty to pay for the construction of the store discharged?

Chapter 12:
Breach and Remedies

WHAT THIS CHAPTER IS ABOUT

Breach of contract is the failure to perform what a party is under a duty to perform. When this happens, the nonbreaching party can choose one or more remedies. Unless damages would be inadequate, that is usually what a court will award.

CHAPTER OUTLINE

I. DAMAGES

Damages compensate a nonbreaching party for the loss of a bargain and, under special circumstances, for additional losses. Generally, the party is placed in the position he or she would have occupied if the contract been performed.

A. TYPES OF DAMAGES

1. Compensatory Damages
Damages compensating a party for the *loss* of a bargain—the difference between the promised performance and the actual performance.

a. Incidental Damages
Expenses that are caused directly by a breach of contract (such as those incurred to obtain performance from another source).

b. Measurement of Compensatory Damages

1) **Sale of Goods**
The usual measure is the difference between the contract price and the market price. If the buyer breaches and the seller has not yet made the goods, the measure is lost profits on the sale.

2) **Sale of Land**

a) **Majority Rule**
If specific performance (see below) is unavailable, or if the buyer breaches, the measure of damages is the difference between the land's contract price and its market price.

b) **Minority Rule**
If the seller breaches and the breach is not deliberate, the buyer recovers any down payment, plus expenses.

3) **Construction Contracts**

a) **Owner's Breach Before, During, or After Construction**
Contractor can recover (1) before construction: only profits (contract price, less cost of materials and labor); (2) during construction: profits, plus cost of partial construction; (3) after construction: the contract price, plus interest.

b) **Contractor's Breach**
Owner can recover, before construction is complete, the cost of completion.

2. **Consequential Damages**
Damages giving an injured party the entire *benefit* of the bargain—foreseeable losses caused by special circumstances beyond the contract. The breaching party must know (or have reason to know) that special circumstances will cause the additional loss.

3. **Punitive Damages**
Damages punishing a guilty party and making an example to deter similar, future conduct. Awarded for a tort, but not for a contract breach.

4. **Nominal Damages**
Damages (such as $1) establishing, when no actual loss resulted, that a defendant acted wrongfully.

B. **MITIGATION OF DAMAGES**
An injured party has a duty to mitigate damages. For example, persons whose jobs have been wrongfully terminated have a duty to seek other jobs. The damages they receive are their salaries, less the income they received (or would have received) in similar jobs.

C. **LIQUIDATED DAMAGES VERSUS PENALTIES**

1. **Liquidated Damages Provision—Enforceable**
Specifies a certain amount to be paid in the event of a breach to the nonbreaching party for the loss.

2. **Penalty Provision—Unenforceable**
Specifies a certain amount to be paid in the event of a breach *to penalize the breaching party*.

3. **How to Determine If a Provision Will Be Enforced**
Ask (1) When the contract was made, was it clear that damages would be difficult to estimate in the event of a breach? (2) Was the amount set as damages a reasonable estimate? If either answer is "no," the provision will not be enforced.

II.   RESCISSION AND RESTITUTION

A. **RESCISSION**
Rescission is an action to undo, or cancel, a contract—to return nonbreaching parties to the positions they occupied prior to the transaction. Rescission is available if fraud, mistake, duress, or failure of consideration is present. The rescinding party must give prompt notice to the breaching party.

B. **RESTITUTION**
To rescind a contract, the parties must make **restitution** by returning to each other goods, property, or money previously conveyed.

III.   SPECIFIC PERFORMANCE
This remedy calls for the performance of the act promised in the contract.

A. **WHEN SPECIFIC PERFORMANCE IS AVAILABLE**
Damages must be an inadequate remedy. If goods are unique, a court will decree specific performance. Specific performance is granted to a buyer in a contract for the sale of land (every parcel of land is unique).

B. **WHEN SPECIFIC PERFORMANCE IS NOT AVAILABLE**
Contracts for sale of goods (other than unique goods) rarely qualify, because substantially identical goods can be bought or sold elsewhere. Courts normally refuse to grant specific performance of personal service contracts.

IV.   REFORMATION
Used when the parties have imperfectly expressed their agreement in writing. Allows the contract to be rewritten to reflect the parties' true intentions.

A. WHEN REFORMATION IS AVAILABLE
(1) In cases of fraud or mutual mistake; (2) to prove the correct terms of an oral contract; (3) if a covenant not to compete is for a valid purpose (such as the sale of a business), but the area or time constraints are unreasonable, some courts will reform the restraints to make them reasonable.

B. WHEN REFORMATION IS NOT AVAILABLE
If the area or time constraints in a covenant not to compete are unreasonable, some courts will throw out the entire covenant.

V. RECOVERY BASED ON QUASI CONTRACT
When there is no enforceable contract, quasi contract prevents unjust enrichment. The law implies a promise to pay the reasonable value for benefits received.

A. WHEN QUASI-CONTRACTUAL RECOVERY IS USEFUL
A party has partially performed under a contract that is unenforceable. The party may recover the reasonable value (fair market value).

B. REQUIREMENTS
The party seeking recovery must show (1) he or she conferred a benefit on the other party, (2) he or she had the reasonable expectation of being paid, (3) he or she did not act as a volunteer in conferring the benefit, and (4) the other party would be unjustly enriched by retaining it without paying.

VI. PROVISIONS LIMITING REMEDIES

A. EXCULPATORY CLAUSES
A provision excluding liability for fraudulent or intentional injury or for illegal acts will not be enforced. An exculpatory clause for negligence contained in a contract made between parties who have roughly equal bargaining positions usually will be enforced.

B. LIMITATION-OF-LIABILITY CLAUSES
Provide that the only remedy for breach is replacement, repair, or refund of the purchase price (or some other limit). Such clauses may be enforced.

C. CONTRACTS FOR SALES OF GOODS
Remedies can be limited (see Chapter 16).

VII. ELECTION OF REMEDIES
A nonbreaching party must choose which remedy to pursue. The purpose of the doctrine is to prevent double recovery. The doctrine has been eliminated in contracts for sales of goods—UCC remedies are cumulative (see Chapter 16).

TRUE-FALSE QUESTIONS
(Answers at the Back of the Book)

____ 1. Damages are designed to compensate a nonbreaching party for the loss of a bargain.

____ 2. Punitive damages are usually not awarded in breach of contract actions.

____ 3. Nominal damages do establish that a defendant acted wrongfully

____ 4. Liquidated damages are uncertain in amount.

____ 5. In rescinding a contract, the parties essentially return to the positions they were in before the contract was formed.

____   **6.** Rescission is not available in a case involving fraud.

____   **7.** On a breach of contract, the nonbreaching party has a duty to mitigate any damages that he or she suffers.

____   **8.** Quasi-contractual recovery is possible only when there is an enforceable contract.

____   **9.** Consequential damages are foreseeable damages that arise from a party's breach of a contract.

____   **10.** Specific performance is the usual remedy when one party has breached a contract for a sale of goods.

FILL-IN QUESTIONS

(Answers at the Back of the Book)

The usual measure of compensatory damages under a contract for a sale of goods is the difference between _____ (the contract price and the market price/the market price and lost profits on the sale). The usual remedy for a seller's breach of a contract for a sale of real estate is _____ (specific performance/rescission and restitution). If this remedy is unavailable or if the buyer breaches, in most states the measure of damages is the difference between _____ (the contract price and the market price/the market price and lost profits on the sale).

MULTIPLE-CHOICE QUESTIONS

(Answers at the Back of the Book)

____   **1.** Ann pays Bob $1,000 to design an intranet for her business office. The next day, Bob tells Ann that he has accepted a job with CompuWeb and cannot design her network, but he does not return her payment. Ann can recover

a. $1,000.
b. Bob's pay from CompuWeb.
c. $1,000 plus Bob's pay from CompuWeb.
d. nothing.

____   **2.** Sue contracts to sell a quantity of CD players to Tom for $1,000, payable in advance. Tom pays the money, but Sue fails to perform. Tom can

a. rescind the contract.
b. obtain restitution of the $1,000 but not rescind the contract.
c. rescind the contract and obtain restitution of the $1,000.
d. none of the above.

____   **3.** Eagle Corporation contracts to sell to Frosty Malts, Inc., six steel mixers for $5,000. When Eagle fails to deliver, Frosty buys mixers from Great Company, for $6,500. Frosty's measure of damages is

a. $6,500.
b. $5,000.
c. $1,500 plus incident al damages.
d. nothing.

____ 4. General Construction contracts to build a store for Home Stores for $1 million. In mid-project, Home repudiates the contract, and General stops working. General incurred costs of $600,000 and would have made a profit of $100,000. General's measure of damages is

a. $1 million.
b. $700,000.
c. $100,000.
d. nothing.

____ 5. Dave contracts with Paul to buy a computer for $1,500. Dave tells Paul that if the goods are not delivered on Monday, he will lose $2,000 in business. Paul ships the computer late. Dave can recover

a. $3,500.
b. $2,000.
c. $1,500.
d. nothing.

____ 6. Jay agrees to sell an acre of land to Kim for $5,000. Kim Jay fails to go through with the deal, when the market price of the land is $7,000. If Kim cannot obtain the land through specific performance, Kim may recover

a. $7,000.
b. $5,000.
c. $2,000.
d. nothing.

____ 7. Ken orally agrees to build three barns for Lora. He builds the first barn, but she fails to pay him. To redress the breach, Ken's best option is

a. damages.
b. quasi-contractual recovery.
c. rescission.
d. specific performance.

____ 8. Jake agrees to sell a warehouse to Kelly. Their contract provides that if Jake fails to close the deal on a certain day, he is to pay a fee equal to half of the price of the warehouse. This clause is

a. a liquidated damages clause.
b. a mitigation of damages clause.
c. a nominal damages clause.
d. a penalty clause.

____ 9. Sam agrees to deliver two tons of copper to United Conversion, Inc., under a contract that states delivery is to be within "15" days when the parties intend "50" days. If United will not amend the contract, Sam may obtain

a. reformation.
b. rescission.
c. specific performance.
d. nothing.

____ 10. Brenda agrees to sell an office building to Carl. When Brenda refuses to complete the deal, Carl uses and recovers damages. Carl can also obtain

a. quasi-contractual recovery.
b. restitution.
c. specific performance.
d. none of the above.

SHORT ESSAY QUESTIONS

1.   What are damages designed to do in a breach of contract situation?

2.   What must parties do to rescind a contract?

ISSUE SPOTTERS

(Answers at the Back of the Book)

1.   Greg contracts to build a storage shed for Holly, who pays Greg in advance, but Greg completes only half the work. Holly pays Ira $500 to finish the shed. If Holly sues Greg, what would be the measure of recovery?

2.   Lyle contracts to sell his ranch to Mary, who is to take possession on June 1. Lyle delays the transfer until August 1. Mary incurs expenses in providing for livestock that she bought for the ranch. When they made the contract, Lyle had no reason to know of the livestock. Is Lyle liable for Mary's expenses in providing for the cattle?

3.   Excel Engineering, Inc., signs a contract to design a jet for Flight, Inc. The contract excludes liability for errors in the design and construction of the jet. An error in design causes the jet to crash. Is the clause that excluded liability enforceable?

Chapter 13:
E-Contracts

WHAT THIS CHAPTER IS ABOUT

E-contracts include any contract entered into in e-commerce, whether business to business (B2B) or business to consumer (B2C), and any contract involving the computer industry. These might be contracts for sales or leases of goods or services, or licensing agreements. This chapter reviews some of the problems of e-contracts.

CHAPTER OUTLINE

I. ONLINE CONTRACT FORMATION
Disputes arising from contracts entered into online concern the terms and the parties' assent to those terms.

A. ONLINE OFFERS
Terms should be conspicuous and clearly spelled out. On a Web site, this can be done with a link to a separate page that contains the details. Subjects include remedies, forum selection, statute of limitations, payment, taxes, refund and return policies, disclaimers, and privacy policies. A click-on acceptance box should also be included.

B. ONLINE ACCEPTANCES
A *shrink-wrap agreement* is an agreement whose terms are expressed inside a box in which a product is packaged. Usually, the agreement is not between a seller and a buyer, but a manufacturer and the product's user. Terms generally concern warranties, remedies, and other issues.

1. Shrink-Wrap Agreements—Enforceable Contract Terms
Courts often enforce shrink-wrap agreements, reasoning that the seller proposed an offer that the buyer accepted after an opportunity to read the terms. Also, it is more practical to enclose the full terms of sale in a box.

2. Shrink-Wrap Agreements—Proposals for Additional Terms
If a court finds that the buyer learned of the shrink-wrap terms *after* the parties entered into a contract, the court might conclude that those terms were proposals for additional terms, which were not part of the contract unless the buyer expressly agreed to them.

3. Click-On Agreements
A *click-on agreement* is when a buyer, completing a transaction on a computer, indicates his or her assent to be bound by the terms of the offer by clicking on a button that says, for example, "I agree." The terms may appear on a Web site through which a buyer obtains goods or services, or on a computer screen when software is loaded.

4. Browse-Wrap Terms
Browse-wrap terms do not require a user to assent to the terms before going ahead with an online transaction. Offerors of these terms generally assert that they are binding without the user's active consent. Critics argue that a user should at least be required to navigate past the terms before they should be considered binding.

II. E-SIGNATURES
How are e-signatures created and verified, and what is their legal effect?

A. E-SIGNATURE TECHNOLOGIES
Methods for creating and verifying e-signatures include—

1. **Digital Signatures**
   Asymmetric (different) cryptographic keys provide private code for one party and public software for another party, who reads the code to verify the first party's identity. A cybernotary issues the keys.

2. **Signature Dynamics**
   One party signs a digital pad with a stylus. A measurement of the signature, with time and date, is encrypted in a biometric token and attached to a document. Another party can use the token to verify the signature.

3. **Other Forms**
   A smart card is a credit-card size device embedded with code that can be read by a computer to establish a person's identity or signature. Other possibilities include retina- and face-scanning.

B. **STATE LAWS GOVERNING E-SIGNATURES**
   Most states have laws governing e-signatures, although the laws are not uniform. The Uniform Electronic Transactions Act (UETA), issued in 1999, was an attempt by the National Conference of Commissioners on Uniform State Laws and the American Law Institute to create more uniformity.

C. **FEDERAL LAW ON E-SIGNATURES AND E-DOCUMENTS**
   In 2000, Congress enacted the Electronic Signatures in Global and National Commerce (E-SIGN) Act to provide that no contract, record, or signature may be denied legal effect solely because it is in an electronic form. Some documents are excluded (such as those governed by UCC Articles 3, 4, and 9.)

III.   PARTNERING AGREEMENTS

Through a partnering agreement, a seller and a buyer agree in advance on the terms to apply in all transactions subsequently conducted electronically. These terms may include access and identification codes. A partnering agreement, like any contract, can prevent later disputes.

IV.   THE UNIFORM ELECTRONIC TRANSACTIONS ACT

The UETA removes barriers to e-commerce by giving the same legal effect to e-records and e-signatures as to paper documents and signatures.

A. **THE SCOPE AND APPLICABILITY OF THE UETA**
   The UETA applies only to e-records and e-signatures in a transaction (an interaction between two or more people relating to business, commercial, or government activities). The UETA does not apply to laws governing wills or testamentary trusts, the UCC (except Articles 2 and 2A), the Uniform Computer Information Transactions Act, and other laws excluded by the states that adopt the UETA.

B. **THE FEDERAL E-SIGN ACT AND THE UETA**

1. **Does the E-SIGN Act Preempt the UETA?**
   If a state enacts the UETA without modifying it, the E-SIGN Act does not preempt it. The E-SIGN Act preempts modified versions of the UETA to the extent that they are inconsistent with the E-SIGN Act.

2. **Can the States Enact Alternative Procedures or Requirements?**
   Under the E-SIGN Act, states may enact alternative procedures or requirements for the use or acceptance of e-records or e-signatures if—

   a.   The procedures or requirements are consistent with the E-SIGN Act.
   b.   The procedures do not give greater legal effect to any specific type of technology.
   c.   The state law refers to the E-SIGN Act if the state adopts the alternative after the enactment of the E-SIGN Act.

C. **HIGHLIGHTS OF THE UETA**
   Individual state versions of the UETA as enacted may vary.

1. **The Parties Must Agree to Conduct Their Transaction Electronically**
   This agreement may be implied by the circumstances and the parties' conduct (for example, giving out a business card with an e-mail address on it). Consent may also be withdrawn.

2. **Parties Can "Opt Out"**
Parties can waive or vary any or all of the UETA, but the UETA applies in the absence of an agreement to the contrary.

3. **Attribution**
The effect of an e-record in a transaction is determined from its context and circumstances. Attribution refers to the identification of a party.

a. **Names and "Signatures"**
A person's name is not necessary to give effect to an e-record, but if, for example, a person types his or her name at the bottom of an e-mail purchase order, that typing qualifies as a "signature" and is attributed to the person.

b. **Relevant Evidence**
Any relevant evidence can prove that an e-record or e-signature is, or is not, attributable to a certain person.

c. **Issues Arising outside the UETA**
State laws other than the UETA apply to issues that relate to agency, authority, forgery, or contract formation.

4. **Notarization**
A document can be notarized by a notary's e-signature.

5. **The Effect of Errors**
If the parties agree to a security procedure and one party does not detect an error because it did not follow the procedure, the conforming party can avoid the effect of the error [UETA 10].

a. **When Other State Laws Determine the Effect of an Error**
Other state laws determine the effect if the parties do not agree on a security procedure.

b. **To Avoid the Effect of an Error**
A party must (1) promptly notify the other party of the error and of his or her intent not to be bound by it and (2) take reasonable steps to return any benefit or consideration received. If restitution cannot be made, the transaction may be unavoidable.

6. **Timing**

a. **When Is an E-Record "Sent"?**
When it is directed from the sender's place of business to the intended recipient in a form readable by the recipient's computer at the recipient's place of business with the closest relation to the deal (or either party's residence, if there is no place of business). Once an e-record leaves the sender's control or comes under the recipient's control, it is sent.

b. **When Is an E-Record "Received"?**
When it enters the recipient's processing system in a readable form—even if no person is aware of its receipt [UETA 15].

TRUE-FALSE QUESTIONS

(Answers at the Back of the Book)

_____ 1. A shrink-wrap agreement is normally not enforced.

_____ 2. A click-on agreement is normally enforced.

_____ 3. State e-signature laws are not uniform.

_____ 4. Under federal law, a signature may be denied legal effect simply because it is in electronic form.

_____ 5. The Uniform Electronic Transactions Act (UETA) is a federal law.

____ 6. The UETA does not apply to a transaction unless the parties agree to apply it.

____ 7. Under the UETA, a person's name is not necessary to give effect to an electronic record.

____ 8. Under the UETA, a contract is enforceable even if it is in electronic form.

____ 9. An e-record is considered received under the UETA only if a person is aware of its receipt.

____ 10. Under the UETA, once an e-record leaves the sender's control or comes under the recipient's control, it is sent.

FILL-IN QUESTIONS

(Answers at the Back of the Book)

Parties _____ (must/need not) participate in e-commerce to make binding contracts, according to the UETA. E-records are valid under the _____ (E-SIGN Act only/UETA only/E-SIGN Act and the UETA). The UETA supports all e-transactions, _____ (and creates/ but does not create) rules for them. The UETA _____ (applies/ does not apply) unless contracting parties agree to use e-commerce in their transactions.

MULTIPLE-CHOICE QUESTIONS

(Answers at the Back of the Book)

____ 1. Alpha Corporation attempts to enter into shrink-wrap agreements with buyers of its products. A shrink-wrap agreement is an agreement whose terms are expressed

a. in code at the end of a computer program.
b. inside a box in which a product is packaged.
c. in small print at the end of a paper contract signed by both parties.
d. on a computer screen.

____ 2. Beta, Inc., includes a shrink-wrap agreement with its products. A court would likely enforce this agreement if a buyer used the product

a. after having had an opportunity to read the agreement.
b. before having had an opportunity to read the agreement.
c. only after actually reading the agreement.
d. none of the above.

____ 3. Gamma Company agrees to sell software to Holly from Gamma's Web site. To complete the deal, Holly clicks on a button that, with reference to certain terms, states, "I agree." The parties have

a. a binding contract that does not include the terms.
b. a binding contract that includes only the terms to which Holly later agrees.
c. a binding contract that includes the terms.
d. no contract.

____ 4. Local Delivery Company and Regional Trucking, Inc., attempt to enter into a contract in electronic form. Under the Electronic Signatures in Global and National Commerce Act (E-SIGN Act), because this contract is in electronic form, it

a. may be denied legal effect.
b. may not be denied legal effect.
c. will be limited to certain terms.
d. will not be enforced.

____   5. International Investments, Inc., enters into contracts in e-commerce and in traditional commerce. The UETA applies, if at all, only to those transactions in which the parties agree to use

   a. e-commerce.
   b. traditional commerce.
   c. e-commerce or traditional commerce.
   d. none of the above.

____   6. American Sales Company and B2C Corporation enter into a contract over the Internet. The contract says nothing about the UETA. The UETA applies to

   a. none of the contract.
   b. only the part of the contract that does not involve computer information.
   c. only the part of the contract that involves computer information.
   d. the entire contract.

____   7. Digital Tech, Inc., e-mails an e-record, as part of a business deal, to E-Engineering Corporation. Under the UETA, an e-record is considered sent

   a. only when it leaves the sender's control.
   b. only when it comes under the recipient's control.
   c. when it leaves the sender's control or comes under the recipient's control.
   d. when it is midway between the sender and recipient.

____   8. New Software, Inc. (NSI), and Open Source Company (OSC) agree to follow a certain security procedure in transacting business. NSI fails to follow the procedure and, for this reason, does not detect an error in its deal with OSC. OSC can avoid the effect of the error

   a. only if NSI's name is affixed to the e-record evidencing the error.
   b. only if OSC takes reasonable steps to return any benefit or consideration received.
   c. under any circumstances.
   d. under no circumstances.

____   9. First Financial Corporation and Great Applications, Inc., enter into a contract that falls under the UETA. The UETA covers contracts that are also covered by

   a. laws governing wills and trusts only.
   b. the Uniform Commercial Code only.
   c. the Uniform Commercial Information Transactions Act only.
   d. none of the above.

____   10. Delta Company and Epsilon, Inc., engage in e-commerce without expressly opting in or out of the UETA. The UETA covers

   a. none of the contract.
   b. only the part of the contract that does not involve e-commerce.
   c. only the part of the contract that involves e-signatures.
   d. the entire contract.

SHORT ESSAY QUESTIONS

1. Are shrink-wrap and click-on agreements enforceable?

2. What are some of the provisions of the UETA?

ISSUE SPOTTERS

(Answers at the Back of the Book)

1. Applied Products, Inc., does business with Best Suppliers, Inc., online. Under the UETA, what determines the effect of the electronic documents evidencing the parties' deal? Is a party's "signature" necessary?

2. Technical Support, Inc., and United Services Corporation enter into a contract that may be subject to the E-SIGN Act and the UETA. Does one of these statutes take precedence over the other?

3. Computer Applications Corporation and Digitized Data, Inc., agree to a contract in e-commerce. Assuming the deal falls under the UETA, what effect might the UETA have in this situation?

CUMULATIVE HYPOTHETICAL PROBLEM
FOR UNIT THREE—INCLUDING CHAPTERS 7–13

(Answers at the Back of the Book)

Doe & Roe is a small accounting firm that provides bookkeeping, payroll, and tax services for small businesses. Java, Inc., is a small manufacturing firm, making and selling commercial espresso machines.

_____ **1.** Java sends e-mail to Doe & Roe, offering to contract for Doe & Roe's services for a certain price. The offer is sent on June 1 and is seen by Doe on June 2. The offer states that it will be open until July 1. This offer

    a. cannot be revoked because it is a firm offer.
    b. cannot be revoked because it is an option contract.
    c. could have been revoked only before Doe saw it.
    d. may be revoked any time before it is accepted.

_____ **2.** Java and Doe & Roe discuss terms for a contract, but nothing is put in writing. If a dispute develops later, and one party files a suit against the other, alleging breach of contract, the court will determine whether or not there is a contract between the parties by looking at

    a. the fairness of the circumstances.
    b. the offeree's subjective intent.
    c. the parties' objective intent.
    d. the parties' subjective intent.

_____ **3.** Java and Doe & Roe sign a written contract for Doe & Roe's services. The contract includes a large arithmetical error. Java later files a breach of contract suit against Doe & Roe, which asserts the mistake as a defense. Doe & Roe will win

    a. if Java wrote the contract.
    b. if the mistake was unilateral and Java knew it.
    c. only if the mistake was due to Java's negligence.
    d. only if the mistake was mutual.

_____ **4.** Java and Doe & Roe sign a written contract for Doe & Roe's services. Java later files a breach of contract suit against Doe & Roe. Doe & Roe could avoid liability on the contract if

    a. the contract has been assigned.
    b. there is an unexecuted accord between the parties.
    c. Java has been discharged by a novation.
    d. none of the above.

____ 5. Java and Doe & Roe sign a written contract for Doe & Roe's services. Java later files a suit against Doe & Roe. Doe & Roe is held to be in breach of contract. The court is most likely to grant relief to Java in the form of

a. damages.
b. specific performance.
c. damages and specific performance.
d. none of the above.

QUESTIONS ON THE FOCUS ON LEGAL REASONING FOR UNIT THREE— *FORD V. TRENDWEST RESORTS, INC.*

(Answers at the Back of the Book)

____ 1. Alpha Corporation enters into an agreement to hire Bob for employment at-will. If Alpha breaches the agreement, under the holding in *Ford v. Trendwest Resorts, Inc.*, Bob is most likely to be awarded

a. damages that represent future earnings.
b. damages that represent lost earnings.
c. nominal damages.
d. nothing.

____ 2. Beta Company enters into an agreement to hire Carol for employment at-will. In the opinion of the majority in *Ford v. Trendwest Resorts, Inc.*, the agreement between Beta and Carol

a. does not change the at-will employment relation between the parties.
b. establishes a claim for lost wages if Beta breaches the agreement *after* Carol starts work.
c. establishes a claim for lost wages if Beta breaches the agreement *before* Carol starts work.
d. establishes a claim for lost wages if Beta breaches the agreement at any time.

____ 3. Gamma, Inc., enters into an agreement to hire Dan for employment at-will. In the opinion of the dissent in *Ford v. Trendwest Resorts, Inc.*, the agreement between Gamma and Dan

a. does not change the at-will employment relation between the parties.
b. establishes a claim for lost wages if Gamma breaches the agreement *after* Dan starts work.
c. establishes a claim for lost wages if Gamma breaches the agreement *before* Dan starts work.
d. establishes a claim for lost wages if Gamma breaches the agreement at any time.

Chapter 14:
The Formation of
Sales and Lease Contracts

WHAT THIS CHAPTER IS ABOUT

This chapter introduces two parts of the Uniform Commercial Code: Article 2, which covers sales of goods, and Article 2A, which covers leases. The chapter also includes a section on contracts for an international sale of goods.

CHAPTER OUTLINE

I. THE SCOPE OF THE UCC

The UCC provides rules to deal with all phases of a commercial sale: Articles 2 and 2A cover contracts for sales or leases of goods; Articles 3, 4, and 4A cover payments by checks, notes, and other means; Article 7 covers warehouse documents; and Article 9 covers transactions that involve collateral.

II. THE SCOPE OF ARTICLE 2—SALES

Article 2 governs contracts for sales of goods.

A. WHAT IS A SALE?

A **sale** is "the passing of title from the seller to the buyer for a price" [UCC 2–106(1)]. The price may be payable in money, goods, services, or land.

B. WHAT ARE GOODS?

Goods are tangible and movable. Legal disputes concern the following—

1. **Goods Associated with Real Estate**

   Goods include minerals or the like and structures, if severance from the land is by the seller (but not if the buyer is to do it); growing crops or timber to be cut; and other "things attached" to realty but capable of severance without material harm to the land [UCC 2–107].

2. **Goods and Services Combined**

   a. **General Rule**

      Services are not included in the UCC. If a transaction involves both goods and services, a court determines which aspect is dominant.

   b. **Special Cases**

      Serving food or drink is a sale of goods [UCC 2–314(1)]. Other goods include unborn animals and rare coins.

C. WHO IS A MERCHANT?

UCC 2–104: Special rules apply to those who (1) deal in goods of the kind involved; (2) by occupation, hold themselves out as having knowledge and skill peculiar to the practices or goods involved in the transaction; (3) employ a merchant as a broker, agent, or other intermediary.

III. THE SCOPE OF ARTICLE 2A—LEASES

Article 2A governs contracts for leases of goods.

A. DEFINITION OF A LEASE

A **lease agreement** is the lessor and lessee's bargain, in their words and deeds, including course of dealing, usage of trade, and course of performance [UCC 2A–103(k)].

B. CONSUMER LEASES

Special provisions apply to leases involving (1) a lessor who regularly leases or sells, (2) a lessee who leases for a personal, family, or household purpose, and (3) total payments of less than $25,000 [UCC 2A–103(1)(e)].

C. FINANCE LEASES

A finance lease involves a lessor (financier) who buys or leases goods from a supplier and leases or subleases them to a lessee [UCC 2A–103(g)]. The lessee must perform, whatever the financier does [UCC 2A–407].

IV. THE FORMATION OF SALES AND LEASE CONTRACTS

The following summarizes how the UCC *changes* the common law of contracts.

A. OFFER

An agreement sufficient to constitute a contract can exist even if verbal exchanges, correspondence, and conduct do not reveal exactly when it became binding [UCC 2–204(2), 2A–204(2)].

1. Open Terms

A sales or lease contract will not fail for indefiniteness even if one or more terms are left open, as long as (1) the parties intended to make a contract and (2) there is a reasonably certain basis for the court to grant an appropriate remedy [UCC 2–204(3), 2A–204(3)].

a. Open Price Term

1) If the parties have not agreed on a price, a court will determine "a reasonable price at the time for delivery" [UCC 2–305(1)].

2) If either the buyer or the seller is to determine the price, the price is to be fixed in good faith [UCC 2–305(2)].

3) If a price is not fixed through the fault of one party, the other can cancel the contract or fix a reasonable price [UCC 2–305(3)].

b. Open Payment Term

When parties do not specify payment terms—

1) Payment is due at the time and place at which the buyer is to receive the goods [UCC 2–310(a)].

2) The buyer can tender payment in cash or a commercially acceptable substitute (a check or credit card) [UCC 2–511(2)].

c. Open Delivery Term

When no delivery terms are specified—

1) The buyer normally takes delivery at the seller's place of business [UCC 2–308(a)]. If the seller has no place of business, the seller's residence is used. When goods are located in some other place and both parties know it, delivery is made there.

2) If the time for shipment or delivery is not clearly specified, a court will infer a "reasonable" time [UCC 2–309(1)].

d. Duration of an Ongoing Contract

A party who wishes to terminate an indefinite but ongoing contract must give reasonable notice to the other party [UCC 2–309(2), (3)].

e. Options and Cooperation Regarding Performance

1) When no specific shipping arrangements have been made but the contract contemplates shipment of the goods, the seller has the right to make arrangements [UCC 2–311].

2) When terms relating to an assortment of goods are omitted, the buyer can specify the assortment [UCC 2–311].

f. Open Quantity Term
If parties do not specify a quantity, there is no basis for a remedy. Exceptions include [UCC 2–306]—

1) Requirements Contract
The buyer agrees to buy and the seller agrees to sell all or up to a stated amount of what the buyer needs or requires. There is consideration: the buyer gives up the right to buy from others.

2) Output Contract
The seller agrees to sell and the buyer agrees to buy all or up to a stated amount of what the seller produces. Because the seller forfeits the right to sell goods to others, there is consideration.

3) The UCC Imposes a Good Faith Limitation
The quantity under these contracts is the amount of requirements or output that occurs during a normal production year.

2. Merchant's Firm Offer
If a merchant gives assurances in a signed writing that an offer will remain open, the offer is irrevocable, without consideration, for the stated period, or if no definite period is specified, for a reasonable period (neither to exceed three months) [UCC 2–205, 2A–205].

a. The offer must be written and signed by the offeror. When a firm offer is contained in a form contract prepared by the offeree, a separate firm offer assurance must be signed as well.

b. The other party need not be a merchant.

B. ACCEPTANCE

1. Any Reasonable Means
When an offeror does not specify a means of acceptance, acceptance can be by any reasonable means [UCC 2–206(1), 2A–206(1)].

2. Promise to Ship or Prompt Shipment

a. Promise or Shipment of Conforming Goods
An offer to buy goods for current or prompt shipment can be accepted by a promise to ship or by a prompt shipment [UCC 2–206(1)(b)].

b. Shipment of Nonconforming Goods
Prompt shipment of nonconforming goods is both an acceptance and a breach, unless the seller (1) seasonably notifies the buyer that it is offered only as an accommodation and (2) indicates clearly that it is not an acceptance.

3. Notice of Acceptance
To accept a unilateral offer, the offeree must notify the offeror of performance if the offeror would not otherwise know [UCC 2–206(2)].

4. **Additional Terms**

   If the offeree's response indicates a definite acceptance of the offer, a contract is formed, even if the acceptance includes terms in addition to, or different from, the original offer [UCC 2–207(1)].

   a. **Not Conditioned on the Offeror's Assent—Battle of the Forms**

      Does the contract include the additional terms?

      1) **When the Seller or Buyer Is a Nonmerchant**

         Additional terms are considered proposals and not part of the contract. The contract is on the offeror's terms [UCC 2–207(2)].

      2) **When Both Parties Are Merchants**

         Additional terms are part of the contract unless (1) the offer expressly states no other terms; (2) they materially alter the original contract; or (3) the offeror objects to the modified terms in a timely fashion [UCC 2–207(2)].

   b. **Conditioned on the Offeror's Assent**

      If the additional terms are conditioned on the offeror's assent, the offeree's response is not an acceptance.

   c. **Additional Terms May Be Stricken**

      Regardless of what parties write down, they have a contract according to their conduct [UCC 2–207(3)]. If they do not act in accord with added terms, the terms are not part of a contract.

C. CONSIDERATION

An agreement modifying a sales or lease contract needs no consideration to be binding [UCC 2–209(1), 2A–208(1)].

1. **Modification Must Be Sought in Good Faith [UCC 1–203]**

2. **When a Modification Must Be in Writing to Be Enforceable**

   a. Contract prohibits changes except by a signed writing.

   b. If a consumer (nonmerchant) is dealing with a merchant, and the merchant's form prohibits oral modification, the consumer must sign a separate acknowledgment [UCC 2–209(2), 2A–208(2)].

   c. Any modification that brings a *sales* contract under the Statute of Frauds must be in writing to be enforceable [UCC 2–209(3)].

D. STATUTE OF FRAUDS

To be enforceable, a sales contract must be in writing if the goods are $500 or more and a lease if the payments are $1,000 or more [UCC 2–201, 2A–201].

1. **Sufficiency of the Writing**

   A writing is sufficient if it indicates the parties intended to form a contract and is signed by the party against whom enforcement is sought. A sales contract is not enforceable beyond the quantity stated. A lease must identify and describe the goods and the lease term.

2. **Transactions between Merchants**

   The requirement of a writing is satisfied if one merchant sends a signed written confirmation to the other.

   a. **Contents of the Confirmation**

      The confirmation must indicate the terms of the agreement, and the merchant receiving it must have reason to know of its contents.

    b. **Objection within Ten Days**

    Unless the merchant who receives the confirmation objects in writing within ten days, the confirmation is enforceable [UCC 2–201(2)].

  3. **Exceptions**

  An oral contract for a sale or lease that should otherwise be in writing will be enforceable in cases of [UCC 2–201(3), 2A–201(4)]—

    a. **Specially Manufactured Goods**

    The seller (or lessor) makes a substantial start on the manufacture of the goods, or makes commitments for it, and the goods are unsuitable for resale to others in the ordinary course of the business.

    b. **Admissions**

    The party against whom enforcement of a contract is sought admits in pleadings or court proceedings that a contract was made.

    c. **Partial Performance**

    Some payment has been made and accepted or some goods have been received and accepted (enforceable to that extent).

E. **PAROL EVIDENCE**

  1. **The Rule**

  If the parties to a contract set forth its terms in a writing intended as their final expression, the terms cannot be contradicted by evidence of any prior agreements or contemporaneous oral agreements.

  2. **Exceptions [UCC 2–202, 2A–202]**

  A court may accept evidence of the following—

    a. **Consistent Additional Terms**

    Such terms clarify or remove ambiguities in a writing.

    b. **Course of Dealing and Usage of Trade**

    The meaning of an agreement is interpreted in light of commercial practices and other surrounding circumstances [UCC 1–205].

    c. **Course of Performance**

    Conduct that occurs under the agreement indicates what the parties meant by the words in their contract [UCC 2–208(1), 2A–207(1)].

  3. **Rules of Construction**

  Express terms, course of performance, course of dealing, and usage of trade are to be construed together when they do not contradict one another. If that is unreasonable, the priority is: (1) express terms, (2) course of performance, (3) course of dealing, and (4) usage of trade [UCC 1–205(4), 2–208(2), 2A–207(2)].

F. **UNCONSCIONABILITY**

  1. **What an Unconscionable Contract (or Clause) Is**

  A contract so one-sided and unfair (at the time it was made) that enforcing it would be unreasonable.

  2. **What a Court Can Do**

  A court can (1) refuse to enforce the contract, (2) enforce the contract without the unconscionable clause, or (3) limit the clause to avoid an unconscionable result [UCC 2–302, 2A–108].

V.   CONTRACTS FOR THE INTERNATIONAL SALE OF GOODS
Contracts for the international sale of goods are governed by the 1980 United Nations Convention on Contracts for the International Sale of Goods (CISG).

A.   APPLICABILITY OF THE CISG
The CISG is to international sales contracts what UCC Article 2 is to domestic sales contracts (except the CISG does not apply to consumer sales). The CISG applies when the parties to an international sales contract do not specify in writing the precise terms of their contract.

B.   COMPARISON OF CISG AND UCC PROVISIONS

1.   Statute of Frauds
International contracts need not be in writing to be enforceable [Art. 11].

2.   Price Term
Must be specified or be determinable from the contract.

3.   Mirror Image Rule
The terms of the acceptance must mirror those of the offer.

4.   Acceptance
When an acceptance is sent, an offer becomes irrevocable, but the acceptance is not effective until it is received. Acceptance by performance does not require notice to the offeror.

TRUE-FALSE QUESTIONS
(Answers at the Back of the Book)

____   1.   Article 2 of the UCC governs sales of goods.

____   2.   Under the UCC, a sale occurs when title passes from a seller to a buyer for a price.

____   3.   The UCC governs sales of services and real estate.

____   4.   Under the UCC, an agreement modifying a contract needs new consideration to be binding.

____   5.   If a contract for a sale of goods is missing a term, it will not be enforceable.

____   6.   An unconscionable contract is a contract so one-sided and unfair, at the time it is made, that enforcing it would be unreasonable.

____   7.   In effect, the CISG is to international sales contracts what Article 2 of the UCC is to domestic sales contracts.

____   8.   Under the UCC, an offer to buy goods can be accepted only by a prompt shipment of the goods.

____   9.   A lease agreement is the lessor and lessee's bargain.

____   10. No oral contract is enforceable under the UCC.

FILL-IN QUESTIONS
(Answers at the Back of the Book)

_____ (Course of dealing/Usage of trade) is a sequence of conduct between the parties that occurred before their agreement and establishes a common basis for their understanding. _____

_____ (Course of dealing/Usage of trade) is any practice or method of dealing having regularity of observance in a place, vocation, or _____ (deal/trade) so as to justify an expectation that it will be observed with respect to the transaction in question. The express terms of an agreement, the course of dealing, and the usage of trade will be construed to be _____(consistent/ inconsistent) with each other whenever reasonable. When that is not possible, the _____ _____ (course of dealing/usage of trade/terms in the agreement) prevail.

MULTIPLE-CHOICE QUESTIONS

(Answers at the Back of the Book)

____   1.   Adam pays Beta Corporation $1,500 for a notebook computer. Under the UCC, this is

   a.   a bailment.
   b.   a consignment.
   c.   a lease.
   d.   a sale.

____   2.   Alpha Electronics, Inc., sells computers, and some computer accessories, to persons who order them. Alpha is a merchant with respect to

   a.   computers only.
   b.   computer accessories only.
   c.   computers and computer accessories.
   d.   none of the above.

____   3.   A-One Products Corporation and Best Manufacturing, Inc., enter into a contract for a sale of goods that does not include a price term. In a suit between A-One and Best over this contract and the price, a court will

   a.   determine a reasonable price.
   b.   impose the lowest market price for the goods.
   c.   refuse to enforce the agreement.
   d.   return the parties to the positions they held before the contract.

____   4.   Coastal Sales Corporation sends its purchase order form to Delta Products, Inc., for sixty display stands. Delta responds with its own form. Additional terms in Delta's form automatically become part of the contract unless

   a.   Coastal objects to the new terms within a reasonable period of time.
   b.   Coastal's form expressly required acceptance of its terms.
   c.   the additional terms materially alter the original contract.
   d.   any of the above.

____   5.   Mountain Boots, Inc., and National Shoe Company orally agree to a sale of 100 pair of hiking boots for $5,000. National gives Mountain a check for $500 as a down payment. At this point, the contract is

   a.   enforceable to at least the extent of $500.
   b.   fully enforceable because it is for specially made goods.
   c.   fully enforceable because it is oral.
   d.   none of the above.

____ 6. Apex Corporation sells two construction cranes to Baker Company, which leases one crane to Construction, Inc., and gives the other crane to Equipment, Inc. Article 2A of the UCC applies to

a. the gift only.
b. the lease only.
c. the sale only.
d. the gift, the lease, and the sale.

____ 7. Bob and Carol dispute the interpretation of an ambiguous clause in their contract. In a suit to determine the meaning of the clause, the court may accept evidence of

a. consistent additional terms only.
b. contradictory terms only.
c. consistent additional terms and contradictory terms.
d. none of the above.

____ 8. Don enters a contract with Ed's Furniture Store. In a later suit, Don claims that a clause in the contract is unconscionable. If the court agrees, it may

a. enforce the contract without the clause.
b. limit the application of the clause to avoid an unconscionable result.
c. refuse to enforce the contract.
d. any of the above.

____ 9. Digital Products, Inc., agrees to buy an unspecified quantity of microchips from Excel Corporation. Excel breaches the contract. Digital can probably

a. enforce the agreement to the amount of a reasonable quantity.
b. enforce the agreement to the amount of Digital's requirements.
c. enforce the agreement to the amount of Excel's output.
d. not enforce the agreement.

____ 10. Lyle in Great Britain orally agrees to sell 100 VCRs at $100 each to Maria in Mexico. Britain and Mexico have adopted the CISG. Lyle fails to deliver. With respect to the deal, Maria can

a. enforce it.
b. not enforce it because it is not in writing.
c. not enforce it because it is not supported by consideration.
d. not enforce it because the price term is not specified.

SHORT ESSAY QUESTIONS

1. For purposes of UCC Article 2, what is a sale? What are goods?

2. Who, for the purposes of UCC Article 2, is a merchant?

ISSUE SPOTTERS

(Answers at the Back of the Book)

1. Ace Autos, a car dealer, writes to Beth, "I have a 1999 Honda Civic that I will sell to you for $4,000. This offer will be kept open for one week." Six days later, Carl tells Beth that Ace sold the car that morning for $5,000. Did Ace breach any contract?

2. E-Design, Inc., orders 150 computer desks. Fine Supplies, Inc., ships 150 printer stands. Is this an acceptance of the offer or a counteroffer? If it is an acceptance, is it a breach of the contract? What if Fine told E-Design it was sending printer stands as "an accommodation"?

3. Truck Parts, Inc. (TPI), often sells supplies to United Service Company (USC), which services trucks. Over the phone, they negotiate for the sale of eighty-four sets of tires. TPI sends a letter to USC detailing the terms and two weeks later ships the tires. Is there an enforceable contract between them?

Chapter 15:
Title and Risk of Loss

What this Chapter Is About

The UCC has special rules involving title, which may determine the rights and remedies of the parties to a sales contract. In most situations, however, issues concerning the rights and remedies of parties to sales or lease contracts are controlled by three other concepts: (1) identification, (2) risk of loss, and (3) insurable interest.

Chapter Outline

I. IDENTIFICATION

For an interest in goods to pass from seller to buyer or lessor to lessee, the goods must (1) exist and (2) be identified as the goods subject to the contract.

A. WHAT IDENTIFICATION IS

Designation of goods as the subject matter of a sales or lease contract.

B. WHY IDENTIFICATION IS SIGNIFICANT

Identification gives the buyer (1) the right to obtain insurance and (2) the right to recover from third parties who damage the goods.

C. WHEN IDENTIFICATION OCCURS

1. According to the Parties' Agreement

Parties can agree when identification will occur (but to pass title and risk of loss, the goods must exist) [UCC 2–501, 2A–217].

2. If the Parties Do Not Specify a Time in Their Contract

a. Existing Goods

If the contract calls for a sale of specific goods already existing, identification occurs when the contract is made.

b. Future Goods

If a sale involves unborn animals or crops to be harvested within twelve months of the contract (or, for crops, during the next harvest season, whichever is further in the future), identification occurs when the goods are conceived, planted, or begin to grow.

c. Goods That Are Part of a Larger Mass

Identification occurs when—

1) **Goods Are Marked, Shipped, or Otherwise Designated**

2) **Exception—Fungible Goods**

A buyer can acquire rights to goods that are alike by physical nature, agreement, or trade usage and that are held by owners in common by replacing the seller as owner [UCC 2–105(4)].

II. PASSAGE OF TITLE

A. WHEN TITLE PASSES

1. According to the Parties' Agreement
Parties can agree on when and under what conditions title will pass.

2. At the Time and Place at Which the Seller Performs
If the parties do not specify a time, title passes on delivery [UCC 2–401(2)]. The delivery terms determine when this occurs.

a. Shipment Contracts
If the seller is required or authorized to ship goods by carrier, title passes at time and place of shipment [UCC 2–401(2)(a)]. All contracts are shipment contracts unless they say otherwise.

b. Destination Contracts
If the seller is required to deliver goods to a certain destination, title passes when the goods are tendered there [UCC 2–401(2)(b)].

c. Delivery without Movement of the Goods
If a buyer is to pick up goods, passing title turns on whether a seller must give a document of title (bill of lading, warehouse receipt).

1) When a Document of Title Is Required
Title passes when and where the document is delivered. The goods do not need to move (for example, they can stay in a warehouse).

2) When No Document of Title Is Required
If the goods have been identified, title passes when and where the contract was made. If the goods have not been identified, title does not pass until identification [UCC 2–401(3)].

B. SALES OR LEASES BY NONOWNERS
Generally, a buyer acquires whatever title the seller has to the goods sold [UCC 2–402, 2–403]. A lessee acquires whatever title a lessor could transfer, subject to the lease [UCC 2A–303, 2A–304, 2A–305].

1. Void Title
If the seller or lessor stole the goods, the buyer or lessee acquires nothing; the real owner can reclaim the goods.

2. Voidable Title
A seller or lessor has voidable title if goods were obtained by fraud, paid for with a check that is later dishonored, bought on credit when the seller was insolvent, or bought from a minor.

a. The Real Owner Can Reclaim the Goods

b. Exception—Good Faith Purchaser or Lessee for Value
The real owner cannot recover the goods [UCC 2–403(1)].

3. The Entrustment Rule
Entrustment includes both delivering goods to a merchant and leaving goods with the merchant for later delivery or pickup [UCC 2–403(3)].

a. Entrusting Goods to a Merchant Who Deals in Goods of the Kind
The merchant can transfer all rights to a buyer or sublessee in the ordinary course of business [UCC 2–403(2), 2A–305(2)].

b. What a Buyer or Sublessee in the Ordinary Course Gets
Only those rights held by the person who entrusted the goods.

III. RISK OF LOSS

The question of who suffers a financial loss if goods are damaged, destroyed, or lost (who bears the *risk of loss*) is determined by the parties' contract. If the contract does not state who bears the risk, the UCC has rules to determine it.

A. DELIVERY WITH MOVEMENT OF THE GOODS—CARRIER CASES

When goods are to be delivered by truck or other paid transport—

1. **Contract Terms**

   a. **F.O.B. (free on board)**—delivery is at seller's expense to a specific location. Risk passes at the location [UCC 2–319(1)].

   b. **F.A.S. (free alongside)**—seller delivers goods next to the ship that will carry them, and risk passes to buyer [UCC 2–319(2)].

   c. **C.I.F. or C.&F. (cost, insurance, and freight)**—seller puts goods in possession of a carrier before risk passes [UCC 2–320(2)].

   d. **Delivery Ex-ship** (from the carrying vessel)—risk passes to buyer when goods leave the ship or are unloaded [UCC 2–322].

2. **Shipment Contracts**

   Risk passes to the buyer or lessee when the goods are delivered to a carrier [UCC 2–509(1)(a), 2A–219(2)(a)].

3. **Destination Contracts**

   Risk passes to the buyer or lessee when the goods are tendered to the buyer at the destination [UCC 2–509(1)(b), 2A–219(2)(b)].

B. DELIVERY WITHOUT MOVEMENT OF THE GOODS

When goods are to be picked up by the buyer or lessee—

1. **If the Seller or Lessor Is a Merchant**

   Risk passes only on the buyer's or lessee's taking possession of the goods.

2. **If the Seller or Lessor Is Not a Merchant**

   Risk passes on tender of delivery [UCC 2–509(3), 2A–219(c)].

3. **If a Bailee Holds the Goods**

   Risk passes when (1) the buyer receives a negotiable document of title for the goods, (2) the bailee acknowledges the buyer's (or in the case of a lease, the lessee's) right to the goods, or (3) the buyer receives a nonnegotiable document of title, presents the document to the bailee, and demands the goods. If the bailee refuses to honor the document, the risk remains with the seller [UCC 2–503(4)(b), 2–509(2), 2A–219(2)(b)].

C. CONDITIONAL SALES

1. **Sale or Return (or Sale and Return)**

   A seller sells goods to a buyer who can set aside the sale by returning any portion of the goods and paying for the goods not returned [UCC 2–326, 2–327].

   a. **Title and Risk Pass to the Buyer with Possession**

   Title and risk stay with the buyer until he or she returns the goods to the seller within the specified time. A sale is final if the buyer fails to return the goods in time. Goods in the buyer's possession are subject to the claims of the buyer's creditors.

    b. Consignment
    A consignment is a sale or return. Goods in the consignee's (buyer's) possession are subject to his or her creditors' claims [UCC 2–326(3)].

  2. Sale on Approval
  A seller offers to sell goods, and the buyer takes them on a trial basis. Title and risk remain with the seller until the buyer accepts the goods.

    a. What Constitutes Acceptance
    Any act inconsistent with the trial purpose or the seller's ownership; or by the buyer's choice not to return the goods on time.

    b. Return
    Return is at the seller's expense and risk [UCC 2–327(1)]. Goods are not subject to the claims of the buyer's creditors until acceptance.

D. RISK OF LOSS WHEN A SALES OR LEASE CONTRACT IS BREACHED
Generally, the party in breach bears the risk of loss.

  1. When the Seller or Lessor Breaches
  Risk passes to the buyer or lessee when the defects are cured or the buyer or lessee accepts the goods in spite of the defects. If, after acceptance, a buyer discovers a latent defect, acceptance can be revoked and the risk goes back to the seller [UCC 2–510(2), 2A–220(1)].

  2. When the Buyer or Lessee Breaches
  Risk shifts to the buyer or lessee (if the goods have been identified), where it stays for a commercially reasonable time after the seller or lessor learns of the breach. The buyer or lessee is liable to the extent of any deficiency in seller or lessor's insurance [UCC 2–510(3), 2A–220(2)].

IV. INSURABLE INTEREST

A party buying insurance must have a "sufficient interest" in the insured item (see Chapter 38). More than one party can have an interest at the same time.

A. INSURABLE INTEREST OF THE BUYER OR LESSEE
A buyer or lessee has an insurable interest in goods the moment they are identified, even before risk of loss passes [UCC 2–501(1), 2A–218(1)].

B. INSURABLE INTEREST OF THE SELLER OR LESSOR
A seller or lessor has an insurable interest in goods as long as he or she holds title or a security interest in the goods [UCC 2–501(2), 2A–218(3)].

V. BULK TRANSFERS

A bulk transfer is a transfer of more than half of a seller's inventory not made in the ordinary course of business [UCC 6–102(1)]. Subject to UCC Article 6, which has been repealed or replaced with revised Article 6 in most states.

TRUE-FALSE QUESTIONS

(Answers at the Back of the Book)

_____ **1.** Before an interest in specific goods can pass from a seller to a buyer, the goods must exist and be identified to the contract.

_____ **2.** Under all circumstances, title passes at the time and place that the buyer accepts the goods.

_____ **3.** Unless a contract provides otherwise, it is normally assumed to be a shipment contract.

____ 4. In a sale on approval, the buyer can set aside the deal by returning the goods.

____ 5. A buyer and a seller cannot both have an insurable interest in the same goods at the same time.

____ 6. A bulk transfer is a transfer of a major part of the inventory not made in the ordinary course of the transferor's business.

____ 7. In a sale on approval, the risk of loss passes to a buyer when the buyer takes possession of the goods.

____ 8. An innocent buyer can acquire title to goods as a good faith purchaser from a thief.

____ 9. Under a destination contract, the risk of loss passes at time and place of shipment.

____ 10. If a seller is a merchant, the risk of loss to goods held by the seller passes to a buyer on delivery.

FILL-IN QUESTIONS

(Answers at the Back of the Book)

_____ (F.A.S./F.O.B.) means that delivery is at a seller's expense to a specific location—the place of shipment or a place of destination. When the term is _____ (F.A.S./F.O.B.) place of *shipment*, risk passes when the seller puts the goods into a carrier's possession. When the term is _____ (F.A.S./F.O.B.) place of *destination*, risk passes when the seller tenders delivery. _____ (F.A.S./F.O.B.) requires a seller at his or her own expense and risk to deliver goods alongside the ship that will transport them at which point risk passes.

MULTIPLE-CHOICE QUESTIONS

(Answers at the Back of the Book)

____ 1. Ron agrees to sell to State University Book Store 1,000 pens. Before an interest in the pens can pass from Ron to the book store, the pens must be

a. in existence only.
b. identified as the specific goods designated in the contract only.
c. in existence and identified as the goods in the contract.
d. none of the above.

____ 2. Alpha Products, Inc., buys ten computers from Beta Sales Corporation. They agree to ship the computers F.O.B. Beta via Gamma Shipping Company. The computers are destroyed in transit. The loss is suffered by

a. Alpha.
b. Beta.
c. Gamma.
d. none of the above.

____ 3. Stan buys a CD player from Tom, his neighbor, who agrees to keep the player until Stan picks it up. Before Stan can get it, the player is stolen. The loss is suffered by

a. Stan only.
b. Tom only.
c. Stan and Tom.
d. none of the above.

____ 4. Retail Floor Stores buys tile from Superior Tile Corporation. Town Storage holds the tile in a warehouse. The tile is delivered to Retail by the transfer of a negotiable warehouse receipt. A fire later damages the tile. The loss is suffered by

  a. Retail.
  b. Superior.
  c. Town.
  d. none of the above.

____ 5. Nora leaves her car with OK Auto Sales & Service for repairs. OK sells the car to Pete, who does not know that OK has no right to sell the car. Nora can recover from

  a. OK only.
  b. Pete only.
  c. OK and Pete.
  d. none of the above.

____ 6. Ed buys a sport utility vehicle (SUV) from Friendly Truck Sales, which agrees to keep the SUV until Ed picks it up. Before Ed can get it, it is stolen. The loss is suffered by

  a. Ed only.
  b. Friendly only.
  c. Ed and Friendly.
  d. none of the above.

____ 7. Omega Engineering, Inc., buys ten drafting tables from Quality Supply Corporation. They agree to ship the tables F.O.B. Omega via State Trucking Company. The tables are destroyed in transit. The loss is suffered by

  a. Omega.
  b. Quality.
  c. State.
  d. none of the above.

____ 8. New Products, Inc. (NPI), agrees to sell one hundred cell phones to Open Source Sales. NPI identifies the goods by marking the crate with red stripes. Before the crate is shipped, an insurable interest exists in

  a. NPI only.
  b. Open Source only.
  c. NPI and Open Source.
  d. none of the above.

____ 9. Standard Goods, Inc., ships fifty defective hard drives to Top Business Corporation. Top rejects the drives and ships them back to Standard, via United Transport, Inc. The drives are lost in transit. The loss is suffered by

  a. Standard.
  b. Top.
  c. United.
  d. none of the above.

____ **10.** Red Apples Corporation agrees to sell forty cases of apples to Sweet Fruit, Inc., under a shipment contract. Red gives the apples to Refrigerated Trucking, Inc. (RTI), which delivers them to Sweet. Title passed when

a. Red agreed to sell the goods.
b. Red gave the goods to RTI.
c. RTI delivered the goods to Sweet.
d. none of the above.

SHORT ESSAY QUESTIONS

1. What is "risk of loss" under the UCC?

2. When does risk pass (a) under a shipment contract; (b) under a destination contract; (c) when the buyer is to pick up the goods and (1) the seller is a merchant and (2) the seller is not a merchant; (d) when a bailee holds the goods?

ISSUE SPOTTERS

(Answers at the Back of the Book)

1. Under a contract between Great Products, Inc., in New York and National Sales Corporation in Dallas, if delivery is "F.O.B. New York," the risk passes when the Great Products puts the goods in a carrier's hands. If delivery is "F.O.B. Dallas," the risk passes when the goods reach Dallas. What if the contract says only that Great Products is "to ship goods at the seller's expense"?

2. Fine Farms in Washington sells Green Produce in Alaska a certain size of apples to be shipped "F.O.B. Seattle." The apples that Fine delivers to the shipping company for transport are too small. The apples are lost in transit. Who suffers the loss?

3. Chocolate, Inc., sells five hundred cases of cocoa mix to Dessert Company, which pays with a bad check. Chocolate does not discover that the check is bad until after Dessert sells the cocoa to Eden Food Stores, which suspects nothing. Can Chocolate recover the cocoa from Eden?

Chapter 16:
Performance and Breach of Sales and Lease Contracts

WHAT THIS CHAPTER IS ABOUT

This chapter examines the basic obligations of a seller and a buyer under a sales contract, and a lessor and a lessee under a lease contract, and the remedies each party has if the contract is breached. The general purpose of the remedies is to put a nonbreaching party "in as good a position as if the other party had fully performed."

CHAPTER OUTLINE

I. **PERFORMANCE OBLIGATIONS**
    The obligations of good faith and commercial reasonableness underlie every contract within the UCC [UCC 1–203]. The obligation of the seller or lessor is to tender and deliver conforming goods. The obligation of the buyer or lessee is to accept and pay for the goods [UCC 2–301, 2A–516(1)].

II. **OBLIGATIONS OF THE SELLER OR LESSOR**
    The seller or lessor must have and hold conforming goods at the disposal of the buyer or lessee and give whatever notice is reasonably necessary to enable the buyer or lessee to take delivery [UCC 2–503(1), 2A–508(1)].

    A. **TENDER OF DELIVERY**
        At a reasonable hour, in a reasonable manner, and the goods must be kept available for a reasonable time [UCC 2–503(1)(a)]. Goods must be tendered in a single delivery unless parties agree otherwise [UCC 2–612, 2A–510] or, under the circumstances, a party can request delivery in lots [UCC 2–307].

    B. **PLACE OF DELIVERY**
        The parties may agree on a particular destination, or their contract or the circumstances may indicate a place.

        1. **Noncarrier Cases**

            a. **Seller's Place of Business**
                If the contract does not designate a place of delivery, and the buyer is to pick up the goods, the place is the seller's place of business or if none, the seller's residence [UCC 2–308].

            b. **Identified Goods That Are Not at the Seller's Place of Business**
                Wherever they are is the place of delivery [UCC 2–308].

        2. **Carrier Cases**

            a. **Shipment Contract**
                The seller must [UCC 2–504]—

                1) Put the goods into the hands of a carrier.

                2) Make a contract for the transport of the goods that is reasonable according to their nature and value.

3) Tender to the buyer any documents necessary to obtain possession of the goods from the carrier.

4) Promptly notify the buyer that shipment has been made.

5) If a seller fails to meet these requirements, and this causes a material loss or a delay, the buyer can reject the shipment.

b. Destination Contract
The seller must give the buyer appropriate notice and any necessary documents of title [UCC 2–503].

C. THE PERFECT TENDER RULE

A seller or lessor must deliver goods in conformity with every detail of the contract. If goods or tender fail in any respect, the buyer or lessee can accept the goods, reject them, or accept part and reject part [UCC 2–601, 2A–509].

D. EXCEPTIONS TO THE RULE

1. Agreement of the Parties
Parties can agree in their contract that, for example, the seller can repair or replace any defective goods within a reasonable time.

2. Cure

a. Within the Contract Time for Performance
If nonconforming goods are rejected, the seller or lessor can notify the buyer or lessee of an intention to repair, adjust, or replace the goods and can then do so within the contract time for performance [UCC 2–508, 2A–513].

b. After the Time for Performance Expires
The seller or lessor can cure if there were reasonable grounds to believe the nonconformance would be acceptable. ("Reasonable grounds" include nonconforming tender with a price allowance.)

c. Substantially Restricts the Buyer's Right to Reject
If the buyer or lessee refuses goods but does not notice of the nature of the defect, he or she cannot later assert the defect as a defense if it is one that could have been cured [UCC 2–605, 2A–514].

3. Substitution of Carriers
If, through no fault of either party an agreed manner of delivery is not available, a substitute is sufficient [UCC 2–614(1)].

4. Installment Contracts

a. Substantial Nonconformity
A buyer or lessee can reject an installment only if a nonconformity substantially impairs the value of the installment and cannot be cured [UCC 2–612(2), 2–307, 2A–510(1)].

b. Breach of the Entire Contract
A breach occurs if one or more nonconforming installments substantially impair the value of the whole contract. If the buyer or lessee accepts a nonconforming installment, the contract is reinstated [UCC 2–612(3), 2A–510(2)]

5. **Commercial Impracticability**
   No breach if performance is impracticable by the occurrence of an unforeseen contingency. If the event allows for partial performance, the seller or lessor must do so, in a fair manner (with notice to the buyer or lessee) [UCC 2–615, 2A–405]

6. **Destruction of Identified Goods**
   When goods are destroyed (through no fault of a party) before risk passes to the buyer or lessee, the parties are excused from performance [UCC 2–613, 2A–221]. If goods are only partially destroyed, a buyer can treat a contract as void or accept damaged goods with a price credit.

7. **Assurance and Cooperation**
   A party with reasonable grounds to believe that the other will not perform may demand adequate assurance, suspend his or her own performance, and with no assurance within thirty days treat the contract as repudiated [UCC 2–609, 2A–401]. When required cooperation is not forthcoming, the other party can do whatever is reasonable, including holding the uncooperative party in breach [UCC 2–311(3)(b)].

III. OBLIGATIONS OF THE BUYER OR LESSEE
The buyer or lessee must make payment at the time and place he or she receives the goods unless the parties have agreed otherwise [UCC 2–310(a), 2A–516(1)].

A. PAYMENT
Payment can be by any means agreed on between the parties [UCC 2–511].

B. RIGHT OF INSPECTION
The buyer or lessee can verify, before making payment, that the goods are what were contracted for. The buyer has no duty to pay if the goods are not what were ordered [UCC 2–513(1), 2A–515(1)].

1. **Time, Place, and Manner**
   Inspection can be in any reasonable place, time and manner, determined by custom of the trade, practice of the parties, and so on [UCC 2–513(2)].

2. **C.O.D. Shipments**
   If a buyer agrees to a C.O.D. shipment or to pay for goods on presentation of a bill of lading, no right of inspection exists [UCC 2–513(3)].

3. **Payment Due—Documents of Title (C.I.F. and C.&F. Contracts)**
   Payment is required on receipt of documents of title, before inspection, and must be made unless the buyer knows the goods are nonconforming [UCC 2–310(b), 2–513(3)].

C. ACCEPTANCE
Acceptance is presumed if a buyer or lessee has a reasonable opportunity to inspect and fails to reject in a reasonable time [UCC 2–606, 2–602, 2A–515].

1. **How a Buyer or Lessee Can Accept**
   A buyer or lessee can accept by words or conduct. Under a sales contract, a buyer can accept by any act (such as using or reselling the goods) inconsistent with the seller's ownership [UCC 2–606(1)(c)].

2. **A Buyer or Lessee Can Accept Only Some of the Goods**
   But not less than a single commercial unit [UCC 2–601(c), 2A-509(1)].

IV. ANTICIPATORY REPUDIATION
The nonbreaching party can (1) treat the repudiation as a final breach by pursuing a remedy or (2) wait, hoping that the repudiating party will decide to honor the contract [UCC 2–610, 2A–402]. If the party decides to wait, the breaching party can retract the repudiation [UCC 2–611, 2A–403].

V. REMEDIES OF THE SELLER OR LESSOR

A. **WHEN THE GOODS ARE IN POSSESSION OF THE SELLER OR LESSOR**

1. **The Right to Cancel the Contract**
A seller or lessor can cancel a contract (with notice to the buyer or lessee) if the other party breaches it [UCC 2–703(f), 2A–523(1)(a)].

2. **The Right to Withhold Delivery**
A seller or lessor can withhold delivery if a buyer or lessee wrongfully rejects or revokes acceptance, fails to pay, or repudiates [UCC 2–703(a), 2A–523(1)(c)]. If a buyer or lessee is insolvent, a seller or lessor can refuse to deliver unless a buyer pays cash [UCC 2–702(1), 2A–525(1)].

3. **The Right to Resell or Dispose of the Goods**

   a. **When a Seller or Lessor Can Resell Goods**
   A seller or lessor still has the goods and the buyer or lessee wrongfully rejects or revokes acceptance, fails to pay, or repudiates the contract [UCC 2–703(d), 2–706(1), 2A–523(1)(e), 2A–527(1)].

   b. **Unfinished Goods**
   A seller or lessor can (1) resell the goods as scrap or (2) finish and resell them (buyer or lessee is liable for any difference in price). The goal is to obtain maximum value [UCC 2–704(2), 2A–524(2)].

4. **The Right to Recover the Purchase Price or Lease Payments Due**
A seller or lessor can bring an action for the price if the buyer or lessee breaches after the goods are identified to the contract and the seller or lessor is unable to resell [UCC 2–709(1), 2A–529(1)].

5. **The Right to Recover Damages**
If a buyer or lessee repudiates a contract or wrongfully refuses to accept, the seller or lessor can recover the difference between the contract price and the market price (at the time and place of tender), plus incidental damages. If the market price is less than the contract price, the seller or lessor gets lost profits [UCC 2–708, 2A–528].

B. **WHEN THE GOODS ARE IN TRANSIT**
A seller or lessor can stop delivery of goods if (1) the buyer or lessee is insolvent or (2) the buyer or lessee is solvent but in breach (if the quantity shipped is a carload, a truckload, or larger) [UCC 2–705, 2A–526].

C. **WHEN THE GOODS ARE IN POSSESSION OF THE BUYER OR LESSEE**

1. **The Right to Recover the Purchase Price or Lease Payments Due**
A seller or lessor can bring an action for the price if the buyer or lessee accepts the goods but refuses to pay [UCC 2–709(1), 2A–529(1)].

2. **The Right to Reclaim the Goods**

   a. **Sales Contracts—Buyer's Insolvency**
   If an insolvent buyer gets goods on credit, the seller can (within ten days) reclaim them. A seller can reclaim any time if a buyer misrepresents solvency in writing within three months before delivery [UCC 2–702(2)].

   b. **Sales Contracts—A Buyer in the Ordinary Course of Business**
   A seller cannot reclaim goods from such a buyer.

   c. **Sales Contracts—Bars the Pursuit of Other Remedies**
   A seller who reclaims gets preferential treatment over a buyer's other creditors (but cannot pursue other remedies) [UCC 2–702(3)].

    d. **Lease Contracts**
    A lessor can reclaim goods from a lessee in default [UCC 2A–525(2)].

VI. REMEDIES OF THE BUYER OR LESSEE

A. WHEN THE SELLER OR LESSOR REFUSES TO DELIVER THE GOODS

When a seller or lessor fails to deliver or repudiates the contract, the buyer or lessee has the following rights.

1. **The Right to Cancel the Contract**
   The buyer or lessee can rescind (cancel) the contract. On notice to the seller, the buyer or lessee is discharged [UCC 2–711(1), 2A–508(1)(a)].

2. **The Right to Recover the Goods**
   A buyer or lessee who paid for goods in the hands of the seller or lessor can recover them if the seller or lessor is insolvent or becomes insolvent within ten days of receiving payment and the goods are identified to the contract. Buyer or lessee must tender any unpaid balance [UCC 2–502, 2A–522].

3. **The Right to Obtain Specific Performance**
   A buyer or lessee can obtain specific performance if goods are unique or damages would be inadequate [UCC 2–716(1), 2A–521(1)].

4. **The Right of Cover**
   The measure of damages is the difference between the cost of cover and the contract price, plus incidental and consequential damages, less expenses saved by the breach [UCC 2–712, 2–715, 2A–518, 2A–520].

5. **The Right to Replevy Goods**
   A buyer or lessee can use replevin if seller or lessor fails to deliver or repudiates and buyer or lessee cannot cover [UCC 2–716(3), 2A–521(3)].

6. **The Right to Recover Damages**
   The measure of damages is the difference between the contract price and, when the buyer or lessee learned of the breach, the market price (at the place of delivery), plus incidental and consequential damages, less expenses saved by the breach [UCC 2–713, 2A–519].

B. WHEN THE SELLER OR LESSOR DELIVERS NONCONFORMING GOODS

1. **The Right to Reject the Goods**
   A buyer or lessee can reject the part of goods that fails to conform to the contract (and rescind the contract or obtain cover) [UCC 2–601, 2A–509].

   a. **Notice Required**
   Notice must be timely, and a buyer or lessee must tell the seller or lessor what the defect is [UCC 2–602(1), 2–605, 2A–509(2), 2A–514].

   b. **Duties of a Merchant Buyer or Lessee**
   Follow the seller or lessor's instructions about the goods [UCC 2–603, 2A–511]. Without instructions, perishable goods can be resold; otherwise they must be stored or returned.

   c. **The Right to Retain and Enforce a Security Interest**
   Buyers who rightfully reject or who justifiably revoke acceptance of goods in their possession have a security interest in the goods. A buyer can recover payments made for the goods and expenses to inspect, transport, and hold the goods, or can resell, withhold delivery, or stop delivery [UCC 2–711, 2–706].

2. **The Right to Revoke Acceptance of the Goods**

a. **Substantial Impairment**
   Any nonconformity must substantially impair the value of the goods *and* either not be seasonably cured or be difficult to discover [UCC 2–608, 2A–517].

b. **Notice of a Breach Must Be within a Reasonable Time**
   Before the goods have undergone substantial change (not caused by their own defects, such as spoilage) [UCC 2–608(2), 2A–517(4)].

3. **The Right to Recover Damages for Accepted Goods**
   Notice of a breach must be within a reasonable time. The measure of damages is the difference between value of goods as accepted and value if they had been as promised [UCC 2–714(2), 2A–519(4)].

VII. LIMITATION OF REMEDIES

Parties can provide for remedies in addition to or in lieu of those in the UCC, or they can change the measure of damages [UCC 2–719, 2A–503]. If a buyer or lessee is a consumer, limiting consequential damages for personal injuries on a breach of warranty is *prima facie* unconscionable.

VIII. STATUTE OF LIMITATIONS

An action for breach of contract under the UCC must be brought within four years of the breach. In their contract, the parties can reduce this period to not less than one year [UCC 2–725(1), 2A–506(1)]. If goods are nonconforming but the buyer accepts them, notice of the breach must be within a reasonable time or all remedies are lost [UCC 2–607(3)(a), 2A–516(3)].

TRUE-FALSE QUESTIONS

(Answers at the Back of the Book)

____ 1. The duties and obligations of the parties to a contract include those specified in their agreement.

____ 2. Generally, under a sales or lease contract, all goods must be tendered in a single delivery.

____ 3. If goods or tender of delivery fails in any way, a buyer or lessee can accept or reject the goods in whole or in part.

____ 4. Unless the parties agree otherwise, a buyer or lessee must pay for goods in advance.

____ 5. If a contract does not specify otherwise, the place for delivery of goods is the buyer's place of business.

____ 6. A buyer or lessee who accepts a delivery of goods cannot withdraw the acceptance.

____ 7. A seller or lessor cannot consider a buyer or lessee in breach until the time for performance has past.

____ 8. In an installment contract, a buyer can reject any installment for any reason.

____ 9. If a buyer or lessee wrongfully refuses to accept or pay for conforming goods, the seller or lessor can cancel the contract and recover damages.

____ 10. If a seller or lessor wrongfully refuses to deliver conforming goods, the buyer or lessee can cancel the contract and recover damages.

FILL-IN QUESTIONS

(Answers at the Back of the Book)

A seller's obligations include holding _____ (conforming/nonconforming) goods at a buyer's disposal _____ (and/or) giving notice reasonably necessary for the buyer to take delivery.

Unless the parties have agreed otherwise, the _____ (seller/buyer) must provide facilities reasonably suited for _____ (delivery/receipt) of the goods. Also, unless the parties have agreed otherwise, a buyer must pay at the time and place of receipt, _____ (even if/unless) the place of shipment is the place of delivery.

MULTIPLE-CHOICE QUESTIONS

(Answers at the Back of the Book)

_____ 1. First Financial Corporation (FFC) orders 100 computers from E-Electronics, Inc. For E-Electronics to tender delivery of the goods, the seller must

   a. only give notice to enable FFC to take delivery.
   b. only hold conforming goods at FFC's disposal .
   c. give notice to FFC and hold conforming goods at FFC's disposal.
   d. none of the above.

_____ 2. Apple Farms contracts for a sale of fruit to Best Groceries, Inc. Apple can enforce its right to payment

   a. only after Best has inspected the goods.
   b. only after Best has had an opportunity to inspect the goods.
   c. only before Best has inspected the goods.
   d. whether or not Best has had the opportunity to inspect the goods.

_____ 3. Kay contracts to sell five laser printers to Lora under a shipment contract. Kay must

   a. only make a reasonable contract for the transport of the goods.
   b. only tender to Lora the documents needed to obtain possession of the goods.
   c. make a reasonable contract for the transport of the goods and tender the documents needed to obtain the goods.
   d. none of the above.

_____ 4. Alpha Stores, Inc., refuses to buy 1,000 DVD players for $80 each from Beta Products Company under their contract, due to a drop in the market price for the players, which can be bought for $40 each. As damages, Beta can recover

   a. $120,000.
   b. $80,000.
   c. $40,000.
   d. $0.

_____ 5. Delta Grocers, Inc., agrees to buy 10,000 potatoes from Eagle Farms. Only half of the shipment conforms to the contract, but conforming potatoes are in short supply in the market. Delta's best course is to

   a. accept the entire shipment.
   b. accept the conforming goods and sue Eagle for the difference between the contract price and the cost of cover.
   c. reject the entire shipment and sue Eagle for specific performance.
   d. suspend payment and wait to see if Eagle will tender conforming goods.

_____ 6. Fine Poultry Corporation agrees to sell 600 frozen chickens to Fast Food, Inc., in three equal installments. In the first installment, 100 chickens are spoiled. Fast Food can

   a. cancel the contract.
   b. recover from Fine Poultry for breach of the entire contract.
   c. reject the first installment only.
   d. use the unspoiled chickens without payment.

____ 7. Adam contracts to buy goods from Beth. Beth wrongfully fails to deliver the goods. Adam can recover damages equal to the difference between the contract price and the market price

a. at the time the contract was made.
b. at the time and place of tender.
c. when Adam learned of the breach.
d. when Adam filed a suit against Beth.

____ 8. Excel Corporation agrees to sell the latest version of its Go! computer game to National Retail Company. Excel delivers an outdated version of Go! (nonconforming goods). National's possible remedies may include

a. recovering damages only.
b. rejecting part or all of the goods, or revoking acceptance only.
c. recovering damages, rejecting goods, or revoking acceptance.
d. none of the above.

____ 9. Engineering, Inc. (EI), agrees to sell specially made parts to Precision Manufacturing Company. EI does not deliver. Due to a market shortage, Precision cannot obtain cover. The buyer's right to recover the parts from EI is

a. novation.
b. replevin.
c. rescission.
d. specific performance.

____ 10. Athletic Goods, Inc. (AGI), agrees to sell sports equipment to Bob's Sports Store. Before the time for performance, AGI tells Bob that it will not deliver. This is

a. anticipatory repudiation.
b. perfect tender.
c. rejection of performance.
d. revocation of acceptance.

SHORT ESSAY QUESTIONS

1. What is a seller's right to cure and how does it affect a buyer's right to reject?

2. What is a buyer's right of cover?

ISSUE SPOTTERS

(Answers at the Back of the Book)

1. Country Fruit Stand orders eighty cases of peaches from Down Home Farms. For no good reason, Down Home delivers thirty cases instead of eighty, and the delivery is late. Does Country have the right to reject the shipment?

2. Great Images, Inc. (GI), agrees to sell Catalog Corporation (CC) 5,000 posters of celebrities, to be delivered on May 1. On April 1, GI repudiates the contract. CC informs GI that it expects delivery. Can CC sue GI without waiting until May 1?

3. Pizza King agrees to buy tomatoes from Quality Farms. When Quality tenders the goods, Pizza King wrongfully refuses to accept. Quality quickly sells the tomatoes to another buyer, for a lower price. Can Quality recover from Pizza King? If so, what's the measure of recovery?

Chapter 17:
Warranties and Product Liability

WHAT THIS CHAPTER IS ABOUT

Some type of warranty that imposes a duty on the seller covers most goods. A breach of the warranty is a breach of the seller's promise. Manufacturers, processors, and sellers may also be liable to consumers, users, and bystanders for physical harm or property damage caused by defective goods. This is product liability.

CHAPTER OUTLINE

I. WARRANTIES

A. WARRANTIES OF TITLE

1. **Good Title**
    Sellers warrant that they have good and valid title and that the transfer of title is rightful [UCC 2–312(1)(a)].

2. **No Liens**
    Sellers warrant that goods are free of a security interest of which the buyer has no knowledge [UCC 2–312(1)(b)]. Lessors warrant no third party will interfere with the lessee's use of the goods [UCC 2A–211(1)].

3. **No Infringements**
    Sellers warrant that the goods are free of any third person's patent, trademark, or copyright claims [UCC 2–312(3)].

    a. **Sales Contract—If the Warranty Is Breached and the Buyer Is Sued**
        The buyer must notify the seller. If the seller agrees in writing to defend and bear all costs, the buyer must let the seller do it (or lose all rights against the seller) [UCC 2–607(3)(b), (5)(b)].

    b. **Lease—If the Warranty Is Breached and the Lessee Is Sued**
        Same as above, except that a consumer who fails to notify the lessor within a reasonable time does not lose any rights against the lessor [UCC 2A–516(3)(b), (4)(b)].

4. **Disclaimer of Title Warranty**
    In a sales contract, a disclaimer can be made only by specific contractual language [UCC 2–312(2)]). In a lease, the disclaimer must be specific, in writing, and conspicuous [UCC 2A–214(4)].

B. EXPRESS WARRANTIES

1. **When Express Warranties Arise**
    A seller or lessor warrants that goods will conform to affirmations or promises of fact, descriptions, samples or models [UCC 2–313, 2A–210].

2. **Basis of the Bargain**
    An affirmation, promise, description, or sample must be part of the basis of the bargain: it must come at such a time that the buyer could have relied on it when agreeing to the contract [UCC 2–313, 2A–210].

3. **Statements of Opinion**

a. Opinions

A statement relating to the value of goods or a statement of opinion or recommendation about goods is not an express warranty [UCC 2–313(2), 2A–210(2)], unless the seller or lessor who makes it is an expert and gives an opinion as an expert.

b. Puffing

Whether a statement is an express warranty or puffing is not easy to determine. Factors include the reasonableness of the buyer's reliance on the statement and the specificity of the statement.

C. IMPLIED WARRANTIES

An implied warranty is derived by implication or inference from the nature of a transaction or the relative situations or circumstances of the parties.

1. Implied Warranty of Merchantability

A warranty automatically arises in every sale or lease of goods by a merchant who deals in such goods that the goods are merchantable [UCC 2–314, 2A–212].

a. Reasonably Fit for Ordinary Purposes

Goods that are merchantable are "reasonably fit for the ordinary purposes for which such goods are used."

b. Characteristics of Merchantable Goods

Average, fair, or medium-grade quality; pass without objection in the market for goods of the same description; adequate package and label, as provided by the agreement; and conform to the promises or affirmations of fact made on the container or label.

2. Implied Warranty of Fitness for a Particular Purpose

Arises when seller or lessor (merchant or nonmerchant) knows or has reason to know the purpose for which buyer or lessee will use goods and knows he or she is relying on seller to select suitable goods [UCC 2–315, 2A–213]. Goods can be merchantable but unfit for a particular purpose.

3. Implied Warranty from Course of Dealing or Trade Usage

An implied warranty may arise from a course of dealing, or when the parties know a well-recognized trade custom, it is inferred that they intended it to apply [UCC 2–314, 2A–212].

D. OVERLAPPING WARRANTIES

1. When Warranties Are Consistent, They Are Cumulative

2. When Warranties Are Inconsistent—

a. Express warranties displace inconsistent implied warranties (except fitness for a particular purpose).

b. Samples take precedence over inconsistent general descriptions.

c. Technical specs displace inconsistent samples or descriptions.

E. THIRD PARTY BENEFICIARIES OF WARRANTIES

1. The Common Law Requires Privity

At common law, privity of contract must exist between a plaintiff and a defendant to bring any action based on a contract.

2. The UCC Eliminates Privity

The UCC includes three optional, alternative provisions eliminating privity with respect to certain types of injuries for certain beneficiaries. Each state may adopt one of the alternatives [UCC 2–318, 2A–216].

F. WARRANTY DISCLAIMERS

1. Express Warranties

A seller can avoid making express warranties by not promising or affirming anything, describing the goods, or using of a sample or model.

a. Oral Warranties

Oral warranties made during bargaining cannot be modified later.

b. Negating or Limiting Express Warranties

A written disclaimer—clear and conspicuous—can negate all warranties not in the written contract [UCC 2–316(1), 2A–214(1)].

2. Implied Warranties

a. General Language

Implied warranties can be disclaimed by the expression "as is" or a similar phrase [UCC 2–316(3)(a), 2A–214(3)(a)].

b. Specific Language

Implied warranty of fitness for a particular purpose: disclaimer must be in writing and be conspicuous (the word *fitness* is not required). Implied warranty of merchantability: disclaimer must mention merchantability; if it is in writing, it must be conspicuous.

3. Buyer's Examination of the Goods

If a buyer examines the goods before entering a contract, there is no implied warranty with respect to defects that a reasonable examination would reveal [UCC 2–316(3)(b), 2A–214(2)(b)]. The same is true if the buyer refuses to examine over the seller or lessor's demand.

4. Unconscionability

Courts view disclaimers with disfavor, especially when consumers are involved, and have sometimes held disclaimers unconscionable [UCC 2–302, 2A–108].

G. MAGNUSON–MOSS WARRANTY ACT

No seller is required to give a written warranty for consumer goods, but if a seller chooses to do so and the cost of the goods is more than—

1. $10

The warranty must be clearly labeled full or limited. A full warranty requires free repair or replacement of defective parts (there is no time limit). A limited warranty is any warranty that is not full.

2. $15

The seller must state (fully and conspicuously in a single document in "readily understood language") the seller's name and address, what is warranted, procedures for enforcing the warranty, any limitations on relief, and that the buyer has legal rights.

II. LEMON LAWS

If a car under warranty has a defect that significantly affects the vehicle's value or use, and it is not remedied by the seller within a specified number of opportunities, the buyer is entitled to a new car, replacement of defective parts, or return of all consideration paid.

III. PRODUCT LIABILITY

A. NEGLIGENCE

If the failure to exercise reasonable care in the making or marketing of a product causes an injury, the basis of liability is negligence.

1. **Privity of Contract between Plaintiff and Defendant Is Not Required**

2. **Manufacturer's Duty of Care**
Due care must be exercised in designing, assembling, and testing a product; selecting materials; inspecting and testing products bought for use in the final product; and placing warnings on the label to inform users of dangers of which an ordinary person might not be aware.

B. **MISREPRESENTATION**
If a misrepresentation (such as intentionally concealing product defects) results in an injury, there may liability for fraud.

C. **STRICT LIABILITY**
Under the doctrine of strict liability, a defendant may be liable for the result of his or her act regardless of intention or exercise of reasonable care.

1. **Requirements of Strict Product Liability**
The requirements for strict product liability, under the *Restatement (Second) of Torts*, Section 402A, are—

   a. **Product Is in a Defective Condition when the Defendant Sells It**

   b. **The Defendant Is Normally in the Business of Selling the Product**

   c. **The Defect Makes the Product Unreasonably Dangerous**
   A product may be so defective if either—

      1) **The Product Is Dangerous beyond the Consumer's Expectation**
      There may have been a flaw in the manufacturing process that led to some defective products being marketed, or a perfectly made product may not have had adequate warning on the label.

      2) **There Is a Less Dangerous, Economically Feasible Alter-native that the Manufacturer Failed to Use**
      A manufacturer may have failed to design a safe product.

   d. **The Plaintiff Incurs Harm to Self or Property by Use of the Product**

   e. **The Defect Is the Proximate Cause of the Harm**

   f. **The Product Was Not Substantially Changed after It Was Sold**

2. **Statutes of Repose**
A statute of repose limits the time in which a suit can be filed. It runs from an earlier date and for a longer time than a statute of limitations.

3. **Market-Share Liability**
Some courts hold that all firms that manufactured and distributed DES (diethylstilbestrol) during a certain period are liable for injuries in proportion to the firms' respective shares of the market.

4. **Other Applications of Strict Liability**
Defendants may be liable to injured bystanders. Suppliers of component parts and lessors may be liable for injuries caused by defective products.

5. *Restatement (Third) of Torts: Products Liability*
This *Restatement* categorizes—

   a. **Manufacturing Defects**
   When a product departs from its intended design even though all possible care was taken (strict liability).

b. **Design Defects**

When a foreseeable risk of harm posed by a product could have been reduced by use of a reasonable alternative design and the omission makes the product unreasonably unsafe. A court would consider such factors as consumer expectations and warnings.

c. **Warning Defects**

When a foreseeable risk of harm posed by a product could have been reduced by providing a reasonable warning and the omission makes the product unreasonably unsafe. Factors include the content and comprehensibility of a warning, and the expected users.

D. **DEFENSES TO PRODUCT LIABILITY**

1. **Assumption of Risk**

In some states, this is a defense if (1) plaintiff knew and appreciated the risk created by the defect and (2) plaintiff voluntarily engaged in the risk, event though it was unreasonable to do so.

2. **Product Misuse**

The use must not be the one for which the product was designed, and the misuse must not be reasonably foreseeable.

3. **Comparative Negligence**

Most states consider a plaintiff's actions in apportioning liability.

4. **Commonly Known Dangers**

Failing to warn against such a danger is not ground for liability.

TRUE-FALSE QUESTIONS

(Answers at the Back of the Book)

_____ 1. Promises of fact made during the bargaining process are express warranties.

_____ 2. A contract cannot include both an implied warranty and an express warranty.

_____ 3. A merchant cannot disclaim an implied warranty of merchantability.

_____ 4. An express warranty can be limited.

_____ 5. Privity of contract between the plaintiff and defendant is required to bring a product liability suit based on negligence.

_____ 6. One of the requirements for a product liability suit based on strict liability is a failure to exercise due care.

_____ 7. In many states, the plaintiff's negligence is a defense that may be raised in a product liability suit based on strict liability.

_____ 8. A warranty of title can be disclaimed or modified only by specific language in a contract.

_____ 9. A manufacturer has a duty to warn about risks that are obvious or commonly known.

_____ 10. Assumption of risk can be raised as a defense in a product liability suit.

FILL-IN QUESTIONS

(Answers at the Back of the Book)

An express warranty _____ (can/cannot) be disclaimed in writing if it is called to the buyer's attention. An implied warranty of fitness for a particular purpose _____ (can/cannot) be disclaimed in writing. An implied warranty of merchantability _____ (can/cannot) be disclaimed in writing. A disclaimer of the implied warranty of fitness for a particular purpose _____ (must/need not) use the word "fitness." A disclaimer of the implied warranty of merchantability _____ (must/need not) include the word merchantability.

MULTIPLE-CHOICE QUESTIONS

(Answers at the Back of the Book)

____ 1. Eagle Skis, Inc., makes and sells skis. In deciding whether the skis are merchantable, a court would consider whether

a. Eagle violated any government regulations.
b. the skis are a quality product.
c. the skis are fit for the ordinary purpose for which such goods are used.
d. the skis are made in an efficient manner.

____ 2. Great Furniture Company makes and sells furniture. To avoid liability for most implied warranties, their sales agreements should note that their goods are sold

a. "as is."
b. by a merchant.
c. for cash only.
d. in perfect condition.

____ 3. Fine Textiles, Inc., sells cloth to Gail by showing her a sample that Fine's salesperson claims is the same as the goods. This statement is

a. an express warranty.
b. an implied warranty.
c. a warranty of title.
d. puffing.

____ 4. Superb Auto Sales sells cars, trucks, and other motor vehicles. A Superb salesperson tells potential customers, "This is the finest car ever made." This statement is

a. an express warranty.
b. an implied warranty.
c. a warranty of title.
d. puffing.

____ 5. A bridge's design is defective and soon after completion it begins to sway in the wind. Everyone stays off, except Carl, who wants to show off. Carl falls from the bridge and sues its manufacturer, who can raise the defense of

a. assumption of risk.
b. commonly known danger.
c. product misuse.
d. none of the above.

____ 6. Kitchen Products, Inc. (KPI), makes knifes and other utensils. Jay is injured while using a KPI knife, and sues the maker for product liability based on negligence. KPI could successfully defend against the suit by showing that

a. Jay's injury resulted from a commonly known danger.
b. Jay misused the knife in a foreseeable way.
c. KPI did not sell the knife to Jay.
d. the knife was not altered after KPI sold it.

    7. Standard Tools, Inc., makes and sells tools. Tina is injured as a result of using a Standard tool. Tina sues Standard for product liability based on strict liability. To succeed, Tina must prove that Standard

    a. was in privity of contract with Tina.
    b. did not use care with respect to the tool.
    c. misrepresented a material fact regarding the tool on which Tina relied.
    d. none of the above.

    8. Yard Work, Inc., makes and sells garden tools. Under the *Restatement (Second) of Torts*, a tool could be unreasonably dangerous

    a. only if, in making the tool, Yard Work failed to use a less dangerous but economically feasible alternative.
    b. only if the tool is dangerous beyond the ordinary consumer's expectation.
    c. if, in making the tool, Yard Work failed to use a less dangerous but economically feasible alternative or if the tool is dangerous beyond the ordinary consumer's expectation.
    d. none of the above.

    9. Fran is in Green's Grocery store when a bottle of Hi Cola on a nearby shelf explodes, injuring her. She can recover from the manufacturer of Hi Cola only if she can show that

    a. she did not assume the risk of the explosive bottle of Hi Cola.
    b. she intended to buy the explosive bottle of Hi Cola.
    c. she was injured due to a defect in the product.
    d. the manufacturer failed to use due care in making the bottle of Hi Cola.

    10. Omega Electronics, Inc., designs and manufacturers CD players. In a product liability suit based on negligence, Omega could be liable for violating its duty of care with respect to a player's

    a. design only.
    b. manufacture only.
    c. design or the manufacture.
    d. none of the above.

SHORT ESSAY QUESTIONS

1. What is the difference between the implied warranty of merchantability and the implied warranty of fitness for a particular purpose?

2. How defective must a product be to support a cause of action in strict liability in a product liability suit?

ISSUE SPOTTERS

(Answers at the Back of the Book)

1. Adam sells a car to Beth. Two months later, Consumer Credit, Inc., tells Beth that it has a security interest in the car, Adam missed three payments, and it is taking the car. Beth says, "I know nothing about any of this. You have to get your money from Adam. You can't take the car." Is Beth right?

2. Delta Corporation makes tire rims, which it sells to Eagle Vehicles, Inc., to put on its cars. One set of rims is defective, which an inspection would reveal. Eagle does not inspect the rims. The car is sold to Fast Auto Sales. Greg buys the car, which is soon in an accident caused by the defective rims and in which Greg is injured. Is Eagle liable?

3.   Real Chocolate Company makes a box of candy, which it sells to Sweet Things, Inc., a distributor. Sweet sells the box to a Tasty Candy store, where Jill buys it. Jill gives it to Ken, who breaks a tooth on a stone the same size and color of a piece of the candy. If Real, Sweet, and Tasty were not negligent, can they be liable for the injury?

CUMULATIVE HYPOTHETICAL PROBLEM FOR UNIT FOUR—INCLUDING CHAPTERS 14–17

(Answers at the Back of the Book)

Alpha Engineering Corporation designs products for companies in the aerospace industry. Beta Computers, Inc., makes and sells hard drives.

____   1.   Alpha writes to Beta to order one hundred hard drives. Beta writes to accept but adds a clause providing for interest on any overdue invoices (a common practice in the industry). If there is no further communication between the parties

a.   Beta has made a counteroffer.
b.   there is a contract but without Beta's added term.
c.   there is a contract that includes Beta's added term.
d.   there is no contract because Alpha did not expressly accept the added term.

____   2.   Beta tenders delivery of the hard drives to Alpha. Alpha says that it cannot take possession immediately but will do so later in the day. Before Alpha takes possession, the goods are destroyed in a fire. The risk of loss

a.   passed to Alpha at the time the contract was formed.
b.   passed to Alpha on Beta's tender of delivery.
c.   remained with Beta, because Alpha had not yet taken possession.
d.   remained with Beta, because title had not yet passed to Alpha.

____   3.   Beta tenders delivery of the hard drives to Alpha. Alpha says that it had decided not to buy them. In Beta's suit against Alpha, Beta can recover the contract price if

a.   Beta does not seek any damages in addition to the contract price.
b.   Beta identified the goods to the contract and a reasonable effort to resell the goods would not succeed.
c.   specific performance is not possible.
d.   the goods have been destroyed and Beta's insurance is inadequate.

____   4.   Alpha tries to put the hard drives into use, but they do not do what Beta promised. In the deal between Alpha and Beta, the most important factor in determining whether an express warranty was created is whether

a.   Beta intended to create a warranty.
b.   Beta made the promises in the ordinary course of business.
c.   Beta's promises became part of the basis of the bargain.
d.   Beta's statements were in writing.

____   5.   Under the UCC, to be subject to an implied warranty of merchantability, Beta's hard drives do NOT need to be

a.   adequately packaged and labeled.
b.   fit for all of the purposes for which Alpha intends to use the goods.
c.   in conformity with any affirmations of fact made on the package.
d.   sold by a merchant.

QUESTIONS ON THE FOCUS ON LEGAL REASONING FOR UNIT FOUR—*PARKER TRACTOR & IMPLEMENT CO. V. JOHNSON*

(Answers at the Back of the Book)

____ 1. Fast Pizza buys a delivery vehicle from Great Motors. The buyer later files a suit against the seller, on the basis of breach of warranty. Under the holding in *Parker Tractor & Implement Co. v. Johnson*, the buyer may be awarded damages even if there is uncertainty in

a. the amount.
b. the cause.
c. the purpose.
d. the reason.

____ 2. Having no written records, Fast Pizza's proof in its suit against Great Motors consists almost entirely of the testimony of the owner and an expert. In the opinion of the majority in *Parker Tractor & Implement Co. v. Johnson*, Fast Pizza may obtain as damages

a. the loss shown by all of Fast Pizza's proof.
b. the loss shown by the owner's testimony only.
c. the loss shown by the expert's testimony only.
d. nothing.

____ 3. According to the dissent in *Parker Tractor & Implement Co. v. Johnson*, Fast Pizza, in its suit against Great Motors, Fast Pizza may obtain as damages

a. the loss shown by all of Fast Pizza's proof.
b. the loss shown by the owner's testimony only.
c. the loss shown by the expert's testimony only.
d. nothing.

Chapter 18:
Negotiability, Transferability, and Liability

WHAT THIS CHAPTER IS ABOUT

A **negotiable instrument** is a written promise or order to pay a sum of money. It is transferred more readily than an ordinary contract, and a person who acquires it is subject to less risk than the assignee of a contract right. This chapter outlines types of negotiable instruments, requirements for negotiability, and the effect of indorsements on negotiation.

CHAPTER OUTLINE

I. **ARTICLE 3 OF THE UCC**
   UCC Article 3 applies to transactions involving negotiable instruments. Since 1990, most states have adopted revised versions of these articles. This outline refers to the revised articles. Both articles were also updated with proposed amendments in 2002 to comport with the Uniform Electronic Transactions Act and the needs of e-commerce.

II. **TYPES OF INSTRUMENTS**

   A. **ORDERS TO PAY**
      The person who signs or makes an order to pay is the **drawer**. The person to whom the order is made is the **drawee**. The person to whom payment is ordered is the **payee**.

      1. **Draft**
         An unconditional written order by one person to another to pay money. The drawee must be obligated to the drawer either by an agreement or through a debtor-creditor relationship to honor the order.

         a. **Time Draft**
            Payable at a definite future time.

         b. **Sight Draft (Demand Draft)**
            Payable on sight (when presented for payment). A draft payable at a stated time after sight is both a time and a sight draft.

         c. **Trade Acceptance**
            A draft in which the seller is both the drawer and the payee. The draft orders the buyer to pay a specified sum of money to the seller, at a stated time in the future.

         d. **Banker's Acceptance**
            A trade acceptance that orders the buyer's bank, rather than the buyer, to pay.

      2. **Check**
         A draft drawn on a bank and payable on demand. A **cashier's check** is a draft in which the bank is both the drawer and drawee.

   B. **PROMISES TO PAY**
      A person who promises to pay is a **maker**. A person to whom the promise is made is a **payee**.

1. **Promissory Note**
    A written promise by one party to pay money to another party.

2. **Certificate of Deposit**
    A note made by a bank promising to repay a deposit of funds with interest on a certain date [UCC 3–104(j)].

III. REQUIREMENTS FOR NEGOTIABILITY

A. FORM AND LOCATION OF SIGNATURE
A signature can be any place on an instrument and in any form (a mark or rubber stamp) that purports to be a signature and authenticates the writing [UCC 1–201(39), 3–401(b)].

B. REQUIREMENTS
To be negotiable, an instrument must [UCC 3–104(a)]—

1. Be in writing.

2. Be signed by the maker or drawer—In any form (a mark or rubber stamp) that purports to be a signature and authenticates the writing [UCC 1–201(39), 3–401(b)].

3. Be an unconditional promise or order to pay—A promise must be more than a mere acknowledgment of a debt (an I.O.U. does not qualify; use of the words "I promise" or "Pay" qualifies) [UCC 3–103(a)(9)].

4. State a fixed amount of money—Variable interest rate notes can be negotiable [UCC 3–104].

5. Be payable on demand or at a definite time.

6. Be payable to order ("to the order of an identified person" or to "an identified person or order") or bearer (does not designate a specific payee), unless it is a check [UCC 3–109].

IV. TRANSFER OF INSTRUMENTS

A. TRANSFER BY ASSIGNMENT
A transfer by assignment (see Chapter 11) gives the assignee only those rights the assignor possessed. Defenses that can be raised against an assignor can normally be raised against an assignee.

B. TRANSFER BY NEGOTIATION
On a transfer by negotiation, the transferee becomes a holder and receives the rights of the previous possessor (and possibly more) [UCC 3–201(a), 3–202(b), 3–203(b), 3–305, 3–306]. An order instrument is negotiated by delivery with indorsement; a bearer instrument is negotiated by delivery only [UCC 3–201(b)].

V. INDORSEMENTS
An **indorsement** is a signature required to negotiate an order instrument.

A. BLANK INDORSEMENT
Specifies no particular indorsee and can consist of a mere signature [UCC 3–205(b)]. Converts an order instrument to a bearer instrument.

B. SPECIAL INDORSEMENT
Names the indorsee [UCC 3–205(a)]. No special words are needed. Converts a bearer instrument to an order instrument.

C. QUALIFIED INDORSEMENT
Disclaims or limits contract liability (see below) (the notation "without recourse" is commonly used) [UCC 3–415(b)]. A blank qualified indorsement requires only delivery for further negotiation. A special qualified indorsement requires indorsement and delivery for further negotiation.

D. RESTRICTIVE INDORSEMENTS

1. Conditional Indorsement

Requires indorsement and delivery for further negotiation. A person paying or taking for value can disregard the condition [UCC 3–206(b)].

2. Prohibitive Indorsement

Need indorsement and delivery for further negotiation [UCC 3–206(a)].

3. For Deposit or Collection Indorsement

Locks the instrument into the bank collection process [UCC 3–206(c)].

4. Trust Indorsement

An indorsement by one who is to hold or use the funds for the benefit of the indorser or a third party [UCC 3–206(d), (e)]. Requires indorsement and delivery for further negotiation.

VI. HOLDER IN DUE COURSE (HDC)

A. HOLDER

A **holder** is a person in possession of an instrument drawn, issued, or indorsed to him or her, to his or her order, or to bearer or in blank [UCC 1–201(20)]. A holder is subject to the same defenses that could be asserted against the transferor (the party from whom the holder obtained the instrument).

B. HOLDER IN DUE COURSE

A holder who meets certain requirements becomes a **holder in due course (HDC)**, and takes an instrument free of all claims to it and most defenses against payment that could be successfully asserted against the transferor.

VII. REQUIREMENTS FOR HDC STATUS

To become an HDC, a person must be a holder and take an instrument (1) for value; (2) in good faith; and (3) without notice that it is overdue, that it has been dishonored, that any person has a defense against it or a claim to it, or that the instrument contains unauthorized signatures, alterations, or is so irregular or incomplete as to call into question its authenticity [UCC 3–302].

VIII. HOLDER THROUGH AN HDC

A. SHELTER PRINCIPLE

A person who does not qualify as an HDC but who acquires an instrument from an HDC or from someone with HDC rights receives the rights and privileges of an HDC [UCC 3–203(b)].

B. LIMITATIONS TO THE SHELTER PRINCIPLE

A holder who was a party to fraud or illegality affecting an instrument or who, as a prior holder, had notice of a claim or defense cannot improve his or her status by repurchasing it from a later HDC [UCC 3–203(b)].

IX. SIGNATURE LIABILITY

Every party (except a qualified indorser) who signs an instrument is primarily or secondarily liable to pay it when it is due.

A. PRIMARY LIABILITY

Only makers and **acceptors** (a drawee who promises to pay an instrument when it is presented later for payment) are primarily liable—they are absolutely required to pay (subject to certain defenses) [UCC 3–305].

B. SECONDARY LIABILITY

Drawers and unqualified indorsers are secondarily liable—they pay only if a party who is primarily liable does not pay. A drawer pays if a drawee does not; an indorser pays if a maker defaults. Secondary liability is triggered by proper presentment, dishonor, and notice of dishonor.

1. **Proper Presentment**

   a. **To the Proper Person**
   A note or CD is presented to the maker; a draft to the drawee for acceptance, payment, or both (whatever is required); a check to the drawee [UCC 3–501(a), 3–502(b)].

   b. **In the Proper Manner**
   Depending on the type of instrument [UCC 3–501(b)]: (1) any commercially reasonable means (oral, written, or electronic; but it is not effective until the demand is received); (2) a clearing-house procedure used by banks; or (3) at the place specified in the instrument.

   c. **Timely**
   Failure to present on time is the most common reason for improper presentment [UCC 3–414(f), 3–415(e), 3–501(b)(4)].

2. **Dishonor**
   Occurs when payment or acceptance is refused or cannot be obtained within the prescribed time, or when required presentment is excused and the instrument is not accepted or paid [UCC 3–502(e), 3–504].

3. **Proper Notice**
   On dishonor, to hold secondary parties liable, notice must be given within thirty days following the day on which a person receives notice of the dishonor (except a bank, which must give notice before midnight of the next banking day after receipt) [UCC 3–503].

C. **UNAUTHORIZED SIGNATURES**
An unauthorized signature does not bind a person whose name is forged unless the person (1) ratifies the signature [UCC 3–403(a)] or (2) was negligent [UCC 3–115, 3–406, 4–401(d)(2)]. An unauthorized signature does bind the *signer* in favor of an HDC [UCC 3–403(a)].

D. **SPECIAL RULES FOR UNAUTHORIZED INDORSEMENTS**
Generally, the loss falls on the first party to take the instrument. The loss falls on the maker or drawer in cases involving—

1. **Imposters**
   Indorsement of an **imposter** (one who induces a maker or drawer to issue an instrument in name of an impersonated payee) can be effective against the drawer [UCC 3–404(a)].

2. **Fictitious Payees**
   Indorsement of a **fictitious payee** (one to whom an instrument is payable but who has no right to receive payment—often, dishonest employees issue such instruments or deceive employers into doing so) can hold employer liable to an innocent holder [UCC 3–404(b)(2)].

X. **WARRANTY LIABILITY**

A. **TRANSFER WARRANTIES**

1. **The Warranties**
   Any person who transfers an instrument for consideration warrants to the transferee and, if the transfer is by indorsement, to all later transferees and holders who take the instrument in good faith [UCC 3–416]—

   a. The transferor is entitled to enforce the instrument.

   b. All signatures are authentic and authorized.

   c. The instrument has not been altered.

   d. The instrument is not subject to a defense or claim that can be asserted against the transferor.

e. The transferor has no knowledge of any insolvency proceedings against the maker, the acceptor, or the drawer of the instrument.

2. **To Whom the Warranties Run**
   Order paper: to any subsequent holder who takes the instrument in good faith. Bearer paper: only to the immediate transferee [UCC 3–416(a)].

B. **PRESENTMENT WARRANTIES**
Any person who obtains payment or acceptance of an instrument warrants to any other person who in good faith pays or accepts it [UCC 3–417(a), (d)]—

1. The person obtaining payment or acceptance is entitled or authorized to enforce the instrument (no missing or unauthorized indorsements).

2. The instrument has not been altered.

3. The person obtaining payment or acceptance has no knowledge that the signature of the issuer of the instrument is unauthorized.

XI. DEFENSES TO LIABILITY

A. **UNIVERSAL DEFENSES**
Valid against all holders, including HDCs and holders who take by HDCs [UCC 3–305, 3–401, 3–403, 3–407].

1. Forgery.

2. Fraud in the execution (when a person is deceived into signing an instrument, believing that it is something else).

3. Material alteration (an alteration that changes the terms between any two parties in any way).

4. Discharge in bankruptcy.

5. Minority (if the contract is voidable).

6. Illegality, mental incapacity, or extreme duress (if contract is void).

B. **PERSONAL DEFENSES**
Personal defenses avoid payment to an ordinary holder (but not an HDC).

1. Breach of contract or breach of warranty.

2. Lack or failure of consideration [UCC 3–303(b), 3–305(a)(2)].

3. Fraud in the inducement (ordinary fraud).

4. Illegality or mental incapacity (if contract is voidable).

5. Discharge by payment or cancellation.

6. Unauthorized completion of an incomplete instrument.

7. Nondelivery of an instrument.

8. Ordinary duress or undue influence (if the contract is voidable).

XII. DISCHARGE FROM LIABILITY

A. **PAYMENT OR TENDER OF PAYMENT**
All parties are discharged if the party primarily liable pays to a holder the amount due in full [UCC 3–602, 3–603]. Payment by any other party discharges only that party and subsequent parties.

B. **CANCELLATION**

A holder can discharge any party by intentionally destroying, mutilating, or canceling an instrument, canceling or striking out a party's signature, or adding words (such as "Paid") to the instrument indicating discharge [UCC 3–604].

C. **IMPAIRMENT OF RIGHT OF RECOURSE**

If a holder adversely affects an indorser's right to recover payment from prior parties, the indorser is discharged [UCC 3–605].

TRUE-FALSE QUESTIONS

(Answers at the Back of the Book)

____ 1. A negotiable instrument can be transferred only by negotiation.

____ 2. A bearer instrument is negotiated by delivery alone.

____ 3. To be negotiable, an instrument must be in writing.

____ 4. An instrument payable to the order of a specific person is not negotiable.

____ 5. A holder in due course (HDC) takes a negotiable instrument free of most of the defenses and claims that could be asserted against the transferor.

____ 6. Personal defenses can be raised to avoid payment to an HDC.

____ 7. Signature liability extends to nearly every person who signs a negotiable instrument.

____ 8. Warranty liability may bind parties who transfer instruments but not parties who only present instruments for payment.

____ 9. A drawer is secondarily liable on an instrument.

____ 10. A holder who has knowledge of a defense against payment on an instrument can become an HDC.

FILL-IN QUESTIONS

(Answers at the Back of the Book)

A person who does not qualify as an HDC _____ (can/cannot) acquire the rights of an HDC if a person who does not qualify as an HDC acquires an instrument from an HDC. A holder who was a party to fraud or illegality affecting an instrument _____ (can/cannot) improve his or her status by repurchasing the instrument from a later HDC. A holder who, as a prior holder, had notice of a claim or defense against the instrument _____ (can/cannot) improve his or her status by repurchasing it from a later HDC.

MULTIPLE-CHOICE QUESTIONS

(Answers at the Back of the Book)

____ 1. Alex makes out a check "Pay to the order of Beth." Beth indorses the check on the back. The check can now be negotiated by

a. delivery only.
b. indorsement only.
c. delivery and indorsement.
d. none of the above.

_____ 2. To pay for a new truck, Eagle Transport Company issues a draft in favor of Fine Motor Sales, Inc. A draft is

a. a promise to pay money.
b. a promise to deliver goods at a future date.
c. a conditional promise to pay money.
d. an unconditional written order to pay money.

_____ 3. Gail indorses a check, "Pay to Highway Equipment Corporation if they deliver the backhoe by June 1, 2003." This indorsement is

a. a blank indorsement.
b. a qualified indorsement.
c. a restrictive indorsement.
d. a special indorsement.

_____ 4. Macro Industries, Inc., issues an instrument in favor of National Credit Corporation. To be negotiable, the instrument need _not_

a. be an unconditional promise or order to pay.
b. be payable on demand or at a specific time.
c. be signed by Macro Industries.
d. recite the consideration given in exchange for it.

_____ 5. Owen executes an instrument is favor of Paula. For the instrument to be negotiable, Owen's signature

a. may be anywhere on the instrument.
b. must be in the lower right hand corner.
c. must be on the back.
d. must not be on the instrument.

_____ 6. Beth gives a $500 note to Carl to deliver a load of apples to Beth's store. On delivery, the apples are spoiled. Beth may defend her decision not to pay the note based on

a. breach of warranty.
b. lack of consideration.
c. fraud in the inducement.
d. undue influence.

_____ 7. Able Company writes a check to Baker Corporation that is drawn on Able's account at City Bank. Baker presents the check to the bank for payment. If the bank accepts the check, the bank is

a. not liable for payment.
b. primarily liable for payment.
c. secondarily liable for payment.
d. simultaneously liable for payment.

_____ 8. Bill writes a check on his account at Community Bank to Donna to pay a preexisting debt. Donna negotiates the check to Ed by indorsement. Before Bill or Donna may be liable on the check, it must be

a. presented for payment only.
b. dishonored, for which notice must be given only.
c. presented for payment and dishonored, for which notice must be given.
d. none of the above.

____   **9.**   Frank signs a note payable to the order of Greg. Greg indorses the note and gives it to Holly as payment for a debt. Holly presents it to Frank, who pays it. Frank's payment discharges

    a.   all of the parties.
    b.   only Frank.
    c.   only Holly.
    d.   none of the above.

____   **10.**   United Business Corporation authorizes Vic to use company checks to buy office supplies. Vic writes a check to Wholesale Supplies, Inc., for $100 over the price of a purchase, for which the seller returns cash. When Wholesale presents the check for payment, it may recover

    a.   nothing.
    b.   the amount stated in the check.
    c.   the amount of the overpayment only.
    d.   the price of the supplies only.

SHORT ESSAY QUESTIONS

1.   How are instruments negotiated?

2.   What are the defenses that may be raised to avoid payment on an instrument?

ISSUE SPOTTERS

(Answers at the Back of the Book)

1.   Mark issues a $500 note to Nora due six months from the date issued. One month later, Nora negotiates the note to Owen for $250 in cash and a check for $250. To what extent is Owen an HDC of the note?

2.   Pat is an accountant with Quality Corporation, but has no authority to sign corporate checks. Pat orders office furniture from Retail Company and pays with a Quality check, signing "Quality Corp. by Pat, accountant." Retail does not know that Pat has no authority to sign the check. Can Quality refuse to pay it?

3.   Roy signs corporate checks for Standard Corporation. Roy makes a check payable to U-All Company, to whom Standard owes no money. Roy signs the check, forges U-All's indorsement, and cashes the check at First State Bank, the drawee. Does Standard have any recourse against the bank for the payment?

Chapter 19:
Checks, the Banking System, and E-Money

WHAT THIS CHAPTER IS ABOUT

This chapter outlines the duties and liabilities that arise when a check is issued and paid. Checks are governed by UCC Articles 3 and 4. If there is a conflict between the articles, Article 4 controls. This outline also covers electronic fund transfers.

CHAPTER OUTLINE

I. **CHECKS**
    A **check** is a draft drawn on a bank, ordering the bank to pay a fixed amount of money on demand [UCC 3–104(f)]. If a bank wrongfully dishonors any of the following special types of checks, the holder can recover expenses, interest, and consequential damages [UCC 3–411].

    A. **CASHIER'S CHECK**
        A check drawn by a bank on itself; negotiable on issue [UCC 3–104(g)].

    B. **TELLER'S CHECK**
        A draft drawn by a bank on another bank, or if drawn on a nonbank, payable at or through a bank [UCC 3–104(h)].

    C. **TRAVELER'S CHECK**
        A check on which a financial institution is both drawer and drawee. The buyer must sign it twice (buying it and using it) [UCC 3–104(i)].

    D. **CERTIFIED CHECK**
        A check accepted by the bank on which it is drawn [UCC 3–409(d)]. When a bank certifies a check, it immediately charges the drawer's account and transfers those funds to its own account. The effect of certification is to discharge the drawer and prior indorsers [UCC 3–414(c), 3–415(d)].

II. **THE BANK-CUSTOMER RELATIONSHIP**

    A. **WHAT A BANK IS**
        A "person engaged in the business of banking, including a savings bank, savings and loan association, credit union or trust company" [UCC 4–105(1)]. Rights and duties of bank and customer are contractual.

    B. **WHAT A CUSTOMER IS**
        A customer is a creditor of the bank (and the bank, a debtor of the customer) when the customer deposits funds in his or her account. A bank acts as an agent for the customer when he or she writes a check drawn on the bank or deposits a check in his or her account for the bank to collect [UCC 4–201(a)].

III. **BANK'S DUTY TO HONOR CHECKS**
    If a bank dishonors a check for insufficient funds, it has no liability. The customer is liable to the payee or holder of the check in a civil suit. If intent to defraud is proved, the customer is also subject to criminal prosecution. If a bank wrongfully dishonors a check, however, it is liable to the customer [UCC 4–402].

A. OVERDRAFTS

If there are insufficient funds in a customer's account, the bank can pay an item drawn on it or dishonor it. If the bank pays, it can charge the customer's account (if the customer has authorized payment) [UCC 4–401(a)]. If a check "bounces," a holder can resubmit it but must notify any indorsers of the first dishonor (or they are discharged).

B. POSTDATED CHECKS

A bank can charge a postdated check against a customer's account if the customer does not give the bank enough notice. If the bank has notice but charges the check anyway, the bank is liable [UCC 4–401(c)].

C. STALE CHECKS

A bank is not obliged to pay an uncertified check presented for payment more than six months after its date [UCC 4–404]. If a bank pays in good faith, it can charge the customer's account for the amount.

D. STOP-PAYMENT ORDERS

1. Who Can Order a Stop Payment and When It Must Be Received

Only a customer or person authorized to draw on the account. Must be received in a reasonable time and manner [UCC 4–403(a), 4–405].

2. How It Can Be Given and How Long It Is Effective

In most states, it can be given orally, but it is binding for only fourteen calendar days unless confirmed in writing. In writing, it is effective for six months, when it may be renewed [UCC 4–403(b)].

3. If the Bank Pays over an Order

It must recredit the customer's account for any loss, including damages for the dishonor of subsequent items [UCC 4–403(c)].

4. The Customer's Risks

Possible liability to payee for the amount of the item (and damages). Defense against payment to a payee may not prevent payment to a subsequent HDC [UCC 3–305, 3–306].

E. DEATH OR INCOMPETENCE OF A CUSTOMER

Until a bank knows of the situation and has time to act, it is not liable for paying items [UCC 4–405]. If a bank knows of a death, for ten days after the date of death it can pay items drawn on or before the date of death (unless a person claiming an interest in the account orders a stop payment).

F. FORGED DRAWERS' SIGNATURES

1. The General Rule

A forged signature on a check has no legal effect as the signature of a drawer [UCC 3–403(a)]. If the bank pays, it must recredit the account.

2. Customer Negligence

If the customer's negligence substantially contributed to the forgery, the bank is not obligated to recredit the account [UCC 3–406(a)].

a. Reducing a Customer's Liability

A customer's liability may be reduced by a bank's negligence (if it substantially contributed to the loss) [UCC 3–406(b)].

b. Timely Examination of Bank Statements Required

The customer must examine the bank statement and canceled checks promptly and report any forged signatures [UCC 4–406(c)].

1) When There's a Series of Forgeries by the Same Wrongdoer

To recover for all items, a customer must report the first forgery to the bank within *thirty* calendar days of receiving the statement and canceled checks [UCC 4–406(d)(2)].

2) When the Bank Is Also Negligent
If the bank fails to exercise ordinary care ("reasonable commercial standards"), it may have to recredit the customer's account for a portion of the loss (on the basis of comparative negligence) [UCC 4–406(e)].

c. **Absolute Time Limit**
A customer must report a forged signature within one year of the date the statement and canceled checks were available [UCC 4–406].

G. FORGED INDORSEMENTS

1. **The General Rule**
If the bank pays a check with a forged indorsement, it must recredit the account (or be held liable for breach of contract) [UCC 4–401(a)].

2. **Timely Examination of Bank Statements Required**
The customer must examine the bank statement and canceled checks and report forged indorsements promptly. Failure to do so within three years relieves the bank of liability [UCC 4–111].

3. **Parties from Whom the Bank May Recover**
The bank can recover for breach of warranty from the bank that cashed the check [UCC 4–207(a)(2)]. Ultimately, the loss usually falls on the first party to take the instrument.

H. ALTERED CHECKS
If the bank fails to detect an alteration, it is liable to its customer for the loss [UCC 4–401(d)(1)].

1. **The Customer's Negligence**
If a bank traces its loss to the customer's negligence or, on successive altered checks, to the customer's failure to discover the first alteration, its liability is reduced (unless it was negligent) [UCC 4–401, 4–406].

2. **Parties from Whom the Bank May Recover**
The bank can recover from the transferor, for breach of warranty. Exceptions involve cashier's, teller's, and certified checks [UCC 3–417(a)(2), 4–208(a)(2), 4–207(a)(2)].

IV.   BANK'S DUTY TO ACCEPT DEPOSITS

A. AVAILABILITY SCHEDULE FOR DEPOSITED CHECKS
Under the Expedited Funds Availability Act of 1987 and Regulation CC—

1. **Funds That Must Be Available the Next Business Day after Deposit**

   a. **The First $100 of Any Deposit and the Next $400 of a Local Check**
   The first $100 must be available for withdrawal on the opening of the next business day. The next $400 of a local check must be available by no later than 5:00 P.M. the next business day.

   b. **Cash Deposits, Wire Transfers, and Certain Checks**
   Funds must be available on the next business day for cash deposits, wire transfers, government checks, the first $100 of a day's check deposits, cashier's checks, certified checks, and checks for which the depositary and payor banks are the same institution.

2. **Funds That Must Be Available within Five Business Days**
All nonlocal checks and nonproprietary ATM deposits, including cash.

3. **Funds That Can Be Held for Eight Days or an Extra Four Days**
Eight days: funds in new accounts (open less than thirty days). Four days: deposits over $5,000 (except government and cashier's checks), accounts with many overdrafts, checks of questionable collectibility (the bank must tell the depositor it suspects fraud or insolvency).

B. THE COLLECTION PROCESS

1. Designation of Banks Involved in the Collection Process
Depositary bank: first bank to receive a check for payment. **Payor bank**: bank on which a check is drawn. **Collecting bank**: bank (except payor bank) that handles a check for collection. **Intermediary bank**: any bank (except payor and depositary banks) involved in the collection process.

2. Check Collection between Customers of the Same Bank
An item payable by a depositary bank that is also the payor bank is an "on-us item." If the bank does not dishonor it by the second banking day, it is considered paid [UCC 4–215(e)(2)].

3. Check Collection between Customers of Different Banks
A depositary bank must arrange to present a check either directly or through intermediary banks to the appropriate payor bank.

   a. Midnight Deadline
   Each bank in the collection chain must pass a check on before midnight of the next banking day following receipt [UCC 4–202(b)].

   b. Deferred Posting and the Midnight Deadline
   Posting of checks received after a certain time can be deferred until the next day [UCC 4–108].

   c. Electronic Check Presentment
   Can be done the same day a check is deposited. The check may be kept at the place of deposit with only information about the check presented for payment under a Federal Reserve agreement, clearinghouse rule, or truncation agreement [UCC 4–110].

V.   ELECTRONIC FUND TRANSFERS

A. CONSUMER FUND TRANSFERS
Governed by Electronic Fund Transfer Act (EFTA) of 1978 and Regulation E.

1. Who Is Subject to the EFTA
Financial institutions that offer electronic fund transfers (EFTs) involving customer asset accounts established for personal, family, or household purposes. Telephone transfers are covered only if they are made pursuant to a prearranged plan involving periodic transfers.

2. Financial Institutions' Responsibilities
Financial institutions must provide customers with—

   a. Receipts
   At the time a transaction is made through an electronic terminal.

   b. Periodic Statements

      1) What They Must Include
      The amounts and dates of transfers, the fees, identification of the terminals, names of third parties involved, and an address and phone number for inquiries and error notices.

      2) How Often They Must Be Provided
      Monthly statements are required for every month in which there is an electronic transfer of funds.

3. Unauthorized Electronic Fund Transfers

   a. What an Unauthorized Transfer Is
   (1) A transfer is initiated by a person who has no actual authority to initiate the transfer; (2) the consumer receives no benefit from it; and (3) the consumer did not furnish the person "with the card, code, or other means of access" to his or her account.

    b. **Customer Liability**
If a debit card is lost or stolen, and misused, a customer is liable for (1) $50—if he or she notifies the bank within two business days of learning of the loss; (2) $500—if he or she does not tell the bank until after the second day; or (3) unlimited amounts—if notice is not within sixty days after transfer appears on customer's statement.

    4. Error Resolution and Damages
The bank must investigate and give the customer a report or be liable for actual damages, court costs, attorneys' fees, punitive damages.

B. COMMERCIAL TRANSFERS

In most states, UCC Article 4A clarifies the rights and liabilities of parties involved in fund transfers not subject to the EFTA or other federal or state statutes. In those states that have not adopted Article 4A, commercial fund transfers are governed by contract law and tort law.

VI. E-MONEY

E-money has the potential to replace physical cash with virtual cash (e-money) in the form of electronic impulses, or digital cash.

A. SMART CARDS

Contain microchips that hold more information than a magnetic stripe on a stored-value card. Less prone to error, and carry and process security programming (such as a digital signature). Debits and credits are automatic and can be immediate.

    1. Deposit Insurance for Smart-Card Balances
Most e-money is not covered by the Federal Deposit Insurance Corporation. If a bank becomes insolvent, an e-money holder is in the position of a general creditor.

    2. Legal Protection for Smart Cards
Some statutes, such as the Federal Trade Commission Act (which prohibits unfair or deceptive practices), and common law principles (such as contract law) extend to e-money.

B. PRIVACY PROTECTION

    1. Right to Financial Privacy Act of 1978
An issuer of e-money may be subject to this act if the issuer is deemed to be (1) a bank by virtue of its holding customer funds or (2) an entity that issues a physical card similar to a credit or debit card.

    2. Financial Services Modernization Act (Gramm-Leach-Bliley Act) of 1999
This act proscribes the disclosure of financial institutions' customer data without notice and an opt-out opportunity.

VII. ONLINE BANKING

There are questions about the application of traditional banking regulations to online banks.

VIII. THE UNIFORM MONEY SERVICES ACT (UMSA)

The UMSA applies to traditional money services the same regulations that apply to other, traditional financial service businesses.

A. TRADITIONAL MONEY SERVICES

Money service businesses do not accept deposits, but issue money orders, traveler's checks, stored-value cards; exchange foreign currency; and cash checks.

B. INTERNET-BASED MONEY SERVICES

    1. Systems Subject to the New Law
May include [UMSA 1–102(c)(21)]—

    a. E-money and Internet payment mechanisms
    b. Internet scrip
    c. Stored-value products (smart, prepaid, and value-added cards)

2. What the UMSA Requires
Persons engaged in money transmission, check cashing, or currency exchange must obtain a license from a state, be examined by state officials, report on their activities to the state, and comply with certain record keeping requirements [UMSA 1–104].

3. Rules That Govern Investments
Money service businesses are covered by rules that govern investments, and must follow "safety and soundness rules," which concern the posting of bonds and annual auditing of their books [see UMSA 2–204].

TRUE-FALSE QUESTIONS

(Answers at the Back of the Book)

____   **1.** A check is a draft drawn on a bank.

____   **2.** If a bank fails to honor a customer's stop-payment order, it may be liable to the customer for more than the amount of the loss suffered by the drawer because of the wrongful payment.

____   **3.** A bank's duty to honor its customer's checks is absolute.

____   **4.** Generally, funds must be available on the next business day for cash deposits.

____   **5.** A bank that fails to investigate an error and report its conclusion promptly to the customer is in violation of the Electronic Fund Transfer Act (EFTA).

____   **6.** A customer must examine the statements provided by the institution handling his or her account and notify it of any errors within sixty days.

____   **7.** The rights and duties of a bank and its customers are contractual.

____   **8.** All funds deposited in all bank accounts must be available for withdrawal no later than the next business day.

____   **9.** A bank that pays a customer's check bearing a forged indorsement must recredit the customer's account.

____   **10.** A forged drawer's signature on a check is effective as the signature of the person whose name is signed.

FILL-IN QUESTIONS

(Answers at the Back of the Book)

A depositor is the _____ (drawee/drawer) of a check. The depositor is the bank's _____ (creditor/debtor) as to the amount on deposit in the depositor's account. The depositor is the bank's _____ (agent/principal) in the deposit contract. The bank is the _____ (drawee/drawer) of a check. The bank is the depositor's _____ (creditor debtor) as to the amount on deposit in the depositor's account. The bank is the depositor's _____ (agent/principal) in the handling of the account and in the collection process.

MULTIPLE-CHOICE QUESTIONS

(Answers at the Back of the Book)

____ 1. First National Bank pays a check on which has been forged the signature of the drawer, Gail, who is the bank's customer. The bank must recredit her account for the entire amount of the check if

  a. Gail's negligence substantially contributed to the forgery.
  b. the amount of the check was less than $50.
  c. the amount of the check was more than $5,000.
  d. the bank's negligence substantially contributed to the forgery.

____ 2. American Bank's cutoff hour is 2 P.M. The bank receives a check drawn on the account of Best Corporation, one of its customers, at 4 P.M. Monday, presented by Carol, not the bank's customer. The bank uses deferred posting. If it decides to dishonor the check, it must do so by midnight

  a. Monday.
  b. Tuesday.
  c. Wednesday.
  d. Thursday.

____ 3. Ann buys three television sets from Bob, paying with a check. When the sets prove defective, Ann orders City Bank, the drawee, to stop payment on the check. This order is valid for fourteen

  a. years.
  b. months.
  c. weeks.
  d. days.

____ 4. First State Bank mistakenly pays one of Gary's checks with a forged indorsement. Gary can recover his loss from the bank if, after receipt of the bank statement, he notifies the bank within three

  a. years.
  b. months.
  c. weeks.
  d. days.

____ 5. Eve writes a check for $600 drawn on her account at First Federal Bank and presents it to Greg. When Greg presents the check for payment, the bank dishonors it. Greg may sue

  a. the bank for dishonoring the check.
  b. Eve on the underlying obligation.
  c. both the bank and Eve.
  d. none of the above.

____ 6. Delta Company issue a payroll check to Ed drawn on its account at First Community Bank. This check will be stale if Ed presents it for payment six

  a. months after it is issued.
  b. months after he indorses.
  c. weeks after he receives it.
  d. weeks after the pay period that it covers.

____   7.   Roy issues a check to Stereo Store in payment on his account. Tina, Stereo's accountant, forges the store's indorsement and deposits the check in her bank account. Town Bank, Roy's bank, pays the check. Roy can recover from

a.   no one.
b.   Tina, but not Town Bank.
c.   Town Bank, which can recover from Tina.
d.   Town Bank, which cannot recover from Tina.

____   8.   Adam pays for a purchase at Beta Computers with a check. Burt, the cashier, steals one of Adam's checks, forges his signature, and County Bank, Adam's bank, pays the check. Adam can recover from

a.   no one.
b.   Burt, but not County Bank.
c.   County Bank, which can recover from Burt.
d.   County Bank, which cannot recover from Burt.

____   9.   Dick loses his bank access card. He realizes his loss the next day but waits a week to call Eagle Bank, his bank. Meanwhile, Erin finds and uses Dick's card to withdraw $5,000 from his account. Dick is responsible for

a. $0.
b. $50.
c. $500.
d. $5,000.

____ 10.   Web Funds, Inc., an e-money issuer, misrepresents the value of its products to the detriment of Jay and other consumers. Web Funds may be liable under

a.   the Federal Trade Commission Act.
b.   the Financial Services Modernization Act.
c.   the Right to Financial Privacy Act.
d.   the Uniform Money Services Act.

SHORT ESSAY QUESTIONS

1.   What are the circumstances in which a customer might be unable to recover from a bank that pays on a forged check drawn on the customer's account?

2.   What are the principal features of the Electronic Fund Transfer Act (EFTA)?

ISSUE SPOTTERS

(Answers at the Back of the Book)

1.   Lyn writes a check for $900 to Mac, who indorses the check in blank and transfers it to Nan. She presents the check to Omega Bank, the drawee bank, for payment. Omega does not honor the check. Is Lyn liable to Nan? Could Lyn be subject to criminal prosecution?

2.   Hal steals a check from Irma, forges her signature, and transfers the check to Jay for value. Unaware that the signature is not Irma's, Jay presents the check to Local Bank, the drawee, which cashes the check. Irma discovers the forgery and insists that the bank recredit her account. Can the bank refuse to recredit the account? If not, can the bank recover the amount paid?

3. Ron writes a check for $700 to Sue. Sue indorses the check in blank and transfers it to Tim, who alters the check to read $7,000 and presents it to Union Bank, the drawee, for payment. The bank cashes it. Ron discovers the alteration and sues the bank. How much, if anything, can Ron recover? From whom can the bank recover this amount?

CUMULATIVE HYPOTHETICAL PROBLEM FOR UNIT FIVE—INCLUDING CHAPTERS 18–19

(Answers at the Back of the Book)

On May 15, 2003, Eve bought the following instrument from Beta Corporation for $1,700. Eve paid for the instrument with check. Eve knew that Alpha, Inc., disputed its liability on the instrument because of Beta's alleged breach of the computer purchase contract referred to on the face of the instrument. On May 20, First National Bank bought the instrument from Eve for $1,900. First National did not know that Alpha disputed its liability. On the back of the instrument is the indorsement "Pay to the order of First National Bank, without recourse [signed] *Eve*".

May 1, 2003

Alpha, Inc., promises to pay to Beta Corp. or bearer $2,000 on June 1, 2003, with interest at the rate of 8 % per year. Alpha may elect to extend the due date to July 1, 2003.

Alpha, Inc.

By ___*C.D. Jones*___

C.D. Jones, president

Re: computer purchase order no. 123, dated May 1, 2003

____ **1.** This instrument is

a. a check.
b. a promissory note.
c. a sight draft.
d. a trade acceptance.

____ **2.** This instrument is

a. negotiable because it refers to the computer purchase agreement.
b. negotiable even though Alpha has the right to extend the due date.
c. nonnegotiable because Alpha has the right to extend the due date.
d. nonnegotiable because it refers to the computer purchase agreement.

____ **3.** First National Bank

a. can negotiate the instrument further only by indorsing it.
b. cannot be an HDC because Eve indorsed without recourse.
c. is an HDC only because Eve indorsed the instrument.
d. is not an HDC because the instrument is nonnegotiable.

____ **4.** First National demands payment on the instrument from Alpha. Alpha refuses, claiming that Beta breached the computer purchase agreement. First National

a. can collect from Alpha because First National is an HDC.
b. can collect from Eve, but not Alpha, because Eve knew of Alpha's claim.
c. cannot collect from Alpha because Eve was not an HDC.
d. cannot collect from Alpha because of Beta's breach.

____   **5.** Beta presents Eve's check for payment, but City Bank, the drawee, refuses to pay. The party with primary liability for payment of the check is

a. Beta.
b. City Bank.
c. Eve.
d. none of the above.

QUESTIONS ON THE FOCUS ON LEGAL REASONING FOR UNIT FIVE— *SCALISE V. AMERICAN EMPLOYERS INSURANCE CO.*

(Answers at the Back of the Book)

____   **1.** Dave delivers a check to Eagle Store, Inc., to pay for a DVD player. Eagle deposits the check in its account with First Federal Bank, which submits the check for collection to United Bank, the drawee bank, which clears the check. Under the holding in *Scalise v. American Employers Insurance Co.,* "payment" occurred when

a. Dave delivered the check.
b. Eagle deposited the check.
c. First Federal submitted the check for collection.
d. United cleared the check.

____   **2.** In the opinion of the majority in *Scalise v. American Employers Insurance Co.,* Dave's debt to Eagle for the DVD player was discharged when

a. Dave delivered the check.
b. Eagle deposited the check.
c. First Federal submitted the check for collection.
d. United cleared the check.

____   **3.** According to the reasoning of the dissent in *Scalise v. American Employers Insurance Co.,* it would be most fair to consider that "payment" occurred when

a. Dave delivered the check.
b. Eagle deposited the check.
c. First Federal submitted the check for collection.
d. United cleared the check.

Chapter 20:
Secured Transactions

WHAT THIS CHAPTER IS ABOUT

This chapter covers transactions in which the payment of a debt is secured (guaranteed) by personal property owned by the debtor or in which the debtor has a legal interest. The importance of being a secured creditor cannot be overemphasized—secured transactions are as basic to modern business as credit.

CHAPTER OUTLINE

I. THE TERMINOLOGY OF SECURED TRANSACTIONS
UCC Article 9 applies to secured transactions.

A. SECURED TRANSACTION
Transaction in which payment of a debt is guaranteed by personal property owned by the debtor or in which the debtor has a legal interest.

B. SECURITY INTEREST, SECURED PARTY, COLLATERAL, AND DEBTOR
A **security interest** is the interest in the collateral that secures payment or performance of an obligation [UCC 1–201(37)]. A **secured party** is a creditor in whose favor there is a security interest in the debtor's collateral [UCC 9–102(a)(72)]. **Collateral** is the subject of a security interest [UCC 9–102(a)(12)]. **Debtor** is the party who owes payment [UCC 9–102(a)(28)].

II. CREATING AND PERFECTING A SECURITY INTEREST
A creditor's two main concerns are, if a debtor fails to pay, (1) satisfaction of the debt through possession or sale of the collateral and (2) priority over other creditors to the collateral.

A. CREATING A SECURITY INTEREST
A creditor's rights attach to collateral, creating an enforceable security interest against a debtor if the following requirements are met [UCC 9–203].

1. Written Security Agreement
(1) It must be written or authenticated (which includes electronic media, or records), (2) describe the collateral, and (3) be signed or authenticated by the debtor [UCC 9–102, 9–108]. Or the secured party must possess the collateral.

2. Secured Party Must Give Value
Value is any consideration that supports a contract [UCC 1–201(44)].

3. Debtor Must Have Rights in the Collateral
The debtor must have an ownership interest or right (current or future legal interest) to obtain possession of the collateral.

B. PERFECTING A SECURITY INTEREST
Perfection is the process by which secured parties protect themselves against the claims of others who wish to satisfy their debts out of the same collateral.

1. Perfection by Filing
Filing is the most common means of perfecting a security interest.

a. **What a Financing Statement Must Contain**
It must contain (1) the names of the debtor and the creditor (a trade name is not sufficient), and (3) a description of the collateral [UCC 9–502, 9–503, 9–506, 9–521].

b. **Where to File a Financing Statement**
Depending on how collateral is classified, filing is with a county (timber, fixtures, etc.) or a state (other collateral) [UCC 9–301(3), 9–502(b)]. The specific office depends on the debtor's location—

   1) Individual debtors: the state of the debtor's residence.
   2) Chartered entity (corporation): state of charter or filing.
   3) Other: state in which business or chief executive office is.

2. **Perfection Without Filing**

   a. **Perfection by Possession**
   A creditor can possess collateral and return it when the debt is paid [UCC 9–310, 9–312(b), 9–313]. For some securities, instruments, and jewelry, this is the only way to perfect.

   b. **Automatic Perfection**

      1) **Purchase-Money Security Interest (PMSI)**
      A PMSI is (1) retained in, or taken by the seller of, goods to secure part or all of the price, or (2) taken by a lender, such as a bank, as part of a loan to enable a debtor to buy the collateral [UCC 9–103(a)(2)].

      2) **Perfection of a PMSI**
      A PMSI in consumer goods is perfected automatically when it is created. The seller need do nothing more.

3. **Effective Time of Perfection**
A financing statement is effective for five years [UCC 9–515]. A continuation statement filed within six months before the expiration date continues the effectiveness for five more years (and so on) [UCC 9–515(d), (e)].

III. THE SCOPE OF A SECURITY INTEREST

A. PROCEEDS
Proceeds include whatever is received when collateral is sold or otherwise disposed of. A secured party has an interest in proceeds that perfects automatically on perfection of the security interest and remains perfected for twenty days after the debtor receives the proceeds. The interest remains perfected for more than twenty days if—

1. A filed financing statement covers the original collateral and the proceeds [UCC 9–315(c), (d)].
2. There is a filed statement that covers the original collateral and the proceeds are identifiable cash proceeds [UCC 9–315(d)(2)].

B. AFTER-ACQUIRED PROPERTY
A security agreement may provide for coverage of **after-acquired property** [UCC 9–204(a)]—collateral acquired by a debtor after execution of a security agreement.

C. FUTURE ADVANCES
A security agreement may provide that future advances against a line of credit are subject to a security interest in the collateral [UCC 9–204(c)].

D. THE FLOATING-LIEN CONCEPT
A **floating lien** is a security agreement that provides for the creation of a security interest in any (or all) of the above. The concept can apply to a shifting stock of goods—the lien can start with raw

materials and follow them as they become finished goods and inventories and as they are sold, turning into accounts receivable, chattel paper, or cash.

IV. PRIORITIES

When several creditors claim a security interest in the same collateral of a debtor, which interest has priority?

A. SECURED PARTIES V. UNSECURED PARTIES

Secured parties (perfected or not) prevail over unsecured creditors and creditors who have obtained judgments against the debtor but who have not begun the legal process to collect on those judgments [UCC 9–201(a)].

B. SECURED PARTIES V. OTHER SECURED PARTIES

1. The General Rule

The first interest to be filed or perfected has priority over other filed or perfected security interests. If none of the interests has been perfected, the first to attach has priority [UCC 9–322(a)(1), (3)].

2. Exception—Commingled or Processed Goods

When goods have lost their identity into a product or mass, security interests attach in a ratio of the cost of the goods to which each interest originally attached to the cost of the total product or mass [UCC 9–336].

3. Exception—Purchase-Money Security Interest (PMSI)

a. Inventory

A perfected PMSI prevails over a previously perfected security interest if the holder of the PMSI perfects and gives the holder of the other interest written notice of the PMSI before the debtor takes possession of the new inventory [UCC 9–324(b)].

b. Software

If software is used in goods subject to a PMSI, priority is according to the classification of the goods [UCC 9–103(c), 9–324(f)].

c. Other Collateral

A perfected PMSI prevails over a previously perfected security interest if the holder of the PMSI perfects before the debtor takes possession of the collateral or within twenty days [UCC 9–324(a)].

C. SECURED PARTIES V. BUYERS

1. The General Rule

A security interest in collateral continues even after the collateral has been sold unless the secured party authorized the sale.

2. Exception—Buyer in the Ordinary Course of Business

Takes goods free of any security interest (unless the buyer knows that the purchase violates a third party's rights) [UCC 9–320(a)].

3. Exception—Buyers of Consumer Goods Purchased outside the Ordinary Course of Business

The buyer must give value and not know of the security interest; the purchase must occur before the secured party perfects by filing [UCC 9–320(b)].

4. Exception—Buyers of Instruments, Documents, or Securities

A holder in due course, a holder to whom a negotiable instrument has been negotiated, and a bona fide purchaser of securities have priority over a previously perfected security interest [UCC 9–330(d), 9–331(a)].

5. **Exception—Buyers of Farm Products**
   A buyer from a farmer has priority over a perfected security interest unless, in some states, the secured party has filed centrally an effective financing statement or the buyer has notice before the sale.

V. RIGHTS AND DUTIES OF DEBTORS AND CREDITORS

A. INFORMATION REQUESTS

When filing, creditors and debtors can ask the filing officer to furnish a copy of the statement with the file number, the date, and the hour [UCC 9–523(a)]. Others (such as prospective creditors) can ask the filing officer to provide a certificate that gives information on possible perfected financing statements [UCC 9–523(c), 9–525(d)].

B. RELEASE, ASSIGNMENT, AND AMENDMENT

A secured party can release all or part of the collateral [UCC 9–512, 9–521(b)], or assign part or all of the security interest [UCC 9–514, 9–521(a)]. A filing can be amended, if both parties agree [UCC 9–512(a)].

C. CONFIRMATION OR ACCOUNTING REQUEST BY DEBTOR

When the debtor asks, the secured party must tell the debtor the amount of the unpaid debt (within two weeks of the debtor's request) [UCC 9–210].

D. TERMINATION STATEMENT

When a debt is paid, the secured party can send a termination statement to the debtor or file it with the original financing statement.

1. **If the Collateral Is Consumer Goods**
   The statement must be filed within one month after the debt is paid, or—if the debtor requests the statement in writing—within twenty days of receipt of the request, whichever is earlier [UCC 9–513(b)].

2. **If the Collateral Is Other Goods**
   The statement must be filed or furnished to the debtor within twenty days after a written request is made by the debtor [UCC 9–513(c)].

VI. DEFAULT

Default is whatever the parties stipulate in their agreement [UCC 9–601, 9–603]. Occurs most often when debtors fail to make payments or go bankrupt.

A. BASIC REMEDIES

1. **Execution and Levy**
   A secured party give up the security interest and proceed to judgment on the debt (this is done if the value of the collateral is less than the debt and the debtor has other assets) [UCC 9–601(a)].

2. **Take Possession of the Collateral**
   A secured party can take possession of the collateral [UCC 9–609(b)] and retain it for satisfaction of the debt [UCC 9–620] or resell it and apply the proceeds toward the debt [UCC 9–610] (see below).

B. SECURED PARTY'S RIGHT TO TAKE POSSESSION OF THE COLLATERAL

A secured party can take possession of the collateral without a court order, if it can be done without a breach of the peace [UCC 9–609(b)]. Generally, this means not going onto the debtor's property, which could be trespass.

C. DISPOSITION OF COLLATERAL

1. **Retention of Collateral by the Secured Party**

a. **Notice**

A secured party must give written notice to the debtor. In all cases except consumer goods, notice must also be sent to any other secured party from whom the secured party has received notice of a claim.

b. **If Debtor or Other Secured Party Objects within Twenty Days**

The secured party must sell or otherwise dispose of the collateral [UCC 9–620(a), 9–621].

2. **Consumer Goods**

If the collateral is consumer goods with a PMSI and the debtor has paid 60 percent or more on the price or loan, the secured party must sell within ninety days [UCC 9–620(e), (f)].

3. **Disposition Procedures**

(1) Disposition must be in a commercially reasonable manner and (2) the debtor must be notified of the sale [UCC 9–610(b)].

a. **Disposition**

After default, a secured party may sell, lease, license, or otherwise dispose of any or all of the collateral. "Commercially reasonable" means the method, manner, time, place, and other terms.

b. **The Secured Party Must Give Written Notice to the Debtor**

In all cases except consumer goods, notice must also be sent to any other secured party from whom the secured party has received notice of a claim [UCC 9–611(b), (c)], unless the collateral is perishable or is customarily sold in a recognized market.

4. **Proceeds from Disposition**

Must be applied to (1) expenses stemming from retaking, storing, or reselling, (2) balance of the debt, (3) junior lienholders, and (4) surplus to the debtor [UCC 9–608(a); 9–615(a), (e)].

5. **Deficiency Judgment**

In most cases, if a sale of collateral does not repay the debt, the debtor is liable for any deficiency. A creditor can obtain a judgment to collect.

6. **Redemption Rights**

Before the secured party retains or disposes of the collateral, the debtor or any other secured party can take the collateral by tendering performance of all secured obligations and paying the secured party's expenses [UCC 9–623].

TRUE-FALSE QUESTIONS

(Answers at the Back of the Book)

_____ 1. A financing statement is not effective if it is filed electronically.

_____ 2. Attachment gives a creditor an enforceable security interest in collateral.

_____ 3. A secured creditor's right to proceeds exists for twenty days after receipt only if the proceeds are forwarded to the secured party.

_____ 4. To be valid, a financing statement does not need to contain a description of the collateral.

_____ 5. When a secured debt is paid, the secured party does not need to file a termination statement in all cases.

_____ 6. The security agreement determines most of the parties' rights and duties concerning the security interest.

_____   7.   A secured party can release the collateral described in a financing statement even if the debtor has not paid the debt.

_____   8.   Default occurs most commonly when a debtor fails to repay the loan for which his or her property served as collateral.

_____   9.   After a default, and before a secured party disposes of the collateral, a debtor cannot exercise the right of redemption.

_____   10.   When two secured parties have perfected security interests in the same collateral, generally the last to perfect has priority.

FILL-IN QUESTIONS

(Answers at the Back of the Book)

1.   Generally, in a secured transaction, the _____ (creditor/debtor) files a financing statement with the appropriate state office. When the debt is paid, the _____ (creditor/debtor) may also send a termination statement to the officer with whom the financing statement was filed.

2.   When two or more secured parties have perfected security interests in the same collateral, generally the _____ (first/last) to perfect has priority. When two conflicting security interests are unperfected, the _____ (first/last) to attach has priority.

MULTIPLE-CHOICE QUESTIONS

(Answers at the Back of the Book)

_____   1.   Alpha Credit Corporation files a financing statement regarding a transaction with Beta Company. To be valid, the financing statement must contain all of the following *except*

a.   a description of the collateral.
b.   the debtor's name.
c.   the debtor's signature.
d.   the secured party's name.

_____   2.   Able Transport, Inc., buys a forklift, but does not make a payment on it for five months. The seller, Baker Equipment Company, repossesses it by towing it from a public street. Able sues Baker for breach of the peace. Able will likely

a.   not prevail because Baker did not use judicial process.
b.   not prevail because the repossession was not a breach of the peace.
c.   prevail because Able did not default on the loan.
d.   prevail because the repossession was a breach of the peace.

_____   3.   Dan owns Eats Café, which he uses as collateral to borrow $10,000 from First State Bank. To be effective, the security agreement must include

a.   a description that reasonably identifies the collateral only.
b.   Dan's signature only.
c.   a description that reasonably identifies the collateral and Dan's signature.
d.   none of the above.

____ 4. Great Trucks, Inc. (GTI), repossesses a truck (not a consumer good subject to a purchase-money security interest) from Highway Trucking Company, and decides to keep it instead of reselling it. GTI sends written notice of this intent to the debtor. GTI must also send notice to

a. only a junior lien claimant who has filed a statutory lien or security interest in the truck.
b. only a secured party from whom GTI has received notice of a claim in the truck.
c. any junior lien claimant who has filed a statutory lien or security interest and any secured party from whom GTI has received notice.
d. none of the above.

____ 5. Irma, a debtor, wants to confirm the amount of his outstanding secured debt with Jiffy Loan Corporation. Irma can ask Jiffy to confirm her view of the debt, without charge, every

a. month.
b. six months.
c. year.
d. none of the above.

____ 6. Kappa Credit, Inc., has a security interest in the proceeds from the sale of collateral owned by Local Stores Company. This interest may remain perfected for longer than twenty days after Local receives the proceeds

a. only if a filed financing statement covers the proceeds.
b. only if the proceeds are identifiable cash proceeds.
c. if a filed financing statement covers the proceeds or the proceeds are identifiable cash proceeds.
d. none of the above.

____ 7. Nick borrows $5,000 from Modern Financial Corporation (MFC), which files a financing statement on May 1, but does not sign a security agreement until he receives the funds on May 5. He also borrows $5,000 from Omega Bank, which advances funds, files a financing statement, and signs a security agreement on May 2. He uses the same property as collateral for both loans. On his default, in a dispute over the collateral, MFC will

a. lose because Omega perfected first.
b. lose because Omega's interest attached first.
c. win because it filed first.
d. win because its interest attached first.

____ 8. Peak Electronics Stores sell consumer products. To create a purchase-money security interest in a home computer bought by Quinn, Peak must

a. assign to a collection agent a portion of Peak's accounts *payable*
b. assign to a collecting agent a portion of Peak's accounts *receivable*
c. extend credit for part or all of the purchase price of the computer.
d. refer Quinn to Rapid Cash Company, a third-party lender.

____ 9. Safe Loans, Inc., wants to perfect its security interest in collateral owned by Tech Corporation. Most likely, Safe should file a financing statement with

a. the city manager.
b. the county clerk.
c. the secretary of state.
d. none of the above.

____ **10.** United Sales Company is incorporated in Virginia, with its chief executive office in Washington. Using its equipment as collateral, United borrows $5,000 from Zip Credit, Inc. To perfect its security interest, Zip should file its financing statement in

  a. Virginia only.
  b. Washington only.
  c. Virginia and Washington.
  d. none of the above.

SHORT ESSAY QUESTIONS

1. What is the floating lien concept?

2. What are a secured party's rights on a debtor's default?

ISSUE SPOTTERS

(Answers at the Back of the Book)

1. Adam needs $500 to buy textbooks, and other supplies. Beth agrees to loan Adam $500, accepting as collateral Adam's computer. They put their agreement in writing. How can Beth let other creditors know of her interest in the computer?

2. Central Sales Company (CSC) borrows $1,000, using its inventory "present and after acquired" as collateral, from Delta Bank, which perfects its interest on May 1. On May 5, CSC buys from Excel Goods, Inc., new inventory in which CSC gives Excel a purchase-money security interest (PMSI). On the same day, Excel perfects its interest and notifies Delta. CSC takes possession of the new inventory on May 7. On June 1, CSC defaults on the loans. Whose security interest has priority?

3. First National Bank loans $5,000 to Gail to buy a car, which is used as collateral to secure the loan. Gail has paid less than 50 percent of the loan, when she defaults. First National could repossess and keep the car, but the bank does not want it. What are the alternatives?

Chapter 21:
Creditors' Rights and Bankruptcy

WHAT THIS CHAPTER IS ABOUT

This chapter sets out the rights and remedies available to a creditor, when a debtor defaults, under laws other than UCC Article 9. This chapter also covers the federal bankruptcy laws.

CHAPTER OUTLINE

I. **LAWS ASSISTING CREDITORS**

    A. **LIENS**
    A **lien** is an encumbrance on property to satisfy a debt or protect a claim for payment of a debt.

        1. **Mechanic's Lien**
        Can be placed by a creditor on real property when a person contracts for labor, services, or materials to improve the property but does not pay.

           a. **When a Creditor Must File a Mechanic's Lien**
           Within a specific period, measured from the last date on which materials or labor were provided (usually within 60 to 120 days).

           b. **If the Owner Does Not Pay**
           The property can be sold to satisfy the debt. Notice of the foreclosure and sale must be given to the debtor in advance.

        2. **Artisan's Lien**
        A security device by which a creditor can recover from a debtor for labor and materials furnished in the repair of personal property.

           a. **The Creditor Must Possess the Property**
           Lien terminates if possession is voluntarily surrendered, unless the lienholder records notice of the lien in accord with state statutes.

           b. **If the Owner Does Not Pay**
           The property can be sold to satisfy the debt. Notice of the foreclosure and sale must be given to the debtor in advance.

        3. **Innkeeper's Lien**
        A security device placed on the baggage of guests for hotel charges that are not paid. The lien terminates when the charges are paid, or the baggage is returned or sold to satisfy the debt.

        4. **Judicial Liens**

           a. **Attachment**
           Attachment is a court-ordered seizure and taking into custody of property before the securing of a judgment for a past-due debt. A sheriff or other officer seizes nonexempt property. If the creditor prevails at trial, the property can be sold to satisfy the judgment.

b. **Writ of Execution**

A **writ of execution** is an order, usually issued by the clerk of court, directing the sheriff to seize and sell any of the debtor's nonexempt property within the court's geographical jurisdiction. Proceeds of the sale pay the debt.

B. GARNISHMENT

Garnishment is when a creditor collects a debt by seizing property of the debtor (such as wages or money in a bank account) that is being held by a third party (such as an employer or a bank). The creditor obtains a judgment against the debtor and serves it on the third party.

C. CREDITORS' COMPOSITION AGREEMENTS

A **creditors' composition agreement** is a contract between a debtor and his or her creditors for discharge of the debtor's liquidated debts on payment of a sum less than that owed.

D. MORTGAGE FORECLOSURE

A **mortgagor** (creditor) can foreclose on mortgaged property if the **mortgagee** (debtor) defaults. Usual method is a judicial sale. Proceeds are applied to the debt. If proceeds do not cover the costs and the debt, the mortgagee can recover the difference from the mortgagor with a deficiency judgment.

E. SURETYSHIP AND GUARANTY

1. **Suretyship**

A promise by a third person to be responsible for a debtor's obligation. Does not have to be in writing. A surety is *primarily* liable—a creditor can demand payment from the surety the moment the debt is due.

2. **Guaranty**

A promise to be *secondarily* liable for the debt or default of another. A guarantor pays only after the debtor defaults and the creditor has made an attempt to collect from the debtor. A guaranty must be in writing unless the main-purpose exception applies (see Chapter 11).

3. **Defenses of the Surety and the Guarantor**

To avoid payment, a surety (guarantor) may use the following defenses.

a. **Material Change to the Contract between Debtor and Creditor**

Without obtaining the consent of the surety (guarantor), a surety is discharged completely or to the extent the surety suffers a loss.

b. **Principal Obligation Is Paid or Valid Tender Is Made**

The surety (guarantor) is discharged from the obligation.

c. **Most of the Principal Debtor's Defenses**

Defenses that cannot be used: debtor's incapacity, bankruptcy, and statute of limitations.

d. **Surety or Guarantor's Own Defenses**

e. **Creditor's Surrender or Impairment of Collateral**

Without the surety's (guarantor's) consent, releases the surety to the extent of any loss suffered from the creditor's actions.

4. **Rights of the Surety and the Guarantor**

If the surety (guarantor) pays the debt—

a. **Right of Subrogation**

The surety (guarantor) has available any remedies that were available to the creditor against the debtor.

    b. **Right of Reimbursement**
The surety (guarantor) is entitled to receive from the debtor all outlays made on behalf of the suretyship arrangement.

    c. **Co-Sureties' Right of Contribution**
A surety who pays more than his or her proportionate share on a debtor's default is entitled to recover from co-sureties.

II.   LAWS ASSISTING DEBTORS

A. HOMESTEAD EXEMPTION
Each state allows a debtor to keep the family home (in some states only if the debtor has a family) in its entirety or up to a specified amount.

B. EXEMPT PERSONAL PROPERTY
Household furniture up to a specified dollar amount; clothing and other possessions; a vehicle (or vehicles); certain animals; and equipment that the debtor uses in a business or trade.

III.   BANKRUPTCY AND REORGANIZATION
Bankruptcy law (1) protects a debtor by giving him or her a fresh start and (2) ensures equitable treatment to creditors competing for a debtor's assets. Bankruptcy proceedings are held in federal bankruptcy courts. Current law is based on the Bankruptcy Reform Act of 1978 (the Bankruptcy Code). Relief can be granted under the Code's Chapter 7, Chapter 11, Chapter 12, or Chapter 13.

IV.   BANKRUPTCY—CHAPTER 7 LIQUIDATION
This is the most familiar type of bankruptcy proceeding. A debtor declares his or her debts and gives all assets to a trustee, who sells the nonexempt assets and distributes the proceeds to creditors.

A. WHO CAN FILE FOR A LIQUIDATION
Any "person"—individuals, partnerships, and corporations (spouses can file jointly)—except railroads, insurance companies, banks, savings and loan associations, certain investment companies, and credit unions.

B. FILING THE PETITION

  1. **Voluntary Bankruptcy**

    a. **Debtor Files a Petition with the Court**
Includes a list of (1) creditors and debts, (2) debtor's financial affairs, (3) debtor's property, (4) current income and expenses.

    b. **Filing of the Petition Constitutes an Order for Relief**
The clerk of the court must give the trustee and creditors notice of the order within not more than twenty days.

    c. **Substantial Abuse**
A court can dismiss a petition if granting it would constitute "substantial abuse" [11 U.S.C. Section 707(b)].

  2. **Involuntary Bankruptcy**
A debtor's creditors can force the debtor into bankruptcy proceedings.

    a. **Who Can Be Forced into Involuntary Proceedings?**
A debtor with twelve or more creditors, three or more of whom (with unsecured claims of at least $11,625) file a petition. A debtor with fewer than twelve creditors, one or more of whom (with a claim of $11,625) files. Not a farmer or a charitable institution.

b.   When Will an Order for Relief Be Entered?

If the debtor does not challenge the petition, the debtor is generally not paying debts as they come due, or a receiver, assignee, or custodian took possession of the debtor's property within 120 days before the petition was filed.

C.   AUTOMATIC STAY

When a petition is filed, an automatic stay suspends all action by creditors against the debtor. A court may grant some relief. The stay does not apply to paternity, alimony, or family maintenance and support claims.

D.   CREDITORS' MEETING AND CLAIMS

Within "not less than ten days or more than thirty days," the court calls a meeting of creditors, at which the debtor answers questions. Within ninety days of the meeting, a creditor must file a proof of claim. The proof lists the creditor's name and address, as well as the amount of the debt.

E.   PROPERTY OF THE ESTATE

1.   What Property Is Included in the Debtor's Estate?

Interests in property presently held; jointly owned property; property transferred in transactions voidable by the trustee; proceeds and profits; after-acquired property; interests in gifts, inheritances, property settlements, and life insurance death proceeds to which the debtor becomes entitled within 180 days after filing.

2.   What Property Is Not Included?

Property acquired after the filing of the petition, except as noted.

F.   EXEMPTED PROPERTY

1.   Federal Law

Exempts such property as interests in a residence to $17,425, a motor vehicle to $2,775, household goods to $9,300, and tools of a trade to $1,750, and the rights to receive Social Security and other benefits.

2.   State Law

Most states preclude the use of federal exemptions; others allow a debtor to choose between state and federal. State exemptions may include different value limitations and exempt different property.

G.   THE TRUSTEE'S ROLE

After the order for relief, an interim trustee is appointed to administer the debtor's property until the first meeting of creditors, when a permanent trustee is elected. A trustee's duty is to collect and reduce to money the property of the estate and distribute the proceeds.

1.   What Are the Trustee's Powers?

A trustee can require persons holding the debtor's property to turn it over to the trustee. A trustee also has the same rights as, for example, a lien creditor with priority over an unperfected secured party.

2.   What Are Voidable Rights?

Any reason that a debtor can use to obtain the return of his or her property can be used by the trustee (fraud, duress, etc.)

3.   What Are Preferences?

A trustee can recover payments made by a debtor (1) within ninety days before the petition and (2) for a preexisting debt.

a.   Insiders or Fraud

If a creditor is an insider (partner, corporate officer, relative) or a transfer is fraudulent, a trustee may recover transfers made within one year before filing.

b. **What Transfers Are Not Preferences?**
Property sold to an innocent third party.

H. PROPERTY DISTRIBUTION

1. **Secured Creditors**
Within thirty days of the petition or before the first creditors' meeting (whichever is first), a debtor must state whether he or she will retain secured collateral (or claim it as exempt, etc.).

2. **Unsecured Creditors**
Paid in the order of priority. The order of priority is—

a. Administrative expenses (court costs, trustee and attorney fees).
b. In an involuntary bankruptcy, expenses incurred by the debtor in the ordinary course of business from the filing of the petition to the appointment of the trustee or the issuance of an order for relief.
c. Unpaid wages, salaries, and commissions earned within ninety days of the petition, to $4,650 per claimant. A claim in excess is a claim of a general creditor (no. i below).
d. Unsecured claims for contributions to employee benefit plans, limited to services performed within 180 days before the petition and $4,650 per employee.
e. Claims by farmers and fishers, to $4,650, against storage or processing facilities.
f. Consumer deposits to $2,100 given to the debtor before the petition to buy, lease, or rent property or services that were not received.
g. Claims for paternity, alimony, maintenance, and support.
h. Taxes and penalties due to the government.
i. Claims of general creditors.
j. Commitments to the Federal Deposit Insurance Corporation, and others, to maintain the capital of an insured depository institution.

I. DISCHARGE
A discharge voids any judgment on a discharged debt and prohibits any action to collect a discharged debt. A co-debtor's liability is not affected.

1. **Exceptions—What Debts May Not Be Discharged?**
Claims for back taxes, amounts borrowed to pay back taxes, goods obtained by fraud, debts that were not listed in the petition, alimony, child support, student loans, certain cash advances, and others.

2. **Objections—What Debtors May Not Receive a Discharge?**
Those who conceal property with the intent to hinder, delay, or defraud a creditor; who fail to explain a loss of assets; or who have been granted a discharge within six years of the filing of the petition.

3. **Revocation of Discharge**
A discharge may be revoked within one year if the debtor was fraudulent or dishonest during the bankruptcy proceedings.

4. **Reaffirmation of Debt**
A reaffirmation of debt is a debtor's agreement to pay an otherwise dischargeable debt. The agreement must be made before a discharge is granted and must be approved by the court. Can be rescinded within sixty days or before the discharge is granted.

V.   BANKRUPTCY—CHAPTER 11 REORGANIZATION
In a Chapter 11 reorganization, the creditors and the debtor formulate a plan under which the debtor pays a portion of the debts, is discharged of the rest, and continues in business.

A. **WHO IS ELIGIBLE FOR RELIEF UNDER CHAPTER 11**

Any debtor (except a stockbroker or a commodities broker) who is eligible for Chapter 7 relief. Used most commonly by corporate debtors. The same principles apply that govern liquidation (automatic stay, etc.).

B. **DEBTOR IN POSSESSION**

On entry of an order for relief, the debtor continues to operate his or her business as a debtor in possession (DIP).

1. **If Gross Mismanagement Is Shown**

The court may appoint a trustee (or receiver) to operate the business. This may also be done if it is in the best interests of the estate.

2. **DIP's Role Is Similar to That of a Trustee in a Liquidation**

The DIP can avoid pre-petition preferential payments and fraudulent transfers and decide whether to cancel pre-petition executory contracts.

C. **CREDITORS' COMMITTEES**

A committee of unsecured creditors is appointed to consult with the trustee or DIP. Certain small businesses can avoid creditors' committees.

D. **THE REORGANIZATION PLAN**

1. **What Must the Plan Do?**

Administer the debtor's assets in the hope of a return to solvency; designate classes of claims and interests; specify the treatment to be afforded the classes; and provide an adequate means for execution.

2. **Who Can File a Plan?**

Only the debtor within the first 120 days (100 days in some cases) after the date of the order for relief. Any other party, if the debtor does not meet the deadline or fails to obtain creditor consent within 180 days.

3. **The Plan Is Submitted to Creditors for Acceptance**

Each class adversely affected by a plan must accept it (two-thirds of the total claims must approve). If only one class accepts, the court may confirm it if it "does not discriminate unfairly" against any creditors. The debtor is given a discharge from all claims not within the plan (except those that would be denied in a liquidation).

VI. BANKRUPTCY—CHAPTER 13 REPAYMENT PLAN

A. **WHO IS ELIGIBLE?**

Individuals (not partnerships or corporations) with regular income and unsecured debts of less than $290,525 or secured debts of less than $871,550.

B. **VOLUNTARY FILING ONLY**

A Chapter 13 case can be initiated by the filing of a voluntary petition only. A trustee is appointed. The automatic stay takes effect (on consumer debts, not business debts).

C. **REPAYMENT PLAN**

The plan must provide for turnover to a trustee of the debtor's future income.

1. **Filing and Confirming the Plan**

Only the debtor can file a plan, which the court will confirm if (1) the secured creditors accept it, (2) it provides that creditors retain their liens and the value of the property to be distributed to them is not less than the secured portion of their claims, or (3) the debtor surrenders the property securing the claim to the creditors.

2. **Payments under the Plan**

The time for payment must be less than three years (five years, with court approval). The payments must be timely, or the court can convert the case to a Chapter 7 liquidation or dismiss the petition. Before completion of payments, the plan may be modified at the request of the debtor, the trustee, or an unsecured creditor.

3. **Objection to the Plan**

Over the objection of the trustee or an unsecured creditor, the court may approve a plan only if (1) the value of the property to be distributed is equal to the amount of the claims, or (2) all the debtor's disposable income during the plan will be used to make payments.

D. DISCHARGE

After completion of all payments, all debts provided for by the plan are discharged. A discharge obtained by fraud can be revoked within one year.

VII. BANKRUPTCY—CHAPTER 12 FAMILY FARMER PLAN

Chapter 12 is nearly identical to Chapter 13. Eligible debtors include a family farmer whose gross income is at least 50 percent farm dependent and whose debts are at least 80 percent farm related (total debt must not exceed $1.5 million), and a partnership or closely held corporation (at least 50 percent owned by a farm family).

TRUE-FALSE QUESTIONS

(Answers at the Back of the Book)

____ 1. A mechanic's lien involves real property.

____ 2. An employer can dismiss an employee due to garnishment for any one debt.

____ 3. A writ of attachment is a court order to seize a debtor's property *before* the entry of a final judgment in a creditor's lawsuit against the debtor.

____ 4. A writ of execution is a court order to seize a debtor's property *after* the entry of a final judgment in a creditor's lawsuit against the debtor.

____ 5. To avoid liability on an obligation to a creditor, a surety cannot use any defenses available to the debtor.

____ 6. A debtor must be insolvent to file a voluntary petition under Chapter 7.

____ 7. The filing of a petition for bankruptcy will not stay most legal actions against the debtor.

____ 8. Filing for bankruptcy under Chapter 13 is less expensive and less complicated than other bankruptcy proceedings.

____ 9. When a business debtor files for Chapter 11 protection, the debtor is not allowed to continue in business.

____ 10. The same principles cover the filing of a liquidation petition and a reorganization proceeding.

FILL-IN QUESTIONS

(Answers at the Back of the Book)

Liquidation is the purpose of Chapter _____ (7/11/13). Reorganization is the purpose of Chapter _____ (7/11/13). Adjustment is the purpose of Chapter _____ (7/11/13). Under Chapter _____ (7/11/13), nonexempt property is sold, with proceeds distributed in a certain priority to classes of creditors, and dischargeable debts are terminated. Under Chapter _____ (7/11/13), a plan for reorganization is submitted, and if it is approved and followed, debts are discharged. Under Chapter _____ (7/11/13), a plan must be approved if the debtor turns over all disposable income for a three-year period, after which debts are discharged. The advantages of Chapter _____ (7/11/13) include the debtor's opportunity for a fresh start. The advantages of Chapter _____ (7/11/13) include the debtor's continuation in business under a plan that allows for reorganization of debts. The advantages of Chapter _____ (7/11/13) include the debtor's continuation in business and discharge of most debts.

MULTIPLE-CHOICE QUESTIONS

(Answers at the Back of the Book)

____ 1. Fran leaves her necklace with Gold Jewelers to be repaired. When Fran returns for the necklace, she says, "I'll pay for the repair later." Gold can

a. keep the necklace for a reasonable time but must return it whether or not Fran pays.
b. keep the necklace until Fran pays.
c. keep the necklace whether or not Fran pays.
d. not keep the necklace.

____ 2. Adam borrows money from Best Credit Company. If Adam defaults, to use attachment as a remedy Best must first

a. commence a suit against Adam.
b. succeed in a suit against Adam.
c. be unable to collect the amount of a judgment against Adam.
d. all of the above.

____ 3. Carol borrows $500 from Delta Loan Corporation. When Carol defaults on the debt, Delta obtains a garnishment order from a court. To satisfy the judgment, the order will likely be served on

a. Carol.
b. Carol's employer.
c. Delta Loan Corporation.
d. the sheriff or other public officer.

____ 4. Eve owes Fred $200,000. A court awards Fred a judgment in the amount of the debt. To satisfy the judgment, Eve's home is sold at public auction for $150,000. The state homestead exemption is $50,000. Fred gets

a. $50,000.
b. $100,000.
c. $150,000.
d. nothing.

____ 5. Great Company wants to borrow money from First State Bank. The bank insists that Hal, Great Company's president, agree to be personally liable for payment if Great defaults. If Hal agrees, he is

a. a guarantor only.
b. a surety only.
c. a guarantor and a surety.
d. none of the above.

____ 6. Ira and Jill agree to act as guarantors on a loan made by Ken. Ken defaults on the payments and Jill refuses to pay. If Ira pays the debt, he can recover from

a. Ken and Jill under the right of reimbursement.
b. Ken and Jill under the right of proportionate liability.
c. Ken under the right of subrogation and Jill under the right of contribution.
d. none of the above.

____ 7. Lora is the sole proprietor of Diners Cafe, which owes debts in an amount more than Lora believes she and the cafe can repay. The creditors agree that liquidating the business would not be in their best interests. To stay in business, Lora could file for bankruptcy under

   a. Chapter 7 only.
   b. Chapter 11 only.
   c. Chapter 13 only.
   d. Chapter 11 or Chapter 13.

____ 8. Mike's monthly income is $2,500, his monthly expenses are $2,100, and his debts are nearly $15,000. If he applied the difference between his income and expenses to pay off the debts, they could be eliminated within three years. The provision in the Bankruptcy Code that covers this plan is

   a. Chapter 7.
   b. Chapter 11.
   c. Chapter 12.
   d. Chapter 13.

____ 9. National Corporation has not paid any of its fifteen creditors, six of whom have unsecured claims of more than $8,000. The creditors can force National into bankruptcy under

   a. Chapter 7 only.
   b. Chapter 11 only.
   c. Chapter 13 only.
   d. Chapter 7 or Chapter 11.

____ 10. Owen files a bankruptcy petition under Chapter 7 to have his debts discharged. The debts most likely to be discharged include claims for

   a. alimony and child support.
   b. back taxes accruing within three years before the petition was filed.
   c. certain fines and penalties payable to the government.
   d. student loans, if the payment would impose undue hardship on Owen.

SHORT ESSAY QUESTIONS

1. What is a lien? What are four ways in which a lien can arise? What is a lienholder's priority compared to other creditors?

2. What are the differences between contracts of suretyship and guaranty contracts?

ISSUE SPOTTERS

(Answers at the Back of the Book)

1. Pat wants to borrow $10,000 from Quality Loan Company to buy a new car, but Quality refuses to lend the money unless Ron cosigns the note. Ron cosigns and makes three of the payments when Pat fails to do so. Can Ron get this money from Pat?

2. Star Company's creditors include Town Bank with a perfected security interest in Star's building and equipment, United Construction with a mechanic's lien on the building that predates Town Bank's interest, and Variety Suppliers, Inc., with an unperfected security interest. Star files a petition for a Chapter 7 liquidation. In what order will the creditors be paid?

3.   Warren is a vice president for Zip Enterprises, Inc. On May 1, Warren loans Zip $10,000. On June 1, Zip repays the loan. On July 1, Zip files for bankruptcy. Ann is appointed trustee. Can Ann recover the $10,000 paid to Warren on June 1?

CUMULATIVE HYPOTHETICAL PROBLEM
FOR UNIT SIX—INCLUDING CHAPTERS 20–21

(Answers at the Back of the Book)

Omega Computers, Inc., sells computers to consumers.

_____   **1.**   Alan fixes the roof of Omega's office building, but Omega does not pay. Bob fixes one of Omega's trucks, but Omega does not pay. Bob does not return the truck to Omega. Alan and Bob place a mechanic's lien and an artisan's lien on Omega's property. Before foreclosure, notice must be given to Omega by

    a.   Alan only.
    b.   Bob only.
    c.   Alan and Bob.
    d.   none of the above.

_____   **2.**   In the course of business, Omega borrows money from First National Bank. The loan is cosigned by Carl as a surety. Omega defaults on the loan, and Carl pays the entire amount. To collect from Omega, Carl has the right of

    a.   contribution.
    b.   exemption.
    c.   exoneration.
    d.   subrogation.

_____   **3.**   Omega buys inventory from Beta Digital Products. Beta finances the purchase, accepts the inventory as security, and perfects its interest. Under UCC Article 9, perfection of a security interest will *not* affect the rights of

    a.   a buyer in the ordinary course of business.
    b.   a subsequent secured creditor.
    c.   the trustee in Omega's bankruptcy.
    d.   all of the above.

_____   **4.**   Omega files a voluntary petition in bankruptcy under Chapter 11. A reorganization plan is filed with the court. Normally, the court will confirm a Chapter 11 plan if it is accepted by

    a.   Omega.
    b.   Omega's secured creditors.
    c.   Omega's shareholders.
    d.   Omega's unsecured creditors.

_____   **5.**   Omega's Chapter 11 plan is confirmed, and a final decree is entered. Omega will

    a.   be discharged from all debts except as otherwise provided by the law.
    b.   be liquidated.
    c.   be operated in business by the bankruptcy trustee.
    d.   not be allowed to continue in the same business.

QUESTIONS ON THE FOCUS ON LEGAL REASONING FOR UNIT SIX— *IN RE STANTON*

(Answers at the Back of the Book)

_____ 1. Ann owns Beta Corporation. On Beta's behalf, Ann borrows money from Corporate Bank in exchange for a mortgage on Ann's house. Ann files for personal bankruptcy. Under the holding in *In re Stanton*, the bank's lien for the money could

   a. be avoided by the bankruptcy trustee to the extent of the entire price of the house.
   b. be avoided by the trustee to the extent of the full amount of the loan.
   c. be avoided by the trustee to the extent of the unpaid amount of the loan.
   d. not be avoided by the trustee.

_____ 2. In the previous question, suppose that the bank continually advanced money on the loan at its option, even after Ann files for bankruptcy. In the opinion of the majority in *In re Stanton*, the bank's post-petition advances would be

   a. eliminated by the trustee.
   b. equal to the trustee.
   c. junior to the trustee.
   d. senior to the trustee.

_____ 3. According to the reasoning of the dissent in *In re Stanton*, the bank's post-petition advances in the previous problem could

   a. be avoided by the trustee to the extent of the entire price of the house.
   b. be avoided by the trustee to the extent of full amount of the advances.
   c. be avoided by the trustee to the extent of the unpaid amount of the entire loan.
   d. not be avoided by the trustee.

Chapter 22:
Agency Relationships

WHAT THIS CHAPTER IS ABOUT

This chapter covers agency relationships, including how they are formed and the duties involved. An agency relationship involves two parties: the principal and the agent. Agency relationships are essential to a corporation, which can function and enter into contracts only through its agents.

CHAPTER OUTLINE

I. AGENCY RELATIONSHIPS

In an agency relationship, the parties agree that the agent will act on behalf and instead of the principal in negotiating and transacting business with third persons.

A. EMPLOYER-EMPLOYEE RELATIONSHIPS
Normally, all employees who deal with third parties are deemed to be agents. Statutes covering workers' compensation and so on apply only to employer-employee relationships.

B. EMPLOYER–INDEPENDENT CONTRACTOR RELATIONSHIPS
Those who hire independent contractors have no control over the details of their physical performance. Independent contractors can be agents.

C. CRITERIA FOR DETERMINING EMPLOYEE STATUS
The greater an employer's control over the work, the more likely it is that the worker is an employee. Another key factor is whether the employer withholds taxes from payments to the worker and pays unemployment and Social Security taxes covering the worker.

II. AGENCY FORMATION

Consideration is not required. A principal must have capacity to contract; anyone can be an agent. An agency can be created for any legal purpose.

A. AGENCY BY AGREEMENT
Normally, an agency must be based on an agreement that the agent will act for the principal. Such an agreement can be an express written contract, can be implied by conduct, or can be oral.

B. AGENCY BY RATIFICATION
A person who is not an agent (or who is an agent acting outside the scope of his or her authority) may make a contract on behalf of another (a principal). If the principal approves or affirms that contract by word or by action, an agency relationship is created by ratification.

C. AGENCY BY ESTOPPEL

1. Principal's Actions
When a principal causes a third person to believe that another person is his or her agent, and the third person deals with the supposed agent, the principal is estopped to deny the agency relationship.

2. **Third Party's Reasonable Belief**
The third person must prove that he or she reasonably believed that an agency relationship existed and that the agent had authority—that an ordinary, prudent person familiar with business practice and custom would have been justified in concluding that the agent had authority.

D. **AGENCY BY OPERATION OF LAW**
An agency relationship in the absence of a formal agreement may occur in family relationships or in an emergency, if the agent's failure to act outside the scope of his or her authority would cause the principal substantial loss.

III. DUTIES OF AGENTS AND PRINCIPALS
The principal-agent relationship is fiduciary.

A. **AGENT'S DUTIES TO THE PRINCIPAL**

1. **Performance**
An agent must perform with reasonable diligence and skill.

2. **Notification**
An agent must notify the principal of all matters concerning the agency.

3. **Loyalty**
An agent must act solely for the benefit of the principal.

4. **Obedience**
An agent must follow all lawful instructions of the principal.

5. **Accounting**
An agent must keep and make available to the principal an account of everything received and paid out on behalf of the principal.

B. **PRINCIPAL'S DUTIES TO THE AGENT**

1. **Compensation**
A principal must pay the agent for services rendered.

2. **Reimbursement and Indemnification**
A principal must (1) reimburse the agent for money paid at the principal's request or for necessary expenses and (2) indemnify an agent for liability incurred because of authorized acts.

3. **Cooperation**
A principal must cooperate with his or her agent.

4. **Safe Working Conditions**
A principal must provide safe working conditions.

IV. AGENT'S AUTHORITY

A. **ACTUAL AUTHORITY**
Express authority may be oral or in writing. Implied authority may be conferred by custom, can be inferred from the position an agent occupies, or is implied as reasonably necessary to carry out express authority.

1. **Equal Dignity Rule**
In most states, if a contract is or must be in writing, an agent's authority to enter into the contract must also be in writing.

2. **Power of Attorney**

A power of attorney can be special or general. An ordinary power terminates on the incapacity or death of the person giving it. A durable power is not affected by the principal's incapacity.

B. APPARENT AUTHORITY

An agent has apparent authority when a principal, by word or action, causes a third party reasonably to believe that an agent has authority, though the agent has no authority. The principal may be estopped from denying it if the third party changes position in reliance.

C. RATIFICATION

A principal can ratify an unauthorized contract or act, if he or she is aware of all material facts. Ratification can be done expressly or impliedly (by accepting the benefits of a transaction). An entire transaction must be ratified; a principal cannot affirm only part.

V. LIABILITY IN AGENCY RELATIONSHIPS

A. LIABILITY FOR CONTRACTS

Who is liable to third parties for contracts formed by an agent?

1. **If an Agent Acts within the Scope of His or Her Authority**

   a. **Disclosed Principal**

   If a principal's identity is known to a third party when an agent makes a contract, the principal is liable. The agent is not liable.

   b. **Partially Disclosed Principal**

   If a principal's identity is not known to a third party when an agent makes a contract but the third party knows the agent is acting for a principal, the principal is liable. In most states, the agent is also liable.

   c. **Undisclosed Principal**

   If the principal's identity is not known to a third party when an agent makes a contract, the principal *and* the agent are liable. Exceptions—

   1) The principal is expressly excluded as a party in the contract.
   2) The contract is a negotiable instrument (check or note).
   3) The performance of the agent is personal to the contract.

2. **If the Agent Has No Authority**

   The principal is not liable in contract to a third party. The agent is liable, unless the third party knew the agent did not have authority.

B. LIABILITY FOR TORTS AND CRIMES

An agent is liable to third parties for his or her torts and crimes. Is the principal also liable?

1. **Liability for Agent's Torts**

   a. **The Doctrine of *Respondeat Superior***

   An employer is liable for harm caused (negligently or intentionally) to a third party by an employee acting within the scope of employment, without regard to the fault of the employer.

   b. **Scope of Employment**

   Factors for determining whether an act is within the scope of employment are—

   1) the time, place, and purpose of the act.
   2) whether the act was authorized by the employer.
   3) whether the act is one commonly performed by employees on behalf of their employers.
   4) whether the employer's interest was advanced by the act.

5) whether the private interests of the employee were involved.
6) whether the employer furnished the means by which an injury was inflicted.
7) whether the employer had reason to know that the employee would do the act in question.
8) whether the act involved the commission of a serious crime.

c. Misrepresentation
A principal is responsible for an agent's misrepresentation made within the scope of the agent's authority.

2. Liability for Independent Contractor's Torts
An employer is not liable for physical harm caused to a third person by an independent contractor's tort (except for hazardous activities, such as blasting operations, transportation of volatile chemicals, and use of poisonous gases, in which strict liability is imposed).

3. Liability for Agent's Crimes
A principal is not liable for an agent's crime, unless the principal participated. In some states, a principal may be liable for an agent's violating, in the course and scope of employment, such regulations as those governing sanitation, prices, weights, and the sale of liquor.

VI. AGENCY TERMINATION

A. TERMINATION BY ACT OF THE PARTIES
An agency ends when the time specified in the agreement expires, its purpose is achieved, a specified event occurs, or by mutual agreement. Both parties have the *power* to terminate an agency, but they may not have the *right* and may therefore be liable for breach of contract.

B. TERMINATION BY OPERATION OF LAW
Circumstances under which an agency terminates by operation of law include death or insanity of either party, destruction of the subject matter of the agency, changed circumstances, bankruptcy of either party, and war between the principal's and agent's countries.

C. NOTICE OF TERMINATION
If an agency terminates by operation of law because of death, insanity, or some other unforeseen circumstance, there is no duty to notify third persons, unless the agent's authority is coupled with an interest. If the parties themselves terminate the agency, the principal must inform any third parties who know of the agency that it has ended.

TRUE-FALSE QUESTIONS

(Answers at the Back of the Book)

_____ 1. Employees who deal with third parties are agents of their employers.

_____ 2. An agent owes his or her principal a duty to act in good faith.

_____ 3. An agent who fails to use reasonable diligence and skill in acting on behalf of his or her principal may be liable for breaching a duty of performance.

_____ 4. If an agent acts within the scope of authority, a disclosed principal is liable to a third party for contracts made by the agent.

_____ 5. A principal is not liable for harm caused to a third party by an agent acting in the scope of his or her employment.

_____ 6. An undisclosed principal is liable to a third party for contracts made by an agent acting within the scope of his or her authority.

_____ 7. Both parties to an agency have the right to terminate the agency at any time.

____   **8.**   If a principal does not ratify an otherwise unauthorized contract, the principal is not bound.

____   **9.**   Information obtained through an agency relationship is confidential.

____   **10.**   When an agent enters into a contract on behalf of a principal, the principal must ratify the contract to be bound.

FILL-IN QUESTIONS

(Answers at the Back of the Book)

An agent's use of reasonable diligence and skill is part of the agent's duty of _____ (obedience/performance). Informing a principal of all material matters that come to the agent's attention concerning the subject matter of the agency is an aspect of the agent's duty of _____ (accounting/notification). Acting solely for the benefit of the principal and not in the interest of the agent or a third party is part of the agent's duty of _____(loyalty/performance). Following all lawful and clearly stated instructions of the principal is an aspect of the agent's duty of _____ (loyalty/obedience). If an agent is required to keep and make available to the principal a record of all property and money received and paid out on behalf of the principal, this is part of the agent's duty of _____ (accounting/notification).

MULTIPLE-CHOICE QUESTIONS

(Answers at the Back of the Book)

____   **1.**   Adam is an officer for Beta Corporation. When acting for Beta in ordinary business situations, Adam is

a. an agent.
b. a principal.
c. an agent and a principal.
d. none of the above.

____   **2.**   Carol is a salesperson who works for Delta Products, Inc. In determining whether Carol is Delta's employee or an independent contractor, the most important factor is

a. the degree of control that Delta exercises over Carol.
b. the distinction between Delta's business and Carol's occupation.
c. the length of the working relationship between Delta and Carol.
d. the method of payment.

____   **3.**   Eagle Company hires Fran, who holds herself out as possessing special accounting skills, to act as its agent. As an agent, Fran must use the degree of skill or care expected of

a. an average, unskilled person.
b. a person having those special skills.
c. a reasonable person.
d. Eagle Company.

____   **4.**   Greg, a salesperson at Home Electronics Company, tells Irma, a customer, "Buy your computer here, and I'll set it up for less than what Home would charge." Irma buys the computer, Greg sets it up, and Irma pays Greg, who keeps the money. Greg has breached the duty of

a. loyalty.
b. notification.
c. obedience.
d. performance.

____   5.   Java Company hires Ken to manage one of its stores. Although their employment agreement says nothing that Ken being able to hire employees to work in the store, Ken has this authority. This is

a.   apparent authority.
b.   express authority.
c.   implied authority.
d.   none of the above.

____   6.   Local Distribution Company employs Mary as an agent. To terminate Mary's authority, Local Distribution must notify

a.   only Mary.
b.   only third parties who know of the agency relationship.
c.   Mary and third parties who know of the agency relationship.
d.   none of the above.

____   7.   National Timber, Inc., employs Owen as an agent. Owen enters into a contract with Pacific Lumber Company within the scope of his authority but without disclosing that he is acting as National's agent. National does not perform. Pacific can recover from

a.   National only.
b.   Owen only.
c.   National or Owen.
d.   none of the above.

____   8.   Quality Products Company requires its customers to pay by check. Ray, a Quality agent, tells customers that they can pay him with cash. Quality learns of Ray's collections, but takes no action to stop them. Ray steals some of the cash. Quality may be liable for the loss under the doctrine of

a.   apparent authority.
b.   express authority.
c.   implied authority.
d.   none of the above.

____   9.   Standard Delivery Company employs Tina as a driver. While driving within the scope of employment, Tina causes an accident in which Vic is injured. Vic can recover from

a.   Standard only.
b.   Tina only.
c.   Standard or Tina.
d.   none of the above.

____   10.   Wendy contracts with Zip Enterprises, Inc., to act as Zip's agent in a fraudulent scheme. Wendy does not successfully complete the scheme. Zip can recover from Wendy for

a.   breach of contract only.
b.   breach of the agent's duty of performance only.
c.   breach of contract and breach of the agent's duty of performance.
d.   none of the above.

SHORT ESSAY QUESTIONS

1.   What are the essential differences among the relationships of principal and agent, employer and employee, and employer and independent contractor? What factors indicate whether an individual is an employee or an independent contractor?

2.   In what situations is a principal liable for an agent's torts?

ISSUE SPOTTERS

(Answers at the Back of the Book)

1.   Ann, owner of Best Goods Company, employs Cathy as an administrative assistant. In Ann's absence, and without authority, Cathy represents herself as Ann and signs a promissory note in Ann's name. In what circumstance is Ann liable on the note?

2.   Don contracts with Eve to buy a certain horse for Eve, who asks Don not to reveal her identity. Don makes a deal with Farm Stables, the owner of the horse, and makes a down payment. Eve fails to pay the rest of the price. Farm Stables sues Don for breach of contract. Can Don hold Eve liable for whatever damages he has to pay?

3.   Great State Bank encourages its depositors to ask its advice concerning their investments. Holly, one of the bank's investment counselors, tells Ira to invest in Jiffy Corporation, although Holly knows its financial situation is precarious. If Ira loses money on the deal, can the bank be held liable?

Chapter 23:
Employment Law

WHAT THIS CHAPTER IS ABOUT

This chapter outlines the most significant laws regulating employment relationships, including those prohibiting employment discrimination.

CHAPTER OUTLINE

I. **WAGE-HOUR LAWS**
    Fair Labor Standards Act of 1938 (FLSA) covers all employees and regulates—

    A. **CHILD LABOR**
        Children under fourteen can deliver newspapers, work for their parents, and work in entertainment and agriculture. Children fourteen and older cannot work in hazardous occupations.

    B. **MAXIMUM HOURS**
        Employees who work more than forty hours per week must be paid no less than one and a half times their regular pay for all hours over forty. Executives, administrators, professionals, outside salespersons are exempt.

    C. **MINIMUM WAGE**
        A specified amount (periodically revised) must be paid to employees in covered industries. Wages include the reasonable cost to furnish employees with board, lodging, and other facilities.

II. **LABOR UNIONS**

    A. **NORRIS-LAGUARDIA ACT**
        Enacted in 1932. Restricts federal courts' power to issue injunctions against unions engaged in peaceful strikes, picketing, and boycotts.

    B. **NATIONAL LABOR RELATIONS ACT (NLRA) OF 1935**
        Established rights to bargain collectively and to strike, and—

        1. **Unfair Employer Practices**
            Prohibits interfering with union activities, discriminating against union employees, refusing to bargain with union, other practices.

        2. **National Labor Relations Board (NLRB)**
            Created to oversee union elections, prevent employers from engaging in unfair practices, investigate employers in response to employee charges of unfair labor practices, issue cease-and-desist orders.

    C. **LABOR-MANAGEMENT RELATIONS ACT (LMRA) OF 1947**
        Prohibits unions from refusing to bargain with employers, engaging in certain types of picketing, featherbedding, and other unfair practices. Preserves union shops, but allows states to pass right-to-work laws, which make it illegal to require union membership for employment.

    D. **LABOR-MANAGEMENT REPORTING AND DISCLOSURE ACT OF 1959**

1. **Union Business**
Requires elections of union officers under secret ballot; prohibits ex-convicts and Communists from holding union office; makes officials accountable for union property; allows members to participate in union meetings, nominate officers, vote in proceedings.

2. **Hot-Cargo Agreements**
Outlaws **hot-cargo agreements** (in which employers agree not to handle, use, or deal in non-union goods of other employers).

III.   WORKER HEALTH AND SAFETY

A.   OCCUPATIONAL SAFETY AND HEALTH ACT OF 1970
Attempts to ensure safe and healthful work conditions for most employees.

1. **Enforcement Agencies**

   a. **Occupational Safety and Health Administration (OSHA)**
   Inspects workplaces and issues safety standards, including standards covering employee exposure to harmful substances.

   b. **National Institute for Occupational Safety and Health**
   Researches safety and health problems and recommends standards for OSHA to adopt.

   c. **Occupational Safety and Health Review Commission**
   Hears appeals from actions taken by OSHA administrators.

2. **Procedures and Violations**
Employees file complaints of OSHA violations (employers cannot retaliate); employers must keep injury and illness records; employers must file accident reports directly to OSHA. Penalties are limited.

B.   WORKERS' COMPENSATION
State laws establish procedure for compensating workers injured on the job.

1. **No State Covers All Employees**
Often excluded are domestic workers, agricultural workers, temporary employees, and employees of common carriers.

2. **Requirements for Recovery**
There must be an employment relationship, and the injury must be accidental and occur on the job or in the course of employment.

3. **Filing a Claim**
An employee must notify the employer of an injury (usually within thirty days), and file a claim with a state agency within a certain period (sixty days to two years) from the time the injury is first noticed.

4. **Acceptance of Workers' Compensation Benefits Bars Suits**
An employee's acceptance of benefits bars the employee from suing for injuries caused by the employer's negligence.

IV.   INCOME SECURITY

A.   SOCIAL SECURITY AND MEDICARE

1. **Social Security**
The Social Security Act of 1935 provides for payments to persons who are retired, widowed, disabled, etc. Employers and employees must contribute under the Federal Insurance Contributions Act (FICA).

2. **Medicare**
   A health insurance program administered by the Social Security Administration for people sixty-five years of age and older and for some under sixty-five who are disabled.

B. **PRIVATE PENSION PLANS**
The Employee Retirement Income Security Act (ERISA) of 1974 empowers the Labor Management Services Administration of the Department of Labor to oversee those who operate private pension funds.

C. **UNEMPLOYMENT INSURANCE**
The Federal Unemployment Tax Act of 1935 created a state system that provides unemployment compensation to eligible individuals.

V. COBRA

The Consolidated Omnibus Budget Reconciliation Act (COBRA) of 1985 prohibits the elimination of a worker's medical, optical, or dental insurance on the termination of most workers' employment. Coverage must continue for up to 18 months (29 months in some cases). A worker pays the premium plus 2 percent.

VI. FAMILY AND MEDICAL LEAVE ACT (FMLA) OF 1993

Employers with fifty or more employees must provide them with up to twelve weeks of family or medical leave during any twelve-month period, continue health-care coverage during the leave, and guarantee employment in the same, or a comparable, position when the employee returns to work.

VII. WRONGFUL DISCHARGE

Under the employment at-will doctrine, either the employer or the employee may terminate an employment relationship at any time and for any reason (unless a contract or the law provides to the contrary).

A. **EXCEPTIONS BASED ON CONTRACT THEORY**
Some courts have held that an implied contract exists between an employer and an employee (if, for example, a personnel manual states that no employee will be fired without good cause). A few states have held that all employment contracts contain an implied covenant of good faith.

B. **EXCEPTIONS BASED ON TORT THEORY**
Discharge may give rise to a tort action for wrongful discharge.

C. **EXCEPTIONS BASED ON PUBLIC-POLICY**
An employer may not fire a worker for reasons that violate a public policy of the jurisdiction (for example, for refusing to violate the law).

VIII. WHISTLEBLOWER STATUTES

An employer cannot fire an employee in violation of a federal or state statute. If so, the employee may bring an action for wrongful discharge. Some state and federal statutes protect whistleblowers from retaliation. The False Claims Act of 1986 gives a whistleblower 15 to 25 percent of proceeds recovered from fraud.

IX. EMPLOYMENT DISCRIMINATION

Discrimination on the basis of race, color, religion, national origin, gender, age, or disability is prohibited. A class of persons defined by one or more of these criteria is known as a **protected class**.

A. **TITLE VII OF THE CIVIL RIGHTS ACT OF 1964**
Prohibits discrimination against employees, applicants, and union members on the basis of race, color, national origin, religion, and gender.

1. **Who Is Subject to Title VII?**
   Employers with fifteen or more employees, labor unions with fifteen or more members, labor unions that operate hiring halls, employment agencies, and federal, state, and local agencies.

2. **Procedures under Title VII**
   (1) Victim files a claim with the Equal Employment Opportunity Commission (EEOC); (2) EEOC investigates and seeks a voluntary settlement; (3) if no settlement is reached, EEOC may sue the employer; (4) if EEOC chooses not to sue, victim may file a lawsuit.

3. **Types of Discrimination**
   Title VII prohibits both intentional and unintentional discrimination.

   a. **Disparate-Treatment Discrimination**
      Intentional discrimination by an employer against an employee.

      1) *Prima Facie* **Case—Plaintiff's Side of the Case**
         Plaintiff must show (1) he or she is member of a protected class, (2) he or she applied and was qualified for the job, (3) he or she was rejected by the employer, (4) employer continued to seek applicants or filled position with person not in protected class.

      2) **Defense—Employer's Side of the Case**
         Employer must articulate a legal reason for not hiring plaintiff. To prevail, plaintiff must show that employer's reason is a pretext and that discriminatory intent motivated the decision.

   b. **Disparate-Impact Discrimination**

      1) **Types of Disparate-Impact Discrimination**
         Because of a requirement or hiring practice, (1) an employer's work force does not reflect the percentage of members of protected classes that characterizes qualified individuals in the local labor market, or (2) members of a protected class are excluded from the employer's work force at a substantially higher rate than nonmembers.

      2) *Prima Facie* **Case—Plaintiff's Side of the Case**
         Plaintiff must show connection between requirement or practice and disparity; no evidence of discriminatory intent is needed.

4. **Discrimination Based on Religion**
   Title VII prohibits employers and unions from discriminating against persons because of their religion.

5. **Discrimination Based on Gender**
   Employers cannot discriminate against employees on the basis of gender (unless the gender of the applicant can be proved essential to the job, etc.). The Pregnancy Discrimination Act of 1978 amended Title VII to include employees affected by pregnancy or related conditions.

6. **Sexual Harassment**

   a. **Forms of Harassment**
      (1) *Quid pro quo* harassment: when promotions, etc., are doled out on the basis of sexual favors; (2) hostile-environment harassment: when an employee is subjected to offensive sexual comments, etc. (Courts are split as to whether plaintiffs can sue for same-gender harassment.)

   b. **Harassment by Supervisors, Co-Workers, or Nonemployees**

      1) **When Is an Employer Liable?**
         If someone harasses an employee, and the employer knew, or should have known, and failed to take immediate corrective action, the employer may be liable.

      2) **Employer's Defense**
         (1) Employer took "reasonable care to prevent and correct promptly any sexually harassing behavior," and (2) employee suing for harassment failed to follow policies and procedures.

7. **Remedies under Title VII**
Reinstatement, back pay, retroactive promotions, damages.

   a. **Compensatory Damages**
   Available only in cases of intentional discrimination. Do not include back pay, interest on back pay, or other Title VII relief.

   b. **Punitive Damages**
   Only if an employer acted with malice or reckless indifference.

   c. **Limitations**
   Total damages are limited to specific amounts against specific employers (from $50,000 against those with one hundred or fewer employees to $300,000 against those with more than five hundred employees).

B. DISCRIMINATION BASED ON AGE

1. **Age Discrimination in Employment Act (ADEA) of 1967**
Prohibits employment discrimination on the basis of age (including mandatory retirement), by employers with twenty or more employees, against individuals forty years of age or older.

2. **Principles Are Similar to Title VII**
Requires the establishment of a *prima facie* case: plaintiff must show that he or she was (1) forty or older, (2) qualified for a position, and (3) rejected in circumstances that infer discrimination. The employer must articulate a legal reason; the plaintiff may show it is a pretext.

3. **State Employers**
Suits against state agencies by state employees for age discrimination are often dismissed because, under the Eleventh Amendment, a state is immune from a suit brought by a private individual in federal court unless the state consents to the suit.

C. DISCRIMINATION BASED ON DISABILITY
Under the Americans with Disabilities Act (ADA) of 1990, an employer cannot refuse to hire a person who is qualified but disabled.

1. **Procedures under the ADA**
A plaintiff must show he or she (1) has a disability, (2) is otherwise qualified for a job and (3) was excluded solely because of the disability. A suit may be filed only after a claim is pursued through the EEOC.

2. **Remedies under the ADA**
Reinstatement, back pay, some compensatory and punitive damages (for intentional discrimination), and certain other relief. Repeat violators may be fined up to $100,000.

3. **What is a Disability?**
"(1) [A] physical or mental impairment that substantially limits one or more of the major life activities . . . ; (2) a record of such impairment; or (3) being regarded as having such an impairment." Includes AIDS, morbid obesity, etc.; not homosexuality or kleptomania.

4. **Reasonable Accommodation**
For person with a disability, employer may have to make a reasonable accommodation (more flexible hours, new job assignment, different training materials or procedures)—but not an accommodation that will cause **undue hardship** (impose "significant difficulty or expense").

D. DEFENSES TO EMPLOYMENT DISCRIMINATION
The first defense is to assert that plaintiff did not prove discrimination. If discrimination is proved, an employer may attempt to justify it as—

1. **Business Necessity**
   An employer may show that there is a legitimate connection between a job requirement that discriminates and job performance.

2. **Bona Fide Occupational Qualification (BFOQ)**
   Another defense applies when discrimination against a protected class is essential to a job—that is, when a particular trait is a BFOQ. Generally restricted to cases in which gender is essential. Race can never be a BFOQ.

3. **Seniority Systems**
   An employer with a history of discrimination may have no members of protected classes in upper-level positions. If no present intent to discriminate is shown, and promotions, etc., are distributed according to a fair seniority system, the employer has a good defense.

E. **AFFIRMATIVE ACTION**
   An affirmative action program attempts to make up for past discrimination by giving members of protected classes preferential treatment in hiring or promotion. Such an employment program cannot use quotas or preferences for unqualified persons, and once it has succeeded, it must be changed or dropped.

F. **STATE STATUTES**
   Most states have statutes that prohibit the kinds of discrimination prohibited under federal legislation. State statutes also often protect individuals who are not protected under Title VII.

TRUE-FALSE QUESTIONS

(Answers at the Back of the Book)

_____ 1. There are no exceptions to the employment "at will" doctrine.

_____ 2. Employers are required to establish retirement plans for their employees.

_____ 3. Federal wage-hour laws cover all employers engaged in interstate commerce.

_____ 4. Whistleblower statutes protect employers from workers' disclosure of the employer's wrongdoing.

_____ 5. Employers can agree with unions not to handle, use, or deal in non-union-produced goods.

_____ 6. In a sexual harassment case, an employer cannot be held liable if an employee did the harassing.

_____ 7. Employment discrimination against persons with a physical or mental impairment that substantially limits their everyday activities is prohibited.

_____ 8. All employers are subject to Title VII of the Civil Rights Act of 1964.

_____ 9. Disparate-treatment discrimination occurs when an employer intentionally discriminates against an employee.

_____ 10. Title VII prohibits employers and unions from discriminating against persons because of their religion.

FILL-IN QUESTIONS

(Answers at the Back of the Book)

Under the employment-at-will doctrine, _____ (either/neither) party may terminate an employment relationship at any time and for any reason _____ (unless/even if) a contract provides to the contrary. An employee who is fired in violation of a federal or state statute _____ (may/may not) bring an action for wrongful discharge. _____ (Some/No) courts have held that an implied contract exists between an employer and an employee. _____ (All/A few states) have held that all employment contracts contain an implied covenant of good faith. An employer _____ (may/may not) fire a worker for reasons that violate a public policy of the jurisdiction.

MULTIPLE-CHOICE QUESTIONS

(Answers at the Back of the Book)

____ 1. Fast Jack is a fast-food restaurant that employs minors. Fast Jack is subject to the federal child labor, minimum-wage, and maximum-hour laws in

a. the Consolidated Omnibus Budget Reconciliation Act.
b. the Fair Labor Standards Act.
c. the Family and Medical Leave Act.
d. the Labor-Management Relations Act.

____ 2. Eve, an employee of CamCorp, is injured. For Eve to receive *workers' compensation*, the injury must be

a. accidental and arise out of a preexisting disease or condition.
b. accidental and occur on the job or in the course of employment.
c. intentional and arise out of a preexisting disease or condition.
d. intentional and occur on the job or in the course of employment.

____ 3. Ron is an employee of National Sales Company. Both Ron and National make contributions to the federal social security system under

a. the Federal Insurance Contributions Act.
b. the Federal Payments Act.
c. the Federal Retirement Income Security Act.
d. the Federal Unemployment Tax Act.

____ 4. ABC Box Corporation provides health insurance for its 150 employees, including Dian. When Dian takes twelve weeks' leave to care for her child, she

a. can continue her heath insurance at her expense.
b. can continue her heath insurance at ABC's expense.
c. is entitled to "leave pay" equal to twelve weeks' of health insurance coverage.
d. loses her heath insurance immediately on taking leave.

____ 5. Mega Corporation provides health insurance for its employees. When Mega closes one of its offices and terminates the employees, the employees

a. are entitled to "severance pay" equal to twelve weeks' of health insurance coverage.
b. can continue their heath insurance at Mega's expense.
c. can continue their heath insurance at their expense.
d. lose their heath insurance immediately on termination of employment.

____ 6. Bob and Carol work for Delta Company. Bob is Carol's supervisor. During work, Bob touches Carol in ways that she perceives as sexually offensive. Carol resists the advances. Bob cuts her pay. Delta is

a. liable, because Bob's conduct constituted sexual harassment.
b. liable, because Carol resisted Bob's advances.
c. not liable, because Bob's conduct was not job-related.
d. not liable, because Carol resisted Bob's advances.

____ 7. Kay, who is hearing impaired, applies for a position with Local Company. Kay is qualified but is refused the job and sues Local. To succeed under the Americans with Disabilities Act, Kay must show that

    a. Kay was willing to make a "reasonable accommodation" for Local.
    b. Kay would not have to accept "significant additional costs" to work for Local.
    c. Local refused to make a "reasonable accommodation" for Kay.
    d. Local would not have to accept "significant additional costs" to hire Kay.

____ 8. Donna applies to Eagle Corporation for an administrative assistant's job, which requires certain typing skills. Donna cannot type but tells Eagle that she is willing to learn. Eagle does not hire Donna, who later sues. To successfully defend against the suit under Title VII, Eagle must show that

    a. being a member of the majority is a BFOQ.
    b. Donna was not willing to learn to type.
    c. Eagle has a valid business necessity defense.
    d. Eagle's work force reflects the same percentage of members of a protected class that characterizes qualified individuals in the local labor market.

____ 9. Standard Corporation terminates Tom, who sues on the basis of age discrimination. To succeed under the Age Discrimination in Employment Act, Tom must show that at the time of the discharge, he was

    a. forty or older.
    b. forty or younger.
    c. replaced with someone forty or older.
    d. replaced with someone forty or younger.

____ 10. National Company requires job applicants to pass certain physical tests. Only a few female applicants can pass the tests, but it they pass, they are hired. To successfully defend against a suit on this basis under Title VII, National must show that

    a. any discrimination is not intentional.
    b. being a male is a BFOQ.
    c. passing the tests is a business necessity.
    d. some men cannot pass the tests.

SHORT ESSAY QUESTIONS

1. What is the employment-at-will doctrine? What are its exceptions?

2. What does the Americans with Disabilities Act require employers to do?

ISSUE SPOTTERS

(Answers at the Back of the Book)

1. Standard Manufacturing Company (SMC) issues an employee handbook that states employees will be discharged only for good cause. One day, Greg, an SMC supervisor, says to Larry, "I don't like your looks. You're fired." Is SMC liable for breach of contract?

2. Phil applies for a job at Quality Corporation for which he is well qualified, but for which he is rejected. Quality continues to seek applicants and eventually fills the position with a person who is not a member of a minority. Could Phil succeed in a suit against Quality for discrimination?

3. Paula, a disabled person, applies for a job at Quantity Corporation for which she is well qualified, but for which she is rejected. Quantity continues to seek applicants and eventually fills the position with a person who is not disabled. Could Paula succeed in a suit against Quantity for discrimination?

CUMULATIVE HYPOTHETICAL PROBLEM FOR UNIT SEVEN—INCLUDING CHAPTERS 22–23

(Answers at the Back of the Book)

Donna, Earl, Frank, Gail, Hal, Ira, Jane, Karen, Larry, and Mike are employees of International Sales Corporation (ISC).

1. Donna, who works in ISC's warehouse, is injured on the job. Donna may NOT collect workers' compensation benefits if she

a. files a civil suit against a third party based on the injury.
b. intentionally caused her own injury.
c. was injured as a result of a co-worker's act.
d. worked for ISC for less than sixty days.

2. Ira voluntarily resigns from ISC. Under COBRA, Ira's group health insurance that was in effect when he worked for ISC

a. ceases if Ira was not at the normal retirement age when he resigned.
b. ceases if Ira was not part of an ISC reduction in force.
c. may be continued for at least eighteen months at Ira's expense.
d. may be continued for at least eighteen months at ISC's expense.

3. Earl retires from ISC at the age of sixty-five. Frank retires at sixty-seven. Because of a disability, Gail, after fifteen years, is unable to continue working for ISC. Hal is discharged from ISC as part of a reduction in force. All of the following benefits are part of Social Security EXCEPT

a. Earl's government retirement payments.
b. Frank's Medicare payments.
c. Gail's government disability payments.
d. Hal's unemployment benefits.

4. Four employees file suits against ISC, alleging discrimination. Title VII of the Civil Rights Act of 1964 covers all of the following EXCEPT Jane's suit alleging discrimination on the basis of

a. age.
b. gender.
c. race.
d. religion.

5. Karen, an ISC manager, wants to institute a policy of mandatory retirement for all employees at age sixty-four. Larry, an ISC manager, wants to discharge Mike, who is age sixty-seven, for cause. Under federal antidiscrimination law

a. only Karen's wish can be granted.
b. only Larry's wish can be granted.
c. both Karen's and Larry's wishes can be granted.
d. none of the above.

QUESTIONS ON THE FOCUS ON LEGAL REASONING FOR UNIT SEVEN—*REDI-FLOORS, INC. V. SONENBERG CO.*

(Answers at the Back of the Book)

____ 1. Nora contracts with Owen on behalf of Nora's principal Pat, without disclosing Pat's identity. Under the holding in *Redi-Floors, Inc. v. Sonenberg Co.*, Owen could pursue a breach of contract claim against

    a. Nora only.
    b. Pat only.
    c. Nora and Pat jointly.
    d. Nora or Pat, but not both.

____ 2. In the previous question, suppose that Owen files claims jointly against Nora and Pat, and that this is unsuccessful. In the opinion of the majority in *Redi-Floors, Inc. v. Sonenberg Co.*, Owen might be able to maintain an action solely against Nora if the court

    a. directed a verdict in Nora's favor.
    b. directed a verdict in Pat's favor.
    c. issued a written judgment order in Nora's favor.
    d. issued a written judgment order in Pat's favor.

____ 3. Under the facts in the previous questions, according to the reasoning of the dissent in *Redi-Floors, Inc. v. Sonenberg Co.*, Owen could not subsequently maintain an action solely against Nora because the court

    a. directed a verdict in Nora's favor.
    b. directed a verdict in Pat's favor.
    c. issued a written judgment order in Nora's favor.
    d. issued a written judgment order in Pat's favor.

Chapter 24:
Sole Proprietorships, Partnerships, and Limited Liability Companies

WHAT THIS CHAPTER IS ABOUT

This chapter sets out the features of two of the major traditional business forms—sole proprietorships and partnerships—and other forms, including limited liability companies (LLCs) and limited liability partnerships (LLPs).

CHAPTER OUTLINE

I. SOLE PROPRIETORSHIPS
The simplest form of business—the owner is the business.

A. ADVANTAGES
The proprietor takes all the profits. Easier to start than other kinds of businesses (few legal forms involved); has more flexibility (proprietor is free to make all decisions); owner pays only personal income tax on profits.

B. DISADVANTAGES
The proprietor has all the risk (unlimited liability for all debts); limited opportunity to raise capital; the business dissolves when the owner dies.

II. THE LAW GOVERNING PARTNERSHIPS
A partnership arises from an agreement between two or more persons to carry on a business for profit. The partnership is governed by this agreement, the principles of agency law, and the Uniform Partnership Act (UPA) or the Revised Uniform Partnership Act (RUPA).

A. DEFINITION OF PARTNERSHIP
"[A]n association of two or more persons to carry on as co-owners a business for profit" [UPA 6(1)].

1. Partnership Status
There are three essential elements to a partnership:

a. A sharing of profits or losses.
b. A joint ownership of the business.
c. An equal right in the management of the business.

2. Entity versus Aggregate

a. **Partnership as an Entity**
A partnership is treated as an entity for certain purposes. For example, generally a partnership can sue and be sued in the firm name. A partnership can own property as an entity.

b. **Aggregate Theory of Partnership**
If a partnership is not regarded as a separate entity, it is treated as an aggregate of the individual partners. For example, a partnership is not a tax-paying entity.

B. PARTNERSHIP FORMATION
A partnership agreement states the intention to create a partnership, contribute capital, share profits and losses, and participate in management.

1. The Partnership Agreement
The agreement can be oral, written, or implied by conduct. Some must be in writing under the Statute of Frauds (see Chapter 10). Partners can agree to any terms that are not illegal or contrary to public policy.

2. Partnership Duration

a. Partnership for a Term
The agreement can specify the duration of the partnership in terms of a date or completion of a particular project. Dissolution without all partners' consent before expiration is a breach of the agreement.

b. Partnership at Will
No duration is set; any partner can dissolve a partnership any time.

3. The Corporation as Partner
Many states have restrictions on corporations becoming partners. The Revised Model Business Corporation Act allows corporations to contract and to incur liabilities; the UPA permits a corporation to be a partner [UPA 2].

4. Partnership by Estoppel
When parties who are not partners hold themselves out as partners and make representations that third persons rely on in dealing with them, liability is imposed. A partner who misrepresents a nonpartner is also liable (and the nonpartner's acts may bind the partnership).

C. RIGHTS AMONG PARTNERS

1. Interest in the Partnership
Unless partners agree otherwise, profits and losses are shared equally [UPA 18(a)]. A partner's interest can be assigned, and creditors can attach it by obtaining a charging order [UPA 28].

2. Management Rights

a. Ordinarily, the Majority Rules
"All partners have equal rights in the management and conduct of partnership business" [UPA 18(e)]. Each partner has one vote.

b. When Unanimous Consent Is Required
(1) Alter the essential nature of the firm's business or capital structure; (2) admit new partners or enter a new business [UPA 18(g), (h)]; (3) assign firm property into a trust for the benefit of creditors; (4) dispose of the firm's goodwill; (5) confess judgment against the firm or submit firm claims to arbitration; (6) undertake any act that would make conduct of partnership business impossible [UPA 9(3)]; or (7) amend the partnership articles.

3. Compensation
Doing partnership business is a partner's duty and not compensable. On the death of a partner, a surviving partner is entitled to compensation to wind up partnership affairs [UPA 18(f)].

4. Inspection of Books
A partner has a right to full information concerning the conduct of partnership business [UPA 20]. Partnership books must be kept at the firm's principal business office [UPA 19].

5. Accounting of Assets
A partner has a right to a formal accounting—

a. When the partnership agreement provides for it.
b. When a partner is wrongfully excluded from the business or books.
c. When a partner withholds profits or benefits belonging to the firm.
d. When circumstances "render it just and reasonable."
e. On dissolution.

6. **Property Rights**

   a. **Right to Share in the Partnership Profits**
   A partner has a right to share in the profits.

   b. **Right to Partnership Property**
   A partner is co-owner with his or her partners of partnership property, holding it as a tenant in partnership [UPA 25(1)].

      1) **Each Partner Has Equal Rights**
      Each partner can possess partnership property for business purposes or in satisfaction of firm debts, but cannot sell, assign, or deal with the property other than for partnership purposes without the consent of all of the partners.

      2) **If a Partner Dies**
      Surviving partners, not the heirs of the deceased, have a right of survivorship to the property (they must account to the decedent's estate for the value [UPA 25(2)]).

D. DUTIES AND LIABILITIES OF PARTNERS

1. **Fiduciary Duties**
   Partners (1) must act in good faith for the benefit of the partnership, (2) must subordinate his or her personal interests to the interests of the firm if a conflict arises, and (3) must account to the partnership for profits or benefits derived in a partnership transaction.

2. **Authority of Partners**
   Agency concepts apply to partners' authority. Implied authority is determined by the character and scope of the partnership business and the customary nature of the business. Normally, partners exercise all implied powers reasonably necessary to carry on the business [UPA 11].

3. **Joint Liability**
   In most states, partners are jointly liable for partnership debts and contracts [UPA 15(b)] (each partner is liable for the entire debt; if one pays, the partnership or the other partners must reimburse that partner [UPA 18(b)]). To bring a successful claim against the partnership, a plaintiff must name all the partners as defendants.

4. **Joint and Several Liability**
   In some states, partners are jointly and severally liable for partnership debts and contracts. In all states, partners are jointly and severally liable for torts and breaches of trust [UPA 15(a)] (partner who commits a tort must reimburse the partnership for any damages it pays).

5. **Liability of Incoming Partner**
   Liable for partnership debts incurred before his or her admission only to the extent of his or her interest in the partnership [UPA 17].

E. PARTNERSHIP TERMINATION
Caused by any change in the relations of the partners that shows unwillingness or inability to carry on partnership business [UPA 29]. To continue the business, a partner can organize a new partnership.

1. **Dissolution**
   Occurs when a partner ceases to associate with the carrying on of the business. Terminates the right of a partnership to exist as a going concern, but the partnership remains long enough to wind up its affairs.

   a. **Dissolution by Acts of Partners**

      1) **Dissolution by Agreement**
         The partnership agreement can state events that will dissolve the firm. Partners can agree to dissolve the partnership early.

      2) **Partner's Power to Withdraw**
         No person can be compelled to be a partner. A partner's withdrawal dissolves the partnership.

      3) **Transfer of a Partner's Interest**
         Transfer of a partner's interest or sale of the interest for the benefit of creditors [UPA 28] leads to judicial dissolution.

   b. **Dissolution by Operation of Law**

      1) **Death**
         Death of a partner dissolves the firm, even if the partnership agreement provides for carrying on the business.

      2) **Bankruptcy**
         Bankruptcy of a partner (or the firm) dissolves a partnership.

      3) **Illegality**
         Dissolution is caused by an event that makes it unlawful for either (1) partnership to continue, unless partners change nature of the business and continue, or (2) any partner to continue.

   c. **Dissolution by Judicial Decree**
      A court can dissolve a partnership for a partner's mental incompetency, incapacity, or improper conduct; if the firm's business can be run only at a loss; or other circumstances [UPA 32].

   d. **Notice of Dissolution**
      Unless the other partners have notice, a withdrawing partner will continue to be bound to all contracts created for the firm. A third person who has extended credit to the partnership must receive actual notice. For others, constructive notice is sufficient.

2. **Winding Up**
   Involves collecting and preserving partnership assets, paying debts, and accounting to each partner for the value of his or her interest. No new obligations can be created on behalf of the partnership.

   a. **Distribution of Assets**
      Priorities for the distribution of a partnership's assets are [UPA 40(b)]: (1) payment to third party creditors; (2) refund of loans made to or for the firm by a partner; (3) return of capital contribution to a partner; and (4) the balance to partners proportionate to their shares in the profits.

   b. **If the Partnership's Liabilities Are Greater Than Its Assets**
      The partners bear the losses in the same proportion in which they shared the profits.

III.   LIMITED LIABILITY COMPANIES

A. THE NATURE OF AN LLC
A limited liability company (LLC) is a hybrid form of business enterprise that offers the limited liability of a corporation with the tax advantages of a partnership.

B. LLC FORMATION
Articles of organization must be filed with the state. Certain information is required.

C. JURISDICTIONAL REQUIREMENTS
An LLC is a citizen of every state of which its members are citizens.

D. ADVANTAGES OF AN LLC
Taxed as a partnership; liability of members is limited to the amount of their investment; members can participate in management; corporations, partnerships, and foreign investors can be members; no limit on the number of members (in many states, one is enough).

E. DISADVANTAGES OF AN LLC
Because the LLC is a new form, little case law exists; until uniform statutes are adopted by most states, an LLC with multistate operations may face difficulties.

F. THE LLC OPERATING AGREEMENT
Provisions relate to management, division of profits, transfer of membership, what events trigger dissolution, and so on. In the absence of an agreement, state statutes govern. If there is no statute, the principles of partnership law apply.

G. MANAGEMENT OF AN LLC

1. Member-Managed LLC
Unless members agree otherwise, all members participate in management and voting rights are usually proportional to capital contributions. An agreement may set governing procedures (in contrast to corporations, which are subject to specific state requirements).

2. Manager-Managed LLC
Members may designate a group to run the firm. If so, the members' interests in the firm may qualify as securities.

IV. LIMITED LIABILITY PARTNERSHIPS
Professionals may organize as a limited liability partnership (LLP) to enjoy the tax advantages of a partnership, while avoiding personal liability for the wrongdoing of other partners.

A. LIABILITY IN AN LLP
In an LLP, professionals avoid personal liability for malpractice of other partners.

B. FAMILY LIMITED LIABILITY PARTNERSHIPS
This is a limited liability partnership (LLP) in which most of the partners are related. All partners must be natural persons or persons acting in a fiduciary capacity for natural persons. Family-owned farms may benefit from this form.

V. LIMITED PARTNERSHIPS
Limited partnerships must include at least one general partner and one or more limited partners. General partners assume management responsibility and liability for all partnership debts.

A. FORMATION OF A LIMITED PARTNERSHIP
The partners sign a certificate of limited partnership, which requires information similar to that found in a corporate charter (see Chapter 25). The certificate is filed with the secretary of state [RULPA 101(7), 201].

B. RIGHTS AND LIABILITIES OF PARTNERS

1. Rights of Limited Partners
Essentially the same rights as general partners. Can generally assign their interests in the partnership [RULPA 702, 704]. Can also sue on behalf of the firm if general partners refuse [RULPA 1001].

2. Liabilities of Limited Partners

a. Limited Liability to Creditors of the Partnership
Liable to the extent of any contribution that is promised to the firm or any part of a contribution that was withdrawn [RULPA 502].

b. Personal Liability for Defects in Formation

1) If a Firm Is Organized in an Improper Manner
If the limited partner fails to withdraw on discovery of the defect, he or she can be personally liable to the firm's creditors.

2) If There Is a False Statement in the Partnership Certificate
If a limited partner knows of the statement, he or she may be liable to any person who relies on it [RULPA 207].

3) How to Avoid Future Liability
File an amendment or corrected certificate or renounce an interest in the profits of the partnership [RULPA 304].

3. Limited Partners and Management
Generally, participating in management results in personal liability for partnership debt, if creditors knew of participation [RULPA 303].

C. DISSOLUTION

1. General Partners—Dissolution
Retirement, death, or mental incompetence of a general partner dissolves the firm, unless continued by other general partners [RULPA 801]. Illegality, expulsion, or bankruptcy of general partner dissolves a firm.

2. Limited Partners—No Dissolution
Death or assignment of interest of a limited partner does not dissolve the firm [RULPA 702, 704, 705], nor does personal bankruptcy.

3. Court Decree
A limited partnership can be dissolved by court decree [RULPA 802].

4. Priority to Assets on Dissolution
(1) Creditors, including partners who are creditors; (2) partners and former partners receive unpaid distributions of partnership assets and, except as otherwise agreed, a return on their contributions and amounts proportionate to their share of distributions [RULPA 201(a)(10), 804].

D. LIMITED LIABILITY LIMITED PARTNERSHIPS
This form is similar to a limited partnership, except that the liability of all partners in a limited liability limited partnership (LLLP) is limited to the amount of their investment in the firm.

VI. SPECIAL BUSINESS FORMS

A. JOINT VENTURE
Treated much like a partnership, but created for a single transaction or limited activity.

B. **SYNDICATE**
A group of individuals financing a project; may exist as a corporation, a partnership, or no legally recognized form.

C. **JOINT STOCK COMPANY**
Usually treated like a partnership (members have personal liability, etc.), but like a corporation, ownership is by shareholders.

D. **BUSINESS TRUST**
Legal ownership and management of the property of the business is in one or more trustees; profits are distributed to beneficiaries, who are not personally responsible for the debts of the trust. Resembles a corporation.

E. **COOPERATIVE**
An association organized to provide an economic service without profit to its members (or shareholders). Incorporated cooperatives are subject to state laws governing nonprofit corporations. Unincorporated cooperatives are often treated like partnerships.

F. **FRANCHISE**
A **franchise** is any arrangement in which the owner of a trademark, a trade name, or a copyright has licensed others to use it in selling goods or services. Not a business form, but a way of doing business: any business form can buy and sell a franchise.

TRUE-FALSE QUESTIONS

(Answers at the Back of the Book)

_____ 1. In a sole proprietorship, the owner and the business are entirely separate.

_____ 2. A partnership is an association of two or more persons to carry on, as co-owners, a business for profit.

_____ 3. In most states, a partnership cannot exist unless a certificate of partnership is filed with a state.

_____ 4. The liability of a general partner for partnership debts is limited to the amount of capital he or she invests in the partnership.

_____ 5. The dissolution of a partnership occurs when any partner ceases to be associated with the carrying on of partnership business.

_____ 6. A limited liability company does not offer the limited liability of a corporation.

_____ 7. In a limited partnership, the liability of each partner is limited to the amount of capital he or she has invested in the partnership.

_____ 8. In a limited liability limited partnership, the liability of each partner is limited to the amount of capital he or she has invested in the partnership.

_____ 9. In a limited liability company, members do not have to participate in the management of the company.

_____ 10. Unless the members agree otherwise, all profits of the LLC will be divided equally.

FILL-IN QUESTIONS

(Answers at the Back of the Book)

In most states, partners _____ (are/are not) subject to joint liability on partnership debts, contracts, and torts. Joint liability means that if a third party sues a partner on a partnership _____ (obligation/tort), the partner has the right to insist that the other partners be sued with him or her. If the third party does not sue all of the partners, those partners who are _____ (not sued/sued) cannot be required to pay a judgment. In that circumstance, the assets of the partnership _____ (can/cannot) be used to satisfy the judgment. The third party's release of one partner _____ (does not release/releases) the other partners. In most states, to bring a successful claim against a partnership on a debt or contract, a plaintiff _____ (may/must) name all the partners as defendants.

MULTIPLE-CHOICE QUESTIONS

(Answers at the Back of the Book)

_____   1.   Adam owns Best Enterprises, a sole proprietorship. Adam's liability for the obligations of the business is

a. limited by state statute.
b. limited to the amount of his original investment.
c. limited to the total amount of capital Adam invests in the business.
d. unlimited.

_____   2.   Carl holds himself out as a partner of Delta Associates, a partnership, even though he has no connection to the firm. Carl obtains a personal loan based on this misrepresentation. Carl's default on the loan will result in

a. Carl being held solely liable for the amount.
b. Delta being held solely liable for the amount.
c. Carl and Delta being held jointly liable for the amount.
d. none of the above.

_____   3.   Holly owns International Imports. She hires Jay as a salesperson, agreeing to pay $10.00 per hour plus 10 percent of his sales. Holly and Jay are

a. partners for the duration of Jay's employment.
b. not partners, because Holly pays Jay an hourly wage.
c. not partners, because Jay does not have an ownership interest or management rights in the business.
d. not partners, because Jay receives a commission, not a share of the profits.

_____   4.   Lora and Mark are partners in New Tech Group. Lora's withdrawal from the partnership will cause

a. the dissolution of the partnership.
b. the temporary suspension of partnership activity.
c. the termination of the partnership's legal existence.
d. none of the above.

_____   5.   Vicky and Warren do business as a partnership under the name United Digital. United

a. is a tax-paying entity.
b. is required to file an information return but is not a tax-paying entity.
c. pays 1/2 of the taxes if there are only two partners.
d. pays 1/3 of the taxes if there are only two partners.

_____   6.   Jay is a limited partner in Kappa Sales, a limited partnership. Jay is liable for the firm's debts

a. in proportion to the total number of partners in the firm.
b. to the extent of his capital contribution.
c. to the full extent of the debts.
d. none of the above.

____   **7.**   Larry is a member of Macro Services, a limited liability company. Larry is liable for the firm's debts

    a. in proportion to the total number of members in the firm.
    b. to the extent of his capital contribution.
    c. to the full extent of the debts.
    d. none of the above.

____   **8.**   Carol and Don form E-Stuff as a limited liability company. They can participate in the firm's management

    a. only to the extent that they assume personal liability for the firm's debts.
    b. only to the extent of the amount of their investment in the firm.
    c. to any extent.
    d. to no extent.

____   **9.**   Drs. Kay and Lyle are partners in a medical clinic, which is organized as a limited liability partnership. Kay manages the clinic. A court holds Lyle liable in a malpractice suit. Kay is liable

    a. in proportion to the total number of partners in the firm.
    b. to the extent of her capital contribution.
    c. to the full extent of the liability.
    d. none of the above.

____   **10.**   Mike, Nora, and Owen want to form a limited partnership. A limited partnership must have at least

    a. one general partner and one limited partner.
    b. one general partner and two limited partners.
    c. two limited partners.
    d. none of the above.

SHORT ESSAY QUESTIONS

1. What are the advantages of doing business as a limited liability company?

2. Compare and contrast the following characteristics of general partnerships and limited partnerships: creation, sharing of profits and loses, liability, capital contribution, management, duration, assignment, and priorities on liquidation.

ISSUE SPOTTERS

(Answers at the Back of the Book)

1. Fred and Gail are partners in a delivery business. When business is slow, without Gail's knowledge, Fred leases the delivery vehicles as moving vans. Because the vehicles would otherwise be sitting idle in a parking lot, can Fred keep the lease money?

2. Hal plans to open a sporting goods store, and to hire Ira and Jill. Hal will invest only his own capital. He does not expect to make a profit for at least eighteen months and to make little profit for the first three years. He hopes to expand eventually. Which form of business organization would be most appropriate?

3. Ace Construction and Bayside Developers form a joint venture. Central Processing and Delta Data form a joint stock company. Efficient Systems and Fast Products form an unincorporated cooperative. What do these forms of business organization have in common?

Chapter 25:
Corporate Formation, Financing, and Termination

WHAT THIS CHAPTER IS ABOUT

This chapter covers corporate rights, powers, classifications, formation, financing, and termination. Most corporations are formed under state law, and a majority of states follow some version of the Revised Model Business Corporation Act (RMBCA).

CHAPTER OUTLINE

I. THE NATURE OF THE CORPORATION

A. THE CONSTITUTIONAL RIGHTS OF CORPORATIONS
A corporation is recognized by the law as a "person" and, under the Bill of Rights, has the same rights as a natural person (see Chapter 1). Only officers and employees have the right against self-incrimination, however, and the privileges and immunities clause does not protect corporations.

B. CORPORATE PERSONNEL
Shareholders elect a board of directors, which is responsible for overall management and hires corporate officers to run daily operations. Shareholders normally are not liable for corporate obligations beyond the extent of their investments.

C. CORPORATE TAXATION
Corporate profits are taxed twice: as income to the corporation and, when distributed as dividends, as income to the shareholders.

D. TORTS AND CRIMINAL ACTS
A corporation is liable for the torts committed by its agents within the course and scope of employment. A corporation may be held liable for the crimes of its employees and agents if the punishment for the crimes can be applied to a corporation.

II. CORPORATE POWERS

A. EXPRESS AND IMPLIED POWERS
Express powers are in (in order of priority) the U.S. Constitution, state constitution, state statutes, articles of incorporation, bylaws, and board resolutions. A corporation has the *implied* power to perform all acts reasonably appropriate and necessary to accomplish its purposes.

B. *ULTRA VIRES* DOCTRINE
Ultra vires acts are beyond the purposes stated in the articles. Most such acts have involved contracts (which generally are enforced [RMBCA 3.04]). Courts usually allow any legal action a firm takes to profit shareholders.

III. CLASSIFICATION OF CORPORATIONS

A. **DOMESTIC, FOREIGN, AND ALIEN CORPORATIONS**
A corporation is a **domestic corporation** in the state in which it incorporated, a **foreign corporation** in other states, and an **alien corporation** in other countries. A foreign corporation normally must obtain a certificate of authority to do business in any state except its home state.

B. **PUBLIC AND PRIVATE CORPORATIONS**
A **public corporation** is formed by the government to meet a political or governmental purpose (the U.S. Postal Service, AMTRAK). A **private corporation** is created for private benefit and is owned by private persons.

C. **NONPROFIT CORPORATIONS**
Corporations formed without a profit-making purpose (private hospitals, educational institutions, charities, and religious organizations).

D. **CLOSE CORPORATIONS**
To qualify as a **close corporation**, a firm must have a limited number of shareholders, and restrict its issue and transfer of stock.

   1. **Advantage**
   Exempt from most of the nonessential formalities of corporate operation (bylaws, annual meetings, etc. [RMBCA 7.32]).

   2. **Management**
   Resembles that of a sole proprietorship or a partnership—one or a few shareholders usually hold the positions of directors and officers.

   3. **Transfer of Shares**
   Often restricted by stipulating that shareholders offer their shares to the corporation or other shareholders before offering them to outsiders.

E. **S CORPORATIONS**

   1. **Requirements**
   Must be a domestic corporation; must not be a member of an affiliated group of corporations; shareholders must be individuals, estates, certain trusts, or (in some cases) corporations; must have thirty-five or fewer shareholders; can have only one class of stock; no shareholder can be a nonresident alien.

   2. **Advantages**
   Shareholders can use corporate losses to offset other income; only a single tax on corporate income is imposed at individual income tax rates at the shareholder level (whether or not it is distributed).

F. **PROFESSIONAL CORPORATIONS**
Generally subject to the law governing ordinary corporations.

   1. **Limited Liability**
   A shareholder in a professional corporation is protected from liability for torts (except malpractice) committed by other members.

   2. **Unlimited Liability**
   A court might regard a professional corporation as a partnership, in which each partner may be liable for the malpractice of the others.

IV. CORPORATE FORMATION

A. **PROMOTIONAL ACTIVITIES**
Promoters take the first steps in organizing a corporation: issue a prospectus (see Chapter 29) and secure the corporate charter (see below).

1. **Promoter's Liability**
Personally liable on preincorporation contracts, unless the contracting party agrees otherwise. This liability continues after incorporation unless the third party releases the promoter or the corporation assumes the contract by novation (see Chapter 11).

2. **Subscriptions**
Subscribers (who agree to buy stock in a future corporation) become shareholders as soon as the corporation is formed or as soon as the corporation accepts their subscription agreement with the promoter.

   a. **Subscribers' Liability**
   A subscription is irrevocable for six months unless the parties agree otherwise [RMBCA 6.20]. In some states, a subscriber can, without liability, revoke an offer to buy before the corporation accepts.

   b. **Corporation's Liability**
   Preincorporation subscriptions are continuing offers to buy stock. On or after its formation, a corporation can choose to accept the offer.

B. INCORPORATION PROCEDURES

1. **State Chartering**
Some states offer more advantageous tax or incorporation provisions.

2. **Articles of Incorporation**
The articles include basic information about the corporation and serve as a primary source of authority for its organization and functions.

   a. **Corporate Name**
   Cannot be the same as, or deceptively similar to, the name of a corporation doing business in the state.

   b. **Duration**
   A corporation can have perpetual existence in most states.

   c. **Nature and Purpose**
   The intended business activities of the corporation must be specified. Stating a general corporate purpose is usually sufficient.

   d. **Capital Structure**
   The amount of stock authorized for issuance; its valuation; and other information as to equity, capital, and credit must be outlined.

   e. **Internal Organization**
   Management structure can be described in bylaws later.

   f. **Registered Office and Agent**
   Usually, the registered office is the principal office of the corporation; the agent is a person designated to receive legal documents on behalf of the corporation.

   g. **Incorporators**
   Incorporators (some states require only one) must sign the articles when they are submitted to the state; often this is their only duty, and they need have no other interest in the corporation.

3. **Certificate of Incorporation (Corporate Charter)**
The articles of incorporation are sent to the appropriate state official (usually the secretary of state). Many states issue a certificate of incorporation authorizing the corporation to conduct business.

4. **First Organizational Meeting (After the Charter Is Granted)**

   a. **Who Holds the Meeting**
   The incorporators or the board; the business conducted depends on state law, the nature of the corporation's business, the provisions of the articles, and the wishes of the promoters.

   b. **Adoption of the Bylaws**
   The most important function of the first organizational meeting.

V.   CORPORATE STATUS

A. IMPROPER INCORPORATION
On the basis of improper incorporation—

1. **Shareholders May Be Personally Liable for Corporate Obligations**
   A person attempting to enforce a contract or bring a tort suit against the corporation could seek to make the shareholders personally liable.

2. **Third Parties May Avoid Liability to the Corporation**
   If a corporation seeks to enforce a contract, the defaulting party who learns of a defect in incorporation may be able to avoid liability.

B. *DE JURE* AND *DE FACTO* CORPORATIONS

1. *De Jure* **Existence**
   Occurs if there is substantial compliance with all requirements for incorporation. In most states, the certificate of incorporation is evidence that all requirements have been met, and neither the state nor a third party can attack the corporation's existence.

2. *De Facto* **Existence**
   The existence of a corporation cannot be challenged by third persons (except the state) if (1) there is a statute under which the firm can be incorporated, (2) the parties made a good faith attempt to comply with it, and (3) the firm has attempted to do business as a corporation.

C. CORPORATION BY ESTOPPEL
If an association that is neither an actual corporation nor a *de facto* or *de jure* corporation holds itself out as being a corporation, it will be estopped from denying corporate status in a lawsuit by a third party.

D. DISREGARDING THE CORPORATE ENTITY
A court may ignore the corporate structure (pierce the corporate veil), exposing the shareholders to personal liability, if—

1. A party is tricked or misled into dealing with the corporation rather than the individual.
2. The corporation is set up never to make a profit or always to be insolvent, or it is too thinly capitalized.
3. Statutory corporate formalities are not followed.
4. Personal and corporate interests are commingled to the extent that the corporation has no separate identity.

VI.   CORPORATE FINANCING

A. BONDS
Bonds are issued as evidence of funds that business firms borrow from investors. A lending agreement called a **bond indenture** specifies the terms (maturity date, interest). A trustee ensures that the terms are met.

B. STOCKS

The most important characteristics of stocks are (1) they need not be paid back, (2) stockholders receive dividends only when voted by the directors, (3) stockholders are the last investors to be paid on dissolution, and (4) stockholders vote for management and on major issues.

VII.   MERGER AND CONSOLIDATION

Whether a combination is a merger or a consolidation, the rights and liabilities of shareholders, the corporation, and its creditors are the same.

A.   MERGER

1.   What a Merger Is

The combination of two or more corporations, often by one absorbing the other. After a merger, only one of the corporations exists.

2.   The Results of a Merger

The surviving corporation has all of the rights, assets, liabilities, and debts of itself and the other corporation. Its articles of incorporation are deemed amended to include changes stated in the articles of merger.

B.   CONSOLIDATION

In a consolidation, two or more corporations combine so that each corporation ceases to exist and a new one emerges. The results of a consolidation are essentially the same as the results of a merger.

C.   PROCEDURE FOR MERGER OR CONSOLIDATION

1.   The Basic Steps

(1) Each board approves the merger or consolidation plan; (2) each firm's shareholders vote on the plan at a shareholders' meeting; (3) the plan is filed, usually with the secretary of state; and (4) the state issues a certificate of merger or consolidation.

2.   Short-Form Merger

A substantially owned subsidiary corporation can merge into its parent corporation without shareholder approval, if the parent owns at least 90 percent of the subsidiary's outstanding stock.

D.   SHAREHOLDER APPROVAL

Actions taken on extraordinary matters (sale, lease, or exchange of all or substantially all corporate assets; amendment to the articles of incorporation; merger; consolidation; dissolution) must be authorized by the board of directors and the shareholders.

E.   APPRAISAL RIGHTS

If provided by statute, a shareholder can dissent from a merger, consolidation, sale of substantially all the corporate assets not in the ordinary course of business, and (in some states) amendments to the articles.

VIII.   PURCHASE OF ASSETS

A.   IS SHAREHOLDER APPROVAL REQUIRED?

A corporation that buys all or substantially all of the assets of another corporation does not need shareholder approval. The corporation whose assets are acquired must obtain approval of its board and shareholders.

B.   ASSUMPTION OF LIABILITY

An acquiring corporation is not responsible for the seller's liabilities, unless there is (1) an implied or express assumption, (2) a sale amounting to a merger or consolidation, (3) a buyer retaining the seller's personnel and continuing the business, or (4) a sale executed in fraud to avoid liability.

IX. PURCHASE OF STOCK

A purchase of a substantial number of the voting shares of a corporation's stock enables an acquiring corporation to control a target corporation. The acquiring corporation deals directly with shareholders to buy shares. A tender offer is a public offer. The offer can turn on the receipt of a specified number of shares by a specified date. The price offered is usually higher than the stock's market price before the offer.

X. TERMINATION

A. DISSOLUTION

Dissolution may be brought about by—

1. **Act of the Legislature in the State of Incorporation**

2. **Expiration of the Time in the Certificate of Incorporation**

3. **Voluntary Approval of the Shareholders and the Board**

4. **Unanimous Approval of the Shareholders**

5. **Court Decree**

    a. In an action brought by the secretary of state or the state attorney general, a corporation may be dissolved for [RMBCA 14.20]—

    1) Failing to comply with corporate formalities or other administrative requirements.
    2) Procuring a charter through fraud or misrepresentation.
    3) Abusing corporate powers (*ultra vires* acts).
    4) Violating the state criminal code after a demand to discontinue the violation has been made by the secretary of state.
    5) Failing to commence business operations.
    6) Abandoning operations before starting up.

    b. In an action by shareholders, a court may dissolve a corporation when a board is deadlocked or for mismanagement [RMBCA 14.30].

B. LIQUIDATION

Corporate assets are converted into cash and distributed among creditors and shareholders according to specific rules.

1. **Board Supervision**
    If dissolution is by voluntary action, the members of the board act as trustees of the assets, and wind up the affairs of the corporation for the benefit of corporate creditors and shareholders.

2. **Court Supervision**
    If dissolution is involuntary, the board does not wish to act as trustee, or shareholders or creditors can show why the board should not act as trustee, a court will appoint a receiver to wind up the corporate affairs.

TRUE-FALSE QUESTIONS

(Answers at the Back of the Book)

____ 1. Generally, a promoter is personally liable on a preincorporation contract.

____ 2. Any power set out in a corporation's charter or bylaws is *ultra vires*.

____ 3. To a corporation, stocks represent corporate ownership.

____ 4. In some states, a close corporation can operate without formal shareholders' or directors' meetings.

____ 5. A corporation is liable for the torts of its agents or officers committed within the course and scope of their employment.

____ 6. Appraisal rights are always available to shareholders.

____ 7. Shareholder approval is not required when a corporation sells all of its assets to another company.

____ 8. Dissolution of a corporation cannot occur without the unanimous approval of its shareholders.

____ 9. In a consolidation, the new corporation inherits all of the rights of the consolidating corporations.

____ 10. A corporation that buys the assets of another corporation always assumes the debts of the selling corporation.

FILL-IN QUESTIONS

(Answers at the Back of the Book)

Those who, for themselves or others, take the preliminary steps in organizing a corporation are _____ (promoters/incorporators). These persons enter into contracts with professionals, whose services are needed in planning the corporation, and are personally liable on these contracts, _____ (unless/even if) the third party issues a release or the corporation assumes the contract. A person who applies to the state on behalf of the corporation to obtain its certificate of incorporation is _____ (a promoter/an incorporator). This person _____ (must/need not) have any interest in the corporation.

MULTIPLE-CHOICE QUESTIONS

(Answers at the Back of the Book)

____ 1. Adam and Beth want to incorporate to sell computers. The first step in the incorporation procedure is to

 a. file the articles of incorporation.
 b. hold the first organizational meeting.
 c. obtain a corporate charter.
 d. select a state in which to incorporate.

____ 2. Great Goods, Inc., is a consumer products firm. As a source of authority for its organization and functions, its articles of incorporation are

 a. a primary source.
 b. a secondary source.
 c. a source of final resort.
 d. not a reliable source.

____ 3. Home Products Company issues common stock for sale to the public. If Ira buys ten shares of the stock, he has a proportionate interest with regard to

 a. control only.
 b. earnings and net assets only.
 c. control, earnings, and net assets.
 d. none of the above.

____ **4.** Jiffy Corporation substantially complies with all conditions precedent to incorporation. Jiffy has

a. corporation by estoppel.
b. *de facto* existence.
c. *de jure* existence.
d. none of the above.

____ **5.** Kate is a shareholder of Local Delivery, Inc. A court might "pierce the corporate veil" and hold her personally liable for Local's debts if

a. Kate's personal interests are commingled with Local's interests to the extent that Local has no separate identity.
b. Local calls too many shareholders' meetings.
c. Local is overcapitalized.
d. none of the above.

____ **6.** Digital Company plans to consolidate with Software Corporation to form DS, Inc. This requires the approval of

a. their board of directors only.
b. their shareholders only.
c. their boards and their shareholders.
d. none of the above.

____ **7.** Alpha Corporation and Beta Company consolidate to form AB, Inc. AB assumes Alpha and Beta's

a. assets only.
b. liabilities only.
c. assets and liabilities.
d. none of the above.

____ **8.** Gamma, Inc., is unprofitable. In a suit against Gamma, a court might order Gamma's dissolution if Gamma does not

a. declare a dividend.
b. make a profit this year.
c. pay its taxes.
d. any of the above.

____ **9.** Spice Corporation and Sugar, Inc., combine so that only Spice remains, as the surviving corporation. This is

a. a consolidation.
b. a merger.
c. a purchase of assets.
d. a purchase of stock.

____ **10.** Macro Sales Corporation and Micro Products Company combine and a new organization, MM, Inc., takes their place. This is

a. a consolidation.
b. a merger.
c. a purchase of assets.
d. a purchase of stock.

SHORT ESSAY QUESTIONS

1. What is the significance of the following as they relate to a company's articles of incorporation: (1) corporate name, (2) nature and purpose, (3) duration, (4) capital structure, (5) internal organization, (6) registered office and agent, and (7) incorporators?

2. What is the process by which a corporation is dissolved and liquidated?

ISSUE SPOTTERS

(Answers at the Back of the Book)

1. Eagle Corporation is formed in one state, but does business through sales representatives in another state, in which it has no office or warehouse. Can the latter exercise jurisdiction over Eagle?

2. The incorporators of Open Source, Inc., want their new firm to have the authority to transact virtually all types of business. Can they grant this authority to their firm?

3. Interstate Corporation asks its shareholders to vote on a proposed merger with Regional, Inc. Jill, an Interstate shareholder, votes against it, but is outvoted by the other shareholders. Is there anything Jill can do to avoid being forced to go along with the transaction?

Chapter 26:
Corporate Directors, Officers, and Shareholders

WHAT THIS CHAPTER IS ABOUT

This chapter outlines the rights and responsibilities of all participants—directors, officers, and shareholders—in a corporate enterprise. Also noted are the ways in which conflicts among these participants are resolved.

CHAPTER OUTLINE

I. **ROLE OF DIRECTORS**

The board of directors governs a corporation. Officers handle daily business.

A. **ELECTION OF DIRECTORS**

1. **Number of Directors**
Set in a corporation's articles or bylaws. Corporations with fewer than fifty shareholders can eliminate the board of directors [RMBCA 8.01].

2. **How Directors Are Chosen**
The first board (appointed by the incorporators or named in the articles) serves until the first shareholders' meeting. Subsequent directors are elected by a majority vote of the shareholders (see below).

3. **Removal of Directors**
A director can be removed for cause by shareholder action (or the board may have the power). In most states, a director cannot be removed without cause, unless the shareholders have reserved the right.

B. **DIRECTORS' QUALIFICATIONS AND COMPENSATION**
A few states have minimum age and residency requirements. Compensation for directors is ordinarily specified in the articles or bylaws.

C. **BOARD OF DIRECTORS' MEETINGS**

1. **Formal Minutes and Notice**
A board conducts business by holding formal meetings with recorded minutes. The dates for regular meetings are usually set in the articles and bylaws or by board resolution, and no other notice is required. Special meetings require notice to all directors.

2. **Quorum Requirements and Voting**
Quorum requirements vary. If the firm specifies none, in most states a quorum is a majority of the number of directors authorized in the articles or bylaws. Voting is done in person, one vote per director.

D. **RIGHTS OF DIRECTORS**

    1. **Participation and Inspection**
       A director has a right to participate in corporate business. A director must have access to all corporate books and records to make decisions.

    2. **Compensation and Indemnification**
       Nominal sums may be paid to directors, and there is a trend to provide more. Most states permit a corporation to indemnify a director for costs and fees in defending against corporate-related lawsuits. Many firms buy insurance to cover indemnification.

E. MANAGEMENT RESPONSIBILITIES

    1. **Areas of Responsibility**
       Major policy and financial decisions; appointment, supervision, pay, and removal of officers and other managerial employees.

    2. **Executive Committee**
       Most states permit a board to elect an executive committee from among the directors to handle management between board meetings. The committee is limited to ordinary business matters.

II. ROLE OF CORPORATE OFFICERS AND EXECUTIVES

Officers and other executive employees are hired by the board. Officers act as agents of the corporation (see Chapter 24).

A. QUALIFICATIONS

At the discretion of the firm; included in the articles or bylaws. A person can hold more than one office and also be a director.

B. RIGHTS AND DUTIES

The rights of corporate officers and other high-level managers are defined by employment contracts. Officers normally can be removed by the board at any time (but the corporation could be liable for breach of contract). Officers' duties are the same as those of directors.

III. DUTIES OF DIRECTORS AND OFFICERS

Directors and officers are fiduciaries of the corporation.

A. DUTY OF CARE

Directors and officers must act in good faith, in what they consider to be the best interests of the corporation, and with the care that an ordinarily prudent person would exercise in similar circumstances.

    1. **Duty to Make Informed and Reasonable Decisions**
       Directors must be informed on corporate matters and act in accord with their knowledge and training. A director can rely on information furnished by competent officers, or others, without being accused of acting in bad faith or failing to exercise due care [RMBCA 8.30].

    2. **Duty to Exercise Reasonable Supervision**
       Directors must exercise reasonable supervision when work is delegated to others.

    3. **Duty to Attend Board Meetings**
       Directors must attend board meetings; if not, he or she should register a dissent to actions taken (to avoid liability for mismanagement).

B. DUTY OF LOYALTY

Directors and officers cannot use corporate funds or confidential information for personal advantage. Specifically, they cannot—

    1. Compete with the corporation.
    2. Usurp a corporate opportunity.

3. Have an interest that conflicts with the interest of the corporation.
4. Engage in insider trading (see Chapter 29).
5. Authorize a corporate transaction that is detrimental to minority shareholders, or (6) sell control over the corporation.
6. Use corporate facilities for personal business.

C. CONFLICTS OF INTEREST

Directors and officers must disclose fully any conflict of interest that might occur in a deal involving the corporation. A contract may be upheld if it was fair and reasonable to the firm when it was made, there was full disclosure of the interest of the officers or directors involved, and it was approved by a majority of disinterested directors or shareholders.

IV. LIABILITY OF DIRECTORS AND OFFICERS

A. THE BUSINESS JUDGMENT RULE

Honest mistakes of judgment and poor business decisions do not make directors and officers liable to the firm for poor results, if the decision complies with management's fiduciary duties, has a reasonable basis, and is within managerial authority and the power of the corporation.

B. LIABILITY FOR TORTS AND CRIMES

Directors and officers are personally liable for their torts and crimes, and may be liable for those of subordinates (under the "responsible corporate officer" doctrine or the "pervasiveness of control" theory). The corporation is liable for such acts when committed within the scope of employment.

V. ROLE OF SHAREHOLDERS

A. SHAREHOLDERS' POWERS

Shareholders own the corporation, approve fundamental corporate changes, and elect and remove directors.

B. SHAREHOLDERS' MEETINGS

Regular meetings must occur annually; special meetings can be called to handle urgent matters.

1. Notice of Meeting Must Be in Writing in Advance

Notice of a special meeting must state the purpose.

2. Proxies

Rather than attend a meeting, shareholders normally authorize third parties to vote their shares. A proxy may be revocable and may have a time limit. When a firm sends proxy materials to its shareholders, it must allow them to vote on pending policy proposals.

C. SHAREHOLDER VOTING

1. Quorum Requirements

At the meeting, a quorum must be present. A majority vote of the shares present is required to pass resolutions. Fundamental changes require a higher percentage.

2. Voting Techniques

Each common shareholder has one vote per share. The articles can exclude or limit voting rights.

a. Cumulative Voting

The number of members of the board to be elected is multiplied by the total number of voting shares. This is the number of votes a shareholder has and can be cast for one or more nominees.

b. Shareholder Voting Agreements

A group of shareholders can agree to vote their shares together. A shareholder can vote by proxy. Any person can solicit proxies.

c. **Voting Trust**
Exists when legal title (recorded ownership on the corporate books) is transferred to a trustee who is responsible for voting the shares. The shareholder retains all other ownership rights.

VI. RIGHTS OF SHAREHOLDERS

A. STOCK CERTIFICATES
Notice of shareholder meetings, dividends, and corporate reports are distributed to owners listed in the corporate books, not on the basis of possession of stock certificates (which most states do not require).

B. PREEMPTIVE RIGHTS
Usually apply only to additional, newly issued stock sold for cash and must be exercised within a specified time (usually thirty days). When new shares are issued, each shareholder is given **stock warrants**.

C. DIVIDENDS
Dividends can be paid in cash, property, or stock. Once declared, a cash dividend is a corporate debt. Dividends are payable only from (1) retained earnings, (2) current net profits, or (3) any surplus.

1. Illegal Dividends
A dividend paid when a corporation is insolvent is illegal and must be repaid. A dividend paid from an unauthorized account or causing a corporation to become insolvent may have to be repaid. In any case, the directors can be held personally liable.

2. If the Directors Fail to Declare a Dividend
Shareholders can ask a court to compel a declaration of a dividend, but to succeed the directors' conduct must be an abuse of discretion.

D. INSPECTION RIGHTS
Shareholders (or their attorney, accountant, or agent) can inspect and copy corporate books and records for a proper purpose, if the request is made in advance [RMBCA 16.02]. This right can be denied to prevent harassment or to protect confidential corporate information.

E. TRANSFER OF SHARES
Any restrictions on transferability must be noted on the face of a stock certificate. Restrictions must be reasonable—for example, a right of first refusal remains with the corporation or the shareholders for only a specified time or a reasonable time.

F. CORPORATE DISSOLUTION
Shareholders can petition a court to dissolve a firm if [RMBCA 14.30]—

1. The directors are deadlocked, shareholders are unable to break the deadlock, and there is or could be irreparable injury to the firm.
2. The acts of the directors or those in control of the corporation are illegal, oppressive, or fraudulent.
3. Corporate assets are being misapplied or wasted.
4. The shareholders are deadlocked in voting power and have failed, for a specified period (usually two annual meetings), to elect successors to directors.

G. SHAREHOLDER'S DERIVATIVE SUIT
If directors fail to sue in the corporate name to redress a wrong suffered by the firm, shareholders can do so (after complaining to the board). Any recovery normally goes into the corporate treasury.

VII. LIABILITY OF SHAREHOLDERS
In most cases, if a corporation fails, shareholders lose only their investment. Exceptions include (see also Chapter 26)—

A. STOCK SUBSCRIPTIONS

Once a subscription agreement is accepted, any refusal to pay is a breach, resulting in personal liability.

B. WATERED STOCK

In most cases, a shareholder who receives watered stock (stock sold by a corporation for less than par value) must pay the difference to the corporation. In some states, such shareholders may be liable to creditors of the corporation for unpaid corporate debts.

VIII. DUTIES OF MAJORITY SHAREHOLDERS

A single shareholder (or a few acting together) who owns enough shares to control the corporation owes a fiduciary duty to the minority shareholders and creditors when they sell their shares.

TRUE-FALSE QUESTIONS

(Answers at the Back of the Book)

____ 1. The business judgment rule immunizes officers from liability for poor decisions that were made in good faith.

____ 2. An officer is a fiduciary of a corporation.

____ 3. Preemptive rights entitle shareholders to bring a derivative suit against the corporation.

____ 4. Only certain funds are legally available for paying dividends.

____ 5. Damages recovered in a shareholder's derivative suit are paid to the shareholder who brought the suit.

____ 6. Generally, shareholders are not personally responsible for the debts of the corporation.

____ 7. Directors, but not officers, owe a duty of loyalty to the corporation.

____ 8. The business judgment rule makes a director liable for losses to the firm in most cases.

____ 9. Shareholders may vote to remove members of the board of directors.

____ 10. Par-value shares have a specific face value.

FILL-IN QUESTIONS

(Answers at the Back of the Book)

A stock certificate may be lost or destroyed, _____(and ownership is/but ownership is not) destroyed with it. A new certificate _____ (can/cannot) be issued to replace one that has been lost or destroyed. Notice of meetings, dividends, and operational and financial reports are all distributed according to the individual _____ _____ (in possession of the certificate/recorded as the owner in the corporation's books).

MULTIPLE-CHOICE QUESTIONS

(Answers at the Back of the Book)

____ 1. Jill is a shareholder of United Manufacturing Company. As a shareholder, Jill does not have a right to

a. compensation.
b. dividends.
c. inspect corporate books and records.
d. transfer shares.

____ 2. The board of directors of Consumer Goods Corporation announces a cash dividend. A cash dividend may not be paid from

a. accumulated surplus.
b. gross profits.
c. net profits.
d. retained earnings.

____ 3. Don and Erin are officers of Fine Products Corporation. As officers, their rights are set out in

a. Don and Erin's employment contracts.
b. international agreements.
c. state corporation statutes.
d. the firm's certificate of authority.

____ 4. Fred is a director of Great Sales, Inc. As a director, Fred owes Great Sales a duty of

a. care only.
b. loyalty only.
c. care and loyalty.
d. none of the above.

____ 5. Holly is a shareholder of Interstate Products, Inc. When the directors fail to act to redress a wrong suffered by Interstate, Holly may file

a. a derivative suit.
b. a preemptive right suit.
c. a proxy suit.
d. a suit of first refusal.

____ 6. Jiffy Corporation uses cumulative voting in its elections of directors. Kay owns 3,000 Jiffy shares. At an annual meeting at which three directors are to be elected, Mary may cast for any one candidate

a. 1,000 votes.
b. 3,000 votes.
c. 9,000 votes.
d. 27,000 votes.

____ 7. Local Business Corporation invests in intrastate businesses. In Local's state, as in most states, the minimum number of directors that must be present before its board can transact business is

a. all of the directors authorized in the articles.
b. a majority of the number authorized in the articles or bylaws.
c. any odd number.
d. none of the above.

____ 8. Micro Manufacturing Company makes and sells computer chips. Like most corporations, Micro's officers are hired by the company's

a. directors.
b. incorporators.
c. officers.
d. shareholders.

____ 9. Nora is a director of Open Source, Inc. Nora has a right to

a. compensation.
b. participation.
c. preemption.
d. none of the above.

____ 10. Pat is a director of Quik Buy, Inc. Without telling Quik Buy, Pat goes into business with Fast Sales, Inc., to compete with Quik Buy. This violates

a. the business judgment rule.
b. the duty of care.
c. the duty of loyalty.
d. none of the above.

SHORT ESSAY QUESTIONS

1. How do the duty of care and the duty of loyalty govern the conduct of directors and officers in a corporation?

2. What are the rights of the shareholders of a corporation?

ISSUE SPOTTERS

(Answers at the Back of the Book)

1. Alpha Corporation's board of directors, who include Beth and Carl (officers of the firm), is deadlocked over whether to market a new product. Dan, a minority shareholder, suspects that Beth and Carl are taking advantage of the deadlock to use corporate assets (offices, equipment, supplies, staff time) to initiate a competing enterprise. Can Dan intervene?

2. Beta Corporation has an opportunity to buy stock in Gamma, Inc. The directors decide that, instead of Beta buying the stock, the directors will buy it. Frank, a Beta shareholder, learns of the purchase and wants to sue the directors on Beta's behalf. Can he do it?

3. Gail is Omega Corporation's majority shareholder. She owns enough stock in Omega that if she were to sell it, the sale would be a transfer of control of the firm. Does she owe a duty to Omega or the minority shareholders in selling her shares?

Chapter 27:
Investor Protection and Online Securities Offerings

WHAT THIS CHAPTER IS ABOUT

The general purpose of securities laws is to provide sufficient, accurate information to investors to enable them to make informed buying and selling decisions about securities. This chapter provides an outline of federal securities laws.

CHAPTER OUTLINE

I. THE SECURITIES AND EXCHANGE COMMISSION (SEC)

The SEC administers the federal securities laws and regulates the sale and purchase of securities.

A. THE SEC'S BASIC FUNCTIONS

1. Require disclosure of facts concerning offerings of certain securities.

2. Regulate national securities trading.

3. Investigate securities fraud.

4. Regulate securities brokers, dealers, and investment advisers.

5. Supervise mutual funds.

6. Recommend sanctions in cases involving violations of securities laws. (The U.S. Department of Justice prosecutes violations.)

B. THE SEC'S EXPANDING REGULATORY POWERS

The SEC's powers include the power to seek sanctions against those who violate foreign securities laws; to suspend trading if prices rise and fall in short periods of time; to exempt persons, securities, and transactions from securities law requirements; and to require more corporate disclosure.

II. SARBANES-OXLEY ACT OF 2002

Imposes strict disclosure requirements and harsh penalties for violations of securities laws.

A. RESPONSIBLE PARTIES

Chief corporate executives (CEOs and CFOs) are responsible for the accuracy and completeness of financial statements and reports filed with the SEC [Sections 302 and 906]. Penalties for knowingly certifying a report or statement that does not meet statutory requirements include up to $1 million in fines and ten years imprisonment ($5 million and twenty years for "willful" certification). Altering or destroying documents is also subject to fines and imprisonment.

B. PUBLIC COMPANY ACCOUNTING OVERSIGHT BOARD

The SEC oversees this entity, which regulates and oversees public accounting firms (see Chapter 31).

C. LIMITATIONS ON PRIVATE ACTIONS

A private action for securities fraud must be brought within two years of the discovery of the violation or five years after the violation, whichever is earlier [Section 804].

III.   SECURITIES ACT OF 1933
Requires that all essential information concerning the issuance (sales) of new securities be disclosed to investors.

A.   WHAT IS A SECURITY?

1.   Courts' Interpretation of the Securities Act
A security exists in any transaction in which a person (1) invests (2) in a common enterprise (3) reasonably expecting profits (4) derived *primarily* or *substantially* from others' managerial or entrepreneurial efforts.

2.   A Security Is an Investment
Examples: stocks, bonds, investment contracts in condominiums, franchises, limited partnerships, and oil or gas or other mineral rights.

B.   REGISTRATION STATEMENT
Before offering securities for sale, issuing corporations must (1) file a registration statement with the Securities and Exchange Commission (SEC) and (2) provide investors with a prospectus that describes the security being sold, the issuing corporation, and the investment or risk. These documents must be written in "plain English."

1.   Contents of a Registration Statement

a. Description of the significant provisions of the security and how the registrant intends to use the proceeds of the sale.
b. Description of the registrant's properties and business.
c. Description of the management of the registrant; its security holdings; its remuneration and other benefits, including pensions and stock options; and any interests of directors or officers in any material transactions with the corporation.
d. Financial statement certified by an independent public accountant.
e. Description of pending lawsuits.

2.   Twenty-Day Waiting Period after Registration
Securities cannot be sold for twenty days (oral offers can be made).

3.   Advertising
During the waiting period, very limited written advertising is allowed. After the period, no written advertising is allowed, except a tombstone ad, which simply tells how to obtain a prospectus.

C.   EXEMPT SECURITIES
Securities that can be sold (and resold) without being registered include—

1.   Small Offerings under Regulation A
An issuer's offer of up to $5 million in securities in any twelve-month period (including up to $1.5 million in nonissuer resales). The issuer must file with the SEC a notice of the issue and an offering circular (also provided to investors before the sale). A company can "test the waters" (determine potential interest) before preparing the circular.

2.   Other Exempt Securities

a. All bank securities sold prior to July 27, 1933.
b. Commercial paper if maturity does not exceed nine months.
c. Securities of charitable organizations.
d. Securities resulting from a reorganization issued in exchange for the issuer's existing securities and certificates issued by trustees, receivers, or debtors in possession in bankruptcy (see Chapter 21).
e. Securities issued exclusively in exchange for the issuer's existing securities, provided no commission is paid (such as stock splits).

    f. Securities issued to finance the acquisition of railroad equipment.

    g. Any insurance, endowment, or annuity contract issued by a state-regulated insurance company.

    h. Government-issued securities.

    i. Securities issued by banks, savings and loan associations, farmers' cooperatives, and similar institutions.

D. EXEMPT TRANSACTIONS

Securities that can be sold without being registered include those sold in transactions that consist of—

1. Limited Offers (Regulation D)

Offers that involve a small amount of money or are not made publicly.

a. Small Offerings

Noninvestment company offerings up to $1 million in a twelve-month period [Rule 504].

b. Blank-Check Company Offerings

Offerings up to $500,000 in any one year by companies with no specific business plans are exempt if (1) no general solicitation or advertising is used, (2) the SEC is notified of the sales, and (3) precaution is taken against nonexempt, unregistered resales [Rule 504a].

c. Small Offerings

Private, noninvestment company offerings up to $5 million in a twelve-month period if (1) no general solicitation or advertising is used; (2) the SEC is notified of the sales; (3) precaution is taken against nonexempt, unregistered resales; and (4) there are no more than thirty-five unaccredited investors. If the sale involves any unaccredited investors, all investors must be given material information about the company, its business, the securities [Rule 505].

d. Private Offerings

Essentially the same requirements as Rule 505, except (1) there is no limit on the amount of the offering and (2) the issuer must believe that each unaccredited investor has sufficient knowledge or experience to evaluate the investment [Rule 506].

2. Small Offerings to Accredited Investors Only

An offer up to $5 million is exempt if (1) no general solicitation or advertising is used; (2) the SEC is notified of the sales; (3) precaution is taken against nonexempt, unregistered resales; and (4) there are no unaccredited investors [Section 4(6)].

3. Intrastate Issues

Offerings in the state in which the issuer is organized and doing business are exempt [Rule 147] if, for nine months after the sale, no resale is made to a nonresident.

4. Resales—"Safe Harbors"

Most securities can be resold without registration. Resales of blank-check company offerings [Rule 504a], small offerings [Rule 505], private offerings [Rule 506], and offers to accredited investors only [Section 4(6)] are exempt from registration if—

a. The Securities Have Been Owned for Three Years or More

If seller is not an affiliate (in control with the issuer) [Rule 144].

b. The Securities Have Been Owned for at Least Two Years

There must be adequate public information about the issuer, the securities must be sold in limited amounts in unsolicited brokers' transactions, and the SEC must be notified of the resale [Rule 144].

c. The Securities Are Sold Only to an Institutional Investor

The securities, on issue, must not have been of the same class as securities listed on a national securities exchange or a U.S. automated interdealer quotation system, and the seller on resale must take steps to tell the buyer they are exempt [Rule 144A].

E. **VIOLATIONS AND PENALTIES**
    The SEC can bring civil actions. The U.S. Department of Justice enforces the criminal provisions. Private parties can also sue. Penalties include fines to $10,000, imprisonment for five years, or both.

IV. SECURITIES EXCHANGE ACT OF 1934
Regulates the markets in which securities are traded by requiring disclosure by Section 12 companies (corporations with securities on the exchanges and firms with assets in excess of $5 million and five hundred or more shareholders).

A. **INSIDER TRADING—SECTION 10(b) AND SEC RULE 10b-5**
    Section 10(b) proscribes the use of "any manipulative or deceptive device or contrivance in contravention of such rules and regulations as the [SEC] may prescribe." Rule 10b-5 prohibits the commission of fraud in connection with the purchase or sale of any security (registered or unregistered).

    1. **What Triggers Liability**
        Any material omission or misrepresentation of material facts in connection with the purchase or sale of any security.

    2. **What Does Not Trigger Liability**
        Under the Private Securities Litigation Reform Act of 1995, financial forecasts and other forward-looking statements do not trigger liability if they include "meaningful cautionary statements identifying factors that could cause actual results to differ materially."

    3. **Who Can Be Liable**
        Those who take advantage of inside information when they know it is unavailable to the person with whom they are dealing.

        a. **Insiders**
            Officers, directors, majority shareholders, and persons having access to or receiving information of a nonpublic nature on which trading is based (accountants, attorneys).

        b. **Outsiders**

            1) **Tipper/Tippee Theory**
                One who acquires inside information as a result of an insider's breach of fiduciary duty to the firm whose shares are traded can be liable, if he or she knows or should know of the breach.

            2) **Misappropriation Theory**
                One who wrongfully obtains inside information and trades on it to his or her gain can be liable, if a duty to the lawful possessor of information was violated and harm to another results.

B. **INSIDER REPORTING AND TRADING—SECTION 16(b)**
    Officers, directors, and shareholders owning 10 percent of the securities registered under Section 12 are required to file reports with the SEC concerning their ownership and trading of the securities.

    1. **Corporation Is Entitled to All Profits**
        A firm can recapture *all* profits realized by an insider on *any* purchase and sale or sale and purchase of its stock in any six-month period.

    2. **Applicability of Section 16(b)**
        Applies to stock, warrants, options, securities convertible into stock.

C. **PROXY STATEMENTS—SECTION 14(A)**
    Regulates the solicitation of proxies from shareholders of Section 12 companies. Whoever solicits a proxy must disclose, in the proxy statement, all of the pertinent facts.

D. VIOLATIONS OF THE 1934 ACT

1. Criminal Penalties

Maximum jail term is twenty-five years; fines up to $5 million for individuals and $2.5 million for partnerships and corporations.

2. Civil Sanctions

a. Insider Trading Sanctions Act of 1984

SEC can bring suit in federal court against anyone violating or aiding in a violation of the 1934 act or SEC rules. Penalties include triple the profits gained or the loss avoided by the guilty party.

b. Insider Trading and Securities Fraud Enforcement Act of 1988

Enlarged the class of persons subject to civil liability for insider-trading violations, increased criminal penalties, and gave the SEC authority to (1) reward persons providing information and (2) make rules to prevent insider trading.

V. REGULATION OF INVESTMENT COMPANIES

The SEC regulates investment companies and mutual funds under the Investment Company Act of 1940, the Investment Company Act Amendments of 1970, the Securities Act Amendments of 1975, and later amendments.

A. WHAT AN INVESTMENT COMPANY IS

Any entity that (1) is engaged primarily "in the business of investing, reinvesting, or trading in securities" or (2) is engaged in such business and has more than 40 percent of the company's assets in investment securities. (Does not include banks, finance companies, and others).

B. WHAT AN INVESTMENT COMPANY MUST DO

Register with the SEC by filing a notification of registration and, each year, file reports with the SEC. All securities must be in the custody of a bank or stock exchange member.

C. WHAT AN INVESTMENT COMPANY CANNOT DO

No dividends may be paid from any source other than accumulated, undistributed net income. There are restrictions on investment activities.

VI. STATE SECURITIES LAWS

All states regulate the offer and sale of securities within individual state borders. Exemptions from federal law are not exemptions from state laws, which have their own exemptions. Under the National Market Securities Improvement Act of 1996, the SEC regulates most national securities activities.

VII. ONLINE SECURITIES OFFERINGS AND DISCLOSURES

Federal and state laws set out the requirements for online initial public offerings. Under SEC interpretations, there is no difference in the disclosure requirements, only in the medium of disclosure, for which there may be new avenues of liability. Also, an online prospectus may not qualify for a Regulation D exemption.

VIII. ONLINE SECURITIES FRAUD

Issues include the use of chat rooms to affect the price of securities, fictitious press releases, and illegal offerings. The First Amendment protects the use of chat rooms. Also, there is a distinction between statements of fact and opinion.

TRUE-FALSE QUESTIONS

(Answers at the Back of the Book)

____ 1. A security that does not qualify for an exemption must be registered before it is offered to the public.

____ 2. Before a security can be sold to the public, prospective investors must be provided with a prospectus.

____ 3. Stock splits are exempt from the registration requirements of the Securities Act of 1933, if no commission is paid.

____ 4. Sales of securities may not occur until twenty days after registration.

____ 5. Private offerings of securities in unlimited amounts that are not generally solicited or advertised must be registered before they can be sold.

____ 6. A proxy statement must fully and accurately disclose all of the facts that are pertinent to the matter on which shareholders are being asked to vote.

____ 7. All states have disclosure requirements and antifraud provisions that cover securities.

____ 8. *Scienter* is not a requirement for liability under Section 10(b) of the Securities Exchange Act of 1934.

____ 9. No one who receives inside information as a result of another's breach of his or her fiduciary duty can be liable under SEC Rule 10b-5.

____ 10. No security can be resold without registration.

FILL-IN QUESTIONS

(Answers at the Back of the Book)

The SEC can award "bounty" payments to persons providing information leading to the _____ (conviction/prosecution) of insider-trading violations. Civil penalties include _____ (double/triple) the profits gained or the loss avoided. Criminal penalties include maximum jail terms of _____ (five/ten) years. Individuals and corporations _____ (may/may not) also be subject to million dollar fines.

MULTIPLE-CHOICE QUESTIONS

(Answers at the Back of the Book)

____ 1. Beth, a director of Alpha Company, learns that an Alpha engineer has developed a new, improved product. Over the next six months, Beth buys and sells Alpha stock for a profit. Of Beth's profit, Alpha may recapture

a. all.
b. half.
c. 10 percent.
d. none.

____ 2. Central Brokerage Associates sells securities. The definition of a security does *not* include, as an element,

a. an investment.
b. a common enterprise.
c. a reasonable expectation of profits.
d. profits derived entirely from the efforts of the investor.

____ 3. Superior, Inc., is a private, noninvestment company. In one year, Superior advertises a $300,000 offering. Concerning registration, this offering is

a. exempt because of the low amount of the issue.
b. exempt because it was advertised.
c. exempt because the issuer is a private company.
d. not exempt.

____ 4. Huron, Inc., makes a $6 million private offering to twenty accredited investors and less than thirty unaccredited investors. Huron advertises the offering and believes that the unaccredited investors are sophisticated enough to evaluate the investment. Huron gives material information about itself, its business, and the securities to all investors. Concerning registration, this offering is

a. exempt because of the low amount of the issue.
b. exempt because it was advertised.
c. exempt because the issuer believed that the unaccredited investors were sophisticated enough to evaluate the investment.
d. not exempt.

____ 5. Ontario, Inc., in one year, advertises two $2.25 million offerings. Buying the stock are twelve accredited investors. Concerning registration, this offering is

a. exempt because of the low amount of the issue.
b. exempt because it was advertised.
c. exempt from registration because only accredited investors bought stock.
d. not exempt from registration.

____ 6. Omega Corporation's registration statement must include

a. a description of the accounting firm that audits Omega.
b. a description of the security being offered for sale.
c. a financial forecast for Omega's nest five years.
d. all of the above.

____ 7. Frank, an officer of Gamma, Inc., learns that Gamma has developed a new source of energy. Frank tells Gail, an outsider. They each buy Gamma stock. When the development is announced, the stock price increases, and they each immediately sell their stock. Subject to liability for insider trading is

a. Frank only.
b. Gail only
c. Frank and Gail.
d. none of the above.

____ 8. National Sales, Inc., wants to make an offering of securities to the public. The offer is not exempt from registration. Before National sells these securities, it must provide investors with

a. a prospectus.
b. a registration statement.
c. a tombstone ad.
d. none of the above.

____ 9. Erie, Inc., is a noninvestment company. In one year, Erie advertises two $1.75 million offerings. Buying the issues are sixty accredited investors and twenty unaccredited investors. Erie gives information about itself, its business, and the securities to unaccredited investors only. Concerning registration, this offering is

a. exempt because of the low amount of the issue.
b. exempt because it was advertised.
c. exempt because the unaccredited investors were informed.
d. not exempt.

____ 10. Great Lakes Company is a private, noninvestment company. Last year, as part of a $250,000 advertised offering, Great Lakes sold stock to John, a private investor. John would now like to sell the shares. Concerning registration, this resale is

    a. exempt because of the low amount of the original issue.
    b. exempt because the offering was advertised.
    c. exempt because all resales are exempt.
    d. not exempt.

SHORT ESSAY QUESTIONS

1. What is the process by which a company sells securities to the public?

2. How is insider trading regulated by Section 10(b), SEC Rule 10b-5, and Section 16(b)?

ISSUE SPOTTERS

(Answers at the Back of the Book)

1. When a corporation wishes to issue certain securities, it must provide sufficient information for an unsophisticated investor to evaluate the financial risk involved. Specifically, the law imposes liability for making a false statement or omission that is "material." What sort of information would an investor consider material?

2. Lee is an officer of Macro Oil, Inc. Lee knows that a Macro geologist has just discovered a new deposit of oil. Can Lee take advantage of this information to buy and sell Macro stock?

3. The Securities Act of 1933, the Securities Exchange Act of 1934, and other securities regulation is federal law. In-State Corporation incorporated in one state, does business exclusively in that state, and offers its securities for sale only in that state. Are there securities laws to regulate this offering?

CUMULATIVE HYPOTHETICAL PROBLEM
FOR UNIT EIGHT—INCLUDING CHAPTERS 24–27

(Answers at the Back of the Book)

    Adam, Beth, and Carl are sole proprietors who decide to pool their resources to produce and maintain an Internet portal Web site, "i-World."

____ 1. Adam, Beth, and Carl decide to form a partnership. They transfer their business assets and liabilities to the firm and start business on May 1, 2001. The parties execute a formal partnership agreement on July 1. The partnership began its existence

    a. on May 1.
    b. on July 1.
    c. when each partner's individual creditors consented to the asset transfer.
    d. when the parties initially decided to form a partnership.

____ 2. After six months in operation, Adam, Beth, and Carl decide to change the form of their partnership to a limited partnership. To form a limited partnership, they must

    a. accept limited liability for all of the partners.
    b. create the firm according to specific statutory requirements.
    c. designate one general partner to be a limited partner.
    d. each make a capital contribution.

____ **3.** Adam, Beth, and Carl's i-World is very successful. In March 2002, they decide to incorporate. The articles of incorporation must include all of the following except

a. the name of a registered agent.
b. the name of the corporation.
c. the names of the incorporators.
d. the names of the initial officers.

____ **4.** In January 2003, Adam, Beth, and Carl decide to issue additional stock in i-World, Inc. The registration statement must include

a. a copy of the corporation's most recent proxy statement.
b. the names of prospective accredited investors.
c. the names of the current shareholders.
d. the principal purposes for which the proceeds from the offering will be used.

____ **5.** The issue of shares that i-World, Inc., plans to make qualifies under Rule 504 of Regulation D of the Securities Act of 1933. Under this rule, i-World

a. may not make the offering through general advertising.
b. may sell the shares to an unlimited number of investors.
c. must offer the shares for sale for more than twelve months.
d. must provide all prospective investors with a prospectus.

QUESTIONS ON THE FOCUS ON LEGAL REASONING FOR UNIT EIGHT—*IN RE MILLER*

(Answers at the Back of the Book)

____ **1.** Alan, a broker, commits securities fraud. According to the majority in *In re Miller*, to impute liability for the fraud under Section 20 of the Securities Exchange Act of 1934 on Alan's supervisor Ben and their employer Carol requires a finding of

a. agency.
b. bankruptcy.
c. partnership.
d. none of the above.

____ **2.** Under the facts in the previous question, according to the dissent in *In re Miller*, to impute liability for the fraud under Section 20 of the Securities Exchange Act of 1934 on Ben and Carol requires a finding of

a. agency.
b. bankruptcy.
c. partnership.
d. none of the above.

____ **3.** In the previous questions, suppose that liability for Alan's act is imputed under Section 20 on Ben and Carol, both of whom file for bankruptcy. In the opinion of the majority in *In re Miller*, a discharge of the debt represented by this liability could be obtained by

a. Ben only.
b. Carol only.
c. Ben and Carol.
d. neither Ben nor Carol.

Chapter 28:
Personal Property and Bailments

WHAT THIS CHAPTER IS ABOUT

This chapter covers the nature of personal property, forms of property ownership, the acquisition of personal property, and bailments. Note that personal property can be tangible (such as a car) or intangible (such as stocks, bonds, patents, or copyrights).

CHAPTER OUTLINE

I. PROPERTY OWNERSHIP
Ownership can be viewed as the rights to possess property and to dispose of it.

A. FEE SIMPLE
A person who holds all of the rights is an owner in fee simple (see Chapter 37); on death, the owner's interest descends to his or her heirs.

B. CONCURRENT OWNERSHIP
Persons who share ownership rights simultaneously are concurrent owners.

1. Tenancy in Common
Each of two or more persons owns an undivided interest (each has rights in the whole—if each had rights in specific items, the interests would be divided). On death, a tenant's interest passes to his or her heirs.

2. Joint Tenancy
Each of two or more persons owns an undivided interest in the property; a deceased joint tenant's interest passes to the surviving joint tenant or tenants. Can be terminated at any time before a joint tenant's death by gift or by sale.

3. Tenancy by the Entirety
Created by a transfer of real property to a husband and wife; neither spouse can transfer separately his or her interest during his or her life.

4. Community Property
Each spouse owns an undivided half interest in property acquired by either spouse during their marriage. Recognized in only some states.

II. ACQUIRING OWNERSHIP OF PERSONAL PROPERTY

A. POSSESSION
An example of acquiring ownership by possession is the capture of wild animals. (Exceptions: (1) wild animals captured by a trespasser are the property of the landowner, and (2) wild animals captured or killed in violation of statutes are the property of the state.)

B. PRODUCTION
Those who produce personal property have title to it. (Exception: employees do not own what they produce for their employers.)

C. GIFTS
A **gift** is a voluntary transfer of property ownership not supported by consideration.

1. **Requirements for an Effective Gift**
   There are three requirements for an effective gift—

   a. **Donative Intent**
      Determined from the language of the donor and the surrounding circumstances (relationship between the parties and the size of the gift in relation to the donor's other assets).

   b. **Delivery**

      1) **Constructive Delivery**
         If a physical object cannot be delivered, an act that the law holds to be equivalent to an act of real delivery is sufficient (a key to a safe-deposit box for the contents of the box, for example).

      2) **Delivery by a Third Person**
         If the person is the donor's agent, the gift is effective when the agent delivers the property to the donee. If the person is the donee's agent, the gift is effective when the donor delivers the property to the agent.

      3) **Giving Up Control**
         Effective delivery requires giving up control over the property.

   c. **Acceptance**
      Courts assume a gift is accepted unless shown otherwise.

2. **Gifts *Inter Vivos* and Gifts *Causa Mortis***
   Gifts *inter vivos* are made during one's lifetime. Gifts *causa mortis* are made in contemplation of imminent death, do not become effective until the donor dies, and are automatically revoked if the donor does not die.

D. **ACCESSION**
Occurs when someone adds value to a item of personal property by labor or materials. Ownership can be at issue if—

1. **Accession Occurs without Permission of the Owner**
   Courts tend to favor the owner over the one who improved the property (and deny the improver any compensation for the value added).

2. **Accession Greatly Increases the Value or Changes the Identity**
   If the accession is in good faith, then the greater the increase, the more likely that ownership will pass to the improver, who must compensate the original owner for the value of the property before the accession.

E. **CONFUSION**
Commingling goods so that one person's cannot be distinguished from another's. Frequently involves fungible goods. If goods are confused due to a wrongful act, the innocent party acquires all. If confusion is by agreement, mistake, or a third party's act, the owners share as tenants in common.

III.   MISLAID, LOST, AND ABANDONED PROPERTY

A. **MISLAID PROPERTY**
Property that has been voluntarily placed somewhere by the owner and then inadvertently forgotten. When the property is found, the owner of the place where it was mislaid (not the finder) becomes the caretaker.

B. **LOST PROPERTY**
Property that is involuntarily left. A finder can claim title against the whole world, except the true owner. Many states require the finder to make a reasonably diligent search to locate the true owner. Es-

tray statutes allow finders, after passage of a specified time, to acquire title to the property if it remains unclaimed.

C. ABANDONED PROPERTY

Property that has been discarded by the true owner, who has no intention of claiming title to it. A finder acquires title good against the whole world, including the original owner. A trespasser does not acquire title, however; the owner of the real property on which it was found does.

IV. BAILMENTS

A bailment is formed by the delivery of personal property, without transfer of title, by a bailor to a bailee, usually under an agreement for a particular purpose, after which the property is returned or otherwise disposed of.

A. ELEMENTS OF A BAILMENT

1. Personal Property
Only personal property is bailable.

2. Delivery of Possession (Without Title)
Bailee must (1) be given exclusive possession and control of the property and (2) knowingly accept it. Delivery may be physical or constructive.

3. Bailment Agreement
The agreement must provide for the return of the property to the bailor or a third person, or for its disposal by the bailee.

B. ORDINARY BAILMENTS

The three types of ordinary bailments are: (1) bailment for the sole benefit of the bailor, (2) bailment for the sole benefit of the bailee, and (3) bailment for their mutual benefit.

1. Rights of the Bailee

a. Right to Control and Possess the Property
This right permits a bailee to recover damages from any third persons for damage or loss to the property.

b. Right to Use the Property
The extent to which a bailee can use property depends on the bailment agreement.

c. Right to Be Compensated
A bailee has a right to be compensated as agreed and to be reimbursed for costs and services in the keeping of the property. To enforce the right, a bailee can put a possessory lien on the property.

d. Right to Limit Liability
Bailees can limit their liability as long as—

1) Limitations Are Called to the Attention of the Bailor
Fine print on the back of a ticket stub is not sufficient.

2) Limitations Are Not Against Public Policy
If a bailee attempts to exclude liability for his or her own negligence, the clause is unenforceable.

2. Duties of the Bailee

a. **Duty of Care**

A bailment for the sole benefit of the bailor requires a slight degree of care; a bailment for the sole benefit of the bailee requires great care. A mutual-benefit bailment requires reasonable care. Failure to use the right amount of care results in tort liability.

b. **Duty to Return Bailed Property**

When a bailment ends, the bailee must relinquish the property. Failure to do so is a breach of contract (unless the property is destroyed, lost, or stolen through no fault of the bailee, or given to a third party with a superior claim) and could be conversion.

c. **Presumption of Negligence**

If the bailee has the property and damage occurs that normally results only from someone's negligence, the bailee's negligence is presumed. The bailee must prove that he or she was not at fault.

3. **Rights of the Bailor**

The bailor's rights are essentially the same as the duties of the bailee.

4. **Duties of the Bailor**

A bailor has a duty to provide the bailee with goods that are free from defects that could injure the bailee. This has two aspects—

a. In a mutual-benefit bailment, the bailor must notify the bailee of all *known* defects and any *hidden* defects that the bailor knew of or could have discovered with reasonable diligence and inspection.

b. In a bailment for the sole benefit of the bailee, the bailor must notify the bailee of any *known* defects.

c. Liability extends to anyone who might be expected to come in contact with the goods. A bailor may also incur liability under UCC Article 2A's implied warranties.

C. **SPECIAL TYPES OF BAILMENTS**

1. **Common Carriers**

Common carriers are publicly licensed to provide transportation services to the general public.

a. **Strict Liability**

Common carriers are absolutely liable, regardless of negligence, for all loss or damage to goods in their possession, except if it is caused by an act of God, an act of a public enemy, an order of a public authority, an act of the shipper, or the nature of the goods.

b. **Limits to Liability**

Common carriers can limit their liability to an amount stated on the shipment contract.

2. **Warehouse Companies**

Warehouse companies are liable for loss or damage to property resulting from negligence. A warehouse company can limit the dollar amount of liability, but the bailor must be given the option of paying an increased storage rate for an increase in the liability limit.

3. **Innkeepers**

Those who provide lodging to the public for compensation as a regular business are strictly liable for injuries to guests.

a. **Hotel Safes**

In many states, innkeepers can avoid strict liability for loss of guests' valuables by providing a safe. Statutes often limit the liability of innkeepers for articles that are not kept in the safe.

b. Parking Facilities

If an innkeeper provides parking facilities, and the guest's car is entrusted to the innkeeper, the innkeeper will be liable under the rules that pertain to parking lot bailments (ordinary bailments).

TRUE-FALSE QUESTIONS

(Answers at the Back of the Book)

____   1. Generally, those who produce personal property have title to it.

____   2. If goods are confused due to a wrongful act and the innocent party cannot prove what percentage is his or hers, the wrongdoer gets title to the whole.

____   3. To constitute a gift, a voluntary transfer of property must be supported by consideration.

____   4. If an accession is performed in good faith, the improver keeps the property as improved, whether or not there has been any change in the value.

____   5. One who finds abandoned property acquires title to it good against the whole world, except the true owner.

____   6. Any delivery of personal property from one person to another creates a bailment.

____   7. A bailee is not responsible for the loss of bailed property in his or her care.

____   8. A bailee has only one duty: to surrender the property at the end of the bailment.

____   9. In some ordinary bailments, bailees can limit their liability.

____   10. Warehouse companies have the same duty of care as ordinary bailees.

FILL-IN QUESTIONS

(Answers at the Back of the Book)

A gift made during the donor's lifetime is a gift _____ (*causa mortis / inter vivos*). A gift _____ (*causa mortis / inter vivos*) is made in contemplation of imminent death. Gifts _____ (*causa mortis / inter vivos*) do not become absolute until the donor dies from the contemplated illness or disease. A gift _____ (*causa mortis / inter vivos*) is revocable at any time up to the death of the donor and is automatically revoked if the donor recovers. A gift _____ (*causa mortis / inter vivos*) is revocable at any time before the donor's death.

MULTIPLE-CHOICE QUESTIONS

(Answers at the Back of the Book)

____   1. Eve designs an Internet home page to advertise her services as a designer of home pages. Tim hires her to design a homepage for his business. Eve has title to

a. her home page only.
b. Tim's home page only.
c. her homepage, Tim's home page, and any other home page she creates.
d. none of the above.

____ **2.** Nancy sells her boat to Chris and Nora. Chris and Nora are not married. The contract of sale says that the buyers each have a right of survivorship in the boat. Chris and Nora own the boat as

a. tenants in common.
b. joint tenants.
c. tenants by the entirety.
d. community property.

____ **3.** Meg wants to give Lori a pair of diamond earrings that Meg has in her safe-deposit box at First National Bank. Meg gives Lori the key to the box and tells her to go to the bank and take the earrings from the box. Lori does so. Two days later, Meg dies. The earrings belong to

a. Lori.
b. Meg's heirs.
c. First National Bank.
d. the state.

____ **4.** John is employed in remodeling homes bought and sold by Best Realty. In one of the homes, John finds an item of jewelry and takes it to Hall Gems, Inc., to be appraised. The appraiser removes some of the jewels. Best title to the jewels that were removed is with

a. John.
b. Hall Gems, Inc.
c. Best Realty.
d. John's employer.

____ **5.** Jane, Mark, and Guy store their grain in three silos. Jane contributes half of the grain, Mark a third, and Guy a sixth. A tornado hits two of the silos and scatters the grain. If each can prove how much he or she deposited in the silos, how much of what is left belongs to each?

a. Jane owns half, Mark a third, and Guy a sixth
b. Because only a third is left, Mark owns it all
c. Because Jane and Mark lost the most, they split what is left equally
d. Jane, Mark, and Guy share what is left equally

____ **6.** Doug wants to give Kim a notebook computer in a locker at the mall. Doug gives Kim the key to the locker and tells her to take the computer. Kim says that she doesn't want the computer and leaves the key on Doug's desk. The next day, Doug dies. The computer belongs to

a. Kim.
b. Doug's heirs.
c. the mall.
d. the state.

____ **7.** Ann parks her car in an unattended lot behind Bob's store, which is closed. Ann locks the car and takes the keys. This is NOT a bailment because

a. no money is involved.
b. no personal property is involved.
c. there is no transfer of possession.
d. neither party signed a contract.

____ **8.** Marcy goes to Don's Salon for a haircut. Behind a plant on a table in the waiting area, Marcy finds a wallet containing $5,000. Who is entitled to possession of the wallet?

a. Marcy because the money was lost
b. Don because the money was mislaid
c. The state under an estray statute
d. The police under the local finders' law

_____   9. Kay checks her coat at a restaurant. Hidden in the sleeve is her purse. By accepting the coat, the restaurant is a bailee of

    a. the coat only.
    b. the purse only.
    c. both the coat and the purse.
    d. none of the above.

_____   10. Adams Corporation ships three loads of goods via Baker Transport Company. Which, if any, of the following losses is Baker liable for?

    a. The first load is lost because Adams failed to package the goods properly.
    b. The second load is lost because the goods are perishable and are shipped too late to survive the transport.
    c. The third load is lost in an accident that is the fault of Baker's driver.
    d. None of the above

SHORT ESSAY QUESTIONS

1. What are the principal features of the forms of concurrent property ownership: tenancies in common, joint tenancies, tenancies by the entirety, and community property?

2. What are the three elements involved in creating a valid gift?

ISSUE SPOTTERS

1. Alpha Corporation sends important documents to Beta, Inc., via Speedy Messenger Service. While the documents are in Speedy's care, a third party causes an accident to Speedy's delivery vehicle that results in the loss of the documents. Does Speedy have a right to recover from the third party for the loss of the documents?

2. Bob leaves his clothes with Corner Dry Cleaners to be cleaned. When the clothes are returned, some are missing and others are greasy and smell bad. Is Corner liable?

3. Omega Corporation ships a load of goods via Peak Transport Company. The load is lost in a hurricane in Florida. Who suffers the loss?

Chapter 29:
Real Property

WHAT THIS CHAPTER IS ABOUT

This chapter covers ownership rights in real property, including the nature of those rights and their transfer. The chapter also outlines the right of the government to take private land for public use, zoning laws, and other restrictions on ownership.

CHAPTER OUTLINE

I. THE NATURE OF REAL PROPERTY

Real property consists of land and the buildings, plants, and trees on it.

A. LAND

Includes the soil on the surface of the earth, natural products or artificial structures attached to it, the water on or under it, and the air space above.

B. AIR AND SUBSURFACE RIGHTS

Limitations on air rights or subsurface rights normally have to be indicated on the deed transferring title at the time of purchase.

1. Air Rights

Flights over private land do not normally violate the owners' rights.

2. Subsurface Rights

Ownership of the surface can be separated from ownership of the subsurface. Conflicts may arise between surface and subsurface owners' interests.

C. PLANT LIFE AND VEGETATION

A sale of land with growing crops on it includes the crops, unless otherwise agreed. When crops are sold by themselves, they are personal property.

D. FIXTURES

Personal property so closely associated with certain real property that it is viewed as part of it (such as plumbing in a building). Fixtures are included in a sale of land if the contract does not provide otherwise.

II. OWNERSHIP OF REAL PROPERTY

A. OWNERSHIP IN FEE SIMPLE

1. Fee Simple Absolute

A fee simple owner has the most rights possible—he or she can give the property away, sell it, transfer it by will, use it for almost any purpose, and possess it to the exclusion of all the world—potentially forever.

2. Fee Simple Defeasible

Conditional ownership ("to A, as long as the property is used for a school"). If condition is not met, the land reverts to the original owner.

B. **LIFE ESTATES**

Lasts for the life of a specified individual ("to A for his life"). A life tenant can use the land (but not commit waste), mortgage the life estate, and create liens, easements, and leases (but no longer than the life estate).

C. **FUTURE INTERESTS**

Residuary interest that an owner retains to retake possession if condition of the fee simple defeasible is not met or when the life estate ends.

1. **Reversions and Remainders**

   If the owner retains ownership of a future interest, it is a reversionary interest. If the owner transfers rights in a future interest to another, it is a remainder ("to A for life, then to B").

2. **Executory Interest**

   An interest that does not take effect immediately on the expiration of another interest ("to A for life and one year after A's death to B").

D. **NONPOSSESSORY INTERESTS**

1. **Easements and Profits**

   Easement: the right of a person to make limited use of another person's land without taking anything from the property. **Profit**: the right to go onto another's land and take away a part or product of the land.

   a. **Easement or Profit Appurtenant**

      Arises when a landowner has a right to go onto (or remove things from) an adjacent owner's land.

   b. **Easement or Profit in Gross**

      Exists when a right to use or take things from another's land does not depend on owning the adjacent property.

   c. **Effect of a Sale of Property**

      The benefit of an easement or profit goes with the land. The burden goes with the land only if the new owner recognizes it, or knew or should have known of it.

   d. **Creation of an Easement or Profit**

      By deed, will, contract, implication, necessity, or prescription.

   e. **Termination of an Easement or Profit**

      Terminates when deeded back to owner of the land burdened, its owner becomes owner of the land burdened, contract terminates, or it is abandoned with the intent to relinquish the right to it.

2. **License**

   The revocable right of a person to come onto another person's land.

III.   TRANSFER OF OWNERSHIP

A. **DEEDS**

Possession and title to land can be passed by deed without consideration.

1. **Requirements**

   (1) Names of the grantor and grantee, (2) words evidencing an intent to convey, (3) legally sufficient description of the land, (4) grantor's (and sometimes spouse's) signature, and (5) delivery.

2. Warranty Deed

Provides the most protection against defects of title—covenants that grantor has title to, and power to convey, the property; that the property is not subject to any outstanding interests that diminish its value; and that the buyer will not be disturbed in his or her possession.

3. Quitclaim Deed

Warrants less than any other deed. Conveys to the grantee only whatever interest the grantor had.

4. Recording Statutes

Recording statutes require transfers to be recorded in public records (generally in the county in which the property is located) to give notice to the public that a certain person is the owner. Many states require the grantor's signature and two witnesses' signatures.

B. WILL OR INHERITANCE

Transfers by will or inheritance are outlined in Chapter 38.

C. ADVERSE POSSESSION

A person who possesses another's property acquires title good against the original owner if the possession is (1) actual and exclusive; (2) open, visible, and notorious; (3) continuous and peaceable for a required period of time; and (4) hostile, as against the whole world.

IV. LIMITATIONS ON THE RIGHTS OF PROPERTY OWNERS

A. EMINENT DOMAIN

The government can take private property for public use. To obtain title, a condemnation proceeding is brought. The Fifth Amendment requires that just compensation be paid for a taking; thus, in a separate proceeding a court determines the land's fair value (usually market value) to pay the owner.

B. ZONING

Under its police power, a state can pass zoning laws to regulate uses of land without having to compensate the landowner. Regulation cannot be (1) confiscatory (or the owner must be paid just compensation); (2) arbitrary or unreasonable (taking without due process under the Fourteenth Amendment); or (3) discriminatory, under the Fourteenth Amendment.

C. ENVIRONMENTAL TAKINGS

Should landowners be compensated when, to protect the environment, the government restricts the use of those owners' property? Court decisions have favored both sides.

D. TAKINGS FOR PRIVATE DEVELOPMENTS

Should governments be allowed to take property from one private party and transfer it to another? This has occurred in cases involving private developers to provide jobs, increase tax revenue, and encourage redevelopment. If the use for which the property is taken furthers only private gain, the taking is unconstitutional.

V. LEASEHOLD ESTATES

Created when an owner or landlord conveys a right to possess and use property to a tenant. The tenant's interest is a leasehold estate.

A. TENANCY FOR YEARS

Created by an express contract by which property is leased for a specific period (a month, a year, a period of years). At the end of the period, the lease ends (without notice). If the tenant dies during the lease, the lease interest passes to the tenant's heirs.

B. PERIODIC TENANCY

Created by a lease that specifies only that rent is to be paid at certain intervals. Automatically renews unless terminated. Terminates, at common law, on one period's notice.

C. TENANCY AT WILL

A tenancy for as long as the landlord and tenant agree. Exists when a tenant for years retains possession after termination with the landlord's consent before payment of the next rent (when it becomes a periodic tenancy). Terminates on the death of either party or tenant's commission of waste.

D. TENANCY AT SUFFERANCE

Possession of land without right (without the owner's permission). Owner can immediately evict the tenant.

VI. LANDLORD-TENANT RELATIONSHIPS

A. CREATING THE LANDLORD-TENANT RELATIONSHIP

1. Form of the Lease

To ensure the validity of a lease, it should be in writing and—

a. Express an intent to establish the relationship.
b. Provide for transfer of the property's possession to the tenant at the beginning of the term.
c. Provide for the landlord to retake possession at the end of the term.
d. Describe the property (include the address).
e. Indicate the length of term and the amount and due dates of rent.

2. Legal Requirements

A landlord cannot discriminate against tenants on the basis of race, color, religion, national origin, or sex. A tenant cannot promise to do something against these (or other) laws.

B. RIGHTS AND DUTIES

1. Possession

a. Landlord's Duty to Deliver Possession

A landlord must give a tenant possession of the property at the beginning of the term.

b. Tenant's Right to Retain Possession

The tenant retains possession exclusively until the lease expires.

c. Covenant of Quiet Enjoyment

The landlord promises that during the lease term no one having superior title to the property will disturb the tenant's use and enjoyment of it. If so, the tenant can sue for damages for breach.

d. Eviction

If the landlord deprives the tenant of possession of the property or interferes with his or her use or enjoyment of it, an eviction occurs. **Constructive eviction** occurs when this results from a landlord's failure to perform adequately his or her duties under the lease.

2. Use and Maintenance of the Premises

a. Tenant's Use

Generally, a tenant may make any legal use of the property, as long as it is reasonably related to the purpose for which the property is ordinarily used and does not harm the landlord's interest. A tenant is not responsible for ordinary wear and tear.

b. Landlord's Maintenance

A landlord must comply with local building codes.

3. Implied Warranty of Habitability

In most states, a landlord must furnish residential premises that are habitable. This applies to substantial defects that the landlord knows or should know about and has had a reasonable time to repair.

4. **Rent**

A tenant must pay rent even if he or she moves out or refuses to move in (if the move is unjustifiable). If the landlord violates the implied warranty of habitability, a tenant may withhold rent, pay for repair and deduct the cost, cancel the lease, or sue for damages.

C. TRANSFERRING RIGHTS TO LEASED PROPERTY

1. **Transferring the Landlord's Interest**

A landlord can sell, give away, or otherwise transfer his or her real property. If complete title is transferred, the tenant becomes the tenant of the new owner, who must also abide by the lease.

2. **Transferring the Tenant's Interest**

Before a tenant can assign or sublet his or her interest, the landlord's consent may be required (it cannot be unreasonably withheld). If the assignee or sublessee later defaults, the tenant must pay the rent.

TRUE-FALSE QUESTIONS

(Answers at the Back of the Book)

_____ 1. A fee simple absolute is potentially infinite in duration and can be disposed of by deed or by will.

_____ 2. The owner of a life estate has the same rights as a fee simple owner.

_____ 3. An easement allows a person to use land and take something from it, but a profit allows a person only to use land.

_____ 4. Deeds offer different degrees of protection against defects of title.

_____ 5. The government can take private property for *public* use without just compensation.

_____ 6. The government can take private property for *private* uses only.

_____ 7. A covenant of quiet enjoyment guarantees that a tenant will not be disturbed in his or her possession of leased property by the landlord or any third person.

_____ 8. If the covenant of quiet enjoyment is breached, the tenant can sue the landlord for damages.

_____ 9. Generally, a tenant must pay rent even if he or she moves out, if the move is unjustifiable.

_____ 10. When a landlord sells leased premises to a third party, any existing leases terminate automatically.

FILL-IN QUESTIONS

(Answers at the Back of the Book)

1. An owner in fee simple absolute who conveys the estate to another in fee simple defeasible retains _____ (a reversionary/an executory) interest. If the conditions of the conveyance are not met, the _____ (next designated heir/original owner) takes ownership of the estate.

2. An owner in fee simple who conveys the estate to another as a life estate retains a _____ (remainder/reversion). When a life estate is conveyed and the grantor has not disposed of the interest in the land remaining after the grantee's life, the grantor retains a _____ (remainder/reversion) that will become possessory on the grantee's death.

3.   When an owner transfers a future interest, the interest in the property held by the buyer or receiver is known as either _____ (a reversionary/an executory) interest or a _____ (remainder/reversion).

MULTIPLE-CHOICE QUESTIONS

(Answers at the Back of the Book)

____   1.   Lou owns two hundred acres next to May's lumber mill. Lou sells to May the privilege of removing timber from his land to refine into lumber. The privilege of removing the timber is

   a.   a license.
   b.   an easement.
   c.   a profit.
   d.   none of the above.

____   2.   Tina conveys her estate "to Al so long as no liquor is consumed on the premises." No liquor is consumed on the premises during Al's life, and the estate passes to Al's heir, Julie. Julie conveys the estate to Mike. Mike opens a bar on the property. The estate

   a.   reverts to Julie.
   b.   reverts to some heir of Al's besides Julie.
   c.   reverts to Tina or Tina's heirs.
   d.   none of the above.

____   3.   Ann owns a cabin on Long Lake. Bob takes possession of the cabin without Ann's permission and puts up a sign that reads "No Trespassing by Order of Bob, the Owner." The statutory period for adverse possession is ten years. Bob is in the cabin for eleven years. Ann sues to remove Bob. She will

   a.   win, because Ann sued Bob after the statutory period for adverse possession.
   b.   win, because Bob did not have permission to take possession of the cabin.
   c.   lose, because Bob acquired the cabin by adverse possession.
   d.   lose, because the no-trespassing sign misrepresented ownership of the cabin.

____   4.   Gina conveys her warehouse to Sam under a warranty deed. Later, Rosa appears, holding a better title to the warehouse than Sam's. Rosa proceeds to evict Sam. Sam can recover from Gina

   a.   the purchase price of the property only.
   b.   damages from being evicted only.
   c.   the purchase price of the property and damages from being evicted.
   d.   none of the above.

____   5.   Evan owns an apartment building in fee simple. Evan can

   a.   give the building away, but not sell it or transfer it by will.
   b.   sell the building or transfer it by a will, but cannot give it away.
   c.   give the building away, sell it, or transfer it by will.
   d.   none of the above.

____   6.   Dan owns a half-acre of land fronting Blue Lake. Rod owns the property behind Dan's land. No road runs to Dan's land, but Rod's driveway runs between a road and Dan's property, so Dan uses Rod's driveway. The right-of-way that Dan has across Rod's property is

   a.   a license.
   b.   an easement.
   c.   a profit.
   d.   none of the above.

_____ **7.** Dave owns an office building. Dave sells the building to P&I Corporation. To be valid, the deed that conveys the property from Dave to P&I must include a description of the property and

    a. only Dave's name and P&I's name.
    b. only words evidencing Dave's intent to convey.
    c. only Dave's signature (witnessed and acknowledged).
    d. words evidencing Dave's intent to convey, Dave's name, P&I's name, and Dave's signature (witnessed and acknowledged).

_____ **8.** Curt operates Diners Cafe in space that he leases in Eagle Mall, which is owned by Fine Property Company. Fine sells the mall to Great Investments, Inc. For the rest of the lease term, Curt owes rent to

    a. Diners Cafe.
    b. Fine Property.
    c. Great Investments.
    d. no one.

_____ **9.** Jim leases an apartment from Maria. With Maria's consent, Jim assigns the lease to Nell for the last two months of the term, after which Nell exercises an option under the original lease to renew for three months. One month later, Nell moves out. Regarding the rent for the rest of the term

    a. no one is liable.
    b. Jim can be held liable.
    c. only Nell is liable.
    d. Maria is liable.

_____ **10.** Sue signs a lease for an apartment, agreeing to make rental payments before the fifth of each month. The lease does not specify a termination date. This is

    a. a periodic tenancy.
    b. a tenancy at sufferance.
    c. a tenancy at will.
    d. a tenancy for years.

SHORT ESSAY QUESTIONS

1. Describe the power of eminent domain and the process by which private property is condemned for a public purpose.

2. What does the implied warranty of habitability require, and when does it apply?

ISSUE SPOTTERS

(Answers at the Back of the Book)

1. Gary owns a commercial building in fee simple. Gary transfers temporary possession of the building to Holding Corporation (HC). Can HC transfer possession for even less time to Investment Company?

2. Ann leases office space in Ted's building for a one-year term. If Ann dies during the period of the lease, what happens to the leased property?

3. Charles sells his house to Dian under a warranty deed. Later, Carol appears, holding a better title to the house than Dian. Carol wants Dian off the property. What can Dian do?

Chapter 30:
Insurance, Wills, and Trusts

WHAT THIS CHAPTER IS ABOUT

Insurance is a contract in which an insurance company promises to pay the insured or a beneficiary if the insured is injured or the insured's property is damaged as a result of a specified contingency. This chapter covers law relating to insurance. This chapter also covers some of the law governing wills and trusts.

CHAPTER OUTLINE

I. **INSURANCE**

A. **RISK MANAGEMENT**
Risk management consists of plans to protect personal and financial interests should some event undermine their security. The most common method is to transfer risk from a business or individual to an insurance company.

B. **CLASSIFICATIONS OF INSURANCE**
Insurance is classified according to the nature of the risk involved.

C. **INSURANCE TERMINOLOGY**
An insurance company is an **underwriter** or an **insurer**; the party covered by insurance is the **insured**; an insurance contract is a **policy**; consideration paid to an insurer is a **premium**; policies are obtained through an **agent** or **broker**.

D. **INSURABLE INTEREST**
To obtain insurance, one must have a sufficient interest in what is insured.

1. **Property Insurance**
One has an insurable interest in property if one would suffer a pecuniary loss from its destruction. This interest must exist *when the loss occurs.*

2. **Life Insurance**
One must have a reasonable expectation of benefit from the continued life of another. The benefit may be related to money or may be founded on a relationship (by blood or affinity).

a. **Key-Person Insurance**
A business (partnership, corporation) can insure the life of an employee who is important to that organization (partner, officer).

b. **When the Insurable Interest Must Exist**
An interest in someone's life must exist *when the policy is obtained.*

E. **THE INSURANCE CONTRACT**

1. **Application**
The application is part of the contract. Misstatements can void a policy, especially if the insurer shows that it would not have issued the policy if it had known the facts.

2. **Effective Date**

A policy is effective when (1) a binder is written, (2) the policy is issued, or (3) a certain time elapses.

a. **When a Policy Is Obtained from a Broker**

A broker is the agent of the applicant. Until the broker obtains a policy, the applicant is normally not insured.

b. **When a Policy Is Obtained from an Agent**

An agent is the agent of the insurer. One who obtains a policy from an agent can be protected from the moment the application is made (under a binder), or the parties may agree to delay coverage until a policy is issued or some condition is met (such as a physical exam).

3. **Provisions and Clauses**

An ambiguity in the policy will be interpreted against the insurer. Some important clauses include—

a. **Coinsurance Clause**

If an owner insures property up to a specified percentage (usually 80 percent) of its value, he or she will recover any loss up to the face amount of the policy. If the insurance is for less than this percentage, the owner is responsible for a proportionate share.

b. **Incontestability Clause**

After a policy has been in force for a certain time (two or three years), the insurer cannot cancel the policy or avoid a claim on the basis of statements made in the application.

4. **Cancellation**

A policy may be canceled for nonpayment of premiums, fraud or misrepresentation, conviction for a crime that increases the hazard insured against, or gross negligence that increases the hazard insured against. An insurer may be required to give advance written notice.

5. **Basic Duties and Rights**

Parties must act in good faith and disclose all material facts. If there is a claim, the insurer must investigate. Insurer and insured must fulfill the terms of the policy.

6. **Defenses against Payment**

Fraud, misrepresentation, violation of warranties, and improper actions that are against public policy or that are otherwise illegal.

II. WILLS

A **will** is a declaration of how a person wants property disposed of after death; it is a formal instrument that must follow certain requirements to be effective.

A. TERMINOLOGY OF WILLS

A **testator** is a person who makes a will; a **probate court** oversees the administration of a will by an **executor** (appointed by the testator in the will) or by an **administrator** (appointed by the court).

B. TYPES OF GIFTS

A gift of real estate by will is a **devise**; the recipient is a **devisee**. A gift of personal property is a **bequest** or **legacy**; a recipient is a **legatee**. Gifts can be specific, general, or residuary. If there are not enough assets to pay all general bequests, an **abatement** reduces the gifts.

C. PROBATE PROCEDURES

Probate: establish the validity of a will and administer the estate. Statutes providing for the distribution of estates vary from state to state. The Uniform Probate Code (UPC) includes rules and procedures for resolving conflicts in settling estates and relaxes some of the will requirements.

1. **Informal Probate**

   In some states, cars, bank accounts, etc., can pass by filling out forms, or property can be transferred by affidavit. Most states allow heirs to distribute assets themselves after a will is admitted to probate.

2. **Formal Probate**

   For large estates, a probate court supervises distribution.

3. **Property Transfers outside the Probate Process**

   Will substitutes include *inter vivos* trusts (see below), life insurance policies with named beneficiaries, and joint tenancies.

D. REQUIREMENTS FOR A VALID WILL

1. **Testamentary Capacity and Intent**

   When a will is made, the testator must be of legal age (in most states, at least eighteen years old) and sound mind (intend the document to be a will, comprehend the property being distributed, and remember family members and others for whom a person normally has affection). If the plan of distribution was the result of improper pressure by another person (undue influence), the will is invalid.

2. **Writing Requirements**

   Generally, a will must be in writing. In a few states, an oral (**nuncupative**) will is valid to pass personal property below a certain value if made in the expectation of imminent death.

3. **Signature Requirements**

   The testator must sign with the intent to validate the will; the signature need not be at the end.

4. **Witness Requirements**

   The number of witnesses (two or three) and other rules vary from state to state. A witness does not have to read the will.

5. **Publication Requirements**

   In a few states, the testator must declare orally to the witnesses that the document they are about to sign is his or her will.

E. REVOCATION OF WILLS

A will is revocable, in whole or in part, by its maker any time during the maker's lifetime by physical act (intentionally obliterating or destroying a will, or directing someone else to do so); by a document (codicil or new will); or by operation of law (marriage, divorce, annulment, birth of a child).

F. INTESTACY LAWS

State statutes regulate how property is distributed when a person dies without a valid will.

1. **Surviving Spouse and Children**

   First, the debts of the decedent are paid out of the estate, and then other assets pass to the surviving spouse and children.

   a. **Legitimate Heirs**

      The spouse receives a share; the children receive the rest (stepchildren are not kin). If no children or grandchildren survive, the spouse receives all of it.

   b. **Illegitimate Children**

      In some states, intestate succession between a father and an illegitimate child can occur only if the child is legitimized by ceremony or was acknowledged by the father.

2. **Other Heirs**

a. Lineal Descendants
If there is no surviving spouse or child, then grandchildren, brothers and sisters, and (in some states) parents share in the property of the estate.

b. Collateral Heirs
If there are no lineal descendants, then nieces, nephews, aunts, and uncles share. If none survive, property goes to the next of kin of collateral heirs (relatives by marriage are not considered kin).

3. Methods of Distribution
Per stirpes: a class or group of distributees take the share that their deceased parent would have been entitled to if that parent lived. *Per capita*: each person takes an equal share of the estate.

III. TRUSTS
Arrangements by which a grantor (settlor) transfers legal title to the trust property to a trustee, who administers the property as directed by the grantor for the benefit of the beneficiaries.

A. ESSENTIAL ELEMENTS OF A TRUST

1. A designated beneficiary.
2. A designated trustee.
3. A fund sufficiently identified to enable title to pass to the trustee.
4. Actual delivery to the trustee with the intention of passing title.

B. EXPRESS TRUSTS

1. *Inter Vivos* Trust
Created by trust deed to exist during the settlor's lifetime.

2. Testamentary Trust
Created by will to come into existence on the settlor's death (if the will is invalid, the trust is invalid). If not named in the will, a trustee is appointed by a court. Trustee's actions are subject to judicial approval.

C. IMPLIED TRUSTS

1. Resulting Trust
Arises when the conduct of the parties raise an inference that the party holding legal title to the property does so for the benefit of another.

2. Constructive Trust
An equitable remedy that enables plaintiffs to recover property from defendants who would otherwise be unjustly enriched. A court declares the legal owner of the property to be a trustee for those entitled to the benefit of the property.

D. SPECIAL TYPES OF TRUSTS

1. Charitable Trust
Designed to benefit a segment of the public or the public in general, usually for charitable, educational, religious, or scientific purposes.

2. Spendthrift Trust
Prevents a beneficiary's transfer of his or her right to future payments of income or capital by placing restraints on the transfer of funds.

3. Totten Trust
Created when one person deposits money in his or her own name as trustee. Revocable at will until the depositor dies or completes the gift.

TRUE-FALSE QUESTIONS

(Answers at the Back of the Book)

____ 1. Risk management involves the transfer of certain risks from an individual or a business to an insurance company.

____ 2. Insurance is classified by the nature of the person or interest protected.

____ 3. An insurance broker is an agent of an insurance company.

____ 4. An insurance applicant is usually protected from the time an application is made, if a premium has been paid, possibly subject to certain conditions.

____ 5. A person can insure anything in which he or she has an insurable interest.

____ 6. A will is revocable only after the testator's death.

____ 7. The testator generally must sign a will.

____ 8. If a person dies without a will, all of his or her property automatically passes to the state.

____ 9. An *inter vivos* trust is a trust created by a grantor during his or her lifetime.

____ 10. A testamentary trust is created by will to begin on the settlor's death.

FILL-IN QUESTIONS

(Answers at the Back of the Book)

When a person dies, a personal representative settles the decedent's affairs. A personal representative named in a will is an _____ (administrator/executor). A personal representative appointed by a court for a decedent who dies without a will, who fails to name a personal representative in a will, who names a personal representative lacking the capacity to serve, or who writes a will that the court refuses to admit to probate is an _____ (administrator/executor).

MULTIPLE-CHOICE QUESTIONS

(Answers at the Back of the Book)

____ 1. Ruth applies to Standard Insurance Company for a fire insurance policy for her warehouse. To obtain a lower premium, she misrepresents the age of the property. The policy is granted. After the warehouse is destroyed by fire, Standard learns the true facts. Standard can

a. not refuse to pay, because an application is not part of an insurance contract.
b. not refuse to pay, because fire destroyed the warehouse.
c. refuse to pay on the ground of fraud in the application.
d. refuse to pay on the ground that fire destroyed the warehouse.

____ 2. Carl is an executive with DigiCom, Inc. Because his death would cause a financial loss to the firm, it insures his life. Later, he resigns to work for a competitor, E-Tech Corporation. Six months later, Carl dies. Regarding payment for the loss, DigiCom can

a. collect, because the firm's insurable interest existed when the policy was obtained.
b. collect if the firm suffered a financial loss when Carl resigned.
c. not collect, because the firm's insurable interest did not exist when a loss occurred.
d. not collect, because the firm suffered no financial loss from Carl's death.

____ **3.** Tom buys a house and obtains from Union Insurance Company a fire insurance policy on the property. If fire destroys the house, to collect payment under the policy, Tom's insurable interest

a. exists only if the property is owned by Tom or a related individual.
b. exists only if the property is owned in fee simple.
c. must exist when the loss occurs.
d. must exist when Union issues the policy and when the loss occurs.

____ **4.** Satellite Communications, Inc., takes out an insurance policy on its plant with United Insurance, Inc. United could cancel the policy

a. for any reason.
b. if any of Satellite's drivers have their driver's licenses suspended.
c. if Satellite begins using grossly careless manufacturing practices.
d. if Satellite's president appears as a witness in a case against United.

____ **5.** Tech Corporation makes computers. To insure its products to cover injuries to consumers if the products prove defective, Tech should buy

a. group insurance.
b. liability insurance.
c. major medical insurance.
d. term life insurance.

____ **6.** Adam's will provides for specific items of property to be given to certain individuals, including employees of his business. The will also provides for certain sums of money to be given to his daughters, Carol and Dian. Because Adam's assets are insufficient to pay in full all of the bequests

a. all of the property must be sold and the proceeds distributed to the heirs.
b. Carol and Dian get nothing.
c. the employees, who are not in a blood relationship with Adam, get nothing.
d. the gifts to Carol and Dian will be reduced proportionately.

____ **7.** Eve dies without a will, but is survived by her brother Frank, her child Gail, and her parents. The party with the first priority to receive Eve's estate is

a. her brother Frank.
b. her child Gail.
c. her parents.
d. the state.

____ **8.** Holly executes a will that leaves all of her property to Ira. Two years later, Holly executes a will that leaves all of her property to Jill. The second will does not expressly revoke the first will. Holly dies. The property passes to

a. Ira, because he was given the property in the first will.
b. Ira, because the second will did not expressly revoke the first will.
c. Jill, because the first will was revoked by the second will.
d. Jill, because two years separated the execution of the wills.

____ **9.** Kelly dies intestate, survived by Lisa, her mother; Mike, her spouse; Nick and Owen, their sons; and Pam, the daughter of Ruth, their daughter, who predeceased her mother. Under intestacy laws

a. Lisa and Mike receive equal portions of Kelly's estate.
b. Mike receives all of Kelly's estate.
c. Mike receives one-third of Kelly's estate, and Nick, Owen, and Pam receive equal portions of the rest.
d. Nick and Owen receive half of Kelly's estate, and Mike receives the rest.

____ **10.** Sam wants Tony and Vic, his sons, to get the benefit of Sam's farm when he dies. Sam can provide for them to get the farm's income, under another party's management, by setting up

a. a constructive trust.
b. an interstate trust.
c. a resulting trust.
d. a testamentary trust.

SHORT ESSAY QUESTIONS

1. What is the concept of insurable interest, and what is its effect on insurance payments?

2. In what ways may a will be revoked?

ISSUE SPOTTERS

(Answers at the Back of the Book)

1. Why is an insurance premium small relative to the amount of coverage that an insurance company offers?

2. Neal applies to Farm Insurance Company for a life insurance policy. On the application, Neal understates his age. Neal obtains the policy, but for a lower premium than he would have had to pay had he disclosed his actual age. The policy includes an incontestability clause. Six years later, Neal dies. Can the insurer refuse payment?

3. Adam is divorced and owns a house. He has no reasonable expectation of benefit from the life of Beth, his ex-spouse, but applies for insurance on her life anyway. He obtains a fire insurance policy on the house and then sells the house. Ten years later, Beth dies and fire destroys the house. Can Adam obtain payment for these events?

CUMULATIVE HYPOTHETICAL PROBLEM FOR UNIT NINE—INCLUDING CHAPTERS 28–30

(Answers at the Back of the Book)

As joint tenants, Eve and Frank own twenty acres of land, on which there is a warehouse surrounded by a fence.

____ **1.** In determining whether the fence is a fixture, the most important factor is

a. the adaptability of the fence to the land.
b. the intent of Eve and Frank.
c. the manner in which the fence is attached to the land.
d. the value of the fence.

____ **2.** Frank wants to sell the land and the warehouse. He executes and delivers a deed to Greg. Eve will

a. own all of the land and the warehouse because she did not sign the deed.
b. own exactly twenty acres and half a warehouse.
c. retain a 1/2 undivided interest in the property.
d. share ownership of the property with Greg as a joint tenant.

____ **3.** For the deed between Frank and Greg to be effective, one of the conditions is that the deed must

a. be delivered by Frank with the intent to transfer title.
b. be recorded within certain statutory time limits.
c. include the sale price.
d. include the signatures of both Frank and Greg.

____ 4. On the warehouse, the owners obtain a $300,000 fire insurance policy from American Insurance Company that includes an 80 percent coinsurance clause. At the time, the warehouse is valued at $400,000. When the warehouse is valued at $500,000, it sustains fire damage of $60,000. Recovery under the policy is

   a. $45,000.
   b. $60,000.
   c. $75,000.
   d. $300,000.

____ 5. International Sales, Inc. (ISI), rents the warehouse from the owners, under a two-year lease that requires ISI to pay the property taxes. At the start of the second year, ISI agrees with J&J Transport to allow it to occupy the warehouse and pay rent to ISI. No one pays the property taxes for the second year. In a suit to collect, the owners would most likely

   a. lose and have to pay the taxes themselves.
   b. prevail against ISI because the agreement with J&J was a sublease.
   c. prevail against ISI and J&J because they are jointly and severally liable.
   d. prevail against J&J because the lease was assigned to J&J.

QUESTIONS ON THE FOCUS ON LEGAL REASONING FOR UNIT NINE—*TAHOE-SIERRA PRESERVATION COUNCIL, INC. V. TAHOE REGIONAL PLANNING AGENCY*

(Answers at the Back of the Book)

____ 1. Washington County imposes a moratorium on building until the completion of the county's land-use plan. According to the majority in *Tahoe-Sierra Preservation Council, Inc. v. Tahoe Regional Planning Agency*, this moratorium is most likely

   a. a taking and must be compensated.
   b. a taking but does not require compensation.
   c. not a taking and does not require compensation.
   d. not a taking but must be compensated.

____ 2. Under the facts in the previous question, according to the dissent in *Tahoe-Sierra Preservation Council, Inc. v. Tahoe Regional Planning Agency*, the moratorium is

   a. a taking and must be compensated.
   b. a taking but does not require compensation.
   c. not a taking and does not require compensation.
   d. not a taking but must be compensated.

____ 3. Suppose that the moratorium in the previous questions is not a taking. According to the majority in *Tahoe-Sierra Preservation Council, Inc. v. Tahoe Regional Planning Agency*, this means that any costs associated with undeveloped land must be borne by

   a. the county government.
   b. the courts.
   c. the federal government.
   d. the landowner.

Chapter 31:
Professional Liability

WHAT THIS CHAPTER IS ABOUT

This chapter outlines the potential common law liability of professionals, the potential liability of accountants under securities laws and the Internal Revenue Code, and the duty of professionals to keep their clients' communications confidential.

CHAPTER OUTLINE

I. POTENTIAL COMMON LAW LIABILITY TO CLIENTS

A. LIABILITY FOR BREACH OF CONTRACT
For a professional's breach of contract, a client can recover damages, including expenses incurred to secure another professional to provide the services and other reasonable and foreseeable losses.

B. LIABILITY FOR NEGLIGENCE
Professionals must exercise the standard of care, knowledge, and judgment generally accepted by members of their professional group.

    1. Accountant's Duty of Care

        a. Comply with Accounting Principles and Standards
        Accountants must comply with generally accepted accounting principles (GAAP) and generally accepted auditing standards (GAAS) (though compliance does not guarantee relief from liability). Violation of either is *prima facie* evidence of negligence. Note: There may be a higher state law standard.

        b. Act in Good Faith
        If an accountant conforms to GAAP and acts in good faith, he or she will not be liable to a client for incorrect judgment.

        c. Investigate Suspicious Financial Transactions
        An accountant who uncovers suspicious financial transactions and fails to investigate the matter fully or to inform his or her client of the discovery can be held liable to the client for the resulting loss.

    2. Attorney's Duty of Care

        a. General Duty
        All attorneys owe a duty to provide competent and diligent representation. The standard is that of a reasonably competent general practitioner of ordinary skill, experience, and capacity.

        b. Specific Responsibilities
        Attorneys must be familiar with well-settled principles of law applicable to a case, discover law that can be found through a reasonable amount of research, and investigate and discover facts that could materially affect the client's legal rights.

C. PROFESSIONALS' LIABILITY FOR FRAUD

1. **Actual Fraud**

   A professional may be liable if he or she intentionally misstates a material fact to mislead his or her client and the client justifiably relies on the misstated fact to his or her injury.

2. **Constructive Fraud**

   A professional may be liable for constructive fraud whether or not he or she acted with fraudulent intent (for example, an accountant who is grossly negligent; gross negligence includes the intentional failure to perform a duty in reckless disregard of the consequences).

II. AUDITORS' LIABILITY TO THIRD PARTIES

Most courts hold that auditors can be held liable to third parties for negligence.

A. THE *ULTRAMARES* RULE

1. **The Privity Requirement**

   An accountant does not owe a duty to a third person with whom he or she has no direct contractual relationship (privity) or no relationship "so close as to approach that of privity."

2. **The "Near Privity" Rule**

   In a few states, if a third party has a sufficiently close relationship or nexus with an accountant, the *Ultramares* privity requirement may be satisfied without establishing an accountant-client relationship.

B. THE *RESTATEMENT* RULE

Most courts hold accountants liable for negligence to persons whom the accountant "intends to supply the information or knows that the recipient intends to supply it" and persons whom the accountant "intends the information to influence or knows that the recipient so intends" [*Restatement (Second) of Torts*, Section 552].

C. LIABILITY TO REASONABLY FORESEEABLE USERS

A few courts hold accountants liable to any users whose reliance on an accountant's statements or reports was reasonably foreseeable.

III. LIABILITY OF ATTORNEYS TO THIRD PARTIES

In some cases, attorneys may be liable to third parties who rely on legal opinions to their detriment.

IV. THE SARBANES-OXLEY ACT OF 2002

This act imposes requirements on a public accounting firm that provides auditing services to an *issuer* (a company that has securities registered under Section 12 of the Securities Exchange Act of 1934; that is required to file reports under Section 15(d) of the 1934 act; or that files—or has filed—a registration statement not yet effective under the Securities Act of 1933).

A. THE PUBLIC COMPANY ACCOUNTING OVERSIGHT BOARD

This board, which reports to the Securities and Exchange Commission, oversees the audit of public companies subject to securities laws to protect public investors and ensure that public accounting firms comply with the provisions of the Sarbanes-Oxley Act.

B. APPLICABILITY TO PUBLIC ACCOUNTING FIRMS

Public accounting firms are firms and associated persons that are "engaged in the practice of public accounting or preparing or issuing audit reports."

1. **Nonaudit Services**

   It is unlawful to perform for an issuer both audit and nonaudit services, which include bookkeeping for an audit client, financial systems design and implementation, appraisal services, fairness opinions, management functions, and investment services.

2. Audit Services

A public accounting firm cannot provide audit services to an issuer if the lead audit partner or the reviewing partner provided those services to the issuer in each of the prior five years, or if the issuer's chief executive officer, chief financial officer, chief accounting officer, or controller worked for the auditor and participated in an audit of the issuer within the preceding year.

3. Reports to an Issuer's Audit Committee

These reports must be timely and indicate critical accounting policies and practices, as well as alternatives discussed, and other communications, with the issuer's management.

C. DOCUMENT DESTRUCTION

The act prohibits destroying or falsifying records to obstruct or influence a federal investigation or in relation to a bankruptcy. Penalties include fines and imprisonment up to twenty years.

V.   LIABILITY OF ACCOUNTANTS UNDER SECURITIES LAWS

A. LIABILITY UNDER THE SECURITIES ACT OF 1933

1. Misstatements or Omissions in Registration Statements

An accountant may be liable for misstatements and omissions of material facts in registration statements (which they often prepare for filing with the Securities and Exchange Commission (SEC) before an offering of securities—see Chapter 33) [Section 11].

a. To Whom an Accountant May Be Liable

Anyone who acquires a security covered by the statement. A plaintiff must show that he or she suffered a loss on the security. There is no requirement of privity or proof of reliance.

b. Due Diligence Defense

An accountant may avoid liability by showing that, in preparing the financial statements, he or she had—

1) Reasonable Grounds to Believe That the Statements Were True

After a reasonable investigation, the accountant believed that the statements were true and omitted no material facts.

2) Followed GAAP and GAAS

Failure to follow GAAP and GAAS is proof of a lack of due diligence.

3) Verified Information Furnished by Officers and Directors

This defense requires that accountants verify information furnished by the offering firm's officers and directors.

c. Other Defenses to Liability

1) There were no misstatements or omissions.
2) The misstatements or omissions were not of material facts.
3) The misstatements or omissions had no causal connection to the purchaser's loss.
4) The purchaser invested in the securities knowing of the misstatements or omissions.

2. Misstatements or Omissions in Other Communications in an Offer

Anyone offering or selling a security may be liable for fraud on the basis of communication to an investor of a misstatement or omission [Section 12(2)].

B. LIABILITY UNDER THE SECURITIES EXCHANGE ACT OF 1934

1. Section 18—False or Misleading Statements in Certain SEC Documents

An accountant may be liable for making or causing to be made in an application, report, document, or registration statement filed with the SEC a statement that at the time and in light of the circumstances was false or misleading with respect to any material fact.

a. **To Whom an Accountant May Be Liable**

Only sellers and purchasers who can prove (1) the statement affected the price of the security and (2) they relied on the statement and were unaware of its inaccuracy.

b. **Defenses**

1) **Proof of Good Faith**

Proof that the accountant did not know the statement was false or misleading. This can be refuted by showing the accountant's (1) intent to deceive or (2) reckless conduct and gross negligence.

2) **Buyer or Seller Knew the Statement Was False or Misleading**

3) **Statute of Limitations Tolled**

An action must be brought within one year after the discovery of facts constituting the cause and within three years after the cause accrues.

2. **Section 10(b) and Rule 10b-5—Misstatements or Omissions**

These laws cover written and oral statements.

a. **Section 10(b)**

Makes it unlawful for any person to use, in connection with the purchase or sale of any security, any manipulative or deceptive device or contrivance in contravention of SEC rules and regulations.

b. **Rule 10b-5**

Makes it unlawful for any person, by use of any means or instrumentality of interstate commerce, to—

1) Employ any device, scheme, or artifice to defraud.

2) Make any untrue statement of a material fact or to omit to state a material fact necessary to make the statements made, in light of the circumstances, not misleading.

3) Engage in any act, practice, or course of business that operates or would operate as a fraud or deceit on any person, in connection with the purchase or sale of any security.

c. **To Whom An Accountant May Be Liable**

Only to sellers or purchasers. Privity is not required. To recover, a plaintiff must prove (1) *scienter*, (2) a fraudulent action or deception, (3) reliance, (4) materiality, and (5) causation.

C. **THE PRIVATE SECURITIES LITIGATION REFORM ACT OF 1995**

1. **Adequate Procedures and Disclosure**

An auditor must use adequate procedures in an audit to detect any illegal acts. If something is detected, the auditor must disclose it to the board, audit committee, or SEC, depending on the circumstances.

2. **Proportionate Liability**

A party is liable only for the proportion of damages for which he or she is responsible.

3. **Aiding and Abetting**

An accountant who knows that he or she is participating in an improper activity and knowingly aids the activity (even by silence) is guilty of aiding and abetting. The SEC may obtain an injunction or damages.

VI. POTENTIAL CRIMINAL LIABILITY OF ACCOUNTANTS

A. THE SECURITIES ACTS

An accountant may be subject to imprisonment of up to five years and a fine of up to $10,000 under the 1933 act and up to $100,000 under the 1934 act. Under the Sarbanes-Oxley Act, for a securities filing accompanied by an accountant's false or misleading certified audit statement, the accountant may be fined up to $5 million and imprisoned up to twenty years.

B. THE INTERNAL REVENUE CODE

1. **Aiding or Assisting in the Preparation of a False Tax Return**

A felony punishable by a fine of $100,000 ($500,000 in the case of a corporation) and imprisonment for up to three years [Section 7206(2)].

2. **Understatement of a Client's Tax Liability**

Liability is limited to one penalty per taxpayer per tax year.

a. **Negligent or Willful Understatement**

A tax preparer is subject to a penalty of $250 per return for negligent understatement and $1,000 for willful understatement or reckless or intentional disregard of rules or regulations [Section 6694].

b. **Aiding and Abetting an Individual's Understatement**

$1,000 per document ($10,000 in corporate cases) [Section 6701].

3. **Other Liability Related to Tax Returns**

A tax preparer may be subject to penalties for failing to furnish the taxpayer with a copy of the return, failing to sign the return, or failing to furnish the appropriate tax identification numbers [Section 6695].

C. STATE LAW

Most states impose criminal penalties for knowingly certifying false or fraudulent reports; falsifying, altering, or destroying books of account; and obtaining property or credit through the use of false financial statements.

VII. WORKING PAPERS

In some states, working papers are the accountant's property. The client has a right of access to them, and they cannot be transferred to another accountant or otherwise disclosed without the client's permission (or a court order). Unauthorized disclosure is a ground for a malpractice suit. Under the Sarbanes-Oxley Act, accountants are required, in some circumstances, to maintain working papers relating to an audit or review for five years. A knowing violation may result in a fine and imprisonment for up to ten years.

VIII. CONFIDENTIALITY AND PRIVILEGE

A. ATTORNEY-CLIENT

The confidentiality of attorney-client communications is protected by law. The client holds the privilege, and only the client may waive it.

B. ACCOUNTANT-CLIENT

In response to a federal court order, an accountant must provide the information sought; there is no privilege. In most states, on a court order, an accountant must disclose information about his or her client. In a few states, no disclosure is allowed (even in a court) without the client's permission.

IX. LIMITING PROFESSIONALS' LIABILITY

Professionals may limit their liability for misconduct of other professionals with whom they work by organizing as a professional corporation (see Chapter 25) or a limited liability partnership (see Chapter 24).

TRUE-FALSE QUESTIONS

(Answers at the Back of the Book)

____ 1. Professionals must exercise the standard of care, knowledge, and judgment observed by their peers.

____ 2. A violation of GAAP and GAAS is *prima facie* evidence of negligence.

____ 3. Compliance with GAAP and GAAS will relieve an accountant of liability.

____ 4. In all states, an accountant is liable to anyone who relies on the accountant's negligently prepared reports.

____ 5. Accountants are not subject to criminal penalties under federal securities laws.

____ 6. A tax preparer may be subject to penalties under the Internal Revenue Code for assisting in filing a false tax return.

____ 7. There is no penalty under the Internal Revenue Code for failing to give the taxpayer a copy of the return.

____ 8. State-provided rights to confidentiality of accountant-client communications are not recognized in federal cases.

____ 9. Under the Private Securities Litigation Reform Act of 1995, a party is liable only for the proportion of damages for which he or she is responsible.

____ 10. For an accountant to be liable to a seller or purchaser for misstatements or omissions under SEC Rule 10b-5, there must be privity.

FILL-IN QUESTIONS

(Answers at the Back of the Book)

Accountants must comply with generally accepted accounting principles (GAAP) and generally accepted auditing standards (GAAS). An accountant who conforms to GAAP and acts in good faith _____ (may/will not) be liable to a client for incorrect judgment. An accountant who uncovers suspicious financial transactions but fails to investigate fully or to inform the client _____ (may/will not) be liable. If a client suffers a loss due to fraud that an accountant negligently fails to discover, the accountant _____ (may/will not) be liable.

MULTIPLE-CHOICE QUESTIONS

(Answers at the Back of the Book)

____ 1. Ann, an accountant, accumulates working papers in performing an audit for her client, Beta Corporation. Ann can release those papers

a. only on the request of another accountant.
b. only with Beta's permission.
c. under any circumstances.
d. under no circumstances.

____ 2. Digital, Inc., asks Ed, an accountant, to prepare its financial statements. Ed conducts the audit negligently. The firm uses the statements to obtain a loan from First National Bank. The loan is not repaid. In most states, Ed is

   a. liable only to Digital for the negligent audit.
   b. liable to any possible foreseeable user of the statements.
   c. liable to the bank if Ed knew the bank would rely on the statements.
   d. liable to the bank only if it was in privity of contract with Ed.

____ 3. Fine Distribution, Inc., includes financial statements prepared by Greg, an accountant, in a registration statement filed with the SEC as part of a public stock offer. Holly buys 100 shares and later suffers losses due to misstatements of fact in the statements. Holly sues Greg under the Securities Act of 1933. Holly will

   a. lose, because Holly relied on the statements.
   b. lose, if Greg and Holly were not in privity.
   c. win, if Greg prepared the statements with knowledge of the misstatements.
   d. win, if the misstatements were material.

____ 4. Dick, an accountant, audits financial statements for Eagle Corporation and issues an unqualified opinion on them. Fran buys 100 shares of Eagle stock and later suffers losses due to misrepresentations in the statements. Fran sues Dick under the Securities Exchange Act of 1934. Fran will

   a. lose, because Fran relied on the statements.
   b. lose, if Dick and Fran were not in privity.
   c. win, if Dick prepared the statements with knowledge of the misstatements.
   d. win, if the misstatements were material.

____ 5. Jack is an accountant. In most states, Jack can be compelled to disclose a client's communication

   a. only on a court order.
   b. only with the client's permission.
   c. under any circumstances.
   d. under no circumstances.

____ 6. In auditing Great Sales Corporation's books, Hal is assisted by Ira, a Great Sales employee. Hal does not discover Ira's theft of Great Sales money because Ira hides records that would reveal it. When Ira absconds with the money, Great Sales sues Hal. Great Sales will

   a. lose, because Hal could not reasonably have been expected to discover the theft.
   b. lose, because Hal is not liable for the results once she has performed.
   c. win, because Hal did not discover the theft.
   d. win, because Hal did not inform Great Sales of the theft.

____ 7. Carol, an accountant, breaches her contract with Diners Cafe, a local restaurant. Damages that Diners may recover include

   a. only penalties imposed for failing to meet deadlines.
   b. only the cost to secure the contracted-for services elsewhere.
   c. penalties for missing deadlines and the cost to secure services elsewhere.
   d. none of the above.

____   8.   Lily is injured in an auto accident, but Mega Insurance, Inc., refuses to pay her claim. She hires Nick, an attorney, who fails to file a suit against Mega before the time for filing runs out. Lily sues Nick. She will

   a.   lose, because clients are ultimately responsible for such deadlines.
   b.   lose, because Nick could not reasonably have been expected to file on time.
   c.   win, because Nick committed malpractice.
   d.   win, because the insurance company refused to pay her claim.

____   9.   Ace Auto Repairs hires Ben, an accountant, to perform an audit, in the course of which Ben accumulates several hundred pages of notes, computations, and other memoranda. After the audit

   a.   Ace has the right to retain all working papers.
   b.   Ben has the right to retain all working papers.
   c.   the working papers are filed with the SEC.
   d.   the working papers must be destroyed.

____   10.   Jane is an accountant whom Kay, a former client, charges with negligence. Jane's defenses include

   a.   only that she was not negligent.
   b.   only that if she was negligent, it was not the proximate cause of Kay's loss.
   c.   that she was not negligent, and if she was negligent, it was not the proximate cause of Kay's loss.
   d.   none of the above.

SHORT ESSAY QUESTIONS

1.   Contrast an accountant's past and present potential common law liability to third persons.

2.   What is the difference between the attorney-client privilege and the accountant-client privilege?

ISSUE SPOTTERS

(Answers at the Back of the Book)

1.   What is a professional liable for, at common law, if he or she *un*intentionally misstates a material fact that misleads a client?

2.   Dave, an accountant, prepares a financial statement for Excel Company, a client, knowing that Excel will use the statement to obtain a loan from the First National Bank. Dave makes negligent omissions in the statement that result in a loss to the bank. Can the bank successfully sue Dave?

3.   Nora, an accountant, prepares a financial statement as part of a registration statement that Omega, Inc., files with the Securities and Exchange Commission before making a public offering of securities. In the statement is a misstatement of material fact not attributable to Nora's fraud or negligence. Pat relies on the misstatement, buys some of the securities, and suffers a loss. Can Nora be held liable to Pat?

QUESTIONS ON THE FOCUS ON LEGAL REASONING FOR UNIT TEN— *KPMG, LLC V. SECURITIES AND EXCHANGE COMMISSION*

(Answers at the Back of the Book)

___ 1. Able Accountants, LLC, loans $50,000 to each of its officers, including Ben. Able's clients include Commercial Innovation, Inc. (CII), which makes Ben its president. CII agrees to pay Able a contingent fee based on CII's future profits. According to the findings of the Securities and Exchange Commission (SEC) in *KPMG, LLC v. SEC*, regarding specific provisions of the American Institute of Certified Public Accountants (AICPA) rules, the Securities Exchange Act of 1934, and the SEC rules, this situation

   a. does not impair anyone's independence.
   b. impairs Able's independence.
   c. impairs Ben's independence.
   d. impairs CII's independence.

___ 2. Under the facts in the previous question, the SEC issues an order to "cease and desist" from "any future violation" of the specific provisions of the Securities Exchange Act of 1934 and the SEC rules. According to the majority in *KPMG, LLC v. SEC*, this order

   a. is not overbroad.
   b. is overbroad because it bans "any future violation."
   c. is overbroad because it is based on past violations.
   d. is overbroad because it is a "sweeping order" to obey the present law.

___ 3. Under the facts in the previous questions, according to the dissent in *KPMG, LLC v. SEC*, the SEC order

   a. can be sustained.
   b. cannot be sustained because the AICPA rules cover only professional services.
   c. cannot be sustained because the SEC rules cover only investment services.
   d. cannot be sustained because the Securities Exchange Act of 1934 covers only sales of securities.

Answers

Chapter 1

True-False Questions

1. T
2. T
3. T
4. T
5. F. The National Conference of Commissioners on Uniform State Laws drafted the Uniform Commercial Code (UCC), and other uniform laws and model codes, and proposed it for adoption by the states. All of the states have adopted most of the UCC, but it is not a federal law.
6. F. This is the definition of civil law. Criminal law relates to wrongs against society as a whole and for which society has established sanctions.
7. T
8. T
9. T
10. F. Commercial speech (advertising) can be restricted as long as the restriction (1) seeks to implement a substantial government interest, (2) directly advances that interest, and (3) goes no further than necessary to accomplish its objective.

Fill-in Questions

with similar facts; precedent; permits a predictable

Multiple-Choice Questions

1. B. The use of precedent—the doctrine of *stare decisis*—permits a predictable, relatively quick, and fair resolution of cases. Under this doctrine, a court must adhere to principles of law established by higher courts.
2. C. The doctrine of *stare decisis* attempts to harmonize the results in cases with similar facts. When the facts are sufficiently similar, the same rule is applied. Cases with identical facts could serve as binding authority, but it is more practical to expect to find cases with facts that are not identical but similar—as similar as possible.
3. A. An order to do or refrain from a certain act is an injunction. An order to perform as promised is a decree for specific performance. These remedies, as well as rescission, are equitable remedies, which are normally awarded only if the usual remedy at law is inadequate. An award of damages (money) is the usual remedy at law.
4. D. Equity and law provide different remedies, and at one time, most courts could grant only one type. Today, most states do not maintain separate courts of law and equity, and a judge may grant either or both forms of relief in any case in which they are

appropriate. Equitable relief is generally granted, however, only if damages (the legal remedy) is inadequate.

5. C. The U.S. Constitution is the supreme law of the land. Any state or federal law or court decision in conflict with the Constitution is unenforceable and will be struck. Similarly, provisions in a state constitution take precedence over the state's statutes, rules, and court decisions.

6. C. In establishing case law, or common law, the courts interpret and apply state and federal constitutions, rules, and statutes. Case law applies in areas that statutes or rules do not cover. Federal law applies to all states, and preempts state law in many areas.

7. A. Law that defines, describes, regulates, or creates rights or duties is substantive law. Law that establishes methods for enforcing rights established by substantive law is procedural law. Criminal law governs wrongs committed against society for which society demands redress.

8. D. International law comes from a variety of sources, and represents attempts to reconcile desires for national authority and profitable commerce. Enforcement of international law can only be accomplished by cooperation, persuasion, or coercion.

9. D. Commercial speech does not have as much protection under the First Amendment as noncommercial speech. Commercial speech that is misleading may be restricted if the restriction (1) seeks to advance a substantial government interest, (2) directly advances that interest, and (3) goes no further than necessary.

10. D. Dissemination of obscene materials is a crime. Speech that harms the good reputation of another, or defamatory speech, is not protected under the First Amendment. "Fighting words," which are words that are likely to incite others to respond with violence, are not constitutionally protected. Other unprotected speech includes other speech that violates criminal laws, such as threats.

Issue Spotters

1. Case law includes courts' interpretations of statutes, as well as constitutional provisions and administrative rules. Statutes often codify common law rules. For these reasons, a judge might rely on the common law as a guide to the intent and purpose of a statute.

2. Yes. Administrative rulemaking starts with the publication of a notice of the rulemaking in the *Federal Register*. A public hearing is held at which proponents and opponents can offer evidence and question witnesses. After the hearing, the agency considers what was presented at the hearing and drafts the final rule.

3. Yes, the law would violate both types of due process. The law would be unconstitutional on substantive due process grounds, because it abridges free-

dom of speech. The law would be unconstitutional on procedural due process grounds, because it imposes a penalty without giving an accused a chance to defend his or her actions.

Chapter 2

True-False Questions

1. T

2. T

3. F. The decisions of a state's highest court on all questions of state law are final. The United States Supreme Court can overrule only those state court decisions that involve questions of federal law.

4. T

5. T

6. T

7. F. A losing party may appeal an adverse judgment to a higher court, but the party in whose favor the judgment was issued may also appeal if, for example, he or she is awarded less than sought in the suit.

8. F. Most lawsuits—as many as 95 percent—are dismissed or settled before they go to trial. Courts encourage alternative dispute resolution (ADR) and sometimes order parties to submit to ADR, particularly mediation, before allowing their suits to come to trial.

9. F. In mediation, a mediator assists the parties in reaching an agreement, but not by deciding the dispute. The mediator emphasizes points of agreement, helps the parties evaluate their positions, and proposes solutions.

10. F. If an arbitration agreement covers the subject matter of a dispute, a party to the agreement can be compelled to arbitrate the dispute. A court would order the arbitration without ruling on the basic controversy.

Fill-in Questions

to dismiss; for judgment on the pleadings; summary judgment

Multiple-Choice Questions

1. A. On a "sliding scale" test, a court's exercise of personal jurisdiction depends on the amount of business that an individual or firm transacts over the Internet. Jurisdiction is most likely proper when there is substantial business, most likely improper when a Web site is no more than an ad, and may or may not be appropriate when there is some interactivity. "Any" interactivity with "any resident" of a state would likely not be enough, however.

2. A. This is part of discovery. Discovery saves time, and the trend is toward more, not less, discovery. Discovery is limited, however, to relevant materials. A party cannot obtain access to such data as another's trade secrets or, in testimony, an admission concerning unrelated matters.

3. C. A corporation is subject to the jurisdiction of the courts in any state in which it is incorporated, in which it has its main office, or in which it does business. In the suit in this question, the court may exercise *in rem* jurisdiction.

4. A. As noted above, a corporation is subject to the jurisdiction of the courts in any state in which it is incorporated, in which it has its main office, or in which it does business. The court may be able to exercise personal jurisdiction or *in rem* jurisdiction, or the court may reach a defendant corporation with a long arm statute. In the right circumstances, this firm might also be involved in a suit in a federal court, if the requirements for federal jurisdiction are met.

5. A. An appeals court examines the record of a case, looking mostly at questions of law for errors by the court below. If it determines that a retrial is necessary, the case is sent back to the lower court. For this reason, an appellant's best ground for an appeal focuses on the law that applied to the issues in the case, not questions concerning the credibility of the evidence.

6. D. The United States Supreme Court is not required to hear any case. The Court has jurisdiction over any case decided by any of the federal courts of appeals and appellate authority over cases decided by the states' highest courts if the latter involve questions of federal law. But the Court's exercise of its jurisdiction is discretionary, not mandatory.

7. B. If a defendant's motion to dismiss is granted, the case is at an end. If the motion is denied, the defendant must then file an answer, or another appropriate response, or a default judgment will be entered against him or her. Of course, the defendant is given more time to file this response. If the motion is granted, the plaintiff is given more time to file an amended complaint.

8. D. Negotiation is an informal means of dispute resolution. Generally, unlike mediation and arbitration, no third party is involved in resolving the dispute. In those two forms, a third party may render a binding or nonbinding decision. Arbitration is a more formal process than mediation or negotiation. Litigation involves a third party—a judge—who renders a legally binding decision.

9. B. In a summary jury trial, the jury's verdict is not binding, as it would otherwise be in a court trial. In a mini-trial, the attorneys argue a case and a third party renders an opinion, but the opinion discusses how a court would decide the dispute. Early neutral case negotiation is what its name suggests, involving a third party who evaluates the disputing parties' positions.

10. C. Online dispute resolution (ODR) is a new type of alternative dispute resolution. Most ODR forums resolve disputers informally and come to nonbonding resolutions. Any party to a dispute being considered in ODR may discontinue the process and appeal to a court at any time.

Issue Spotters

1. Yes. Submission of the dispute is mandatory, but compliance with a decision is voluntary.

2. Dean could file a motion for a directed verdict. This motion asks the judge to direct a verdict for Dean on the ground that Jan presented no evidence that would justify granting Jan relief. The judge grants the motion if there is insufficient evidence to raise an issue of fact.

3. This is not necessarily the end of their case. Either a plaintiff or a defendant, or both, can appeal a judgment to a higher court. An appellate court can affirm, reverse, or remand a case, or take any of these actions in combination. To appeal successfully, it is best to appeal on the basis of an error of law, because appellate courts do not usually reverse on findings of fact.

Chapter 3

True-False Questions

1. T

2. T

3. T

4. F. According to utilitarianism, it is the consequences of an act that determine how ethical the act is. Applying this theory requires determining who will be affected by an act, assessing the positive and negatives effects of alternatives, and choosing the alternative that will provide the greatest benefit for the most people. Utilitarianism is premised on acting so as to do the greatest good for the greatest number of people. An act that affects a minority negatively may still be morally acceptable.

5. T

6. F. In situations involving ethical decisions, a balance must sometimes be struck between equally good or equally poor courses of action. The choice is often between equally good alternatives—benefiting shareholders versus benefiting employees, for example—and sometimes one group may be adversely affected. (The legality of a particular action may also be unclear.)

7. T

8. F. Simply obeying the law will not meet all ethical obligations. The law does not cover all ethical requirements. An act may be unethical but not illegal. In fact, compliance with the law is at best a moral minimum. Furthermore, there is an ethical aspect to almost every decision that a business firm makes.

9. T

10. F. Bribery is also a legal issue, regulated in the United States by the Foreign Corrupt Practices Act. Internationally, a treaty signed by the members of the Organization for Economic Cooperation and Development makes bribery of public officials a serious crime. Each member nation is expected to enact legislation implementing the treaty.

Fill-in Questions

Religious standards; Kantian ethics; the principle of rights

Multiple-Choice Questions

1. C. Business ethics focus on the application of moral principles in a business context. Different standards are not required. Business ethics is a subset of ethics that relates specifically to what constitutes right and wrong in situations that arise in business.

2. A. Traditionally, ethical reasoning relating to business has been characterized by two fundamental approaches—duty-based ethics and utilitarianism, or outcome-based ethics. Duty-based ethics derive from religious sources or philosophical principles. These standards may be absolute, which means that an act may not be undertaken, whatever the consequences.

3. A. Under religious ethical standards, it is the nature of an act that determines how ethical the act is, not its consequences. This is considered an *absolute* standard. But this standard is tempered by an element of compassion (the "Golden Rule").

4. D. In contrast to duty-based ethics, outcome-based ethics, or utilitarianism, involves a consideration of the consequences of an action. Utilitarianism is premised on acting so as to do the greatest good for the greatest number of people.

5. D. Utilitarianism requires determining who will be affected by an action, assessing the positive and negatives effects of alternatives, and choosing the alternative that will provide the greatest benefit for the most people. This approach has been criticized as tending to reduce the welfare of human beings to plus and minus signs on a cost-benefit worksheet.

6. A. A corporation, for example, as an employer, commonly faces ethical problems that involve conflicts among itself, its employees, its customers, its suppliers, its shareholders, its community, or other groups. Increasing wages, for instance, may benefit the employees and the community, but reduce profits and the ability of the employer to give pay increases in the future, as well as decreasing dividends to shareholders. To be considered socially responsible, when making a decision, a business firm must take into account the interests of all of these groups, as well as society as a whole.

7. B. In any profession, there is a responsibility, both legal and ethical, not to misrepresent material facts, even at the expense of some profits. This is a clear ethical standard in the legal profession and in the accounting profession.

8. A. In part because it is impossible to be entirely aware of what the law requires and prohibits, the best course for a business firm is to act responsibly and in good faith. This course may provide the best defense if a transgression is discovered. Striking a balance between what is profitable and what is legal and ethical can be difficult, however. A failure to act legally or ethically can result in a reduction in profits, but a failure to act in the profitable interest of the firm can also cause profits to suffer. *Optimum* profits are the maximum profits that a firm can realize while staying within legal and ethical limits.

9. D. The principle of rights theory of ethics follows the belief that persons have fundamental rights. This belief is implied by duty-based ethical standards and Kantian ethics. The rights are implied by the duty that forms the basis for the standard (for example, the duty not to kill implies that persons have a right to live), or by the personal dignity implicit in the Kantian belief about the fundamental nature of human beings. Not to respect these rights would, under the principle of rights theory, be morally wrong.

10. C. The Foreign Corrupt Practices Act prohibits any U.S. firm from bribing foreign officials to influence official acts to provide the firm with business opportunities. Such payments are allowed, however, if they would be lawful in the foreign country. Thus, to avoid violating the law, the firm in this problem should determine whether such payments are legal in the minister's country.

Issue Spotters

1. The answer depends on which system of ethics is used. Under a duty-based ethical standard, it may not be the consequences of an act that determine how ethical the act is; it may be the nature of the act itself. Stealing would be unethical regardless of whether the fruits of the crime are given to the poor. In contrast, utilitarianism is premised on acting so as to do the greatest good for the greatest number of people. It is the consequences of an act that determine how ethical the act is.

2. Maybe. On the one hand, it is not the company's "fault" when a product is misused. Also, keeping the product on the market is not a violation of the law, and stopping sales would hurt profits. On the other hand, suspending sales could reduce suffering and could stop potential negative publicity if sales continued.

3. When a corporation decides to respond to what it sees as a moral obligation to correct for past discrimination by adjusting pay differences among its employees, an ethical conflict is raised between the firm and its employees and between the firm and its shareholders. This dilemma arises directly out of the effect such a decision has on the firm's profits. If satisfying this obligation increases profitability, then the dilemma is easily resolved in favor of "doing the right thing."

Cumulative Hypothetical Problem for Unit One—Including Chapters 1–3

1. C. The power of judicial review is the power of any state or federal court to review a statute and declare it unconstitutional. Courts can also review the actions of the executive branch, which includes administrative agencies, to determine their constitutionality. A statute or rule that is declared unconstitutional is void. The power of judicial review is not expressly stated in the Constitution but is implied.

2. A. Mediation involves the a third party, a mediator. The mediator does not decide the dispute but only assists the parties to resolve it themselves. Although the mediator does not render a legally binding decision, any agreement the parties reach may be legally binding.

3. D. These state and federal courts would all have jurisdiction over the defendant. The customer's state could exercise jurisdiction over the firm through its long arm statute. The firm's state would have jurisdiction over it as a resident. A federal court could hear the case under its diversity jurisdiction: the parties are residents of different states and the amount in controversy is at least $75,000.

4. A. Damages, or money damages, is a remedy at law. Remedies in equity include injunctions, specific performance, and rescission. The distinction arose because the law courts in England could not always grant suitable remedies, and so equity courts were created to grant other types of relief. The U.S. legal system derives from the English system.

5. D. Ethics is the study of what constitutes right or wrong behavior. It focuses on the application of moral principles to conduct. In a business context, ethics involves the application of moral principles to business conduct. Legal liability is a separate question and may, or may not, indicate unethical behavior. Profitability is also a separate issue. *Optimum* profitability is the *maximum* profitability a business may attain within the limits of the law *and* ethics.

Questions on the Focus on Legal Reasoning for Unit One—*Kasky v. Nike, Inc.*

1. D. The majority set out a three-part test for determining whether speech is commercial. The three elements included the speaker, the intended audience, and the content of the message. The court seemed to emphasized the source of the speech as the dominant element. None of the other answer choices were mentioned.

2. B. The dissent argued that commercial speech should be distinguished by its content only, not by its content, the identity of the speaker, and the intended audience, as the majority held. The dissent asserted in part that "the inherent worth of the speech in terms of its capacity for informing the public does not depend upon the identity of its source" and that corporate and other business speakers contribute to the types of ideas that the First Amendment "seeks to foster."

3. D. The majority felt that its holding would have no chilling effect on commercial speech or public debate. Because commercial speech is based on a profit motive, it is "more hardy than noncommercial speech" and not likely to be much inhibited by this case. The dissent disagreed, arguing that this case "would have an undoubted chilling effect on speech," inhibiting businesses' ability to participate in debates over matters of public concern.

Chapter 4

True-False Questions

1. T
2. F. A reasonable apprehension or fear of *immediate* harmful or offensive contact is an assault.
3. T
4. F. Puffery is seller's talk—the seller's *opinion* that his or her goods are, for example, the "best." For fraud to occur, there must be a misrepresentation of a *fact*.
5. T
6. F. To establish negligence, the courts apply a reasonable person standard to determine whether certain conduct resulted in a breach of a duty of care.
7. T
8. F. This is not misconduct, in terms of a wrongful interference tort. Bona fide competitive behavior is permissible, whether or not it results in the breaking of a contract or other business relation.
9. T
10. F. Some states have statutes prohibiting or regulating the use of spam. Also, the sending of spam may constitute trespass to personal property, and could be curtailed by private lawsuits. What the government can do to restrict spam may be limited by the First Amendment's protection for freedom of speech, however.

Fill-in Questions

1. negligence;
2. defense of assumption of risk

3. contributory;
4. comparative

Multiple-Choice Questions

1. B. Joe committed a battery and may have committed an assault. For an intentional tort, what matters is the actor's intent regarding the consequences of an act or his or her knowledge with substantial certainty that certain consequences will result. Motive is irrelevant, and the other person's fear is not a factor in terms of the actor's intent.

2. A. To delay a customer suspected of shoplifting, a merchant must have probable cause (which requires more than a mere suspicion). A customer's concealing merchandise in his or her bag and leaving the store without paying for it would constitute probable cause. Even with probable cause, a merchant may delay a suspected shoplifter only for a reasonable time, however.

3. B. Trespass to land occurs when a person, without permission, enters onto another's land, or remains on the land. An owner does not need to be aware of an act before it can constitute trespass, and harm to the land is not required. A trespasser may have a complete defense, however, if he or she enters onto the land to help someone in danger.

4. B. The basis of the tort of defamation is publication of a statement that holds an individual up to contempt, ridicule, or hatred. Publication means that statements are made to or within the hearing of persons other than the defamed party, or that a third party reads the statements. A secretary reading a letter, for example, meets this requirement. But the statements do not have to be read or heard by a specific third party. (Whether someone is a public figure is important only because a public figure cannot recover damages for defamation without proof of actual malice.)

5. A. The standard of a business that invites persons onto its premises is a duty to exercise reasonable care. Whether conduct is unreasonable depends on a number of factors, including how easily the injury could have been guarded against. A landowner has a duty to discover and remove hidden dangers, but obvious dangers do not need warnings.

6. C. To commit negligence, a breach of a duty of care must cause harm. If an injury was foreseeable, there is causation in fact. This can usually be determined by the but-for test: but for the wrongful act, the injury would not have occurred. Thus, an actor is not necessarily liable to all who are injured. Insurance coverage and business dealings are not factors.

7. B. Strict liability is liability without fault. This is imposed on dangerous activities when they (1) involve potentially serious harm to persons or property, (2) involve a high degree of risk that cannot be completely guarded against by the exercise of reasonable

care, and (3) are activities not commonly performed in the area. The other choices represent irrelevant factors.

8. D. Advertising is bona fide competitive behavior, which is not a tort even if it results in the breaking of a contract. Obtaining more customers is one of the goals of effective advertising. Taking unethical steps to interfere with others' contracts or business relations could constitute a tort, however.

9. D. Under the Communications Decency Act, an Internet service provider (ISP) may not be held liable for defamatory statements made by its customers online. Congress provided this immunity as an incentive to ISPs to "self-police" the Internet for offensive material.

10. D. Trespass to personal property is intentional physical contact with another's personal property that causes damage. Sending spam through an Internet service provider (ISP) is intentional contact with the ISP's computer systems. A negative impact on the value of the ISP's equipment, by using its processing power to transmit e-mail, constitutes damage (the resources are not available for the ISP's customers). Also, service cancellations harm an ISP's business reputation and goodwill.

Issue Spotters

1. Yes. Adam is guilty of battery—an unexcused, harmful, or offensive physical contact intentionally performed. A battery may involve contact with any part of the body and anything (a blouse, in this problem) attached to it.

2. Yes. Trespass to personal property occurs when an individual unlawfully harms another's personal property or otherwise interferes with the owner's right to exclusive possession and enjoyment.

3. No. As long as competitive behavior is bona fide, it is not tortious even if it results in the breaking of a contract. The public policy that favors free competition in advertising outweighs any instability that bona fide competitive activity causes in contractual or business relations. To constitute wrongful interference with a contractual relationship, there must be (1) a valid, enforceable contract between two parties; (2) the knowledge of a third party that this contract exists; and (3) the third party's intentionally causing the breach of the contract (and damages) to advance the third party's interest.

Chapter 5

True-False Questions

1. T
2. F. A copyright is granted automatically when a qualifying work is created, although a work can be registered with the U.S. Copyright Office.

3. T

4. T

5. F. Anything that makes an individual company unique and would have value to a competitor is a trade secret. This includes a list of customers, a formula for a chemical compound, and other confidential data.

6. F. Trade names cannot be registered with the federal government. They are protected, however, under the common law (when used as trademarks or service marks) by the same principles that protect trademarks.

7. F. A copy does not have to be the same as an original to constitute copyright infringement. A copyright is infringed if a substantial part of a work is copied without the copyright holder's permission.

8. F. A trademark may be infringed by an intentional or unintentional use of a mark in its entirety, or a copy of the mark to a substantial degree. In other words, a mark can be infringed if its use is intended or not, and whether the copy is identical or similar. Also, the owner of the mark and its unauthorized user need not be in direct competition.

9. T

10. F. Proof of a likelihood of confusion is not required in a trademark dilution action. The products involved do not even have to be similar. Proof of likely confusion is required in a suit for trademark infringement, however.

Fill-in Questions

70; 95; 120; 70

Multiple-Choice Questions

1. B. A firm that makes, uses, or sells another's patented design, product, or process without the owner's permission commits patent infringement. It is not required that an invention be copied in its entirety. Also, the object that is copied does not need to be trademarked or copyrighted, in addition to being patented.

2. A. The user of a trademark can register it with the U.S. Patent and Trademark Office, but registration is not necessary to obtain protection from trademark infringement. A trademark receives protection to the degree that it is distinctive. A fanciful symbol is the most distinctive mark.

3. B. Ten years is the period for later renewals of a trademark's registration. The life of a creator plus seventy years is a period for copyright protection. No intellectual work is protected forever, at least not without renewal. To obtain a patent, an applicant must satisfy the U.S. Patent and Trademark Office that the invention or design is genuine, novel, useful, and not obvious in light of contemporary technology. A patent is granted to the first person to create whatever is to be patented, rather than the first person to file for a patent.

4. A. Copyright protects a specific list of creative works, including literary works, musical works, sound recordings, and pictorial, graphic, and sculptural works. Although there are exceptions for "fair use," a work need not be copied in its entirety to be infringed. Also, to make a case for infringement, proof of consumers' confusion is not required, and the owner and unauthorized user need not be direct competitors.

5. D. Business processes and information that cannot be patented, copyrighted, or trademarked are protected against appropriation as trade secrets. These processes and information include production techniques, as well as a product's idea and its expression.

6. C. Trademark law protects a distinctive symbol that its owner stamps, prints, or otherwise affixes to goods to distinguish them from the goods of others.

7. B. A certification mark certifies the region, materials, method of manufacture, quality, or accuracy of goods or services. A collective mark is a certification mark used by members of a cooperative, association, or other organization (a union, in this problem). A service distinguishes the services of one person or company from those of another. A trade name indicates part or all of a business's name.

8. D. This is not copyright infringement because no copyright is involved. This is not cybersquatting because no one is offering to sell a domain name to a trademark owner. (It is also unlikely that this violates the Anticybersquatting Consumer Protection Act because there is no indication of "bad faith intent.") Trademark dilution occurs when a trademark is used, without the owner's without permission, in a way that diminishes the distinctive quality of the mark. That has not happened here.

9. C. The Berne Convention provides some copyright protection, but its coverage and enforcement was not as complete or as universal as that of the TRIPS (Trade-Related Aspects of Intellectual Property Rights) Agreement. The Paris Convention allows parties in one signatory country to file for patent and trademark protection in other signatory countries.

10. A. Publishers cannot put the contents of their periodicals into online databases and other electronic resources, including CD-ROMs, without securing the permission of the writers whose contributions are included.

Issue Spotters

1. The owner of the customer list can sue its competitor for the theft of trade secrets. Trade secrets include customer lists. Liability extends to those who misappropriate trade secrets by any means, including modems.

2. This is patent infringement. A software maker in this situation might best protect its product, save litigation costs, and profit from its patent by the use of a license. In the context of this problem, a license would grant permission to sell a patented item. (A license can

be limited to certain purposes and to the licensee only.)

3. Yes. This may be an instance of trademark dilution. Dilution occurs when a trademark is used, without permission, in a way that diminishes the distinctive quality of the mark. Dilution does not require proof that consumers are likely to be confused by a connection between the unauthorized use and the mark. The products involved do not have to be similar. Dilution does require, however, that a mark be famous when the dilution occurs.

Chapter 6

True-False Questions

1. T
2. F. Felonies are crimes punishable by imprisonment of a year or more (in a state or federal prison). Crimes punishable by imprisonment for lesser periods (in a local facility) are classified as misdemeanors.
3. F. These are elements of the crime of robbery. (Robbery also involves the use of force or fear.) Burglary requires breaking and entering a building with the intent to commit a crime. (At one time, burglary was defined to cover only breaking and entering the dwelling of another at night to commit a crime.)
4. F. This is an element of larceny. The crime of embezzlement occurs when a person entrusted with another's property fraudulently appropriates it. Also, unlike robbery, embezzlement does not require the use of force or fear.
5. T.
6. F. The crime of bribery occurs when a bribe is offered. Accepting a bribe is a separate crime. In either case, the recipient does not need to perform the act for which the bribe is offered for the crime to exist. Note, too, that a bribe can consist of something other then money.
7. F. The recipient of the goods only needs to know that the goods are stolen. The recipient does not need to know the identity of the thief or of the true owner to commit this crime. Thus, not knowing these individuals' identities is not a defense.
8. T
9. T
10. T

Fill-in Questions

unreasonable; probable; due process of law; jeopardy; trial; trial by; witnesses; bail and fines

Multiple-Choice Questions

1. D. A person who wrongfully or fraudulently takes and carries away another's personal property commits larceny. Unlike burglary, larceny does not involve breaking and entering. Unlike embezzlement, larceny requires that property be taken and carried away from the owner's possession. Unlike forgery, larceny does not require the making or altering of a writing. Unlike robbery, larceny does not involve force or fear.
2. C. The elements of most crimes include the performance of a prohibited act and a specified state of mind or intent on the part of the actor.
3. C. Fraudulently making or altering a writing in a way that changes another's legal rights is forgery. Forgery also includes changing trademarks, counterfeiting, falsifying public documents, and altering other legal documents.
4. B. Embezzlement involves the fraudulent appropriation of another's property, including money, by a person entrusted with it. Unlike larceny, embezzlement does not require that property be taken from its owner.
5. D. The standard to find a criminal defendant guilty is beyond a reasonable doubt. This means that each juror must be convinced, beyond a reasonable doubt, of the defendant's guilt. The standard in most civil cases is a preponderance of the evidence.
6. C. The federal crime of mail fraud has two elements: a scheme to defraud by false pretenses, and mailing, or causing someone else to mail, a writing for the purpose of executing the scheme. It would also be a crime to execute the scheme by wire, radio, or television transmissions.
7. B. In considering the defense of entrapment, the important question is whether a person who committed a crime was pressured by the police to do so. Entrapment occurs when a government agent suggests that a crime be committed and pressure an individual, who is not predisposed to its commitment, to do it.
8. C. A person in police custody who is to be interrogated must be informed that he or she has the right to remain silent; anything said can and will be used against him or her in court; and he or she has the right to consult with an attorney. The person also must be told that if he or she is indigent, a lawyer will be appointed. These rights may be waived if the waiver is knowing and voluntary.
9. C. If, for example, a confession is obtained after an illegal arrest, the confession is normally excluded. Under the exclusionary rule, all evidence obtained in violation of the constitutional rights spelled out in the Fourth, Fifth, and Sixth Amendments normally is excluded, as well as all evidence derived from the illegally obtained evidence. The purpose of the rule is to deter police misconduct.
10. B. A formal charge issued by a grand jury is an indictment. A charge issued by a magistrate is called an information. In either case, there must be sufficient evidence to justify bringing a suspect to trial. The arraignment occurs when the suspect is brought before

the trial court, informed of the charges, and asked to enter a plea.

Issue Spotters

1. No. A mistake of fact, as opposed to a mistake of law, will constitute a defense if it negates the mental state required for the crime. The mental state required for theft involves the knowledge that the property is another's and the intent to deprive the owner of it.
2. Yes. With respect to the gas station, she has obtained goods by false pretenses. She might also be charged with forgery, and most states have special statutes covering illegal use of credit cards.
3. Yes. The National Information Infrastructure Protection Act of 1996 amended the Counterfeit Access Device and Computer Fraud and Abuse Act of 1984. The statute provides that a person who accesses a computer online, without permission, to obtain classified data (such as consumer credit files in a credit agency's database) is subject to criminal prosecution. The crime has two elements: accessing the computer without permission and taking data. It is a felony if done for private financial gain. Penalties include fines and imprisonment for up to twenty years. The victim of the theft can also bring a civil suit against the criminal to obtain damages and other relief.

Cumulative Hypothetical Problem for Unit Two—Including Chapters 4–6

1. B. Intellectual property law protects such intangible rights as copyrights, trademarks, and patents, which include the rights that an individual or business firm has in the products it produces. Protection for software comes from patent law and from copyright law. Protection for the distinguishing trademarks on the software come from, of course, trademark law.
2. C. Of these choices, the firm most likely violated tort law, which includes negligence and strict liability, both as distinct torts and as a part of product liability. Negligence requires proof of intent. Strict liability does not. These firms may also have breached their contracts and their warranties, topics which are discussed in the next Unit.
3. B. This is cyber theft. Accessing a computer online, without authority, to obtain classified, restricted, or protected data, or attempting to do so is prohibited by the National Information Infrastructure Protection Act of 1996. Penalties include fines and imprisonment for up to twenty years.
4. A. A corporation can be held liable for the crimes of its employees, officers, or directors. Imprisonment is not possible, in a practical sense, as a punishment for a corporation. A business firm can be fined or denied certain privileges, however.
5. C. Corporate officers can be held personally liable for the crimes they commit, whether or not the crimes were committed for their personal benefit or on their firm's behalf. Also, corporate officers can be held liable for the actions of employees under their supervision. Furthermore, a court can impose criminal liability on a corporate officer in those circumstances regardless of whether he or she participated in, directed, or even knew about a given crime.

Questions on the Focus on Legal Reasoning for Unit Two—*Pinsonneault v. Merchants & Farmers Bank & Trust Co.*

1. C. The majority stated that "business owners are in the best position to appreciate the crime risks that are posed on their premises." They have no general duty to protect all others from the criminal acts of third persons, but "they do have a duty to implement reasonable measures to protect their patrons from criminal acts when those acts are foreseeable."
2. B. The majority and the dissent agreed that in this case, the bank owed a duty to its patrons to take security steps against the reasonably foreseeable criminal acts of third parties. The majority concluded, after a review of the lower court's record, that the bank had met its duty.
3. A. As noted in the previous answer, the dissent agreed with majority that the bank owed a duty to its patrons to protect them from the reasonably foreseeable criminal acts of third parties. The dissent concluded, however, after a review of the trial court record, that the bank had not met this duty. The basis for the disagreement was the dissent's different interpretation of the facts.

Chapter 7

True-False Questions

1. F. All contracts involve promises, but all promises do not establish contracts. (A contract is an agreement that can be enforced in court.) Contract law reflects which promises society believes should be legally enforced, and assures parties to private contracts that the agreements they make will be enforceable.
2. T
3. T
4. F. A bilateral contract is accepted by a promise to perform. A unilateral contract is formed when the offeree (the party who receives the offer) completes the requested act or other performance.
5. F. An oral contract is an express contract, which may be written or oral. In an express contract, the terms are fully stated in words. In an implied contract, it is the conduct of the parties that creates and defines the terms.
6. F. An unenforceable contract is a valid contract that cannot be enforced due to certain defenses. A voidable contract is a valid contract in which one or

both of the parties has the option of avoiding his or her legal obligations.

7.   T
8.   T
9.   T
10.   F. A quasi contract is imposed by a court to avoid the unjust enrichment of one party at the expense of another. Quasi contracts are not true contracts.

Fill-in Questions

objective; objective; did; circumstances surrounding

Multiple-Choice Questions

1.   C. Freedom of contract refers to the law's recognition that most every individual may enter freely into contractual arrangements. This freedom is expressed in Article I, Section 10 of the U.S. Constitution.
2.   B. One party has performed; the other has not. The contract is executed on the one side and executory on the other, and classified as executory. Once the delivered goods are paid for, the contract will be fully executed.
3.   C. In considering an implied-in-fact contract, a court looks at actions leading up to what happened. If, for example, the plaintiff furnished services, expecting to be paid, which the defendant should have known, and the defendant had a chance to reject the services and did not, the court would hold that the parties had an enforceable implied-in-fact contract.
4.   A. An obligation to pay will be imposed by law to prevent one party from being unjustly enriched at another's expense. This is the doctrine of quasi contract. The doctrine will not be applied, however, if there is a contract covering the matter in dispute. Also, there are some circumstances in which parties will not be forced to pay for benefits "thrust" on them, particularly if this is done over their protest.
5.   B. According to the objective theory of contracts, a party's intent to enter into a contract is judged by outward, objective facts as they would be interpreted by a reasonable person, rather than by the party's own subjective intentions. A reasonable person in the position of a party receiving an offer can know what is in the offer only from what is offered. A court might consider the circumstances surrounding a transaction, and the statements of the parties and the way they acted when they made their contract.
6.   A. An express contract is a contract in which the terms are fully expressed in words, but those words do not necessarily have to be in writing. A contract that is implied from conduct is an implied-in-fact contract. Implied-in-law, or quasi, contracts are not actual contracts but are imposed on parties by courts.
7.   A. The primary purpose of the rules for the interpretation of contracts is to determine the parties' intent from the language used in their agreement and to give effect to that intent. A court will not ordinarily interpret a contract according to what the parties later claim was their intent when they contracted.
8.   C. One of the rules for the interpretation of contracts is that evidence of course of performance, course of dealing, and custom and usage of trade may be admitted to clarify the meaning of ambiguous terms. This evidence is given weight (or priority) in that order.
9.   B. A voidable contract is a valid contract that can be avoided at the option of one or both of the parties. If a party with the option chooses to avoid the contract, both parties are released from their obligations under it. If a party with the option elects to ratify the contract, both parties must perform.
10.   C. Like the definition of a promise, a contract can be defined as an agreement to do or refrain from doing some legal act now or in the future. Mutual promises can make up an agreement, and an agreement that can be enforced in a court is a contract.

Issue Spotters

1.   Under the objective theory of contracts, if a reasonable person would have thought that the offeree accepted the offeror's offer when the offeree signed and returned the letter, a contract was made, and the offeree is bound. This depends in part on what was said in the letter (was it a valid offer?) and what was said in response (was it a valid acceptance?). Under any circumstances, the issue is not whether either party subjectively believed that they did, or did not, have a contract.
2.   Yes. A person who is unjustly enriched at the expense of another can be required to account for the benefit under the theory of quasi contract. The parties here did not have a contract, but the law will impose one to avoid the unjust enrichment.
3.   No. This "contract," although not fully executed, is for an illegal purpose and therefore void. A void contract gives rise to no legal obligation on the part of any party. A contract that is void is no contract. There is nothing to enforce.

Chapter 8

True-False Questions

1.   T
2.   F. One of the elements for a valid offer is that the terms be definite enough to be enforced by a court. This is so a court can determine if a breach had occurred and, if so, what the appropriate remedy would be. An offer might invite a specifically worded acceptance.
3.   T
4.   F. Irrevocable offers (offers that must be kept open for a period of time) include option contracts.

Other irrevocable offers include a merchant's firm offer and, under the doctrine of promissory estoppel, an offer on which an offeree has changed position in reliance.

5. F. The mirror image rule requires that the terms of an offeree's acceptance must exactly match the terms of the offeror's offer to form a valid contract. Any other response effectively rejects the offer, terminating it. An offeree may, of course, include a counteroffer with his or her rejection.

6. F. Normally, silence does not operate as an acceptance, but it can be an acceptance when: an offeree takes the benefit of offered goods or services (even though he or she had an opportunity to reject and knew that they were offered with the expectation of compensation); the parties have had prior dealings in which the offeree has led the offeror reasonably to understand that the offeree will accept all offers unless he or she sends notice to the contrary; or if one has agreed that his or her failure to respond will constitute acceptance.

7. F. Normally, courts will not question the adequacy of consideration, if the consideration is legally sufficient, unless it is so grossly inadequate as to "shock the conscience" of the court or so unfair as to indicate the existence of fraud, duress, incapacity, undue influence, or a lack of bargained-for exchange.

8. T

9. F. Promises based on "past" consideration (that is, promises made with respect to events that have already happened) are unenforceable. These promises lack the element of bargained-for consideration.

10. T

Fill-in Questions

serious; offeror; reasonably definite; offeree

Multiple-Choice Questions

1. D. When an acceptance is made conditional, it constitutes a rejection, but the conditions state a counteroffer. A counteroffer is both a rejection of an original offer and a simultaneous making of a new offer.

2. A. Generally, an offer may be revoked any time before acceptance. Most offers are revocable, even if they say that they are not, as long as the revocation is communicated to the offeree before acceptance. This may be done by express repudiation or by acts that are inconsistent with the offer and that are made known to the offeree (such as a sale to someone else about which the offeree learns).

3. C. An acceptance is effective if it is timely. Under the mailbox rule, using a mode of communication expressly or impliedly authorized by the offeror makes an acceptance effective when sent. If no mode is expressly stated, the mail is acceptable. Here, the offeror

did not specify a certain mode, so the mode that the offeree used to accept was a reasonable means.

4. A. The promisee was not legally obligated to undertake the act, and the promisor was not legally obligated to pay the promisee until the performance was completed. The act undertaken was both detrimental to the promisee and beneficial to the promisor. Also, consideration must be bargained for. Performance or a promise is bargained for if, as in this problem, the promisor seeks it in exchange for his or her promise and the promisee gives it in exchange for that promise.

5. C. Generally, a promise to do what one already has a legal duty to do is not legally sufficient consideration, because no legal detriment or benefit has been incurred or received. This is the preexisting duty rule. Unforeseen difficulties may qualify as an exception to this rule, but an increase in ordinary business expenses, which is a type of risk usually assumed in doing business, does not qualify as an unforeseen difficulty.

6. A. Two parties can mutually agree to rescind their contract, at least to the extent that it is executory, and agree to a new contact. If the rescission and the making of the new contract are simultaneous, and a dispute later arises, the court may have to decide whether to apply the preexisting duty rule, but that seems unlikely in the circumstances described in this problem.

9. D. The injured party signed a valid, enforceable release. No fraud was involved. Consideration was given in the form of the uninjured party's promise to pay in return for the injured party's promise not to sue for a larger amount.

8. C. A person who reasonably relies on the promise of another to that person's detriment can recover under the doctrine of promissory estoppel (also called detrimental reliance). There must be (1) a promise, (2) reliance on the promise, (3) reliance of a substantial, definite nature, and (4) justice in the enforcement of the promise.

9. A. To constitute consideration, the value of whatever is exchanged for the promise must be legally sufficient. Its economic value (its "adequacy") is rarely the basis for a court's refusal to enforce a contract.

10. A. In a covenant not to sue, the parties substitute a contractual obligation for some other type of legal action, such as a tort. A covenant not to sue does not always bar further recovery, unlike a release.

Issue Spotters

1. No. Taking into consideration the owner's frustration and the obvious difference between the value of the car and the "stated" price, a reasonable person would realize that the offer was not made with serious intent and that the party who "paid" the price did not have an agreement.

2. No. The offer was revoked before it was accepted. Revocation of an offer may be implied by conduct inconsistent with the offer. When the corporation hired someone else, and the offeree learned of the hiring, the offer was revoked. The acceptance was too late.

3. Yes. Under the doctrine of detrimental reliance, or promissory estoppel, the promisee is entitled to payment of $5,000 from the promisor on graduation. There was a promise, on which the promisee relied, the reliance was substantial and definite (the promisee went to college for the full term, incurring considerable expenses, and will likely graduate), and it would only be fair to enforce the promise.

Chapter 9

True-False Questions

1. T
2. T
3. F. A person who enters into a contract when he or she is intoxicated can avoid the contract only if he or she was so intoxicated as to fail to comprehend the legal consequences of entering into the deal. Note, though, that the intoxication need not have been involuntary.
4. F. A minor is personally liable for his or her torts. In some circumstances, the minor's parents may also be held liable, if, for example, the tort was malicious or committed at the direction of the parent.
5. T
6. T
7. T
8. F. An illegal contract is void. A court will not enforce it on behalf of any party to it.
9. F. A contract with an unlicensed practitioner may be enforceable if the purpose of the statute is to raise government revenues, but not if the statute's purpose is to protect the public from unlicensed practitioners.
10. F. A covenant not to compete may be upheld if the length of time and the size of the geographic area in which the party agrees not to compete are reasonable. A court may in fact reform these terms to make them reasonable and then enforce them as reformed.

Fill-in Questions

ratification; disaffirm; indicates; ratification

Multiple-Choice Questions

1. B. Ratification is the act of accepting and giving legal force to an obligation that was previously not enforceable. A minor may disaffirm a contract within a reasonable time after attaining majority, however, particularly if the minor returns the consideration received, does not take possession of the subject matter of the contract, or otherwise takes steps that would be inconsistent with ratification.
2. B. If a person was intoxicated enough to lack mental capacity, the contract is voidable at his or her option. Being intoxicated enough to lack mental capacity means being so impaired as not to comprehend the consequences of entering into a contract. Otherwise, the contract is enforceable. Under no circumstances would the contract be void.
3. D. Only a guardian can enter into legally binding contracts on a person's behalf if the person has been adjudged mentally incompetent by a court. Any contract entered by the incompetent person is void. If the person has not been so adjudged, however, a contract may be enforceable if the person either knew it was a contract or understood its legal consequences.
4. C. To disaffirm a contract, a minor must return whatever he or she received under it. In a state in which there is also an obligation to return the other party to the position he or she was in before the contract, the minor must also pay for any damage to the goods.
5. D. The general rule is that an illegal contract is unenforceable. Thus, if an illegal agreement is executory, with the illegal part not yet performed, the party whose performance has not been rendered can withdraw. The person cannot be held in breach, and the contract cannot be enforced.
6. D. This promise (a covenant not to compete) is enforceable, because it is no broader than necessary for the other party's protection. Such promises may be considered contracts in restraint of trade, illegal on grounds of public policy, when they are broader than necessary (particularly in terms of geographic area and time), or are not accompanied by a sale of a business.
7. D. A contract with an unlicensed party is illegal and not enforceable by either party to it if the purpose of the licensing statute is to protect the public from unauthorized practitioners. If the purpose of the statute is to raise government revenues, however, the contract is enforceable.
8. B. The reasonableness of a covenant not to compete, accompanied by the sale of a business or included in an employment contract, is determined by the length of time and the size of the area in which the party agrees not to compete. In some cases, a court might even reform overly restrictive terms to prevent any undue burdens or hardships.
9. A. An exculpatory clause (a contract clause attempting to absolve a party of negligence or other wrongs) is often held unconscionable, especially in a case involving a lease of real property, or in which an employer is attempting to avoid liability for injury to an employee, or in which a business important to the public interest is seeking its enforcement.

10. D. A contract with an unlicensed individual may be enforceable depending on the nature of the applicable licensing statute. If the statute bars the enforcement of such contracts, of course they are not enforceable. They are also not enforceable if the statute's purpose is to protect the public from unlicensed practitioners. Otherwise, if the statute is intended only to raise revenue, such contracts may be enforceable.

Issue Spotters

1. A minor may effectively ratify a contract after he or she reaches the age of majority either expressly or impliedly. Failing to disaffirm an otherwise enforceable contract within a reasonable time after reaching the age of majority would also effectively ratify it. Nothing a minor does before attaining majority, however, will ratify a contract.

2. The criminal in this problem can recover none of the payments to the law enforcement official. Their contract was an illegal contract and, as such, unenforceable by either party to it and neither party can recover damages or the relief if the contract has been executed.

3. No. Generally, An exculpatory clause (a clause attempting to absolve parties of negligence or other wrongs) is not enforced if the party seeking its enforcement is involved in a business that is important to the public as a matter of practical necessity, such as an airline. Because of the essential nature of these services, they have an advantage in bargaining strength and could insist that anyone contracting for their services agree not to hold them liable.

Chapter 10

True-False Questions

1. T
2. F. If the parties to both sides of a contract are mistaken as to the same material fact, either party can rescind the contract at any time. This is a bilateral, or mutual, mistake. Either party can enforce a contract, however, if the mistake relates to the later market value or quality of the object of the contract.
3. T
4. F. Proof off injury is not needed to rescind a contract for fraud. Proof of injury is required, however, to recover damages on the basis of fraud.
5. T
6. F. The Statute of Frauds requires that contracts for all transfers of interests in land be in writing to be enforceable. Included are sales, mortgages, leases, and other transfers. The purpose is to ensure that there is reliable evidence of the contracts and their terms.
7. F. The UCC's Statute of Frauds requires that contracts for sales of goods priced at $500 or more must

be in writing to be enforceable. Of course, there are exceptions. Oral contracts for customized goods, for example, may be enforced in some circumstances, as may oral contracts between merchants that have been confirmed in writing.
8. F. A misrepresentation of material fact can take the form of words or actions. In other words, misrepresentation by conduct alone is enough on which to base an action for fraud. Concealing a fact that is material to a contract constitutes such conduct. Failing to volunteer pertinent information will not qualify, however, unless the information concerns a serious defect or problem that the buyer cannot reasonably be suspected to know.
9. T
10. F. Under the parol evidence rule, if the parties' contract is completely integrated into a writing (which they intend to be the embodiment of their agreement), evidence of their prior negotiations, prior agreements, or contemporaneous oral agreements that contradicts or varies the terms of their contract is not admissible at trial.

Fill-in Questions

ancillary; primary; must; need not

Multiple-Choice Questions

1. C. Generally, a unilateral mistake—a mistake on the part of only one of the parties—does not give the mistaken party any right to relief. There are two exceptions. One exception occurs when the other party knew or should have known that a mistake was made. The second occurs when a mistake is due to a mathematical mistake, such as in this problem. Both exceptions must involve material facts (and not relate solely to the later market value or quality of the object of the contract).
2. C. This statement is none of the other choices because it is a statement of opinion, and thus is not generally subject to a claim of fraud or any of the other causes of action listed here. A fact is objective and verifiable. Puffery often involves vague assertions of quality. Affirmatively concealing a material fact, failing to respond when asked, and in some cases failing to volunteer pertinent facts may constitute fraud, however. Taking advantage of a party with whom one is in a confidential relationship to influence their entering into a "good deal" might constitute undue influence. Threats of physical harm may amount to duress.
3. D. When parties contract, their agreement establishes the value of the object of their transaction for the moment. Each party is considered to assume the risk that the value will change or prove to be different from what he or she thought. In this case, the buyer assumed the risk of a drop in the price. If instead the mistake had involved a material fact and had been

mutual, the buyer may have been able to avoid the contract (or enforce it).

4.   B. The problem states the elements of fraudulent misrepresentation: misrepresentation of a material fact, intent to deceive, and the innocent party's justifiable reliance on the misrepresentation. The misrepresentation must be an important factor in inducing the party to contract—reliance is not justified if the party knows or should know the truth. The defrauded may elect to rescind or enforce the contract. Damages are recoverable on proof of injury.

5.   D. Fraud involves misrepresentation that is intended to mislead another. The perpetrator must know or believe that the assertion is not true. Representations of future facts, statements of opinion, and most laypersons' statements about the law are generally not subject to claims of fraud. People are assumed to know the law. An exception occurs when the misrepresenting party is in a profession known to require a greater knowledge of the law than the average person possesses.

6.   C. Either party can enforce this oral contract. A contract that cannot be performed within one year must be in writing to be enforceable. Because the employee was hired to work for six months, the contract can be performed within a year and does not need to be in writing to be enforced.

7.   D. Under the Statute of Frauds, a contract for the sale of an interest in land must be in writing to be enforceable. A party to an oral contract involving an interest in land cannot force the other party to buy or sell the property.

8.   D. A collateral promise must be in writing to be enforceable unless the main purpose of the party making the promise is to secure a benefit for himself or herself. Here, the problem does not include such a purpose. (A collateral promise is a secondary, or ancillary, promise to a primary, or principal, contractual relationship—a third party's promise to assume the debt of a primary party to a contract, for example.)

9.   C. A collateral promise need not be in writing to be enforceable if the main purpose of the guarantor is to secure a benefit for himself or herself. Here, the problem includes such a purpose.

10.   C. Under the UCC, an oral contract for goods priced at $500 or more is enforceable to the extent that the buyer accepts delivery of the goods (or the seller accepts payment). Note that there must be delivery or payment for this exception to the Statute of Frauds to apply.

Issue Spotters

1.   Yes. Rescission may be granted on the basis of fraudulent misrepresentation. The elements of fraud include an intent to deceive, or *scienter*. *Scienter* exists if a party makes a statement recklessly, without regard to whether it is true or false, or if a party says or implies that a statement is made on some basis such as

personal knowledge or personal investigation when it is not. An action for fraud can be maintained when a party who unknowingly misstates a material fact later learns of the misstatement but does not reveal it.

2.   No. This is economic duress exerted on a party. A threat to break a contract on the eve of the deadline in this problem is sufficiently coercive to constitute duress. Duress involves coercive conduct—forcing a party to enter into a contract by threatening the party with a wrongful act.

3.   A court might conclude that under the doctrine of promissory estoppel, the employer is estopped from claiming the lack of a written contract as a defense. This oral contract may be enforced because the employer made a promise on which the employee justifiably relied in moving, the reliance was foreseeable, and injustice can be avoided only by enforcing the promise. If the court strictly enforces the Statute of Frauds, however, the employee may be without a remedy because a contract that cannot be performed within one year from the day after its making must be in writing to be enforceable.

Chapter 11

True-False Questions

1.   F. Intended beneficiaries have legal rights in contracts under which they benefit. An intended beneficiary is a party whom the contracting parties intended to benefit. Third parties who benefit from a contract only incidentally (incidental beneficiaries) normally do not have rights under the contract.

2.   F. In an assignment, the party assigning the rights is the *assignor*. The *obligor* is the party who was originally obligated to perform for the assignor. The party who receives the rights on an assignment is the *assignee* (who may also be the *obligee*). In a delegation, the party delegating the duties is the *delegator* (also the *obligator*) and the party assuming the duties is the *delegatee*.

3.   F. A right under a personal service contract cannot normally be assigned. Also, a right cannot ordinarily be assigned if a statute expressly prohibits its assignment, a contract stipulates that it cannot be assigned, or assignment would materially increase or alter the risk of the obligor.

4.   T

5.   T

6.   T

7.   T

8.   F. A material breach of contract (which occurs when performance is not at least substantial) excuses the nonbreaching party from performance of his or her contractual duties and gives the party a cause of action to sue for damages caused by the breach. A *minor* breach of contract does not excuse the nonbreaching

party's duty to perform, however, although it may affect the extent of his or her performance and, like any contract breach, allows the nonbreaching party to sue for damages.

9.   F. An executory contract can be rescinded. If it is executory on both sides, it can be rescinded solely by agreement. In any case, the parties must make a new agreement, and this agreement must qualify as a contract. (The parties' promises not to perform are consideration for the new contract.)

10.   T

Fill-in Questions

an assignment; a delegation; assigned; assign

Multiple-Choice Questions

1.   B. An incidental beneficiary cannot enforce a contract between two other parties. An example of such a contract would be a consumer's agreement to buy a new car from an auto dealer. The car's manufacturer would indirectly benefit under this contract, but could not enforce it if, for example, the consumer refused to pay the dealer.

2.   C. The rights of an intended third party beneficiary to a contract vest when the original parties cannot rescind or change the contract without the third party's consent. This occurs when the beneficiary learns of the contract and manifests assent to it. This also occurs when the beneficiary changes position in reliance on the contract.

3.   B. The party originally entitled to the payment of the money is the assignor, the party who agreed to pay is the obligor, and the party who receives the right to the payment is the assignee. An assignee has a right to demand performance from an obligor, but the assignee takes only those rights that the assignor originally had, and these rights are subject to defenses that the obligor has against the assignor. The obligor's consent is not necessary for an effective assignment.

4.   C. A right cannot normally be assigned if the assignment would materially increase or alter the risk of the obligor (the different circumstances represented by different persons with different property alter the risk in this problem). A right under a personal service contract cannot normally be assigned, but this is not a personal service contract, which requires a service unique to the person rendering it (an insurance policy is unlikely to qualify).

5.   C. Delegating a duty does not normally free the delegator of the obligation to perform if the delegatee does not do so. Ordinarily, if a delegatee fails to perform, the delegator remains liable to the obligee. Of course, the obligee must accept performance from the delegatee if it is forthcoming. Note that here, this is not a personal service contract, which would prohibit

its delegation, nor is its delegation prohibited by any other circumstance.

6.   B. For mutual rescission, the parties must make a contract that satisfies the legal requirements, which include consideration. Promises not to perform as originally agreed can constitute consideration when a contract is executory. If it is executed on one side, however, additional consideration or restitution is necessary.

7.   A. An accord is an executory contract to perform an act to satisfy a contractual duty that has not been discharged (that is, to provide and accept performance different from what was originally promised). An accord suspends the original obligation. A satisfaction is the performance of the accord. If a party does not perform under an accord, the nonbreaching party can bring an action based on either the accord or the original contract.

8.   C. A novation substitutes a new party for an original party, by agreement of all the parties. The requirements are a previous valid obligation, an agreement of all the parties to a new contract, extinguishment of the old obligation, and a new contract (which must meet the requirements for a valid contract, including consideration).

9.   D. Accord and satisfaction, agreement, and operation of law are valid bases on which contracts are discharged, but most contracts are discharged by the parties' doing what they promised to do. A contract is fully discharged by performance when the contracting have fully performed what they agreed to do (exchange services for payment, for example).

10.   D. This contract is discharged by objective impossibility of performance. On this basis, a contract may be discharged if, after it is made, performance becomes objectively impossible because, as in this problem, a change in the law renders performance illegal. This is also the result if one of the parties dies or becomes incapacitated, or the subject matter of the contract is destroyed. Circumstances that would not qualify include nonpayment because a certain bank is closed, a labor strike, and bad weather (which would more likely only temporarily suspend performance).

Issue Spotters

1.   Yes. When one person makes a promise with the intention of benefiting a third person, the third person can sue to enforce it. This is a third party beneficiary contract. The third party (the one to whom, in this problem, the money is owed) is the intended beneficiary.

2.   Yes. When an assignor successfully assigns a right to receive payment, the assignor's right to the payment is extinguished, and the assignee acquires the right to enforce payment from the obligor.

3.   No. The builder has substantially performed its duties under the contract. Assuming this performance was in good faith, the builder could thus successfully sue for the value of the work performed. For the sake of justice and fairness, the buyer will be held to the duty to pay, less damages for the deviation from the contract deadline.

Chapter 12

True-False Questions

1. T
2. T
3. F. An award of nominal damages, though usually small inn amount, establishes that a breaching party acted wrongfully. Also, nominal damages may be awarded when no actual loss results from a breach of contract (but the breach must still be proved).
4. F. Liquidated damages are certain amounts of money estimated in advance of, and payable on, a breach of contract. *Liquidated* means determined, settled, or fixed.
5. T
6. F. Rescission is available in cases involving fraud, mistake, duress, or failure of consideration. Both parties must make restitution to each other by returning whatever benefit was conveyed in execution of their contract. If the actual item cannot be returned, an equivalent amount in money must be paid.
7. T
8. F. There can be no enforceable contract if the doctrine of quasi contract is to be applied. Under this doctrine, to prevent unjust enrichment, the law implies a promise to pay the reasonable value for benefits received in the absence of an enforceable contract. This recovery is useful when one party has partially performed under a contract that is unenforceable.
9. T
10. F. Damages is the usual on breach of contracts for sales of goods. To obtain specific performance, damages must *not* be an adequate remedy. If goods are unique, or a contract involves a sale of land, damages would not adequately compensate an innocent party for a breach of contract, so specific performance is available.

Fill-in Questions

the contract price and the market price; specific performance; the contract price and the market price

Multiple-Choice Questions

1. A. The failure of one party to perform under a contract entitles the other party to rescind the contract. Both parties, however, must make restitution (return goods, property, or money previously conveyed). Here, on breaching the contract, which entitled the employer to rescind the deal, the contractor did not return the amount of the employer's payment.
2. C. A breach of contract by failing to perform entitles the nonbreaching party to rescind the contract, and the parties must make restitution by returning whatever benefit they conferred on each other, particularly when the breaching party would otherwise be unjustly enriched.
3. C. Under a contract for a sale of goods, the usual measure of compensatory damages is the difference between the contract price and the market price, plus incidental damages. On a seller's breach, the measure includes the difference between what the seller would have been owed if he or she had performed and what the buyer paid elsewhere for the goods.
4. B. The measure of damages on breach of a construction contract depends on which party breaches and when the breach occurs. If, as in this problem, the owner (buyer) breaches during construction, normally the contractor (seller) may recover its profit plus the costs incurred up to the time of the breach.
5. B. On the seller's breach of a contract, the buyer is entitled to be compensated for the loss of the bargain. Here, the buyer will receive what was contracted for, but it will be late. When, as in this problem, a seller knew that the buyer would lose business if the goods were not delivered on time, the loss of the bargain is the consequential damages (the amount lost as a foreseeable consequence of the breach).
6. C. Specific performance is an award of the act promised in a contract. This remedy is granted when the legal remedy (damages) is inadequate. Damages are generally inadequate for a buyer on the breach of a contract for a sale of land, because every piece of land is considered unique. If specific performance is not available, however, as when the land cannot be sold by the contracting seller, damages are possible, and their measure is the benefit of the buyer's bargain (the difference between the contract price and the market price of the land at the time of the breach).
7. B. A quasi contract may be imposed when a party has partially performed under a contract that is unenforceable. (An oral contract, the terms of which cannot be performed within one year, is unenforceable under the one-year rule of the Statute of Frauds.) To obtain quasi-contractual relief, a party must show that (1) he or she conferred a benefit on another, (2) he or she conferred the benefit with the reasonable expectation of being paid, (3) he or she did not act as a volunteer in conferring the benefit, and (4) the party receiving the benefit would be unjustly enriched by retaining the benefit without paying for it.
8. D. The clause is a penalty clause and, as such, it is unenforceable. To determine whether a clause is a liquidated damages clause or a penalty clause, consider first whether, when the contract was made, damages would clearly be difficult to estimate in the event of a breach. Second, consider whether the amount set as

damages is a reasonable estimate. Two "yeses" mean the clause is enforceable. One "no" means the provision is an unenforceable penalty. Here, the damages on the seller's breach would not be difficult to estimate, nor is the amount set in the contract a reasonable estimate of those damages.

9.   A. Reformation permits a contract to be rewritten to reflect the parties' actual intentions when they have imperfectly expressed their agreement in writing. This often applies in a case of fraud or mutual mistake (in a land sale contract, for example, when the property's legal description is erroneous). To prevent hardship, a court may also reform a covenant not to compete to convert its unreasonable terms into reasonable ones.

10.   D. Under the election of remedies doctrine, a nonbreaching party must choose which remedy to pursue. Here, the innocent party chose damages. The purpose of the doctrine is to prevent double recovery: a party may not recover twice for the same harm. Note that this doctrine has been eliminated in contracts for sales of goods. In other words, under the UCC, double recovery is not possible, but remedies are cumulative (choosing to pursue one remedy does not foreclose the pursuit of others).

Issue Spotters

1.   A nonbreaching party is entitled to his or her benefit of the bargain under the contract. Here, the innocent party is entitled to be put in the position she would have been in if the contract had been fully performed. The measure of the benefit is the cost to complete the work ($500). These are compensatory damages.

2.   No. To recover damages that flow from the consequences of a breach but that are caused by circumstances beyond the contract (consequential damages), the breaching party must know, or have reason to know, that special circumstances will cause the nonbreaching party to suffer the additional loss. That was not the circumstance in this problem.

3.   This clause is known as an exculpatory clause. In many cases, such clauses are not enforced, but to be effective in any case, all contracting parties must have consented to it. A clause excluding liability for negligence may be enforced if the contract was made by parties in roughly equal bargaining positions, as two large corporations would be.

Chapter 13

True-False Questions

1.   F. Courts usually do enforce shrink-wrap agreements. The reasoning is that the shrink-wrap terms constitute an offer, proposed by a seller and accepted by a buyer after the buyer had an opportunity to review the terms.

2.   T

3.   T

4.   F. Under the Electronic Signatures in Global and National Commerce (E-SIGN) Act, which Congress passed in 2000, no contract, record, or signature can be denied legal effect simply because it is in an electronic form (although some documents are specifically excluded).

5.   F. The UETA, like the Uniform Computer Information Transactions Act (UCITA), was drafted by the National Conference of Commissioners on Uniform State Laws and the American Law Institute as a proposal of legislation for the states to enact individually. Most states have enacted the UETA. (Only a couple of states have enacted the UCITA.)

6.   F. Parties to a transaction can waive or vary any or all of the provisions of the UETA (that is, they can opt out or choose not to have it apply), but the UETA applies in the absence of an agreement to the contrary. The parties must have agreed to conduct their transaction electronically, however.

7.   T

8.   T

9.   F. Under the UETA, an e-record is considered received when it enters the recipient's processing system in a readable form, even if no person is aware of its receipt.

10.   T

Fill-in Questions

need not; E-SIGN Act and the UETA; but does not create; does not apply

Multiple-Choice Questions

1.   B. The terms of a shrink-wrap agreement typically concern warranties, remedies, and other issues. The other answer choices in this question represent locations of the terms in click-on agreements, in "fine print," and in computer code that may not be readable by humans. A shrink-wrap agreement is typically between the manufacturer of hardware or software and its user.

2.   A. Shrink-wrap agreements have not always been enforced. The most important consideration is the time at which the manufacturer communicated the terms to the end-user. If they are proposed after a contract is entered into, they can be construed as proposals for additional terms, to which the consumer must expressly agree.

3.   C. A binding contract can be created by clicking on, for example, an "I agree" button if an opportunity is provided to read the terms before the button is clicked. If the terms are not revealed until after an agreement is made, however, it is unlikely that, as in cases involving shrink-wrap agreements, they would

be considered part of the deal. Here, the problem states that the button referred to the terms, meaning the buyer knew, or should have known, what was being agreed to.

4.   B. Under the E-SIGN Act, no contract, record, or signature may be denied legal effect solely because it is in electronic form. An e-signature is as valid as a signature on paper, and an e-document is as valid as a paper document. One possible complication is that state laws on e-signatures are not uniform. Most state have enacted the Uniform Electronic Transactions Act (UETA) but with individual modifications.

5.   A. The UETA does not apply unless the parties agree to use e-commerce in their transaction. The UETA does support all electronic transactions, but it does not provide rules for them.

6.   D. To fall under the UETA, the parties to a contract must agree to conduct their transaction electronically. The UETA then applies in the absence of an agreement between the parties to the contrary, although they can waive or vary any or all of its provisions. Whether the contract involves computer information is irrelevant under the UETA.

7.   C. To be "sent," an e-record must be properly directed from the sender's place of business to the intended recipient, in a form readable by the recipient's computer, at the recipient's place of business. This location is the recipient's place of business with the closest relation to the transaction. If a party does not have a place of business, the party's residence is used. An e-record is received when it enters the recipient's processing system in a readable form, even if no person is aware of the receipt

8.   B. If the parties to a deal subject to the UETA agree to a security procedure and one party fails to detect an error because it does not follow the procedure, the other party may be able to avoid the effect of the error. To do so, the conforming party must (1) promptly notify the other party of the error and of his or her intent not to be bound by it and (2) take reasonable steps to return any benefit or consideration received. If there can be no restitution, the transaction may not be avoidable. (If the parties do not agree on a security procedure, other state laws determine the effect of the mistake.)

9.   D. The UETA applies only to e-records and e-signatures in a transaction (an interaction between two or more people relating to business, commercial, or government activities). The UETA does not apply to laws governing wills or testamentary trusts, the UCC (except Articles 2 and 2A), the Uniform Computer Information Transactions Act, and other laws excluded by the states that adopt the UETA.

10.   D. The UETA is like most other uniform acts that apply in the business context. For contracts that fall within its scope, it applies in the absence of an agreement to the contrary. Parties who would otherwise be covered by the UETA can agree to opt out of all or part of the act and agree not to be covered by it, however, or vary any or all of its provisions. The parties must have agreed to conduct their transaction electronically, however.

Issue Spotters

1.   The effect of an e-record is determined from its context and circumstances. Any relevant evidence can prove that an e-record is, or is not, the act of a party to a deal. A party's name or "signature" on an e-record is not necessary to give effect to it, although a party's name typed on, for example, an e-mail purchase order, qualifies as a "signature" and is attributable to the party.

2.   If a state enacts the UETA without modifying it, the E-SIGN Act does not preempt it. The E-SIGN Act preempts modified versions of the UETA to the extent that they are inconsistent with the E-SIGN Act. Under the E-SIGN Act, states may enact alternative procedures or requirements for the use or acceptance of e-records or e-signatures if the procedures or requirements are consistent with the E-SIGN Act, the procedures do not give greater legal effect to any specific type of technology, and the state law refers to the E-SIGN Act if the state adopts the alternative after the enactment of the E-SIGN Act.

3.   First, it might be noted that the UETA does not apply unless the parties to a contract agree to use e-commerce in their transaction. In this deal, of course, the parties used e-commerce. The UETA removes barriers to e-commerce by giving the same legal effect to e-records and e-signatures as to paper documents and signatures. The UETA it does not include rules for those transactions, however.

Cumulative Hypothetical Problem for Unit Three—Including Chapters 7–13

1.   D. An offeror can revoke an offer for a bilateral contract, which is what this offer is, any time before it is accepted. This may be after the offeree is aware of the offer.

2.   C. Courts impose an objective, or reasonable, analysis in determining whether or not a contract was made and in interpreting its terms. This is known as the objective theory of contracts.

3.   B. A mutual mistake of fact may be a ground for relief, but it is not the only mistake for which relief may be granted. Although a party to a contract is not normally granted relief for a unilateral mistake, if the other party knew, or should have known, of the mistake, the law allows for relief.

4.   C. A novation completely discharges a party to a contract. Another party assumes the discharged party's obligations. If a party has assigned his or her rights under a contract, he or she may still be liable in the event the assignee defaults. A *executed* accord

would allow a party to avoid liability under a contract, but an *unexecuted* accord does not.

5. A. Damages, the remedy at law, is the usual remedy for a breach of contract. Specific performance is granted only if the remedy at law is inadequate, as it is when, for example, the goods that are the subject of a contract are unique. Courts are also reluctant to award specific performance in cases involving contracts for services.

Questions on the Focus on Legal Reasoning for Unit Three—*Ford v. Trendwest, Inc.*

1. C. In the *Ford* case, the court reasoned that "[w]hen the parties contracted for at-will employment, Ford had no greater expectations than an at-will employee, and Trendwest had no fewer rights than an at-will employer. . . . Nothing in this contract changed the at-will employment relationship." The court concluded that "lost earnings cannot measure damages for the breach of an employment at-will contract because the parties to such a contract do not bargain for future earnings. By its very nature, at-will employment precludes an expectation of future earnings."

2. A. The majority in the *Ford* case stated that "[a]n employee's expectations under an employment at-will contract are no different from the employment itself." An at-will employee may be terminated at any time for any reason. Nothing in an agreement to hire an individual for employment at-will "change[s] the at-will employment relationship."

3. D. The dissent in the *Ford* case reasoned that if an employer "promises . . . specific treatment in specific situations and an employee is induced thereby to . . . not actively seek other employment, those promises are enforceable." If they are breached, "the mere fact an employer could have fired the employee without liability the next day or under some other circumstance not amounting to breach of contract does not render . . . a claim for lost wages speculative."

Chapter 14

True-False Questions

1. T
2. T
3. F. If a transaction involves only a service, the common law usually applies (one exception is the serving of food or drink, which is governed by the UCC). When goods and services are combined, courts have disagreed over whether a particular transaction involves a sale of goods or a rendering of service. Usually, a court will apply the law that applies to whichever feature is dominant. Article 2 does not cover sales of real estate, although sales of goods associated with real estate, including crops, may be covered. A contract for a sale of minerals, for example, is considered a contract for a sale of goods if the severance is to be made by the seller.

4. F. Unlike the common law rule that contract modification must be supported by new consideration, the UCC requires no consideration for an agreement modifying a contract.

5. F. A contract will be enforceable, and a writing will be sufficient under the UCC's Statute of Frauds, if it indicates that a contract was intended, if it includes a quantity term, and—except for transactions between merchants—if it is signed by the party against whom enforcement is sought. Most terms can be proved by oral testimony or be supplied by the UCC's open term provisions (for example, price, delivery, and payment terms). A contract is not enforceable beyond the quantity of goods shown in the writing, however, except for output and requirements contracts.

6. T
7. T
8. F. A seller can accept an offer to buy goods for current or prompt shipment by promptly *shipping* the goods or by promptly *promising* to ship the goods. Of course, under the mirror image rule, an offer must be accepted in its entirety without modification, or there is no contract. Under the UCC, additional terms may become part of the contract if both parties are merchants (though not if at least one party is a nonmerchant).

9. T
10. F. Under the UCC, oral contracts for specially manufactured goods may be enforceable. Also, an oral contract for a sale or lease of goods may be enforceable if the party against whom enforcement is sought admits in court pleadings or proceedings that a contract was made. Partial performance of a contract for a sale or lease of goods may also support the enforcement of an oral contract, at least to the extent of that performance.

Fill-in Questions

Course of dealing; Usage of trade; trade; consistent; terms in the agreement

Multiple-Choice Questions

1. D. A sale is defined in the UCC as "the passing of title from the seller to the buyer for a price." The price may be payable in money or in goods, services, or real estate. A lease involves the transfer of possession and use, not title, in exchange for rental payments. (Article 2A of the UCC applies to leases.)

2. C. A merchant is a person who acts in a mercantile capacity, possessing or using expertise specifically related to the goods being sold. A merchant for one type of goods is not necessarily a merchant for another type, however. The test is whether the merchant holds himself or herself out by occupation as having knowledge or skill unique to the goods in the transaction.

3. A. Under the UCC, a sales contract will not fail for indefiniteness even if one or more terms are left open, as long as the parties intended to make a contract and there is a reasonably certain basis for the court to grant an appropriate remedy. If the price term is left open, for example, and the parties cannot later agree on a price, a court will set the price according to what is reasonable at the time for delivery. If one of the parties is to set the price, it must be set in good faith. If it is not fixed, the other party can set the price or treat the contract as canceled.

4. D. In a transaction between merchants, additional terms in the acceptance of an offer become part of a contract *unless* they qualify as one of these exceptions.

5. A. The contract is subject to the Statute of Frauds, and thus should be in writing to be fully enforceable. (Initialed notes, among other things, may constitute a sufficient writing.) A contract that is subject to the Statute of Frauds but is not in writing will be enforceable, however, under the partial performance exception when payment is made and accepted (at least to the extent of the payment actually made). Other enforceable exceptions include admissions in court and contracts for specially made goods (if they are not suitable for sale to others and if substantial steps have been taken toward their manufacture).

6. B. A lease involves a lessor who leases (or buys) goods from a supplier and leases (or subleases) them to a lessee. In other words, a lessor sells the right to the possession and use of goods under a lease. Sales are subject to Article 2 of the UCC. Gifts are not subject to the UCC.

7. A. A contract in writing that was intended to be a final expression cannot be contradicted by evidence of prior agreements or contemporaneous oral agreements. Some evidence outside the contract is admissible, however. Besides the evidence noted in the correct answer, evidence of what the parties did under the contract (their course of dealing and their course of performance) and the usage in their trade (commercial practices) is also admissible.

8. D. An unconscionable clause is one that is so unfair and one-sided that it would be unreasonable to enforce it. When considering such a clause, a court can choose among the answers choices in this problem. To assess unconscionability, a court may weigh such factors as a high price, a consumer's level of education, and his or her capacity to compare prices.

9. D. Contracts without specified quantities are not enforceable under the UCC. The UCC includes a number of open-term provisions that can be used to fill the gaps in a contract. Terms for delivery, payment, and price can be proved by evidence, or whatever is reasonable will be determined. The quantity of goods must be expressly stated, however, or a court cannot award a remedy.

10. A. Under the CISG (which governs this transaction) an international contract for a sale of goods need not be in writing to be enforceable nor is consideration a requirement. Those are two of the differences between the CISG and the UCC (which requires consideration for a contract for a sale of goods and a writing for contracts involving goods priced at $500 or more). Also, the price term is specified in the deal in this problem.

Issue Spotters

1. Yes. Under the UCC, if a merchant gives assurances in a signed writing that an offer will remain open, the offer is irrevocable. The car dealer in this problem is a merchant who promised to keep an offer open for seven days and did not do so.

2. A shipment of nonconforming goods constitutes an acceptance and a breach, unless the seller seasonably notifies the buyer that the nonconforming shipment does not constitute an acceptance and is offered only as an accommodation. Without the notification, the shipment is an acceptance and a breach. Thus, here, the shipment was both an acceptance and a breach.

3. Yes. In a transaction between merchants, the requirement of a writing is satisfied if one of them sends to the other a signed written confirmation that indicates the terms of the agreement, and the merchant receiving it has reason to know of its contents. If the merchant who receives it does not object in writing within ten days after receipt, the writing will be enforceable against him or her even though he or she has not signed anything.

Chapter 15

True-False Questions

1. T

2. F. Title passes at the time and place at which the seller delivers the goods—unless the parties agree otherwise, which is always an option under the UCC.

3. T

4. F. This is the definition of a sale or return.

5. F. A buyer has an insurable interest in goods the moment they are identified to the contract by the seller. A seller has an insurable interest in goods as long as he or she has title. After title has passed, a seller who has a security interest in goods retains an insurable interest. Thus, a buyer and a seller can both have an insurable interest in goods at the same time.

6. T

7. F. In a sale on approval, title and risk of loss passes when the buyer accepts the goods. In contrast, in a sale or return, title and risk pass when the buyer receives possession of the goods..

8. F. Generally, a buyer acquires whatever title the seller has to the goods. If a seller (or lessor) stole the goods, he or she has no title, and the buyer (or lessee, who might otherwise acquire a valid leasehold interest) gets nothing. The real owner can reclaim the goods from the buyer or the thief.

9. F. Under a *shipment* contract, the risk of loss (and title) passes from seller to buyer at time and place of shipment. Under a destination contract, risk of loss (and title) passes when the goods are tendered at a certain destination.

10. T

Fill-in Questions

F.O.B.; F.O.B.; F.O.B.; F.A.S.

Multiple-Choice Questions

1. C. These are the requirements for identification. Title and risk of loss cannot pass from seller to buyer until the goods are identified to the contract. Other actions on the part of a seller, such as arranging for shipment or obtaining insurance, do not determine when an interest in goods passes.

2. B. This agreement (F.O.B.) is a shipment contract under which the seller is not required to deliver the goods to the buyer's location, but only to place them into the possession of a carrier. Under this shipment contract, the risk of loss passes when the seller gives the goods to the carrier.

3. A. When goods are to be picked up by a buyer, if a seller is a nonmerchant, risk passes on the seller's tender of delivery (unless the parties agree otherwise). The goods were tendered before the theft, so the buyer suffers the loss. If the seller is a merchant, the risk of loss passes when the buyer takes possession of the goods.

4. A. If a bailee holds goods for a seller and the goods are delivered without being moved, under a negotiable document of title, the risk of loss passes when the buyer receives the document. If the document is nonnegotiable, however, more is required to transfer the risk: the buyer must also have had a reasonable time to present the document and demand the goods. In either case, the risk can also pass on the bailee's acknowledgment of the buyer's right to possess the goods. In any case, if the bailee refuses to recognize the buyer's right, the loss stays with the seller.

5. A. Entrusting goods to a merchant who deals in goods of the kind gives the merchant power to transfer all rights to a buyer in the ordinary course of business. The owner of the car has good title against the dealer, but a buyer in the ordinary course of business can acquire, in good faith, good title from the merchant. This title is good against even the original owner. Note that had a thief stolen the car from the original owner and left it with the dealer, the later

buyer would not have good title against the original owner.

6. B. When goods are to be picked up by a buyer, if a seller is a merchant, the risk of loss does not pass to the buyer until the buyer takes possession of the goods (unless the parties agree otherwise). The goods were tendered before the theft, but the buyer did not take possession.

7. B. Under a destination contract, the risk of loss passes when the seller tenders delivery at the specified destination. Here, the destination was the buyer, and the goods were destroyed before they reached that location. Also, note that "F.O.B." indicates that the seller bears the cost of the transport to the specified destination.

8. C. A buyer has an insurable interest in goods as soon as they are identified to the contract, even before the risk of loss passes. A seller has an insurable interest as long as he or she still has title to the goods. More than one party can have an insurable interest at the same time.

9. A. Generally, the party who breaches a contract bears the risk of loss. Here, the seller breached by shipping defective goods. The risk would have passed to the buyer if the buyer accepted the goods in spite of their defects. (If the buyer had accepted the goods and then discovered the defects, the buyer could have revoked its acceptance, which would have transferred the risk back to the seller.)

10. B. Under a shipment contract, if the contracting parties do not specify a time for title to pass, then it passes on delivery of the goods to the carrier.

Issue Spotters

1. The result would be the same as if the contract stated, "F.O.B. New York." For the risk of loss to remain with the seller, a seller must specifically agree to deliver goods to a particular destination. Remember, all contracts are assumed to be shipment contracts unless they state otherwise.

2. The seller suffers the loss. If goods are so nonconforming that a buyer has the right to reject them, the risk of loss will not pass from the seller to the buyer until the defects are cured or the buyer accepts the defective goods. Here, the defects had not been cured and the buyer had not yet accepted the goods. Note that if the goods were shipped and arrived at the buyer's location, the risk would remain with the seller because the goods were defective.

3. No. A seller has voidable title if the goods that he or she is selling were paid for with a bad check (a check that is later dishonored). Normally, a buyer acquires only the title that the seller had, or had the power to transfer, but a seller with voidable title can transfer good title to a good faith purchaser (one who buys in good faith without knowledge that the seller did not have the right to sell the goods). Under those circumstances, an original owner cannot recover goods from a good faith purchaser. Here, the ultimate buyer is a good faith purchaser.

Chapter 16

True-False Questions

1. T
2. T
3. T
4. F. If the parties do not agree otherwise, the buyer or lessee must pay for the goods at the time and place of their receipt (subject, in most cases, to the buyer or lessee's right to inspect). When a sale is on credit, a buyer must pay according to credit terms, not when the goods are received. Credit terms may provide for payment within thirty days, for example. A credit period usually begins on the date of shipment.
5. F. If a contract does not state where goods are to be delivered, and the buyer is to pick them up, the place for delivery is the seller's place of business (unless the parties know that the goods are elsewhere, in which case the place of their delivery is their location). Shipment and destination contracts are subject to different rules that depend on their terms.
6. F. A buyer or lessee who accepts nonconforming goods can revoke the acceptance, but only notifying the seller or lessor, which must occur within a reasonable time and before goods have, for example, spoiled. If the goods are perishable, the buyer or lessee must follow any reasonable instructions of the seller or lessor regarding the goods. (This is also the case when the buyer or lessee rejects the goods.)
7. F. If, before the time for performance, a buyer or lessee clearly communicates his or her intent not to perform, the seller or lessor can suspend performance and wait to see if the other will perform, or the seller or lessor can treat the anticipatory repudiation as a breach, suspend performance, and pursue a remedy.
8. F. A buyer can reject an installment only if its nonconformity *substantially impairs* the value of the installment and it cannot be cured (in which case, the seller has breached the contract).
9. T
10. T

Fill-in Questions

conforming; and; buyer; receipt; even if

Multiple-Choice Questions

1. C. The parties to a contract can stipulate the time, place, and manner of delivery. In the absence of specific details, however, the seller or lessor's obligation is to tender delivery at a reasonable hour and in a rea-sonable manner. The buyer must be notified, and the goods must be kept available for a reasonable time.
2. B. Unless the contract provides otherwise, a buyer (or lessee) has an absolute right to inspect tendered goods before making payment, to verify that they are as ordered. If they are not as ordered, the buyer has no duty to pay, and the seller cannot enforce any right to payment.
3. C. It is the seller's obligation to tender delivery of goods. Under a shipment contract, a seller must make a reasonable contract for the transportation of goods, tender to the buyer whatever documents are necessary to obtain possession of goods from the carrier, and notify the buyer that shipment has been made.
4. C. If a buyer repudiates a contract or wrongfully refuses to accept goods, a seller can sue for damages equal to the difference between the contract price and the market price at the time and place of tender. The seller can also recover incidental damages, which include the cost of transporting the goods. If the market price is less than the contract price, damages include the seller's lost profits.
5. B. Under the circumstances in this problem, the buyer's best course is to attempt to obtain substitute goods for those that were due under the contract. When a buyer is forced to obtain cover, the buyer can recover from the seller the difference between the cost of the cover and the contract price, plus incidental and consequential damages, less whatever expenses (such as delivery costs) were saved as a result of the seller's breach.
6. C. In an installment contract, a buyer can reject an installment only if a nonconformity substantially impairs the value of the installment and cannot be cured. Thus, among the answer possibilities here, the rejection of the first installment is the best choice. This deviation might be curable, however, by an adjustment in price or by a shipment of conforming goods, so an answer that suggested these alternatives might represent an even better choice.
7. C. A buyer (or lessee) can sue for damages when a seller (or lessor) repudiates the contract or fails to deliver the goods, or when the buyer has rightfully rejected or revoked acceptance of the goods. The place for determining the price is the place at which the seller was to deliver the goods. The buyer may also recover incidental and consequential damages, less expenses saved due to the breach.
8. C. Depending on the circumstances, when a seller or lessor delivers nonconforming goods, the buyer or lessee can reject the part of the goods that does not conform (and rescind the contract or obtain cover). The buyer or lessee may instead revoke acceptance, or he or she may recover damages, for accepted goods.
9. B. Replevin is an action to recover specific goods in the possession of a party who is wrongfully withholding them. When a seller (or lessor) refuses to deliver (or repudiates the contract), the buyer or lessee

may maintain an action to replevy the goods. The buyer or lessee must show, however, an inability to cover.

10.   A. If, before the time of performance, a party to a contract informs the other party that he or she will not perform, the nonbreaching party can treat the repudiation as a final breach and seek a remedy or wait, for a commercially reasonable time, hoping that the breaching party will decide to honor the contract. In either case, the nonbreaching party can suspend his or her performance.

Issue Spotters

1.   Yes. A seller is obligated to deliver goods in conformity with a contract in every detail. This is the perfect tender rule. The exception of the seller's right to cure does not apply here, because the seller delivered too little too late to take advantage of this exception.

2.   Yes. In a case of anticipatory repudiation, a buyer (or lessee) can resort to any remedy for breach even if the buyer tells the seller (the repudiating party in this problem) that the buyer will wait for the seller's performance.

3.   If a buyer wrongfully refuses to accept conforming goods, the seller can recover damages. The measure is the difference between the contract price and the market price (at the time and place of tender), plus incidental damages. If the market price is less than the contract price, the seller gets lost profits.

Chapter 17

True-False Questions

1.   T
2.   F. Warranties are not exclusive. A contract can include an implied warranty of merchantability, an implied warranty of fitness for a particular purpose, and any number of express warranties.
3.   F. Unless the circumstances indicate otherwise, the implied warranty of merchantability (and the implied warranty of fitness for a particular purpose) can be disclaimed by such expressions as "as is" and "with all faults." Express warranties can also be disclaimed.
4.   T
5.   F. An action based on negligence does not require privity of contract. At one time, there was a requirement of privity in product liability actions based on negligence, but this requirement began to be eliminated decades ago. Privity of contract is also not a requirement to bring a suit based on strict product liability.
6.   F. In an action based on strict liability, a plaintiff does not have to prove that there was a failure to exercise due care. That distinguishes an action based on strict liability from an action based on negligence,

which requires proof of a lack of due care. A plaintiff must show, however, that (1) a product was defective, (2) the defendant was in the business of distributing the product, (3) the product was unreasonably dangerous due to the defect, (4) the plaintiff suffered harm, (5) the defect was the proximate cause of the harm, and (6) the goods were not substantially changed from the time they were sold.

7.   T
8.   T
9.   F. There is no duty to warn about such risks. Warnings about such risks do not add to the safety of products and could make other warnings seem less significant. In fact, a plaintiff's action in the face of such a risk can be raised as a defense in a product liability suit.
10.   T

Fill-in Questions

can; can; can; need not; must

Multiple-Choice Questions

1.   C. An implied warranty of merchantability arises in every sale of goods by a merchant who deals in goods of the kind. It makes no difference whether the merchant knew of or could have discovered a defect that makes a product unsafe. The warranty is that the goods are "reasonably fit for the ordinary purposes for which such goods are used." The efficiency and the quality of their manufacture, and the manufacturer's compliance with government regulations, are not factors that directly influence this determination.
2.   A. To disclaim an implied warranty of fitness for a particular purpose, a warranty must be conspicuous, but the word *fitness* does not have to be used. A disclaimer of the implied warranty of merchantability must mention *merchantability*. Warranties of title, however, can be disclaimed only by specific language (for example, a seller states that it is transferring only such rights as it has in the goods), or by circumstances that indicate no warranties of title are made.
3.   A. A seller crates an express warranty by representing the condition of the goods through a promise, a description, a model, or a sample, as in this problem. Regarding the other choices, an implied warranty is not express. A warranty of title concerns a seller's rights in the goods, and not their quality. Puffing is an expression of opinion that is not a statement of fact ("the best that money can buy," for example).
4.   D. This is a statement of opinion (puffing). Puffing creates no warranty. If the salesperson had said something factual about the vehicle (its miles per gallon, its total mileage, whether it had been in an accident, etc.), it would be more than puffing and could qualify as an express warranty.

5.   A. Assumption of risk is a defense in an action based on product liability if the plaintiff knew and appreciated the risk created by the defect and voluntarily undertook the risk, even though it was unreasonable to do so.

6.   A. A manufacturer may be held liable if its product is unsafe as a result of negligence in the manufacture or if the design makes it unreasonably dangerous for the use for which it is made. A manufacturer also has a duty to warn and to anticipate reasonably foreseeable misuses. An injury must not have been due to a change in the product after it was sold, but there is no requirement of privity. There is no liability, however, with respect to injuries caused by commonly known dangers, even if the manufacturer does not warn against them.

7.   D. In a product liability action based on strict liability, the plaintiff does not need to prove that anyone was at fault. Privity of contract is also not an element of an action in strict liability. A plaintiff does have to show, however, in a suit against a seller, that the seller was a merchant engaged in the business of selling the product on which the suit is based. Note that recovery is possible against sellers who are processors, assemblers, packagers, bottlers, wholesalers, distributors, retailers, or lessors, as well as against manufacturers.

8.   C. These choices concern the defective condition of a product that causes harm to a plaintiff. A product may be unreasonably dangerous due to a flaw in the manufacturing process, a design defect, or an inadequate warning.

9.   C. All courts extend the doctrine of strict liability to injured bystanders. A defendant does not have to prove that the manufacturer or seller failed to use due care, nor is there a requirement of privity (or "intent" with regard to entering into privity). The defense of assumption of risk does not apply, because one cannot assume a risk that one does not know about.

10.   C. If a manufacturer fails to use due care to make a product safe, the manufacturer may be liable for product liability based on negligence. This care must be used in designing the product, selecting the materials, producing the product, inspecting and testing any components, assembling the product, and placing warnings on the product.

Issue Spotters

1.   No. A creditor with a valid security interest can repossess goods from a subsequent purchaser. If a creditor repossesses goods, however, a buyer who had no actual knowledge of the security interest can recover from the seller for breach of warranty. Thus, the creditor in this problem can repossess the car from the ultimate buyer, who can recover from the seller-borrower.

2.   Yes. The manufacturer is liable for the injuries to the user of the product. A manufacturer is liable for its failure to exercise due care to any person who sustains an injury proximately caused by a negligently made (defective) product. In this problem, the failure to inspect is a failure to use due care. Of course, the maker of the component part may also be liable.

3.   Yes. Under the doctrine of strict liability, persons may be liable for the results of their acts regardless of their intentions or their exercise of reasonable care (that is, regardless of fault). There is no requirement of privity.

Cumulative Hypothetical Problem for Unit Four—Including Chapters 14–17

1.   C. The modification would not be considered a rejection. Under UCC 2–207, a merchant can add an additional term to a contract, with his or her acceptance, as part of the contract, unless the offeror expressly states otherwise.

2.   C. If nothing is stated in a contract about the risk of loss, then the UCC determines when the risk of loss passes. Under the UCC, if there are no contract terms to the contrary, the risk of loss passes on delivery, if the seller is a merchant.

3.   B. Under UCC 2–709, a seller can demand enforcement of a contract if the buyer breaches, the goods have been identified, and the seller cannot resell the goods for a reasonable price. From the perspective of the seller, recovery of the contract price is specific performance.

4.   C. A seller makes an express warranty by providing an assertion, an affirmation, a promise, or a similar statement about the quality of the goods that becomes a part of the basis of the bargain. The promises may be oral, and the seller's intent is not relevant.

5.   B. To be subject to the UCC's implied warranty of merchantability, goods must be fit for their ordinary or intended use, but they do not need to be fit for ALL of the possible purposes that a buyer might have in mind. The other choices are part of this implied warranty.

Questions on the Focus on Legal Reasoning for Unit Four—*Parker Tractor & Implement Co. v. Johnson*

1.   A. In the *Parker* case, the court reasoned that "it is enough that sufficient facts are given from which the [court] may safely make at least a minimum estimate" of the amount of damages. Damages are speculative "only when the cause is uncertain, not when the amount is uncertain."

2.   A. The majority in the *Parker* case held that lost business profits can be awarded if the data of their estimation are so definite that they can be ascertained reasonably by calculation. In estimating those damages, the court reasoned that they could be calculated using the testimony of the injured party if that was the best evidence available.

3. D. The dissent in the *Parker* case reasoned that more substantial proof is necessary to obtain damages. The weight to be given the proof—the scarcity of documentary evidence, the arguably self-serving testimony of the plaintiff, the non-existent proof of some points—was the issue over which the court in the *Parker* case disagreed.

Chapter 18

True-False Questions

1. F. A negotiable instrument can be transferred by assignment or negotiation. When a transfer fails to qualify as a negotiation, it becomes an assignment and is governed by the rules of assignment under contract law.
2. T
3. T
4. F. This is an order instrument. Order instruments that meet the requirements for negotiability are negotiable. An instrument that contains any indication that does not purport to designate a specific payee (for example, "payable to bearer") is a bearer instrument. A bearer instrument that meets the requirements for negotiability is also negotiable. When an instrument is not negotiable, it may be transferred by assignment.
5. T
6. F. Personal defenses (such as breach of contact or breach of warranty) can be used to avoid payment to an ordinary holder, but only universal defenses are good against an HDC.
7. T
8. F. All transferors of negotiable instruments, including those who present instruments for payment, make certain implied warranties regarding the instruments. For example, a person who transfers an instrument for payment warrants to any other person who in good faith accepts or pays the instrument, with some exceptions, that the instrument has not been altered.
9. T
10. F. A holder who knows or has reason to know of a claim to an instrument or a defense against payment on it cannot become an HDC. Furthermore, such a holder cannot change his or her status by selling the instrument and repurchasing it from a later HDC in an attempt to take advantage of the shelter principle.

Fill-in Questions

can; cannot; cannot

Multiple-Choice Questions

1. A. Before the payee indorsed the back of the check, it was an order instrument. It could be negotiated further only with the payee's signature (and with delivery). After the check was indorsed, it became a bearer instrument and could be negotiated by delivery alone. If a bearer instrument is lost, it can be negotiated by whoever finds it.
2. D. A draft is created when the party creating it orders another party to pay money, usually to a third party. The drawee (the party on whom the draft is drawn) must be obligated to the drawer, either by an agreement or through a debtor-creditor relationship, for the drawee to be obligated to the drawer to honor the draft. A trade acceptance is a draft; a check is a draft.
3. C. A restrictive indorsement requires the indorsee to comply with certain instructions regarding the funds involved (but it does not restrict the negotiation of the instrument). A blank indorsement specifies no particular indorsee and can be a simple signature. A qualified indorsement disclaims contract liability on the instrument (for example, an indorser adding "without recourse" to his or her signature is a qualified indorsement). A special indorsement names the indorsee ("pay to Adam") with the signature of the indorser.
4. D. All of the other answer choices are among the requirements for negotiability. The other requirements are that an instrument must be in writing (on something permanent and portable—a shirt might be acceptable but not, for example, a cow), must state a fixed amount of money, and must be payable to order or to bearer, unless it is a check.
5. A. The location of the maker or drawer's signature does not affect the negotiability of an instrument. Also, a signature may, among other things, be a trade name or may consist of thumbprint, a handwritten statement, or a rubber stamp.
6. A. When there is a breach of warranty concerning the underlying contract for which a negotiable instrument (the note) was issued, the maker can refuse to pay the note. This is a personal defense, not good against an HDC, but the party who accepted the note was not an HDC, but the other contracting party who took the note with knowledge of the claim against it. The other choices are also personal defenses, but they do not fit the facts in this problem.
7. B. Makers of notes and acceptors of negotiable instruments are primarily liable. (Drawers—and indorsers—have secondary liability.) A drawee (the bank in this problem) becomes primarily liable becomes an acceptor, which occurs when, as here, it accepts a check for payment.
8. C. Based on their signatures on an instrument, a drawer and a payee-indorser have secondary liability. Parties who are secondarily liable promise to pay only if the following events occur: (1) the instrument is properly and timely presented; (2) the instrument is dishonored; and (3) notice of dishonor is given in a timely manner to the secondarily liable party.

9. A. All of the parties on a note are discharged if the maker of a note (the party primarily liable on it) pays to a holder the amount due in full. Payment by any other party, however, discharges only that party and later parties, however.

10. B. The issuer of the check in this problem was authorized to use an employer's checks to pay for certain items. Assuming the seller knew of this agency relationship, the principal (the employer) is liable for the amount of the check. There is nothing in the facts here to suggest that the seller had notice of a defense to payment on the check, or notice that the amount of the check was materially altered, either of which would have prevented it from becoming an HDC and changed the liability of the parties.

Issue Spotters

1. This party is an HDC to the full extent of the note. One of the requirements for becoming an HDC is taking an instrument for value. A party may attain HDC status to the extent that he or she gives value for the instrument. Paying with cash or with a check is giving value.

2. Yes. As in cases of forgery, in which the person whose name is used is not liable, this firm can assert the defense of the unauthorized signature against any HDC, because the employee exceeded authority in signing the check on behalf of the firm.

3. No. When a drawer's employee provides the drawer with the name of a fictitious payee (a payee whom the drawer does not actually intend to have any interest in an instrument), a forgery of the payee's name is effective to pass good title to subsequent transferees.

Chapter 19

True-False Questions

1. T

2. F. If a bank pays a check over a customer's proper stop-payment order, the bank is obligated to recredit the customer's account, but only for the amount of the actual loss suffered by the drawer because of the wrongful payment.

3. F. A bank's duty to honor its customer's checks is not absolute (although when a bank receives an item payable from a customer's account, but there are insufficient funds in the account to cover the amount, the bank can choose to pay it and charge the customer's account). Failing to pay an overdraft will not subject the bank to criminal prosecution, though a person who writes a bad check may be prosecuted (and sued).

4. T

5. T

6. T

7. T

8. F. Under the Expedited Funds Availability Act of 1987, there are different availability schedules for different funds, depending on such factors as the location of the bank on which an item is drawn, what type of item it is, the age and activity of an account, and the amount of the item.

9. T

10. F. A forged drawer's signature on a check has no legal effect as the signature of the party whose name is signed. If the bank pays the check, the bank must recredit the customer's account (unless the customer's negligence contributed substantially to the forgery).

Fill-in Questions

drawer; creditor; principal; drawee; debtor; agent

Multiple-Choice Questions

1. D. When a bank pays a check on a drawer's forged signature, generally the bank is liable. This is particularly true when the bank's negligence substantially contributes to the forgery. If the customer's negligence contributed to the forgery, however, the bank may not be liable. The amount of the check does not affect liability.

2. C. Each bank in the collection chain, including the depositary bank, must pass the check on before receipt. Under the deferred posting rule, a check received after a bank's cutoff hour, can be considered received the next day.

3. D. This is assuming the drawer's state allows oral stop-payment orders. If a drawee bank pays a check over a customer's stop-payment order, the bank is obligated to recredit the account of the customer, but the bank is liable for no more than the actual loss suffered by the drawer.

4. A. A bank that pays a customer's check bearing a forged indorsement must recredit the customer's account or be liable to the drawer customer for breach of contract. A customer has a duty to examine returned checks and corresponding bank statements, however, and must report any forged indorsements within three years.

5. B. A drawee bank's contract is with its customer, not with those who present its customers' checks for payment. Thus, a drawee bank is not liable to a holder who presents a check for payment, even if the drawer has sufficient funds on deposit to pay the check. The holder's recourse is against the drawer, who may subsequently hold the bank liable for a wrongful refusal to pay.

6. A. A bank is not obligated to pay a stale, uncertified check. If the bank decides to pay it, however, the bank might consult the customer first or simply pay it an d charge the customer's account of the amount.

7. C. If a drawee bank cashes a customer's check over a forged indorsement, or fails to detect an alteration on a check of its customer-drawer and cashes the check, the bank is liable for the loss. (The customer's negligence can shift the loss, however.) The bank may be able to recover some of the loss from the forger, if he or she can be found.

8. C. If a drawee bank cashes a customer's check over the customer's (drawer's) forged signature, the bank is liable for the loss. (Of course, this is assuming that the customer's negligence did not cause the loss—the customer's negligence can shift the loss, as noted above.) The bank may be able to recover at least some of the loss from the forger, however.

9. C. The customer is liable for this amount because the bank was not notified that the card was missing until after the withdrawal. If a customer does not inform the institution within less than two business days after learning of a card's loss or theft, the customer's liability for unauthorized transactions is up to $500.

10. A. Though it is not yet entirely clear which laws apply to e-money, the Federal Trade Commission (FTC) Act, as well as the other statutes mentioned here, and common law principles (such as contract law) do extend to new forms of debits and credits. The FTC Act applies to the facts in this problem—this act prohibits unfair or deceptive practices. The other statutes apply in other circumstances.

Issue Spotters

1. Yes, to both questions. In a civil suit, a drawer is liable to a payee or to a holder of a check that is not honored. If intent to defraud can be proved, the drawer can also be subject to criminal prosecution for writing a bad check.

2. Yes, to both questions. The general rule is that a bank must recredit a customer's account when it pays on a forged signature. The bank has no right to recover from a holder who, without knowledge, cashes a check bearing a forged drawer's signature, however. Thus, the bank in this problem cannot collect from its customer or from the party who cashed the check. The bank's recourse is to look for the thief.

3. The drawer is entitled to $6,300—the amount to which the check was altered ($7,000) less the amount that the drawer ordered the bank to pay ($700). The bank may recover the this amount from the party who presented the altered check for payment.

Cumulative Hypothetical Problem for Unit Five—Including Chapters 18–19

1. B. A promissory note is a written promise by one party to pay money to another party. This instrument is not a draft: there is no drawee. Because it is not a draft, it cannot be a sight draft, a check, or a trade acceptance, all of which are drafts.

2. B. This instrument meets all of the requirements for negotiability: it is in writing, it is signed by the maker, it is an unconditional promise to pay a fixed amount of money, it is payable to bearer, and it is payable at a definite time. The extension clause does not affect its negotiability because, although the right to extend is given to the maker, the period of the extension is specified.

3. A. The instrument is negotiable, but it can be negotiated further only by the bank's indorsement, because it was converted from a bearer instrument to an order instrument with the indorsement to pay to the order of the bank. Because it was a bearer instrument, it could have been negotiated by delivery only, without indorsement. The indorsement "without recourse" does not affect the negotiability of the instrument.

4. A. The bank is an HDC because it took the instrument (1) for value, (2) in good faith, and (3) without notice that any person had a defense against payment on it. The party from whom the bank bought the instrument was not an HDC, however, because that party did take the instrument with knowledge of the contract dispute.

5. D. No party to a check has primary liability with respect to payment on it. The drawer is secondarily liable to the payee. If the drawer has sufficient grounds, he or she may sue the drawee for wrongful dishonor, but the payee cannot successfully sue the drawee.

Questions on the Focus on Legal Reasoning for Unit Five—*Scalise v. American Employers Insurance Co.*

1. A. In the *Scalise* case, the court held that if a check is honored and paid on presentment, the date of the payment of the underlying obligation is the date of the delivery of the check. The court acknowledged that the debt is not discharged until the check is paid, but reasoned that once that happened, payment occurred as of "the moment of the delivery of the check."

2. A. The majority in the *Scalise* case held that if a check is honored and paid on presentment, the date of the payment for the underlying obligation is the date of the delivery of the check. The majority cited the principle that "the giving of a draft by a debtor to his creditor does not discharge the debt itself until the draft is paid, it being a means adopted to enable the creditor to obtain payment of the debt and remaining, until honored or paid, but evidence of the indebtedness." But the majority reasoned that "payment by check is ordinarily understood to constitute payment for an obligation as of the moment of delivery of the check, provided that the check is honored upon its presentment."

3. D. Contrary to the majority, the dissent in the *Scalise* case reasoned that "[t]he giving of a check by a debtor to his creditor does not discharge the debt until the check is paid" and indicated that this is when "payment" occurs. Otherwise, "the plaintiff's time to exercise his rights . . . begins to run before he even has any such rights."

Chapter 20

True-False Questions

1.   F. Perfection is the process by which secured parties protect themselves against the claims of third parties who may wish to have their debts satisfied out of the same collateral. In most situations, this process involves filing a financing statement with a state official. That filing may be accomplished by a paper filing or electronically.
2.   T
3.   F. A security interest in proceeds perfects automatically and remains perfected, in most cases, for at least twenty days after the debtor's receipt of the proceeds.
4.   F. The financing statement must include the names of the debtor and creditor, and describe the collateral. Also, to avoid problems arising from different descriptions, a secured party can repeat the security agreement's description in the financing statement or file the two together.
5.   T
6.   T
7.   T
8.   T
9.   F. A debtor who has defaulted has redemption rights. Before the secured party decides to retain the collateral or before it is disposed of, the debtor can take back the collateral by tendering performance of all secured obligations and paying the secured party's expenses. (Other secured parties have this same right.)
10.   F. When more than one creditor claims a security interest in the same collateral, the first interest to be filed takes priority. The first to attach has priority if none of the interests has been perfected.

Fill-in Questions

1.   creditor; creditor
2.   first; first

Multiple-Choice Questions

1.   C. A *financing statement* must provide the names of the debtor and the creditor and describe the collateral covered by the security agreement. Filing a financing statement (which is the most common means of perfecting a security interest) gives notice to other creditors of the secured party's interest.
2.   B. In those cases in which it is otherwise available, the right of self-help repossession can generally be exercised so long as the secured party does not commit trespass onto land, assault, battery, or break-ing and entering. Here, the repossession occurred on a public street and did not involve any commission of the other crimes.
3.   C. To be effective, a written security agreement must (1) be signed by the debtor, (2) contain a description of the collateral, and (3) the description must reasonably identify the collateral. This meets one of the three requirements for an enforceable security interest. The other requirements are that creditor's giving something of value to the debtor, and the debtor having rights in the collateral. Once these requirements are met, the interest attaches. A security interest is enforceable when attachment occurs.
4.   C. To retain collateral that a secured party repossessed on a debtor's default, the secured party must notify the debtor and (in all cases except consumer goods) any other secured party of whom the party has notice of a claim, as well as junior lien claimants who filed their liens or security interests ten days before the debtor consented to the retention. If the debtor or other secured party objects within twenty days, the collateral must be sold, or otherwise disposed of. If the collateral is sold, the first priority of the proceeds are the fees stemming from the secured party's preparation for the sale.
5.   B. The secured party has fourteen days to reply. More frequent requests must be paid for. Among other rights and duties of the parties, if the secured party assigns its interest in the debtor's collateral, the assignee can become the secured party of record through the filing of a uniform amendment form, which is also required for the secured party's release of the debtor. If the debtor pays the debt and asks for a termination statement, the secured party has twenty days to comply.
6.   C. A secured party's security interest in collateral includes an interest in the proceeds (whatever is received) from the sale, exchange, or other disposal of the collateral. This interest perfects automatically and remains perfected for twenty days. Ways to extend this period are listed in the answer. It should be noted, too, that the initial effective term of the filing of a financing statement is a period of five years, and this can be extended for another five years by the filing of a continuation statement before the expiration of the original filing.
7.   C. The first security interest to be filed or to be perfected has priority over other filed or perfected security interests. Although the first lender was not the first to provide funds to the debtor, it was the first to file its financing statement. Priority between perfected security interests is nearly always determined by the time of perfection (which is usually by filing). Note, though, that perfection may not protect a secured party's interest against the claim of a buyer in the ordinary course of business, and some others.
8.   C. A purchase-money security interest (PMSI) is created (1) when a seller retains or takes a security

interest in collateral to secure part or all of the purchase price of property serving as collateral, or (2) when some other party (such as a bank) takes a security interest in the collateral to secure the party's advances or other obligation that is actually used by the debtor to acquire rights in or to use the collateral.

9.   C. In most states, filing is in a central office (of the state in which the debtor is located). When collateral consists of timber to be cut, fixtures, or collateral to be extracted, a filing in the county in which the collateral is located is typically required. Of course, if perfection is by a pledge (possession), no filing is necessary.

10.   A. The filing of a security interest in a corporate debtor's collateral should be done in the state in which the debtor is incorporated. For individual debtors, however, the place of filing is the state of the debtor's principal residence. Of course, the perfection of an interest in some types of collateral, such as negotiable instruments, can only be accomplished by taking possession of the property.

Issue Spotters

1.   A creditor can put other creditors on notice by perfecting its interest: by filing a financing statement in the appropriate public office, or by taking possession of the collateral until the debtor repays the loan.

2.   The PMSI has priority. When two or more secured parties have perfected security interests in the same collateral, the first to perfect has priority (unless a state statute provides otherwise). There are exceptions to this general rule, however, concerning a PMSI. As in this question, a PMSI has priority, even if it is second in time of perfection when it attaches to inventory, it is perfected, and proper written or authenticated notice is given to other security-interest holders on or before the time that the debtor takes possession of the inventory. All of these occurred in this question.

3.   When collateral is consumer goods with a PMSI, and the debtor has paid less than 60 percent of the debt or the purchase price, the creditor can dispose of the collateral in a commercially reasonable manner, which generally requires notice of the place, time, and manner of sale. A debtor can waive the right to notice, but only after default. Before the disposal, a debtor can redeem the collateral by tendering performance of all of the obligations secured by it and by paying the creditor's reasonable expenses in retaking and maintaining it.

Chapter 21

True-False Questions

1.   T

2.   F. This is prohibited under federal law. Garnishment of an employee's wages for any one indebtedness cannot be a ground for dismissal of an employee.

3.   T

4.   T

5.   F. This is the most important concept in suretyship: a surety can use any defenses available to a debtor (except personal defenses) to avoid liability on the obligation to the creditor. Note, though, that a debtor does need not to have defaulted on the underlying obligation before a surety can be required to answer for the debt. Before a *guarantor* can be required to answer for the debt of a debtor, the debtor must have defaulted on the underlying obligation, however.

6.   F. Any individual can be a debtor under Chapter 7, and any debtor who is liable on a claim held by a creditor may file for bankruptcy under Chapter 7.

7.   F. The filing of a bankruptcy petition, voluntary or involuntary, automatically stays most litigation and other actions by creditors against the debtor and his or her property. A creditor may ask for relief from the stay, but a creditor who willfully violates the stay may be liable for actual damages, costs, and fees, as well as punitive damages.

8.   T

9.   F. Under Chapter 11, the creditors and the debtor formulate a plan under which the debtor pays some of the debts, the other debts are discharged, and the debtor is then allowed to continue in business.

10.   T

Fill-in Questions

7; 11; 13; 7; 11; 13; 7; 11; 13

Multiple-Choice Questions

1.   B. The jeweler can keep the necklace until the customer pays for the repair. If the customer fails to pay, the jeweler has an artisan's lien on the necklace for the amount of the bill and can sell the necklace in satisfaction of the lien.

2.   A. The creditor in this problem can use prejudgment attachment. Attachment occurs at the time of or immediately after commencement of a suit but before entry of a final judgment. The court issues a writ of attachment, directing the sheriff or other officer to seize property belonging to the debtor. If the creditor prevails at trial, the property can be sold to satisfy the judgment. (A writ of execution can be used after all of the conditions represented by the answer choices in this problem have been met.)

3.   B. Garnishment is a collection remedy directed at a debtor's property or rights held by a third person. A garnishment order can be served on a judgment debtor's employer (or bank) so that part of the debtor's paycheck (or account) will be paid to the creditor.

4.   B. The debt is $200,000. The amount of the homestead exemption ($50,000) is subtracted from the sale price of the house ($150,000), and the remainder

($100,000) is applied against the debt. Proceeds from the sale of any nonexempt personal property could also be applied against the debt. The debtor gets the amount of the homestead exemption, of course.

5. C. A guarantor is secondarily liable (that is, the principal must first default). Also, in this problem, if the president were, for example, the borrower's only salaried employee, the guaranty would not have to be in writing under the main-purpose exception to the Statute of Frauds. A surety is primarily liable (that is, the creditor can look to the surety for payment as soon as the debt is due, whether or not the principal debtor has defaulted). Usually, also, in the case of a guarantor, a creditor must have attempted to collect from the principal, because usually a debtor would not otherwise be declared in default.

6. C. A guarantor has the right of subrogation when he or she pays the debt owed to the creditor. This means that any right the creditor had against the debtor becomes the right of the guarantor. A guarantor also has the right of contribution, when there are one or more other guarantors. This means that if he or she pays more than his or her proportionate share on a debtor's default, the guarantor is entitled to recover from the others the amount paid above the guarantor's obligation. This problem illustrates how these principles work.

7. D. Under Chapter 11, creditors and debtor plan for the debtor to pay some debts, be discharged of the rest, and continue in business. Under Chapter 13, with an appropriate plan, a small business debtor can also pay some (or all) debts, be discharged of the rest, and continue in business. A petition for a discharge in bankruptcy under Chapter 11 may be filed by a sole proprietor, a partnership, or a corporation; a petition for a discharge under Chapter 13, however, may be filed only by a sole proprietor, among these business entities.

8. D. Under Chapter 13, a debtor can submit a plan under which he or she continues in possession of his or her assets, but turns over disposable income for a three-year period, after which most debts are discharged. When applicable, a Chapter 13 plan must provide for the surrender of all collateral to the creditors. Note that a court will not refuse to approve a Chapter 13 plan on the objection of a creditor or a trustee if the property to be distributed under the plan is ore than the amount of the creditors' claims.

9. D. Under Chapter 7 or Chapter 11, a corporate debtor (or an individual debtor or a partnership, but not a farmer or a charitable institution) who has twelve or more creditors can be forced into bankruptcy by three or more of them, who collectively have unsecured claims for at least a certain amount. (The amount is periodically increased.) A debtor with less than twelve creditors can be involuntarily petitioned into bankruptcy by one or more of them, if the petitioner (or petitioners) has a claim for at least a certain amount.

10. D. Claims that are not dischargeable in bankruptcy include the claims listed in the other answer choices: claims for back taxes accruing within three years before the bankruptcy, claims for alimony and child support, and claims for certain student loans. There are many others.

Issue Spotters

1. Yes. In this problem, the party who assured the lender of payment on behalf of the debtor is a surety. A surety has a right of reimbursement from the debtor for all outlays the surety makes, as here, on behalf of the suretyship arrangement.

2. The order of their priority is the party with the mechanic's lien, the party with the perfected security interest, and, lastly, the party with the unperfected security interest. Mechanic's liens (and artisan's liens) have priority over perfected security interests. Secured parties have the next highest priority. Unsecured creditors are generally paid last, if at all.

3. Yes. A debtor's payment to a creditor made for a preexisting debt, within ninety days (one year in the case of an insider or fraud) of the bankruptcy filing, can be recovered if it gives a creditor more than he or she would have received in the bankruptcy proceedings.

Cumulative Hypothetical Problem for Unit Six—Including Chapters 20–21

1. C. A mechanic's lien can be placed by a creditor on real property when a person contracts for labor to repair the property but does not pay. An artisan's lien entitles a creditor to recover from a debtor for the repair of personal property. In both cases, the property can be sold to satisfy the debt, but notice of the foreclosure and sale must first be given to the debtor.

2. D. With the right of subrogation, a surety, or a guarantor, may pursue any remedies that were available to the creditor against the debtor. These rights include collection of the debt. A right of contribution is available to a co-surety, who pays more than his or her proportionate share of a debt, to recover from any other co-sureties. An exemption, in the context of a debt, is property that a debtor can protect from being used to pay the debt. Exoneration is not a term that applies to this circumstance.

3. A. Unless a buyer in the ordinary course of business knows that a purchase violates a third party's rights, the buyer takes goods free of any security interest. This is an exception to the general rule that a security interest in collateral continues even after the collateral is sold.

4. B. Only a debtor can file a plan under Chapter 11, but for the court to confirm it, the secured creditors

must accept it. There is another condition that the plan must meet. It must provide that creditors retain their liens and the value of the property to be distributed to them is not less than the secured portion of their claims, or the debtor must surrender to the creditors the property securing those claims.

5. A. A Chapter 11 plan must provide for the full payment of all claims entitled to priority and the same treatment of each claim within a particular class. After the payments are completed, all debts provided for by the plan are discharged.

Questions on the Focus on Legal Reasoning for Unit Six—*In re Stanton*

1. D. In the *Stanton* case, the court held that the creditor's lien was not avoidable by the bankruptcy trustee because it was not the corporation that filed a petition in bankruptcy. In other words, the automatic stay provision did not apply. The court in that case reasoned that when money is loaned to a non-bankrupt corporation that the debtor owns, "[a] business relationship of stock ownership does not . . . extend the automatic stay to non-bankrupts."

2. C. The majority in the *Stanton* case reasoned, regarding a lender's lien's priority in these circumstances, that "where the advances of promised loan moneys are, under an agreement to lend money, largely optional," as they would be in this problem, "liens attaching prior to an optional advance would thus be superior." In other words, the bankruptcy trustee would be senior to the bank's lien for advances made after the debtor filed for personal bankruptcy because the trustee would "attach" before those later advances.

3. B. The dissent in the *Stanton* case reasoned in this context that the Bankruptcy Code's automatic stay provision "barred the debtors' attempt to use their house as collateral without prior court approval because, in continuing to use their house as collateral for [the corporation's] debts on post-petition advances, the debtors incurred debt within the meaning of" that provision.

Chapter 22

True-False Questions

1. T
2. T
3. T
4. T
5. F. An agent is liable for his or her own torts, but a principal may also be liable under the doctrine of *respondeat superior*. The key is whether the tort is committed within the scope of employment. One of the

important factors is whether the act that constituted the tort was authorized by the principal.

6. T
7. F. The parties to an agency may always have the *power* to terminate the agency at any time, but they may not always have the *right*. If a party who terminates an agency does not have the right to do so, he or she may be liable for breach of contract.

8. T
9. T
10. F. One of the main attributes of an agency relationship is that the agent can enter into binding contracts on behalf of the principal. When an agent acts within the scope of his or her authority in entering a contract, the principal is bound, whether the principal's identity was disclosed, partially disclosed, or undisclosed to the other party to the contact.

Fill-in Questions

performance; notification; loyalty; obedience; accounting

Multiple-Choice Questions

1. A. Agency law is essential to the existence of most business entities, including corporations, because without agents, most firms could not do business. A corporate officer who serves in a representative capacity, as in this problem, is an agent. The corporation is the principal. For a contract to be binding on the firm, it needs only to be signed by the agent and to be within the scope of the officer's authority.

2. A. There is a long list of factors that courts can consider in determining whether an individual is an employee or an independent contractor, and all of the choices in this question are among those factors. The most important factor, however, is the degree of control that the employer has over the details of the work.

3. B. In performing an agency, an agent is expected to use reasonable diligence and skill, which is the degree of skill of a reasonable person under similar circumstances. If an agent claims special skills, such as those of in this problem, he or she is expected to use those skills.

4. A. An agent's duties to a principal include a duty to act solely in the principal's interest in matters concerning the principal's business. This is the duty of loyalty. The agent must act solely in the principal's interest and not in the interest of the agent, or some other party. It is also a breach of the duty of loyalty to use a principal's trade secrets or other confidential information (but not acquired skills) even after the agency has terminated.

5. C. Implied authority can be conferred by custom, inferred from the agent's position, or inferred as reasonably necessary to carry out express authority. In determining whether an agent has the implied authority to do a specific act, the question is whether it is reasonable for the agent to believe that he or she has the authority.

6. C. Until an agent is notified of the principal's decision to terminate the agency relationship, the agent's authority continues. Similarly, third parties with whom the agent deals must be informed of the termination to end the agent's apparent authority, as regards those third parties. Unless an agency is in writing, in which case it must be terminated in writing, an agent can learn of a termination through any means.

7. C. When an agent enters into a contract within the scope of his or her authority, the principal is liable, whether or not the principal's identity was disclosed. The agent is also liable as a party to the contract when neither the identity of the principal nor the fact of the agency is disclosed.

8. A. Apparent authority exists when a principal causes a third party reasonably to believe that an agent has the authority to act, even if the agent does not otherwise have the authority to do so. If the third party changes positions in reliance on the principal's representation, the principal may be estopped from denying the authority. Thus, here, the principal could not hold the customers liable for failing to pay.

9. C. An agent (or employee) is liable for his or her own torts, whether or not they were committed within the scope of a principal's employment. The principal is also liable under the doctrine of *respondeat superior* when a tort is within the scope of the employment. One of the important factors in determining liability is whether the agent was on the principal's business or on a "frolic of his or her own."

10. D. An agency relationship can be created only for a legal purpose. An agency relationship created for an illegal purpose, such as a scheme to defraud, is unenforceable. Also, it should be kept in mind that although a principal must have contractual capacity, an agent does not need it. Even a person who is legally incompetent can be an agent.

Issue Spotters

1. A person in whose name a contract is made by one who is not an agent may be liable on the contract if he or she approves or affirms that contract. In other words, the employer-principal would be liable on the note in this problem on ratifying it.

2. Yes. A principal has a duty to indemnify an agent for liabilities incurred because of authorized and lawful acts and transactions and for losses suffered because of the principal's failure to perform his or her duties.

3. Probably. A principal is liable for a loss due to an agent's knowing misrepresentation if the representation was made within the scope of the agency and the agent's scope of authority.

Chapter 23

True-False Questions

1. F. Employment "at will" means that either party may terminate the employment at any time, with or without good cause. There are many exceptions to this doctrine, enacted by state legislatures and Congress, or created by the courts. These include exceptions based on contract or tort theories, or public policy.

2. F. Employers are free to offer employees no benefits. Federal and state governments participate in insurance programs designed to protect employees and their families by covering some of the financial impact of retirement, disability, death, and hospitalization.

3. T

4. F. A "whistleblower" is one who reports wrongdoing. These statutes protect employees who report their employers' wrongdoing from retaliation on the part of those employers.

5. F. Secondary boycotts, including hot-cargo agreements, which are described in the question, are illegal.

6. F. An employer may be liable even though an employee did the harassing, if the employer knew, or should have known, and failed to take corrective action, or if the employee was in a supervisory position.

7. T

8. F. Title VII covers only employers with fifteen or more employees, labor unions with fifteen or more members, labor unions that operate hiring halls, employment agencies, and federal, state, and local agencies.

9. T

10. T

Fill-in Questions

either; unless; may; Some; A few states; may not

Multiple-Choice Questions

1. B. Child labor, minimum-wage, and maximum-hour provisions are included in the Fair Labor Standards Act (also known as the Wage-Hour Law), covering virtually all employees. The employer may also be subject to the other laws given as choices in this problem, but those laws concern other rights and duties of employees and employers.

2. B. Intentionally inflicted injuries are not covered by workers' compensation. Many states cover problems arising out of preexisting conditions, but that is not part of the test for coverage. To collect benefits, an employee must notify the employer of an injury and file a claim with the appropriate state agency.

3. A. The Federal Unemployment Tax Act of 1935 concerns the system that provides unemployment

compensation. The Employee Retirement Income Security Act (ERISA) of 1974 concerns the regulation of private pension plans.

4. B. Under the Family and Medical Leave Act (FMLA) of 1993, employees can take up to twelve weeks of family or medical leave during any twelve-month period and are entitled to continued health insurance coverage during the leave. Employees are also guaranteed the same, or a comparable, job on returning to work.

5. C. Under the Consolidated Omnibus Budget Reconciliation Act (COBRA) of 1985, most workers' medical, optical, or dental insurance is not automatically eliminated on termination of employment. The workers can choose to continue the coverage at the employer's group rate, if they are willing to pay the premiums (and a 2 percent administrative fee).

6. A. Sexual harassment occurs when, in a workplace, an employee is subject to comments or contact that is perceived as sexually offensive. An employer may be liable even though an employee did the harassing. If the employee was in a supervisory position, as in this problem, for an employer to be held liable, a tangible employment action may need to be proved. Here, the employee's pay was cut.

7. C. An employer who is subject to the Americans with Disabilities Act cannot exclude arbitrarily a person who, with reasonable accommodation, could do what is required of a job. A disabled individual is not required to reasonably accommodate an employer. Also, the standard is not "significant additional costs," to either the employer or the disabled individual.

8. C. Here, the employer would seem to have a valid business necessity defense. It appears reasonable that administrative assistants be able to type. An employer can insist that, to be hired, a job applicant possess the actual skills required for a job. Except for an applicant's willingness or unwillingness to acquire certain skills, the other answer choices might be legitimate defenses in other circumstances.

9. A. The Age Discrimination in Employment Act (ADEA) of 1967 requires, for the establishment of a *prima facie* case, that at the time of the alleged discrimination, the plaintiff was forty or older, was qualified for the job, and was discharged or otherwise rejected in circumstances that imply discrimination. The difference between a *prima facie* case under the ADEA and under Title VII is that the ADEA does not require a plaintiff to show that someone who is not a member of a protected class filled the position at the center of the claim.

10. C. The employer's best defense in this problem would be that being able to pass the tests is a business necessity—it is a necessary requirement for the job. Discrimination may be illegal even if it is not intentional, and whether or not all men pass the tests is not relevant to whether there is discrimination against women. If the employer hires some women for the job,

it could not argue successfully that gender is a BFOQ for the job.

Issue Spotters

1. Yes. Some courts have held that an implied employment contract exists between employer and employee under an employee handbook that states employees will be dismissed only for good cause. An employer who fires a worker contrary to this promise can be held liable for breach of contract.

2. Yes, if he is a member of a protected class. These circumstances would then include all of the elements of a *prima facie* under Title VII of the Civil Rights Act of 1964: (1) the applicant is a member of a protected class, (2) he applied and was qualified for an open position, (3) he was rejected, and (4) the employer continued to seek applicants or filled the position with a person who is not in a protected class. The employer would then have to offer a legitimate reason for its action, and the applicant would have to show that this is a pretext, that discriminatory intent was the motivation.

3. Yes, if she can show that she was not hired solely because of her disability. The other elements for a discrimination suit based on a disability are that the plaintiff (1) has a disability and (2) is otherwise qualified for the job. Both of these elements appear to be satisfied in this problem.

Cumulative Hypothetical Problem for Unit Seven—Including Chapters 22–23

1. B. The requirements for recovery under state workers' compensation laws include the existence of an employment relationship and an accidental injury that occurs on the job or within the scope of employment. Accepting benefits precludes an employee from suing his or her employer, but it does not bar the employee from suing a third party for causing the injury.

2. C. At the termination of most workers' employment, their group health insurance cannot be terminated, and may be continued for as much as twenty-nine months in some cases, if the worker is willing to pay the premium plus an administrative cost. There is no additional requirement that the employee be at the "normal" retirement age or that he or she be part of a general layoff.

3. D. The Social Security Act of 1935 provides payments for persons who are retired or disabled. The Social Security Administration is a federal agency that also administers the Medicare program. Unemployment benefits, however, are part of a state system created by the Federal Unemployment Tax Act of 1935.

4. A. Title VII of the Civil Rights Act of 1964 covers many forms of discrimination, including discrimination based on gender, race, religion, color, and national origin. But Title VII does not prohibit discrimination based on age, which is the subject of the Age Discrimination in Employment Act of 1967.

5.   B. The Age Discrimination in Employment Act of 1967 prohibits discrimination against persons age forty or more. This includes mandatory retirement of such individuals. In most circumstances, however, an employer can discharge an employee for cause, regardless of his or her age, without running afoul of this, or any other, federal antidiscrimination law.

Questions on the Focus on Legal Reasoning for Unit Seven—*Redi-Floors, Inc. v. Sonenberg Co.*

1.   D. In the *Redi-Floors* case, the majority explained out that "if an agent buys in his own name, without disclosing his principal, and the seller subsequently discovers that the purchase was, in fact, made for another, he may, at his choice, look for payment either to the agent or the principal." In the words of the court, a seller "who has once elected, can claim no right to make a second choice," however.

2.   A. It would likely depend on the grounds for the verdict. In the reasoning of the majority in the *Redi-Floors* case, however, "it is the plaintiff who is entitled to elect against which of the defendants, principal or agent, to take the judgment." In this *Redi-Floors* case, "the trial court's erroneous granting of a directed verdict deprived the plaintiff of its right to elect which defendant it would proceed against."

3.   D. The dissent in the *Redi-Floors* case reasoned that the seller made its decision against whom to pursue an action when the contracting party "procured a judgment order which was reduced to writing against" the principal. Obtaining that judgment "constituted an election of alternative remedies that precluded plaintiff from pursuing the excluded remedy against" the agent. "As the plaintiff may not obtain judgment against both, he must make an election *prior to judgment.*"

Chapter 24

True-False Questions

1.   F. In a sole proprietorship, the owner and the business are the same. The owner receives all of the profits, and the income of the business is taxed as the owner's personal income. If the owner dies, the business is automatically dissolved.

2.   T

3.   F. A partnership is formed through an agreement among the partners. If this agreement satisfies the definition of partnership, nothing more is needed for a partnership to exist. The partnership agreement does not need to be in writing, except as otherwise required under the Statute of Frauds.

4.   F. Partners are subject to personal liability for the debts and obligations of a partnership, and this is whether or not they have participated in its management. On the firm's dissolution, its creditors have the top priority in the distribution of the firm's assets. If those assets are not sufficient to pay the creditors, the partners are liable for the difference.

5.   T

6.   F. One of the chief advantages of a limited liability company (LLC) is that it offers the limited liability of a corporation. Because an LLC also offers the tax advantages of a partnership, many businesses are using this form of organization.

7.   F. The liability of the limited partners in a limited partnership is limited to the amount of their investment in the firm, but the liability of the general partners is the same as that of the partners in a general partnership (unlimited).

8.   T

9.   T

10.   T

Fill-in Questions

are; obligation; sued; cannot; releases; must

Multiple-Choice Questions

1.   D. There are no limits on the liability of the owner of a sole proprietorship for the debts and obligations of the firm. A sole proprietorship has greater organizational flexibility, however, than other forms of business organization.

2.   A. Under a partnership by estoppel theory, a person who is not a partner, but who represents himself or herself as a partner, is liable to a third person who acts in reasonable reliance on that representation. If one of the actual partners had consented to the misrepresentation, however, the firm would also be liable.

3.   C. This arrangement for the payment of an employee (a base wage and a sales commission) does not make the employee a partner in the employer's business. There are three attributes of a partnership: sharing profits, joint ownership of a business, and an equal right in the management of the business. None of these are present here.

4.   A. Dissolution of a partnership precipitated by the withdrawal of a partner is not always the end of the firm's business, which may be continued by the remaining partners. Dissolution is only the first step towards the termination of the firm's legal existence. The other steps are covered by the winding up of the partnership's affairs.

5.   B. For most purposes, a partnership is regarded as an entity. A partnership can sue and collect judgments in its own name (rather than in the names of the individual partners). A partnership can own real estate in its name. For federal income tax purposes, how-

ever, a partnership is considered an aggregate: the firm pays no income tax. The partners pay taxes individually.

6. B. Ordinarily, limited partners are liable for the debts of their limited partnerships only to the extent of their capital contributions to the firms. A general partner, in contrast, may be held personally liable for the full amount of the firm's obligations.

7. B. Normally, the members of a limited liability company are liable for the debts of their company only to the extent of their investment in the firm, like corporate shareholders or limited partners. Sole proprietors and general partners, in contrast, may be personally liable for the full amount of their firms' obligations.

8. C. One of the advantages of the limited liability company (LLC) form of business organization is that its members are not personally liable for the debts of their firm regardless of the extent of their participation in management (unlike a limited partnership). In fact, unless agreed otherwise, an LLC's management will be considered to include all members. Another advantage is that there is generally no limit on the number of members that a firm can have (unlike an S corporation).

9. B. Professionals who organize as a limited liability partnership avoid personal liability for the wrongdoing of other partners. They have only the same liability as a limited partner in a limited partnership.

10. A. Also, the partners must sign a certificate of limited partnership, which must then be filed with the appropriate state official, usually the secretary of state.

Issue Spotters

1. No. Under the partners' fiduciary duty, a partner must account to the partnership for any personal profits or benefits derived without the consent of all the partners in connection with the use of any partnership property. Here, the leasing partner may not keep the money.

2. When a business is relatively small and is not diversified, employs relatively few people, has modest profits, and is not likely to expand significantly or require extensive financing in the immediate future, the most appropriate form for doing business may be a sole proprietorship.

3. There are differences between these forms of business organization, but all of them are treated under the law like partnerships. The differences include that the members of joint ventures have less authority than partners, and the members of a joint stock company are not agents of each other. Also, a joint stock company has many of the characteristics of a corporation: (1) ownership by shares of stock, (2) managed by directors and officers, and (3) perpetual existence.

Chapter 25

True-False Questions

1. T

2. F. Powers set out in corporate documents (and in the laws of the state of incorporation and state and federal constitutions) are express powers. Acts of a corporation that exceed its express and implied powers are called *ultra vires* (which means "beyond the powers"). Legal and illegal acts can be *ultra vires*.

3. T

4. T

5. T

6. F. Appraisal rights are available only when a statute specifically provides for them. The rationale for appraisal rights is that shareholders should not be forced to become owners of corporations that are different from the ones in which they originally invested

7. F. Shareholder approval is not normally required to buy all, or substantially all, of another corporation's assets. It is necessary, however, that the selling corporation's shareholders approve the sale of all or substantially all of its assets to another corporation.

8. F. Dissolution can occur by this means, but there are many other ways to bring about the dissolution of a corporation. Also, liquidation, which is the other step in the termination of a corporation, can be performed without court supervision.

9. T

10. F. Ordinarily, a corporation that purchases the assets of another corporation does not assume the other's liabilities. In some cases, however, the purchasing corporation may be held responsible for the seller's liabilities (for example, if the purchasing corporation continues the seller's business with the same personnel).

Fill-in Questions

promoters; unless; an incorporator; need not

Multiple-Choice Questions

1. D. State incorporation laws vary, so looking for the state that offers the most favorable provisions for a particular firm is important. There are some principles that states commonly observe, however. For example, in all states a firm can have perpetual existence, but cannot do business under the same, or even a similar, name as an existing firm.

2. A. Articles of incorporation serve as a primary source of authority for its organization and functions. The information contained in the articles includes the firm's operating name, its duration, its nature and purpose, its capital structure (including the value and classes of corporate stock), its registered office and agent (who receives legal documents on the firm's behalf), and the date of its annual shareholders' meeting (which is not likely to appear in the corporation's charter).

3.   C. Common stock represents an interest in a corporation with regard to all of these aspects in proportion to the number of shares owned out of the total number of shares issued. Common stock represents the true ownership of a corporation. Preferred shareholders have priority to the payment of any dividends (they do not have a right to dividends) but may not have the right to vote. Common stockholders are the last to receive payment for their investment, however, on the dissolution of the corporation.

4.   C. The certificate of incorporation is viewed as evidence that the firm has met the requirements for corporate existence. A *de facto* corporation is one as to which there is a defect in complying with state law, but among other things, there was a good faith attempt to comply. A firm that does not have a certificate of incorporation may be held to be a corporation by estoppel when a third party contracts with it and it should not otherwise by allowed to avoid liability.

5.   A. Other factors that a court may use to pierce the corporate veil include that a party is tricked or misled into dealing with the firm rather than the individual, that the firm is too thinly capitalized (not overcapitalized), and that the firm holds too few (not too many) shareholders' meetings.

6.   C. Directors and shareholders must approve a consolidation (or a merger). Corporate officers do not have to approve either a merger or a consolidation. In both cases, a state must also issue a certificate of consolidation or merger. A court approval's is not required, however.

7.   C. In either a merger or consolidation, the surviving corporation acquires all of the assets and assumes all of the debts of its predecessors (the corporations that formed it).

8.   C. A corporation's failure to comply with administrative requirements could also result in a court-ordered dissolution. Filing an annual report is an administrative requirement. Dissolution may be ordered if a corporation fails to commence business operations after forming. Other reasons include obtaining a corporate charter through fraud and abuse of corporate powers. Failure to declare a dividend and failure to earn a profit are not grounds for which a court would order a dissolution, if the directors are otherwise complying with their fiduciary duties

9.   B. This combination is a merger (one, but only one, corporation continues to exist). In a consolidation, an entirely new corporation acquires all of the assets and liabilities of the consolidating, disappearing corporations.

10.   A. This combination is a consolidation (a new entity takes the place of the consolidating, disappearing firms). In a merger, one of the merging entities continues to exist.

Issue Spotters

1.   A foreign corporation must have sufficient minimum contacts with a state for it to exercise jurisdiction. Doing business within a state is generally considered to constitute sufficient contact, as a firm does when it sells or advertises in a state, or otherwise places goods in the stream of commerce. Thus, a court in which a firm does business can exercise jurisdiction over it even if it was not incorporated in that state.

2.   Broad authority to conduct business can be granted in a corporation's articles of incorporation. For example, the term "any lawful purpose" is often used. This can be important because acts of a corporation that are beyond the authority given to it in its articles or charter (or state statutes) are considered illegal, *ultra vires* acts.

3.   Shareholders who disapprove of a merger or a consolidation may be entitled to be paid fair value for their shares. These are known as appraisal rights.

Chapter 26

True-False Questions

1.   T
2.   T
3.   F. Preemptive rights consist of preferences given to shareholders over other purchasers to buy shares of a new corporate issue in proportion to the number of shares that they already hold. This allows a shareholder to maintain his or her proportionate ownership share in the corporation. Generally, these rights are granted (or withheld) in the articles of incorporation.
4.   T
5.   F. Any damages recovered in a shareholder's derivative suit are normally paid to the corporation on whose behalf the shareholder or shareholders exercised the derivative right.
6.   T
7.   F. Officers and directors owe the same fiduciary duties to the corporations for which they work. They both owe a duty of loyalty. This duty requires them to subordinate their personal interests to the welfare of the corporation.
8.   F. The business judgment rule immunizes directors (and officers) from liability for poor business decisions and other honest mistakes that cause a corporation to suffer a loss. Directors are not immunized from losses that do not fit this category, however.
9.   T
10.   T

Fill-in Questions

but ownership is not; can; recorded as the owner in the corporation's books

Multiple-Choice Questions

1. A. There is no such right. This is also not a right of directors, except as specified in the articles of incorporation. The ownership of a corporation by shareholders also does not include rights of actual ownership of specific corporate property.

2. B. Dividends may be paid from the other sources listed here. Once declared, a dividend becomes a debt enforceable at law like any other debt. Generally, state law allows dividends to be paid as long as a corporation can pay its other debts as they come due and the amount of the dividend is not more than the net worth of the corporation.

3. A. Officers and other executive employees are hired by a corporation's board of directors. The rights of the officers and other high-level managers are defined by their employment contracts with the corporation.

4. C. Directors must exercise care in their duties. For example, they are expected to use a reasonable amount of supervision over corporate officers and employees when they delegate work. Their liability for breach of this duty could be grounded in negligence or mismanagement of corporate personnel. They are also expected to be loyal: faithful to their obligations and duties.

5. A. A shareholder's derivative suit is a claim filed on behalf of the corporation. Such a suit may allege, for example, that officers or directors misused corporate assets. Of course, any damages that are awarded must be paid to the corporation. Preemptive rights, rights of first refusal, and proxies relate to the sale, purchase, and voting of shares of stock.

6. C. Cumulative voting can often be used in the election of directors to enhance the power of minority shareholders in electing a representative. In calculating a shareholder's votes under the cumulative voting method, in this problem, Mary's number of shares is multiplied by the number of directors to be elected.

7. B. Unless a state statute provides to the contrary, a quorum of directors must be present to conduct corporate business, such as the declaration of a dividend. A quorum is a majority of the number of directors authorized in the firm's articles or bylaws. The rule is one vote per director.

8. A. The board of directors hires the company's officers and other managerial employees, and determines their compensation. Ultimate responsibility for all policy decisions necessary to the management of corporate affairs also rests with the directors.

9. B. Directors' main right is their right to participate in board meetings. Directors also have a right to inspect corporate books and to be indemnified in defense of some lawsuits (regardless of the outcome of the suit). Rights that directors do not have include a right to compensation. That is, directors may be compensated for their efforts, but they have no inherent right to it. "Preemption" is not a right.

10. C. Under their duty of loyalty, directors cannot compete with their corporation or have an interest that conflicts with the interest of the corporation. Owning the stock of a competitor would also constitute an interest that conflicts with the interest of the corporation on whose board a director serves.

Issue Spotters

1. Under these circumstances, a minority shareholder can petition a court to appoint and receiver and liquidate the assets of the corporation.

2. Yes. A shareholder can bring a derivative suit on behalf of a corporation, if some wrong is done to the corporation. Normally, any damages recovered go into the corporate treasury.

3. Yes. A single shareholder—or a few shareholders acting together—who owns enough stock to exercise *de facto* control over a corporation owes the corporation and minority shareholders a fiduciary duty when transferring those shares.

Chapter 27

True-False Questions

1. T
2. T
3. T
4. T
5. F. Rule 506, issued under the Securities Act of 1933, provides an exemption for these offerings, if certain other requirements are met. This is an important exemption, applying to private offerings to a limited number of sophisticated investors.
6. T
7. T
8. F. *Scienter* is not a requirement for liability under Section 16(b) of the Securities Exchange Act of 1934, but it is required for liability under Section 10(b) and under Rule 10b-5.
9. F. Anyone who receives inside information as a result of an insider's breach of his or her fiduciary duty can be liable under Rule 10b-5, which applies in virtually all cases involving the trading of securities. The key to liability is whether the otherwise undisclosed information is *material*.
10. F. Most securities can be resold without registration. Also, under Rule 144 and 144A ("Safe harbor" provisions), there are specific exemptions for securities that might otherwise require registration with the SEC.

Fill-in Questions

prosecution; triple; ten; may

Multiple-Choice Questions

1. A. This purchase and sale is a violation of Section 16(b) of the Securities Exchange Act of 1934. When a purchase and sale is within a six-month period, as in this problem, the corporation can recover all of the profit. Proof of *scienter* is not required.

2. D. Under the Securities Act of 1933, a security exists when a person invests in a common enterprise with the reasonable expectation of profits derived primarily or substantially from the managerial or entrepreneurial efforts of others (not from the investor's own efforts).

3. A. Because of the low amount of the issue, it qualifies as an exemption from registration under Rule 504. No specific disclosure document is required, and there is no prohibition on solicitation. If the amount had been higher than $1 million but lower than $5 million, this offer might have qualified for an exemption under Regulation A, which requires notice to the SEC and an offering circular for investors.

4. D. The amount of this offering is too high to exempt it from the registration requirements except possibly under Rule 506 or Section 4(6). This issuer advertised the offering, however, and Rule 506 prohibits general solicitation. Thus, without filing a registration statement, the issuer could not legally solicit *any* investors (whatever it may have believed about the unaccredited investors). This offering does not qualify under Section 4(6), because unaccredited investors participated.

5. D. This issue might qualify under Rule 505 or Section 4(6), except that again, the issuer advertised the offering, which it cannot do and remain exempt from registration. In other words, the amount of this offering disqualified the issuer from advertising it without filing a registration statement.

6. B. A registration statement must supply enough information so that an unsophisticated investor can evaluate the financial risk involved. The statement must explain how the registrant intends to use the proceeds from the sale of the issue. Also, besides the description of management, there must be a disclosure of any of their material transactions with the firm. A certified financial statement must be included.

7. C. A corporate officer is a traditional inside trader. The outsider in this problem is a tippee who is liable because the tippee knew of the officer's misconduct. Liability here is based on the fact that the information was not public. Liability might be avoided if those who know the information wait for a reasonable time after its public disclosure before trading their stock.

8. A. Of course, the offering must be registered with the SEC before it can be sold, and this requires a registration statement. Investors must be given a prospectus that describes the security, the issuing corporation, and the risk of the security. A tombstone ad tells an investor how and where to obtain the prospectus.

9. D. The chief problem with this offering is that the issuer advertised it. Under Rule 506, private offerings in unlimited amounts may qualify for an exemption from registration, but no general solicitation is permitted without registration. Even if this issuer complied with all other SEC requirements, however, it should have given the required information to *all* investors, not only the unaccredited investors. (This offering does not qualify under Section 4(6), because unaccredited investors participated.)

10. A. Most resales are exempt from registration if they are undertaken by persons other than issuers or underwriters. Resales of restricted securities acquired under Rule 504a, Rule 505, Rule 506, or Section 4(6) may trigger registration requirements, but the original sale in this problem came under Rule 504.

Issue Spotters

1. The average investor is not concerned with minor inaccuracies but with facts that if disclosed would tend to deter him or her from buying the securities. This would include facts that have an important bearing on the condition of the issuer and its business (liabilities, loans to officers and directors, customer delinquencies, and pending lawsuits).

2. No. The Securities Exchange Act of 1934 extends liability to officers and directors in their personal transactions for taking advantage of inside information when they know it is unavailable to the persons with whom they are dealing.

3. Yes. All states have their own corporate securities laws ("blue sky" laws).

Cumulative Hypothetical Problem for Unit Eight—Including Chapters 24–27

1. A. A partnership is an association of two or more persons who manage a business and share profits. Here, the partnership began when the parties combined their assets and commenced business. Before that time, there was no sharing of profits, no joint ownership of a business, and no equal right in the management of a business (because there was no business). The execution of a formal partnership agreement is not necessary, nor is the consent of creditors.

2. B. Unlike general partnerships, which can come into existence even when the parties do not intend to form a partnership, a limited partnership can only be created pursuant to the provisions of a state statute. This statute sets out exactly what partners must do to form a limited partnership, which must include at least one general partner who assumes personal liability for the debts of the firm.

3. D. The information that each state requires to be in articles of incorporation differs somewhat, but the

information represented by the choices in this problem is generally required. It is not necessary to name the initial officers in the articles. Other information that might be required includes the number of authorized shares. Other information that is not required includes quorum requirements.

4. D. Other information that must be included in a registration statement, under the Securities Act of 1933, includes a description of the issuer's business, a description of the security, the capital structure of the business, the underwriting arrangements, and the certified financial statements.

5. B. Rule 504 exempts certain stock offerings from the registration requirements of the Securities Act of 1933. To qualify, a noninvestment company offering may not exceed $1 million in any twelve-month period, the Securities and Exchange Commission must be notified of the sale.

Questions on the Focus on Legal Reasoning for Unit Eight—*In re Miller*

1. A. In the reasoning of the majority in the *In re Miller* case, fraud in such cases as this problem "could be imputed only on a finding of agency." The court held, however, that "Section 20(a) extends liability well beyond traditional [agency] doctrines, providing expansive remedies in a highly regulated industry."

2. D. The dissent in the *In re Miller* case reasoned that a finding of agency is not necessary to impose liability under Section 20. The dissent would have imputed liability in the circumstances described in these questions, and would have held that the debt represented by that liability was not dischargeable in bankruptcy.

3. C. In the *In re Miller* case, the majority reasoned that there is "nothing in the Bankruptcy Code or the securities laws indicating that these two separate provisions of law should be combined" to impose liability on a fraudulent broker's innocent employer and declare that liability a non-dischargeable debt under the Bankruptcy Code. "Section 20(a) [of the Securities Exchange Act] extends liability well beyond traditional doctrines, providing expansive remedies in a highly regulated industry." However, "the Bankruptcy Code addresses actual, traditional fraud, and we are not persuaded that it should be read in such a way as to encompass the nontraditional liability imposed under [Section] 20(a)."

Chapter 28

True-False Questions

1. T

2. F. If goods are confused due to a wrongful act, it is the *wrongdoer* who must prove what percentage of the whole belongs to him or her to acquire title to any of the goods. Otherwise, the *innocent party* gets title to the whole.

3. F. The essence of a gift is that it is a voluntary transfer without consideration. The elements of a gift are donative intent, delivery, and acceptance.

4. F. If an accession is performed in good faith, ownership depends on the change in the value of the property. The greater the increase, the more likely that the improver will own the property.

5. T

6. F. To constitute a bailment, a delivery must be of possession without any transfer of title and there must be an agreement that the property be returned or otherwise disposed of according to the owner's directions.

7. F. In most cases, a bailee is subject to a reasonable standard of care. Depending on the specific type of bailment, that standard may range from slight care (bailment for the sole benefit of the bailor) to great care (bailment for the sole benefit of the bailee).

8. F. A bailee has *two* basic responsibilities: to take proper care of the property and to surrender or dispose of the property at the end of the bailment.

9. T

10. T

Fill-in Questions

inter vivos; causa mortis; causa mortis; causa mortis; inter vivos

Multiple-Choice Questions

1. A. Personal property includes such items as computer software and home pages. Those who produce personal property have title to it. Because the creator of the property produced it, she owns it. There is an exception, however. Employees do not own what they produce for their employers. Here, she was hired to create property for another; the other owns what she created.

2. B. A right of survivorship, in which a deceased joint tenant's interest passes to the surviving joint tenant, is the distinguishing feature of a joint tenancy. Generally, to acquire or own property as joint tenants, the owners must specify that as the form they want their ownership to take. If these buyers had not specified that form, they would own the property as tenants in common.

3. A. The three elements for an effective gift are donative intent, delivery, and acceptance. Here, the giver had the intent, and the recipient clearly accepted, if delivery was effective, which it was. Delivery of the key to the box was constructive delivery of the earrings. Thus, the gift would have been effective even if the giver had died before the recipient had taken them from the box.

4. A. The finder found what appears to be lost property. Generally, the finder of lost property has good title against all *but the true owner*. Therefore, the finder in this problem has title.

5. A. When goods are commingled, and the goods are lost, the owners bear the loss in the same proportion that they contributed to the whole. This is assuming that they can prove how much they contributed to the whole. Thus, the parties take out the same proportions that they put in.

6. B. The three elements for an effective gift are donative intent, delivery, and acceptance. Here, the giver had the intent and clearly delivered the object of the gift (by constructive delivery). Thus, the gift would have been effective if the recipient accepted it. Acceptance is generally presumed unless proven otherwise. In the problem, the recipient announced that she did not want the gift and left they key in the possession of the donor. In this case, there was no gift. The property belongs to the donor's heirs.

7. C. A bailee must be given exclusive possession and control of the property and knowingly accept it. Here, there is no delivery of possession. Regarding the other choices, money does not need to be involved for a transaction to be a bailment, a car is personal property, and a signed contract is not necessary for a bailment (the bailment agreement may be oral).

8. B. The wallet appears to have been placed behind the plant intentionally and thus is classified as mislaid property. The owner of the premises on which mislaid property is found is entitled to possession as against the finder.

9. A. A bailment involves delivery of personal property in such a way that the bailee is given, and knowingly accepts, exclusive possession and control over it. By accepting the coat, the restaurant is given exclusive possession and control over the purse, but it the restaurant does not *knowingly* accepts the purse.

10. C. A common carrier is liable for damage caused by the willful acts of third persons or by an accident. Thus, the transport company is liable for the loss of the last load. The other losses are caused by acts of the shipper and must be borne by the shipper.

Issue Spotters

1. Yes. A bailee's right of possession, even though temporary, permits the bailee to recover damages from any third persons for damage or loss to the property.

2. Yes. An ordinary bailee owes a duty to take proper care of the clothes left in its charge. To recover from a party who does not fulfill his or her duty of care, the injured party must normally prove a lack of care. In this case, that would be difficult, because the bailor is unaware as to why the property was returned in bad condition. Under the law of bailments, proof of damage or loss raises a presumption that a bailee is

guilty of negligence (or conversion), and the bailee must prove that he or she exercised due care.

3. The shipper suffers the loss. A common carrier is liable for damage caused by the willful acts of third persons or by an accident. Other losses must be borne by the shipper (or the recipient, depending on the terms of their contract). This shipment was lost due to an act of God.

Chapter 29

True-False Questions

1. T
2. F. The owner of a life estate has the same rights as a fee simple owner except that the value of the property must be kept intact for the holder of the future interest.
3. F. An easement merely allows a person to use land without taking anything from it, while a profit allows a person to take something from the land.
4. T
5. F. Under the Fifth Amendment to the U.S. Constitution, when taking private property, the government is required to pay the owner just compensation.
6. F. The government has the power to take private property, but the purposes for which such property may be taken must be *public*.
7. T
8. T
9. T
10. F. A landlord can sell, give away, or otherwise transfer his or her property without affecting a tenant's obligations under a lease, except that the tenant becomes the tenant of the new owner.

Fill-in Questions

1. reversionary; original owner
2. reversion; reversion
3. an executory; remainder

Multiple-Choice Questions

1. C. A *profit* is the right to go onto land in possession of another and take away some part of the land itself or some product of the land. In contrast, an easement is a right to make limited use of another person's land without taking anything from the property. A license is a revocable right to come onto another person's land.

2. C. Once the condition in a fee simple defeasible fails, the owner of the conditional estate is divested of rights, and the estate reverts to the original owner or his or her heirs. This right of the owner and his or her heirs is a reversionary interest.

3. C. This situation meets all the requirements for acquiring property by adverse possession: the possession was (1) actual and exclusive; (2) open, visible, and notorious; (3) continuous and peaceful for the statutory period; and (4) hostile, against the whole world, including the original owner.

4. C. Warranty deeds include a number of promises, including a covenant of quiet enjoyment, which guarantees that the buyer will not be disturbed in his or her possession of the land by the seller or any third persons. If this covenant is breached, the buyer can recover from the seller the purchase price and any damages for the eviction.

5. C. The rights that accompany ownership in fee simple include the right to sell the land or give it away, as well as the right to use the land for whatever purpose the owner sees fit, subject, of course, to the law's limitations.

6. B. An easement is a right to make limited use of another's real property without taking anything from it. In this problem, it is an easement by necessity—the owner needs access to his property. The right to take something from the property is a profit. A revocable right to come onto the property is a license.

7. D. A valid deed must contain the names of the grantee (buyer) and grantor (seller), words evidencing an intent to convey the property, a legally sufficient description of the property, and the grantor's (and usually the spouse's) signature.

8. C. When a landlord transfers his or her interest in leased property, the tenant becomes the tenant of the new owner. It is to this new owner that the tenant owes rent. Both parties must continue to follow the terms of the lease.

9. B. An assignment does not relieve an assigning tenant from the obligation to pay rent during the original term or during an extension under an option in the original lease.

10. A. A lease that does not specify how long it is to last but does specify that rent is to be paid at certain intervals creates a periodic tenancy. The tenancy is automatically renewed for each rental period unless it has been properly terminated.

Issue Spotters

1. Yes. An owner of a fee simple has the most rights possible—he or she can give the property away, sell it, transfer it by will, use it for almost any purpose, possess it to the exclusion of all the world, or as in this case, transfer possession for any period of time. The party to whom possession is transferred can also transfer his or her interest (usually only with the owner's permission) for any lesser period of time.

2. When a tenant dies, the lease passes to the tenant's heirs as personal property. Of course, the heirs (and the owner of the property) must continue to abide by the terms of the lease.

3. This is a breach of the warranty deed's covenant of quiet enjoyment. The buyer can sue the seller and recover the purchase price of the house, plus any damages.

Chapter 30

True-False Questions

1. T

2. F. Insurance is classified according to the nature of the risk involved.

3. F. A broker is the agent of the applicant. If the broker fails to obtain coverage and the applicant is damaged as a result, the broker is liable for the loss.

4. T

5. T

6. F. A will is revocable by the testator (or by operation of law) at any time during his or her life.

7. T

8. F. Intestacy statutes regulate how property is distributed when a person dies without a will. These statutes typically provide that after payment of the decedent's debts, the remaining property passes to the decedent's surviving wife, children, or other relatives. If there are no living relatives, the property passes to the state.

9. T

10. T

Fill-in Questions

executor; administrator

Multiple-Choice Questions

1. C. An insurance company evaluates risk factors based on the information in an insurance application. For this reason, misrepresentation can void a policy, especially if the company can show that it would not have extended insurance if it had known the facts.

2. A. The insurable interest in life insurance must exist at the time the policy is obtained. Under a key-person life insurance policy, it will not matter if the key person is no longer in the business's employ at the time of the loss (the person's death).

3. C. To recover for a loss under a property insurance policy, an insurable interest in the property must exist when the loss occurs. It does not make any difference whether or not the property is owned in fee simple, or by an individual, or when an insurance policy is issued.

4. C. Property insurance can be canceled for gross negligence that increases the hazard insured against. Other reasons for canceling insurance include non-payment of premiums, fraud or misrepresentation, and conviction for a crime that, like gross negligence, increases the hazard insured against.

5. B. Liability insurance protects against liability imposed on a company resulting from injuries to the person or property of another. Coverage under a liability policy may also include expenses involved in recalling and replacing a product that has proved to be defective.

6. D. When assets are insufficient to pay in full all that a will provides, the gifts of general property, such as sums of money, are reduced proportionately. Thus, the gifts to the testator's daughters will be reduced. This is known as abatement.

7. B. Under intestacy statutes, each state regulates how property is distributed when a person dies without a will. These statutes attempt to carry out the likely intent of the decedent, setting out rules by which the deceased's natural heirs (such as children, siblings, parents, or other family members) inherit his or her property.

8. C. If an express declaration of revocation is missing from a second will, the wills are read together, and if a disposition in the second will is inconsistent with the prior will, the language of the second will controls.

9. C. A surviving spouse usually receives a share of the estate—one-half if there is also a surviving child and one-third if there are two or more children, and the remaining property passes to the children and the children of deceased children.

10. D. Under a testamentary trust, which is set up in a will, a designated, court-approved trustee would manage the property for the daughters' benefit.

Issue Spotters

1. Insurance companies use the principle of risk pooling. The risk that an event will occur requiring payments under an insurance contract is spread among a large number of people to make the premiums small compared with the coverage offered.

2. No. An incorrect statement as to the age of an insured is a misrepresentation. Under an incontestability clause, however, after a policy has been in force for a certain time (usually two or three years), the insurer cannot cancel the policy or avoid a claim on the basis of statements made in the application.

3. No. To obtain insurance, one must have a sufficiently substantial interest in whatever is to be insured. One has an insurable interest in property if one would suffer a pecuniary loss from its destruction. This interest must exist *when the loss occurs*. To obtain insurance on another's life, one must have a reasonable expectation of benefit from the continued life of the other. The benefit may be founded on a relationship, but "ex-spouse" alone is not such a relationship. An interest in someone's life must exist *when the policy is obtained*.

Cumulative Hypothetical Problem for Unit Nine—Including Chapters 28–30

1. B. The most important factor in determining whether an item is a fixture is the intent of the owners. Other factors include whether the item can be removed without damaging the real property, and whether the item is sufficiently adapted so as to have become a part of the real property. If removal would irreparably damage the property, the item may also be considered a fixture.

2. C. If a joint tenant transfers his or her interest by deed to a third party, the third party becomes a tenant in common with the remaining joint tenant or tenants. (If there is more than one remaining joint tenant, they are still joint tenants among themselves.)

3. A. The elements for a transfer of real property ownership by deed include the names of the grantor and grantee, the intent of the grantor to convey ownership, the legal description of the property, the signature of the grantor, delivery, and acceptance. Elements that are not required include consideration, the signature of the grantee, a recording of the deed, and a purchase price.

4. A. Under a coinsurance provision, the amount of recovery is the amount of the loss multiplied by the quotient of the amount of insurance and (the total value of the property multiplied by a specified percentage). Here, the specified percentage is 80 percent, the total value of the property is $500,000, the amount of insurance is $300,000, and the loss is $60,000. The amount of recovery is $45,000—$60,000 x [$300,000/ ($500,000 x 80 percent)]. (Note that a coinsurance provision reduces the amount of a recovery only in a case of partial loss and then only if the insured has less insurance than the specified percentage.)

5. B. If a tenant transfers only part of a lease (that is, if the tenant transfer the right to occupy leased premises for less than the whole term) the arrangement is a sublease. (If the transfer is for the whole term, it is an assignment.) In a sublease, the original tenant is still liable to the landlord for the rent and other conditions of the original lease despite the transfer of the right to occupy the property.

Questions on the Focus on Legal Reasoning for Unit Nine—*Tahoe-Sierra Preservation Council, Inc. v. Tahoe Regional Planning Agency*

1. C. The majority in *Tahoe-Sierra Preservation Council, Inc. v. Tahoe Regional Planning Agency*, reasons that "a temporary restriction that merely causes a diminution in value is not" a taking of property. "Logically, a fee simple estate cannot be rendered valueless by a temporary prohibition on economic use, because the property will recover value as soon as the prohibition is lifted." Moratoria "are used widely among land-use planners." The Court added, however, that factors such as "the good faith of the planners, the reasonable expectations of the landowners," and "the actual impact of the moratorium on property values" should be weighed in the balance.

2. A. The dissent in *Tahoe-Sierra Preservation Council, Inc. v. Tahoe Regional Planning Agency*, argues that when a property owner is forced "to leave his property economically idle, he has suffered a taking," whether that idleness is "temporary" or "permanent." The dissent fears that if this principle is not applied, a government has "every incentive" to label a ban on development "temporary" and "repeatedly [extend] the 'temporary' prohibition into a long-term ban on all development" This would let a government "do by regulation what it cannot do through eminent domain—i.e., take private property without paying for it."

3. D. Under the holding in *Tahoe-Sierra Preservation Council, Inc. v. Tahoe Regional Planning Agency*—which is that a building moratorium like that described in these questions is not a taking and does not require compensation—property owners are not owed compensation for a local government's temporary ban on further development of their property. A property owner might thus have to bear the financial burden of undeveloped land as long as a local regulatory body deems.

Chapter 31

True-False Questions

1. T
2. T
3. F. Compliance with GAAP and GAAS may be required, but it is no guarantee of freedom from liability. Also, there may be a higher standard of conduct under a state statute or judicial decision.
4. F. The majority view is that accountants are subject to liability for negligence to foreseeable users. In some states, however, the view is to extend liability only to users whose use of, and reliance on, an accountant's statements or report was reasonably foreseeable.
5. F. Under the securities acts, an accountant may be subject to criminal penalties for willful violations.
6. T
7. F. Tax preparers may be subject to penalties if they fail to furnish a taxpayer with a copy of the return.
8. T
9. T
10. F. No, privity is not required. To recover, a plaintiff must prove five elements, including *scienter*, a fraudulent act or deception, reliance, materiality, and causation.

Fill-in Questions

will not; may; may

Multiple-Choice Questions

1. B. Working papers are the property of the accountant whose work they represent, but working papers cannot be released without the permission of the client for whom they were accumulated.
2. C. Generally, an auditor can be held liable to a third party for negligence. In most states, however, an accountant is liable only to users whom the accountant knew or should have known about. In some states, privity is required; in others, "near privity" is the requirement. This question and answer are based on a question that appeared in the CPA exam in 1997.
3. D. Under the Securities Act of 1933, an accountant may be liable for any false statement of material fact or omission of a material fact in a registration statement. The other elements indicated in the other choices are not requirements for liability under this statute.
4. C. Under the Securities Exchange Act of 1934, an accountant may be liable for any false statement of material fact or omission of a material fact made with the intent to defraud. An accountant may also be liable for failing to disclose to a client facts that give reason to believe misstatements have been made or fraud has been committed.
5. A. In most states, under a court order an accountant must disclose information about his or her client, including communications between the accountant and the client.
6. A. The client assigned the employee who was committing the wrongful act to assist the accountant, who failed to discover the wrongdoing because the employee covered it up. The client's loss was thus due to the client's own error. This generally reduces or eliminates any potential liability on the part of the accountant.
7. C. Besides the cost to obtain the accountant's contracted-for services elsewhere and the amount of any penalties for failing to meet deadlines, the client may recover other reasonable and foreseeable losses.
8. C. In this problem, the attorney failed to exercise reasonable care and professional judgment, thereby breaching the duty of care owed to clients. If a statute of limitations runs out, a client can no longer file a suit and loses a potential award of damages.
9. B. In a number of states, working papers remain the property of the accountant. These papers may act as crucial evidence in case the accountant needs to defend himself or herself against charges of negligence or fraud. At the same time, because the working papers reflect the client's financial situation, the client has the right of access to them. Also, in some circum-

stances, audit papers must be retained for as long as five years.

10. C. Another possible defense that an accountant or other professional may assert against a charge of negligence, in a state that allows contributory negligence as a defense, is that the client was negligent.

Issue Spotters

1. Unintentionally misstating a material fact may lead to liability based on constructive fraud. A professional may be liable for constructive fraud whether or not he or she acted with fraudulent intent. Constructive fraud may exist, for instance, if a professional intentionally fails to perform a duty in reckless disregard of the consequences.

2. Yes. In these circumstances, when the accountant knows that the bank will use the statement, the bank is a foreseeable user. A foreseeable user is a third party within the class of parties to whom an accountant may be liable for negligence.

3. No. In the circumstances described in the problem, the accountant will not be held liable to a purchaser of the securities. To avoid liability, however, the accountant must prove that he is free of fraud and negligence.

Questions on the Focus on Legal Reasoning for Unit Ten—*KPMG, LLC v. Securities and Exchange Commission*

1. B. Like the facts in the *KPMG* case, this situation could be held to violate generally accepted auditing standards (GAAS), which require

accountants to be independent of their clients. In the *KPMG* case, the SEC ruled that the loan and the contingent fee, which is proscribed by AICPA Rule 302, impaired the accounting company's independence. This violates SEC Rule 2-02(b) of Regulation S-X, which mandates compliance with GAAS. In the case, the SEC also concluded that the accounting firm caused its client to violate Section 13(a) of the Securities Exchange Act of 1934 and SEC Rule 13a-1, which require reports certified by *independent* public accountants.

2. A. In the *KPMG* case, the accounting firm argued in part that the order was overbroad because it was not more narrowly directed toward specific violations of the provisions of the statutes and rules concerned. The majority reasoned in part that Section 21C of the Securities Exchange Act authorizes a cease-and-desist order to prohibit *"any* future violation" of a provision violated in the case before the court. Also, the order in this case extended "only to a subset of the violations comprehended by the rules and statutory provisions involved, namely those that are independence related."

3. B. According to the dissent in the *KPMG* case, "[t]he SEC's contingent fee finding was clearly erroneous." The dissent reasoned that AICPA Rule 302 covers only "professional" services. The SEC's interpretation of the rule in issuing the cease-and-desist order, should receive no deference, according to the dissent, "because we have no hint that Congress intended the SEC to fill in gaps left by AICPA" and all the SEC "has is its general requirement that accountants be independent."

Notes